Jazz: An American Journey

Brian Harker
Brigham Young University

PEARSON
Prentice
Hall

Upper Saddle River, NJ. 07458

Library of Congress Cataloging-in-Publication Data

Harker, Brian.
  Jazz: an American journey/Brian Harker.
    p. cm.
  ISBN 0-13-098261-X
    1. Jazz—History and criticism—Textbooks. 2. Jazz—Social aspects—Textbooks. I. Title.

ML3506.H35 2005
781.65'09—dc22   2004050371

Editor-in-Chief: Sarah Touborg
Senior Acquisitions Editor: Christopher T. Johnson
Editorial Assistant: Evette Dickerson
Executive Marketing Manager: Sheryl Adams
Director of Production & Manufacturing: Barbara Kittle
Managing Editor: Joanne Riker
Production Editor: Laura A. Lawrie
Production Liaison: Jean Lapidus
Manufacturing Manager: Nick Sklitsis
Prepress & Manufacturing Buyer: Benjamin D. Smith
Art Director: Carmen DiBartolomeo
Interior & Cover Design: Carmen DiBartolomeo
Photo Researcher: Francelle Carapetyan
Image Permission Coordinator: Craig A. Jones
Cover Image: Jazz Band Performing / Wally McNamee. © Wally McNamee/CORBIS.
Compositor: Interactive Composition Corporation (ICC)
Printer/Binder: Courier Companies, Inc.
Cover Printer: Phoenix Color Corporation

To Sally, Daniel, and Robbie

Credits and acknowledgments borrowed from other sources and reproduced, with permission, in this textbook appear on appropriate on page 351.

Pearson Education LTD.
Pearson Education Singapore, Pte. Ltd
Pearson Education, Canada, Ltd
Pearson Education—Japan

Pearson Education Australia PTY, Limited
Pearson Education North Asia Ltd
Pearson Educación de Mexico, S.A. de C.V.
Pearson Education Malaysia, Pte. Ltd

10 9 8 7 6 5 4 3 2
ISBN 0-13-098261-X

Contents

Preface

This textbook grew out of an assignment I received several years ago to teach a jazz history course for nonmusic majors. General Education guidelines encouraged teachers to place their subjects within broad humanistic settings, to help students make connections with historical events they may have studied elsewhere, and to reveal cultures relevant to the topic being addressed. When asked if jazz history could be taught in this way, I responded affirmatively. Studying jazz in context uncovers relationships with economics, politics, and other social dimensions, particularly at the site of watershed historical events—the Great Migration of southern blacks to northern cities, World War I and World War II, the Great Depression, the Cold War, the civil rights movement, among others. Students' understanding of jazz should illuminate many aspects of twentieth-century culture they encounter in other courses.

Moreover, the emphasis on context makes it possible to see how social conditions gave birth to musical style. It helps to know, for instance, that the defining paradigms of Booker T. Washington and W. E. B. Du Bois established basic attitudes toward race throughout the century. These attitudes decisively affected the evolution of jazz style, particularly its transformation from entertainment to art. Such connections can be made all along the line: vaudeville inspired the antic quality of much early jazz, the ability to hire more musicians for less money supported the rise of big bands during the Depression, the drive by American blacks for political freedom in the early sixties found its counterpart in free jazz, and so forth.

The conviction that jazz can and should be presented within a vivid historical setting reflects the direction of much jazz scholarship of recent years. But as I began examining materials to use in the class, I realized that few textbooks attempted to provide such a setting. Most were concerned to present a more or less abstract evolution of musical style, occasionally addressing historical issues, but more often discussing the players and composers from critical perspectives outside the time periods being treated. Seeing the need for a survey that would tell the story of jazz holistically, situating the music within its natural home in American history and culture, I embarked upon this book. I hope the results of my efforts prove helpful to others who teach jazz in the university as well.

I have organized the book into fifteen-year segments that correspond roughly to fundamental changes in both American society and jazz, as shown in the following timeline.

Chronology

1900	Theodore Roosevelt becomes president (1901)
	The United States becomes world power
	Beginnings of ragtime and the blues
1914	Outbreak of World War I; Great Migration intensifies
	First New Orleans jazz bands move north, setting the stage for the Jazz Age
1929	Stock market crash; onset of Great Depression
	Beginnings of the Swing Era
1945	End of World War II
	Introduction of bebop to the public
1960	John F. Kennedy elected president; civil rights movement intensifies
	Rise of free jazz
1975	Richard M. Nixon resigns (1974); Vietnam War ends
	Leading fusion bands dissolve
	Emergence of neo-bop movement
1990	End of the Cold War
	Jazz becomes increasingly institutionalized, eclectic, international

This chronology is divided into six parts: Origins, Early Jazz, Swing, Bop, Free Jazz to Fusion, and Postmodern Jazz (see Contents). Each part begins with a chapter on historical context to introduce the period. Additionally, most chapters open with a brief section on historical and cultural setting. The first part, Origins (c. 1900–1914), discusses the social conditions among African Americans that led to the rise of jazz, the influence of ragtime and the blues, and the formative role of New Orleans. The second part, Early Jazz (c. 1914–1929), treats the development of early jazz in Chicago and New York, the emergence of Louis Armstrong, and so forth.

Each chapter has pedagogical aids to further illuminate the subject. These include **Contemporary Voices** boxes containing quotations from people who lived during the period in question, boxes titled **Great Debates** summarizing important controversies among jazz critics and scholars, and **Chronology** boxes listing influential events—both musical and otherwise—for individual parts. Other boxes treat **record labels, venues,** and **offstage personalities.** One unique feature of this book is a series of **historical maps** indicating regions, cities, communities, and venues that proved especially hospitable to jazz. Period **photographs, album covers,** and **cartoons** give a visual sense of the attitudes and customs that surrounded the music. **Birth and death dates** in parentheses mark the first substantive mention of significant figures, and important **names and terms** are highlighted in the text.

Context, of course, has no purpose without a text. The "text" for this book is a series of fifty-five outstanding jazz recordings collected in an available **three-CD set.** Most of the recordings are classics in that they represent leading musicians' best or most influential work according to longstanding critical consensus. Indeed, a third of the selections are taken from the now-defunct *Smithsonian Collection of Classic Jazz,* a widely used anthology before its discontinuance several years ago. Some of the more recent recordings have not yet had the chance to stand the test of time and thus reflect a more subjective selection process. Some recordings were chosen to represent a particular style; others to illustrate a historical pattern. (For instance, Charlie Barnet's "Cherokee," from the Swing Era, should help prepare students to understand Charlie Parker's "Koko," a modern jazz treatment of the "Cherokee" chord progression.) All recordings are discussed in detail, and thirty-five are represented visually in a **Listening Chart** (see below). The twenty recordings *without* listening charts provide students the opportunity to create their own diagrams of the music. In addition to the three-CD recording set, this book can be packaged at no extra cost *with* the **Prentice Hall Jazz Collection,** a single CD compiled by David Cutler.

Together, the two anthologies contain sixty-seven outstanding jazz recordings. Because this book is designed for nonmusicians, I have omitted musical notation and overly technical musical analysis. However, the Introduction includes a **discussion of musical elements**—melody, harmony, rhythm, timbre, texture, dynamics, and form—and establishes a basic vocabulary of musical terms which appear frequently in later chapters.

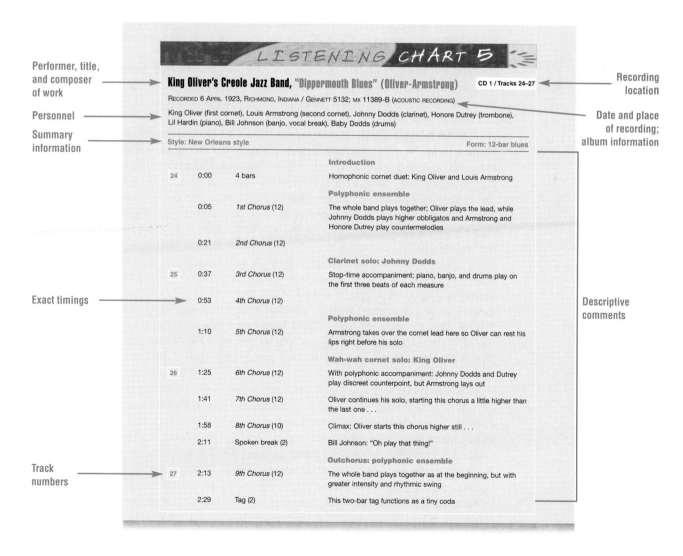

This book presents the history of jazz in narrative form, emphasizing chronology, cause and effect, and the human dramas that contributed to the shaping of musical style. As much as possible, I have tried to relate the story of jazz from the point of view of the original participants, often quoting the musicians, critics, promoters, and audiences that lived at the time the music was being made. Occasionally, later critical perspectives are used to show how a particular artist is viewed today or to contrast early and late views of the music. More typically, I have tried to avoid anachronisms in order to portray the development of jazz as faithfully as possible in historical terms.

As an introduction to jazz history, this book is not intended to be a definitive or comprehensive treatment. Accordingly, I have attempted to do more with less—to discuss fewer musicians in greater detail or within a richer historical context. The book devotes a full chapter to each of five seminal figures: Louis Armstrong, Duke Ellington, Charlie Parker, Miles Davis, and John Coltrane. Less influential musicians are treated in chapters on various styles or movements (bebop, cool jazz, hard bop, etc.). In keeping with their leading role, black players receive the most attention, but white musicians are not overlooked. The part on Swing, for instance, contains a chapter on white bands led by Benny Goodman, Artie Shaw, and Charlie Barnet. The contributions of women to jazz have been limited but powerful within their area of concentration. In the first chapter on singing—the one arena dominated by women—I assess the role of women in jazz generally. The book addresses styles and genres occasionally slighted in other histories, including contemporary big bands, Latin jazz, soul jazz, neo-bop, smooth jazz, acid jazz, and world fusion. Three chapters are devoted to jazz after 1975.

At this point perhaps a word of explanation is in order about the title—*Jazz: An American Journey.* I do not mean to imply that only Americans played or listened to jazz. Indeed, jazz bands in locations as farflung as Europe and Australia date back to the 1920s at least. Nor did Americans numerically outweigh jazz musicians and audiences from other countries; quite the contrary, in fact. But I don't believe it can be disputed that Americans both invented and developed jazz in all its major stylistic manifestations. The vast majority of innovative performers lived and worked primarily in the United States. Many books have been and will be written telling the story of jazz in other countries (a story that is arousing new and compelling interest with regard to exciting musical developments taking place in those countries today). But this book, as an introduction to the subject, dwells on the most historically influential figures in jazz history—the figures, mostly American, that largely set the standard for the rest of the world. Thus, our journey together will be primarily an American journey, focusing on people, places, and events that took place within the United States.

Like many textbooks, this one relies heavily on the scholarship and interpretations of other writers. I benefitted from the work of many experts on individual musicians and bands: Lawrence Gushee on Jelly Roll Morton, Mark Tucker and John Hasse on Duke Ellington, Jeffrey Magee on Fletcher Henderson, Jeffrey Taylor on Earl Hines, Richard Sudhalter on Bix Beiderbecke, Ross Firestone on Benny Goodman, Vladimir Simosko on Artie Shaw, John Chilton on Sidney Bechet and Coleman Hawkins, Lewis Porter on Lester Young, Stuart Nicholson, Donald Clarke, and Leslie Gourse on Billie Holiday and Ella Fitzgerald, Alyn Shipton on Dizzy Gillespie, Carl Woideck on Charlie Parker, Ted Gioia on Dave Brubeck, Gary Giddins on the Modern Jazz Quartet, Nick Catalano on Clifford

Brown, Gene Santoro on Charles Mingus, Jack Chambers on Miles Davis, John Litweiler on Ornette Coleman, Peter Pettinger on Bill Evans, Eric Nisensen and Lewis Porter on John Coltrane, Donald L. Maggin on Stan Getz, Leslie Gourse on Joe Williams and Wynton Marsalis. I also learned much from authorities on periods and styles. Scott DeVeaux's landmark work, *The Birth of Bebop: A Musical and Social History,* provided the historical basis for much of the material on swing and early modern jazz. In addition, I would like to acknowledge the work of Gunther Schuller and William Howland Kenney on early jazz, Schuller and David W. Stowe on swing, Richard Sudhalter on white jazz, Ted Gioia on West Coast jazz, David H. Rosenthal and Kenny Mathieson on hard bop and soul jazz, John Litweiler, Ekkehard Jost, and A. B. Spellman on free jazz, John Roberts Storm on Latin jazz, and Stuart Nicholson on jazz-rock and neo-bop.

I am grateful to Chris Johnson at Prentice Hall, who encouraged me to write the book in the first place, and to my production and copy editor Laura Lawrie, who shepherded the project to its completion. I thank the anonymous readers who reviewed the manuscript, as well as the colleagues, friends, and family members who read and commented on portions of the work: Ian Bent, Steve Call, Herbert Harker, Rand Harker, Scott Harker, and Steven Johnson. Michael Hicks read the entire manuscript and helped in many other ways besides. Thanks to my father, Herbert Harker, who drew the maps. I am grateful to Hans Klarer for allowing me to tell his story in the Introduction. A special thanks also goes to David Murray for answering one of my queries about his work with the World Saxophone Quartet. Jay Lawrence and Justin Cash shared with me their knowledge of jazz in the 1990s. Edward A. Berlin and Thomas Riis kindly answered questions about early popular songs. I learned about New Orleans *charivari* from a talk Mark McKnight gave at a conference on American music. Francelle Carapetyan secured licensing rights for the illustrations; Tom Laskey, of Sony Music, produced the 3-CD recording set. Denae Coco and Joseph Hoffman helped with research. I would like to acknowledge my particular indebtedness to the late Mark Tucker for all he taught me about jazz and scholarship, without which this book would not have been possible. Finally, I am grateful to my wife, Sally, and my boys, Daniel and Robbie, for their loving support and encouragement during the process of writing.

Brian Harker

Introduction

On October 31, 1957, a twenty-five-year-old commercial artist named Hans Klarer left his home in Zurich, Switzerland, boarded the Queen Elizabeth, and sailed for New York. Upon arriving a week later, he immediately left his bags at a YMCA and called a taxi. "Take me to Birdland," he told the driver excitedly. Hans Klarer had come to the United States for nothing so mundane as to pursue the American dream. He had come to hear the best live jazz in the world and to meet the musicians who played it.

Hans had grown up listening to swing bands on Voice of America, a shortwave radio program broadcast from the United States to Europe and other industrialized parts of the world. Over the years he became an avid record collector. The first sounds of modern jazz repelled him, but he quickly acclimated to the new style. He and his friends even adopted the sartorial image of the European bebop devotee: long hair, high-water pants, striped socks. Once in New York, Hans regularly patronized the top nightclubs: Jazz Gallery, Café Bohemia, and the Village Vanguard, as well as Birdland. He heard big bands—Count Basie, Maynard Ferguson, Woody Herman, Stan Kenton. And he reveled in the rich variety of small groups, including those of Miles Davis, Bud Powell, Horace Silver, and Gerry Mulligan. It was, he recalled, a jazz lover's paradise.

Hans still lives in New York. He likes nothing better than to regale his friends with memories of what he clearly views as a golden age of jazz history—the period from swing to the sixties that occupies the central portion of this book.

A Controversial Music

Hans Klarer's story of immigration for jazz may sound dramatic, but the passion behind it is not unusual. Many jazz players and fans speak of their first contact with the music as something akin to religious conversion or romantic love. Such strong feelings have naturally led to partisan disagreements. Every critic or fan has experienced the shock of hearing a favorite record maligned by a fellow commentator.

Not surprisingly, the history of jazz has been fraught with controversy. In the 1920s, fundamentalists and freethinkers argued over the moral propriety of jazz. With the birth of jazz criticism in the 1930s, battle lines were drawn between insiders who debated the musical merits of individual bands and soloists. Writers in the 1940s fought over the issue of authenticity: Was swing a commercial corruption of "the real jazz" born in New Orleans? Was bebop a betrayal of the jazz tradition? In the 1950s, as the civil rights movement heated up, the question turned to race: What distinguished "black" from "white" jazz? And, reformulating an older problem, what was the proper relation between jazz and classical music? Could the two ever be reconciled? Then in the 1960s the tone became anxious as free jazz seemingly drove a generation of listeners into the burgeoning pop market. Was jazz dying? Some thought so when mainstream artists began wedding the music to rock and funk. Yet jazz continues to be played today and remains a topic of healthy dispute. Many vital issues of the past still interest us, but we see them through the continually shifting perspective of our own time. As ever, the arguments focus on interpretation: What is the *meaning* of this remarkably durable music?

Jazz in the Academy

Given this legacy of impassioned discourse, one might expect jazz to find a natural home in the academy. Yet, although colleges have offered performance courses in jazz for decades, most curricula have whole-heartedly embraced jazz history, theory, and composition only recently. Even today, some members of the jazz community—mostly performers—question the relevance of jazz in the university. They feel that as an emotional, intuitive art, jazz should not be strapped to the dissection table of intellectual analysis. They are in good company: both Louis Armstrong and Duke Ellington evidently felt the same way.

Even so, a multitude of eminent jazz artists now routinely serve on university or conservatory faculties, often in adjunct capacities. The steadily growing roster includes Oscar Peterson, Clark Terry, JoAnne Brackeen, Jim Hall, Billy Taylor, Jimmy Heath, Gunther Schuller, and, most prominently, Wynton Marsalis. These educators take the position that jazz deserves—and can withstand—just as much serious attention as any other musical tradition in Western culture. They believe that jazz looks richer, not poorer, under close scrutiny. And they believe students come away enriched for having studied jazz in an academic setting.

In the best of all possible worlds we might wish to follow the example of Hans Klarer and learn about jazz directly from the people who created it. But given the constraints of time, space, and money, most students cannot hope for such utopian adventures. Moreover, in the last half-century historians have constructed a vision of the music's long-range development that even Birdland could not provide. By combining historical perspective with the immediacy of classic recordings, this book aims to strike a balance between objective scholarship and firsthand experience with the music.

Definitions

One of the most intractable problems facing the student of jazz has to do with definitions. What, precisely, *is* jazz? Let's start with etymology. The word "jazz" was apparently used colloquially in the first decade of the twentieth century to mean pep, vitality, or the sex act. The first known printed usage appeared in 1913. A San Francisco sportswriter used the word to describe the spirit and energy of certain baseball players: "Everybody [on the team] has come back full of the old 'jazz'." During World War I, New Orleans musicians used the word (with various spellings) in the names of their bands: Stein's Dixie Jass Band, Original Dixieland Jass Band, New Orleans Jazz Band. By 1917, a New York journalist could report that "a strange word has gained widespread use in the ranks of our producers of popular music. It is 'jazz,' used mainly as an adjective descriptive of a band." To this music dancers "shake and jump and writhe in ways to suggest a return to the medieval jumping mania."

Since that time, the question of how to define jazz has produced much of the controversy referred to above. Some call it "America's classical music"; others refer to it as the art music of black Americans. One often hears that it must be improvised, that it must "swing," or that it must be rooted in the blues. At various times in the music's history writers have questioned the validity of commercially successful jazz, convinced as they are that jazz must reflect folk or patently artistic sensibilities. Some consider jazz a process (*how* one plays), others a product (*what* is played). Most probably view it as a primarily musical phenomenon; but one prominent commentator insists that jazz is "mostly about race, sexuality, and spectacle." Understandably frustrated by the obsession with categorizing, some jazz musicians have simply rejected the term.

As this book proceeds it will become clear that jazz is indeed an inadequate term for the bewildering array of musical styles covered by it. For present purposes we will view jazz as an American musical tradition that began in the early twentieth century and continues today, a tradition with multiple meanings determined by whatever generation was using the word at any given time. Paul Whiteman in the 1920s understood "jazz" to be something very different from what Cecil Taylor understood by it in the 1960s.

The Evolution of Jazz Style

Most accounts of jazz history depict an evolutionary process in which the music changes from one generation to the next, producing a succession of styles: Dixieland, swing, bebop, cool jazz, hard bop, free jazz, Latin jazz, soul jazz, fusion, acid jazz, and so forth. Many factors have affected the evolution of jazz style. Some are transitory, involving accidents of history or the influence of one musician on another. Other factors have exerted a more or less continuous impact. In this book, three of these will appear as recurring themes: racial ideology, European classical influence, and cross-instrumental influences.

Racial Ideology

With few exceptions, most of the major innovators, composers, and soloists in jazz have been black. In this sense jazz can be seen as fundamentally an expression of the African American experience. In the early twentieth century, black Americans fought for social equality through primarily economic means. It was thought that economic self-reliance would win the black community admiration, respect, and eventually social and political freedom. But the white establishment erected high barriers to black financial success. Prejudice kept most blacks in manual labor or service occupations; only a small minority broke into the professional world.

In the fields of entertainment and sports, however, blacks found occupations with fewer social barriers and greater financial rewards. Jazz began as one of these occupations. During this period jazz provided light entertainment or dance music. It was, in short, a **functional music,** fulfilling a social purpose outside itself. Like singers, dancers, jugglers, and comedians, jazz musicians aspired to succeed in show business. Indeed, in addition to playing their instruments many of them sang, danced, told jokes, or took acting roles in Hollywood movies.

functional music music that fulfills a social purpose outside itself.

Yet, by World War II, it had become obvious that the entertainment industry was determined to block the progress of all but the most prominent black jazz musicians. Bitterness set in among young players that paralleled a broader disillusionment in the black community. Gradually, for both jazz musicians and black society, the emphasis shifted from economic to political goals. The civil rights movement made clear that blacks were no longer willing to wait for fair treatment; they would demand it as American citizens. In jazz this attitude produced new styles of music no longer intended to entertain or ingratiate but to edify, challenge, or provoke. Performers and audiences increasingly viewed jazz as an **art music,** meant primarily for attentive listening. The political overtones of postwar jazz increased as the civil rights movement grew.

European Classical Influence

Notwithstanding the fact of black dominance, jazz is undeniably a product, also, of the confrontation between African American and European American musical traditions. Western *classical music*—art music for the concert hall—has been influential on several levels. In the 1920s and 1930s, classical composers such as Igor Stravinsky, Maurice Ravel, and Aaron Copland experimented with jazz idioms in their works for orchestra. Working from the opposite direction, jazz musicians from Paul Whiteman to Claude Thornhill to the Modern Jazz Quartet absorbed classical elements into their jazz pieces. With few exceptions, these attempts to fuse jazz and classical idioms remained at an experimental level, exerting little lasting influence on jazz style.

In other, subtler ways, however, classical traditions have made a profound and enduring impact. Above all, jazz musicians have perennially sought to improve their instrumental skill through European training, technique, and repertory. The influence of classical pedagogy on jazz musicians began with New Orleans Creoles and extended down to the generation of Wynton Marsalis (b. 1961), the first musician to receive a Grammy Award in both jazz and classical categories. Instruments with already strong ties to European music have benefitted the most; the evolution of jazz piano style, for instance, has shown the greatest debt to classical training. The saxophone, by contrast, with an extremely limited classical tradition, has developed in a manner far more independent of European pedagogy.

Cross-Instrumental Influences

Another important engine of stylistic change has been the influence of one instrument's distinctive idiom on another. This process especially spurred the rise in *virtuosity* (high instrumental skill) during the early years of jazz. Some instruments assimilated foreign idioms more readily than others. Usually the pattern has been for traditionally less agile instruments to coopt the style of more fluent ones. Trombone players imitated trumpet players, trumpet players imitated clarinetists and saxophonists, and woodwind players imitated pianists and guitarists.

Pianists dominated the arena of technical facility, having drawn much of their virtuosity from classical training. Yet sometimes an individual's musical personality was strong enough to trump idiom; players of all instruments imitated the trumpeter Louis Armstrong and the saxophonist Charlie Parker, for instance. Jazz musicians generally prospered by adapting their playing to the strengths of their most formidable competitors, whether those strengths were determined by instrumental idiom or personal idiosyncrasy.

art music music meant primarily for attentive listening.

A Few Basic Concepts

In order to understand the music discussed in this book, readers will need to master a basic vocabulary of musical terms and concepts. We will define the principles first and then see how they apply to a particular piece.

Rhythm

Let's begin with **rhythm,** a vital element of any jazz performance. Rhythm refers to the patterns of sound durations produced by the various instruments. In jazz, an especially prominent aspect of rhythm is the **beat.** This term refers to the division of musical time into regular recurring units. It is the pulse or "heartbeat" of the music, the thump-thump-thump-thump to which you tap your foot.

We use the word **tempo** to describe the speed of the beat. Classical music identifies tempo with Italian terms such as *Andante, Moderato,* and *Allegro,* but these have never gained widespread currency in jazz. To describe a fast piece, jazz musicians often use the words *uptempo* or *jump tune.* A slow piece (that is not a blues) is called a *ballad.*

Almost all music, including jazz, manifests what is called **meter,** the organization of the beat into regular recurring patterns. Most jazz is in *duple* or *quadruple meter,* meaning that the beat falls into groups of two or four. The most common meter in jazz is a quadruple meter known as 4/4 (pronounced "four-four") time. Some jazz after World War II is in *triple meter* (groups of three beats) or more complex meters, but these remain exceptional cases. The groups of beats themselves are called **measures** or **bars.** Thus, four bars in 4/4 time contain sixteen beats.

Now we come to one of the most important aspects of jazz rhythm—a sense of **swing.** Swing resists definition, even in technical terms, but listeners can easily learn to recognize it. Swing is a propulsive rhythmic intensity that seems to carry the music forward. It is that aspect of a performance that makes you want to tap your foot, bob your head, or—if you are an extrovert—get up and dance.

Although hard to define, swing has two easily recognizable characteristics. First, it implies an underlying rhythmic structure that subdivides each beat into two unequal parts: a long note and a short note (specifically, a note half as long as the first one). This subdivision produces what we call "eighth notes"— so-named because you can count eight of them in any bar in 4/4 time. Eighth notes with unequal durations, such as we have just described, are called *swing eighth notes.* Eighth notes with equal durations are called *straight eighth notes.* Whether explicit in the outward melodies or only implied by the rhythm section, swing eighth notes create an "eight-to-the-bar" rhythmic pattern that is a hallmark of the swing effect.

A second characteristic of swing is **syncopation.** This word refers to the accentuation of rhythms that ordinarily go unaccented. In 4/4 time beats 1 and 3 are normally strong, or accented, while beats 2 and 4 are weak, or unaccented. Thus, we count ONE two THREE four, ONE two THREE four. The strong beats are called *downbeats;* the weak beats *upbeats.* Syncopation occurs when musicians play accents on the upbeats and on rhythms between the beats.

Melody

Now let's turn our attention to **melody.** First we must address the matter of **pitch**— the "highness" or "lowness" of a sound as determined by the speed of the sound's vibrations. For instance, a woman generally sings (and speaks) at a higher pitch

rhythm the durational patterns of sound and silence in a piece of music.

beat (or pulse) the division of musical time into regular, recurring units; also: any one of those units.

tempo the speed of the beat.

meter the organization of the beat into regular, recurring patterns.

measure (or bar) the regular groupings of beats in a given meter; e.g., in 4/4 time, sixteen beats add up to four measures.

swing the propulsive rhythmic intensity in a jazz performance defined, in part, by accented upbeats and an alternating long-short / long-short rhythmic pattern at the eighth-note level.

syncopation the accentuation of rhythms that ordinarily go unaccented.

melody a linear succession of pitches that we hear as a coherent unit.

pitch (1) the "highness" or "lowness" of a sound as determined by the speed of the sound's vibration; (2) a discrete unit within the pitch spectrum; sometimes called a *note.*

level than a man does. The Western musical system divides the pitch spectrum into discrete units which are themselves called "pitches" or notes. Technically, a *note* is a pitch that is written down or *notated*, but musicians often use the terms interchangeably. **Notation,** by the same logic, consists of music that is written down.

Melody, then, may be defined as a succession of pitches (and rhythms) that we recognize as a coherent unit; the tune to "Twinkle, Twinkle, Little Star" is a good example. A **motive** is a short musical idea that serves as a building block of melody; melodies often consist of two or three motives linked together. ("Twinkle, Twinkle" has only one motive—a seven-note rhythmic pattern: short-short-short-short-short-short-LONG—that repeats over and over.) Here are some other useful concepts relating to melody: interval, scale, and octave. An **interval** is the vertical distance (that is, the highness-lowness relationship) between any two pitches. Two adjacent white keys on the piano keyboard are said to be a "second" apart, or at the interval of a second. Count out three adjacent white keys and the distance between the first and last keys is a third. Count out four white keys and you have a fourth, and so on. A **scale** is an abstract collection of pitches from which musicians draw to create melodies. Play seven adjacent white keys in succession (from left to right) on the piano and you will have created some version of the *diatonic scale*—the most common scale in Western music, including jazz. Now play one more white key, making eight keys in all; you may notice that this last note seems in some sense to duplicate the first note of the scale: it sounds the same, only higher. The interval between these two notes is called an **octave** (or the interval of an "eighth").

Harmony

Whereas melody refers to the linear or horizontal succession of pitches in time, **harmony** refers to their simultaneous sounding. In jazz and other types of Western music, most harmony is based on the *chord,* a harmonic entity usually comprising from three to seven pitches, each lying a third apart from the next one. Chords show up in various ways in a jazz performance, but are played most explicitly by the pianist or guitarist (or both) in the band.

Harmony also refers to more large-scale pitch relationships in a piece of music. Here the important concept to understand is **key.** The key of a piece is its tonal center, or central pitch around which all other pitches seem to gravitate. To get a feel for this elusive concept, think about the end of the song "Somewhere Over the Rainbow," from the classic film *The Wizard of Oz*. Imagine that after Judy Garland sang "If happy little bluebirds fly beyond the rainbow, why, oh why, caaan't—" that she ended the song there and never sang the last note on "I." Wouldn't you feel frustrated as a listener? Wouldn't the piece seem incomplete, unresolved, as if the ending had been aborted? That desire we have to hear the last note in a song reflects our strong sense of key. Another way to understand this concept is to go to the piano, play a note, then sing a simple melody starting on that note. Now choose a different note to start on (not the octave!) and sing it again. You have just sung the same melody in two different keys. The process of changing from one key to another is called **modulation.**

A concept related to key is that of **mode.** There are two modes pertinent to this book: *major* and *minor*. The important chords in a piece of music determine its mode. In general, major chords sound bright and open; minor chords sound darker and more unstable. In a similar way, a piece of music in major mode often seems cheerful, while one in minor mode can arouse more complex

---

notation music that is written down, i.e., in *notes*.

motive a short musical idea that serves as a building block for melodies, often through repetition and development.

interval the vertical distance (i.e., the "highness-lowness" relationship) between any two pitches.

scale an abstract collection of pitches from which musicians draw to create melodies.

octave the interval of an eighth.

harmony (1) the simultaneous sounding of two or more pitches; (2) more abstractly, the system of pitch relationships in a given piece.

key in most jazz before c. 1960, the tonal center, or central pitch, around which all other pitches seem to gravitate.

modulation the process of changing from one key to another.

mode a harmonic quality conveying certain emotional effects in a piece: *major mode* often sounds bright or happy; *minor mode* sounds darker, more complex.

emotions. You can compare these two modes by singing to yourself "Happy Birthday," a song in major mode, followed by "Greensleeves," a song in minor mode. As you ponder the curious effects of mode, remember that other factors contribute to the emotional makeup of a piece as well.

Two final concepts related to harmony are consonance and dissonance. **Consonance** refers to a state of harmonic rest, whereas **dissonance** refers to harmonic tension. The most consonant interval is the octave. Major and minor chords are also consonant harmonies, though the latter contains slightly more tension. To experience dissonance, go to the piano and play a black key and an adjacent white key at the same time. This harsh interval is called a *half-step.* Now play all the notes within an octave, both white and black, in succession from left to right. Not including the octave itself, you should have played a total of twelve notes. These twelve notes constitute the *chromatic scale.* Music that features portions of the chromatic scale is said to be "chromatic" or to manifest "chromaticism." Such passages often are perceived to have a high level of dissonance, being composed entirely of *half-steps.*

Tone Color

The aspect of music that allows you to distinguish between one instrument and another is called **tone color** (or **timbre**). Some of the most magical effects in jazz derive from the interaction of tone colors. This interaction is governed by two factors: instrumentation and orchestration. **Instrumentation** refers to the particular instruments the composer or musicians have chosen for the performance. The principal instruments used in jazz include the following:

Brass
trumpet/cornet
trombone

Woodwinds
clarinet
soprano saxophone
alto saxophone
tenor saxophone
baritone saxophone

Rhythm section instruments
piano
guitar/banjo
string bass/tuba
drums

As shown here, these instruments are often divided into families according to their constructive material (brass, woodwinds) or musical function (rhythm). You also should note that musicians commonly use four different types of saxophone, which correspond roughly to the four standard vocal ranges and are ordered from highest and smallest (soprano) to lowest and largest (baritone).

Orchestration refers to the way a composer or arranger uses the instruments in a given piece, deciding which ones play the melody, which ones the harmony, how they are combined, and so forth. Unlike mere instrumentation, orchestration is an art in itself, requiring exquisite sensitivity to nuances of musical color and texture.

consonance a state of harmonic rest.

dissonance a state of harmonic tension.

tone color (or timbre) that dimension of a sound that allows you to distinguish between one instrument and another; also: the inherent sound of a particular instrument.

instrumentation the particular instruments chosen for a given piece or performance.

orchestration the way a composer or arranger uses the available instruments in a given piece.

Texture

Texture refers to the overall musical fabric created by the simultaneous presentation of musical lines. If you have a group of instruments all playing a single melody, the texture is *monophonic;* musicians refer to this as playing in **unison.** Two or more melodies sounding simultaneously create **polyphony** or **counterpoint** (adj., *contrapuntal*), whereas one melody with any kind of accompaniment is called **homophony.** Most jazz performances feature subtle combinations of these three basic textures.

In this book, we will use the term "homophony" to refer to cases in which a group of instruments plays the same rhythms at the same time but with harmony lines added to the melody. This kind of texture is sometimes called *chordal homophony* because it produces chords under every melody note. You often hear chordal homophony in church, for instance, when some people sing the melody of a hymn while others sing harmony parts in the same rhythms.

Dynamics

We use the word **dynamics** to refer to the patterns of loud and soft in the music. Classical music has developed a vocabulary of Italian terms pertaining to dynamics, which jazz musicians have generally found to be more useful than those relating to tempo. Some of these include: *forte* (loud), *piano* (soft), *crescendo* (gradually louder), and *decrescendo* (gradually softer).

Form

The **form,** or shape, of a piece is determined by three principles: repetition, contrast, and variation. *Repetition* is when an element is repeated identically. *Contrast* is when a second element is new, distinctly different from the first. And *variation* is when the second element introduces some new aspects but also retains some similarity with the first element.

We use letters of the alphabet to designate the various sections of a piece of music. The first element is A, a contrasting element is B, a variation of the first element is A′, a second contrasting element is C, and so forth. Because the most common form in jazz is AABA, we will use this form as our example. In most pieces in this form, each section has the same length—thirty-two beats or eight bars. Thus, the entire AABA structure normally lasts thirty-two bars.

Most jazz pieces in AABA form have a *cyclical* structure, meaning that this basic design repeats (with variations) several times in the course of the piece. Each statement of the AABA form is called a **chorus.** The first chorus usually presents the main melody; subsequent choruses often feature soloists. In the absence of the melody, what unites all the choruses? The common denominator is a fundamental **chord progression,** a thirty-two-bar sequence of chords that defines the AABA chorus structure and can be heard "underneath" surface differences like changes of orchestration and the absence of the main melody. Musicians use the word **cadence** to describe the sense of resolution that occurs near the end of a chord progression or other formal section of music.

Improvisation versus Composition

Pure **composition** is when every detail of a performance is worked out in advance; pure **improvisation** is when every detail is invented on the spot. Jazz musicians typically use a mixture of predetermined and spontaneous elements. As one way of understanding this process, imagine yourself having an informal

---

texture the overall musical fabric created by the simultaneous presentation of musical lines (or parts).

unison the texture produced by a group of instruments all playing the same melody.

polyphony (or counterpoint) a texture of two or more melodies proceeding simultaneously.

homophony a texture often defined as melody with accompaniment.

dynamics the patterns of loud and soft in music.

form the shape of a piece of music, as determined by its patterns of repetition, contrast, and variation.

chorus a fundamental chord progression (usually 8, 12, 16, 24, or 32 bars long) that repeats again and again, cyclically, over the course of a jazz performance.

chord progression in any given piece, a repeating sequence of chords that provide the harmonic basis for jazz arrangements and improvisation.

cadence a melodic and/or harmonic gesture that creates a sense of resolution at the end of a melody, chord progression, or other formal section of music.

composition the process of creating a piece of music in advance of its first performance.

improvisation the process of spontaneously creating a musical statement during the act of performance.

conversation with a friend at lunch. Unless you wrote down beforehand every word of your conversation (pure composition) or communicated in a language you both invented on the spot (pure improvisation), you would bring a combination of rehearsed and spontaneous elements to your conversation. Jazz musicians "improvise" in a manner very similar to our impromptu use of language.

Improvisation and composition imply different methods of musical transmission. A great deal of jazz composition forms part of a **notated tradition** in which the notes are preserved by writing them down. Improvisation, by contrast, usually stems from an **aural tradition** that is passed from one player to another through memorized recreations of live performances. The advent of recording technology in the twentieth century bridged these two traditions by making possible a permanent record of live music but one that is accessible only by ear.

Putting It All Together: A Practice Analysis

To illustrate these principles we will now examine a classic jazz recording from 1941, Duke Ellington's performance of "Take the 'A' Train," a piece by Billy Strayhorn.

Let's start, first of all, by listening to the piece from beginning to end.

Now, let's back up and listen again, slowly and carefully this time, focusing on certain details of the performance. As we do, please refer frequently to **Listening Chart 1,** a diagram that divides the piece visually into seven different parts:

Introduction
Main melody
Muted trumpet solo: Ray Nance
Transition
Open trumpet solo: Ray Nance
(Partial) main melody
Coda

The purpose of the *introduction* is to capture the listener's attention and prepare the main material. Here, Duke Ellington plays a short, simple solo on piano while Sonny Greer accompanies on drums. You can hear the **beat** clearly marked by the bass drum in the introduction and you can "feel" it continuously thereafter. The piece moves along at a medium **tempo**—not too fast, not too slow. Can you figure out the **meter?** It's in 4/4 time, a meter you can verify for yourself by counting the beats in groups of four from the beginning of the recording (**Track 1**):

1 2 3 4   2 2 3 4   3 2 3 4   4 2 3 4 . . . etc.

By the end of four groups of four you should be through the piano introduction and ready to begin the main melody. Hence, the piano introduction lasts for sixteen beats—or four bars:

bar 1   bar 2   bar 3   bar 4
1 2 3 4   2 2 3 4   3 2 3 4   4 2 3 4 . . . etc.

The next part is the *main melody,* in AABA form. The saxophones play this melody in **unison** while the trumpets and trombones provide punchy *background figures* (**Track 2,** 0:05–0:50). Are you tapping your foot by now? If so,

notated tradition a method of musical transmission that involves preserving musical details by writing them down.

aural tradition a method of musical transmission that involves passing music from one generation to another through memorized recreations of live performances.

LISTENING CHART 1

Duke Ellington and His Famous Orchestra, "Take the 'A' Train" (Strayhorn)

CD 1 / Tracks 1–10

RECORDED 15 FEBRUARY 1941, HOLLYWOOD / VICTOR 27380; MX 055283-1

Wallace Jones, Ray Nance (trumpets), Rex Stewart (cornet), Lawrence Brown, Tricky Sam Nanton (trombones), Juan Tizol (valve trombone), Johnny Hodges, Otto Hardwick (alto saxophones), Barney Bigard (clarinet), Ben Webster (tenor saxophone), Harry Carney (baritone saxophone), Duke Ellington (piano), Fred Guy (guitar), Jimmy Blanton (bass), Sonny Greer (drums)

Style: Big band swing   **Form: AABA song form**

			Introduction
1	0:00	4 bars = 16 beats	Piano solo: Duke Ellington; bass drum indicates the *beat*, marking four pulses for each bar: thump-thump-thump-thump
		1st Chorus	**Main Melody**
2	0:05	A (8 bars = 32 beats)	Saxophones play the A-section of main melody *in unison;* trumpets and trombones play punchy background figures
3	0:13		An entire bar of *swing eighth notes*
	0:17	A (8 bars)	*A-section repeated*
4	0:28	B (8 bars)	Saxophones play B-section (bridge) of main melody in unison; trombones play background figures
	0:40	A (8 bars)	Saxophones: the A-section of main melody in unison; brass: background figures
		2nd Chorus	**Muted Trumpet Solo: Ray Nance**
5	0:51	A (8)	*Polyphonic texture (first 4 bars):* Ray Nance's solo lines + saxophone *countermelody;* Nance plays with a *mute* in his trumpet
	1:02	A (8)	*A-section repeated:* saxophone countermelody the same, Nance's solo different
6	1:14	B (8)	*Homophonic texture:* Nance continues, with saxophones playing sustained *chords*
	1:25	A (8)	*Polyphonic texture (first 4 bars):* Nance continues, saxophones return to A-section countermelody
			Transition
7	1:37	5 bars: 3 + 3 + 3 + 3 + 4	Full ensemble in *triple meter* (except for the last bar); music *modulates* from the original key to a new one

		3rd Chorus		**Open Trumpet Solo: Ray Nance**
		A (8) (New key)		*Call-and-response:* Saxophones (call) vs. Nance (response)
8	1:42	*Call* (4)	1st half	Saxophones play rising line in *chordal homophony;* the line is *syncopated* and consists of a complete *diatonic scale*
	1:45		2nd half	Saxophones immediately follow rising line with a burst of rapidly falling notes—a descending *chromatic line*
9	1:47	*Response* (4)		Nance plays an *open horn* solo (without a mute)
	1:54	A (8)		*A-section repeated:* Saxophone line the same, Nance's solo different
	2:05	B (8)		Nance continues, as ensemble builds to climax behind him
		Main Melody (Partial Reprise)		
10	2:16	A (8)		Saxophones: the A-section of main melody in unison; brass: background figures
		Coda		
	2:27	A (8)		The A-section played again, but softer (use of *dynamics*)
	2:38	A′ (8)		The A-section played again, still softer—then the piece ends

you have probably discovered the wonderful sense of **swing** that the Ellington orchestra generates on this recording. In fact, you can hear an entire bar of **swing eighth notes** in the saxophone part at the end of the first A-section (**Track 3,** 0:13–0:14). During the B-section (also called the *bridge*) the trumpets drop out and allow the trombones to accompany the saxophone melody by themselves (**Track 4**).

In the next part—the second **chorus** of the AABA form—Ray Nance plays a *muted trumpet solo* (**Track 5**). Nance uses a *mute,* a cone-shaped metal object that fits into the bell of the trumpet, to give his sound a ritzy metallic effect. In the first half of each A-section composer Strayhorn calls for a **polyphonic** texture: while Nance plays his solo, the saxophones add what might be called a *countermelody* in the background. The saxophones are clearly subordinate to Nance; still, the saxophone line carries a melodic importance that raises it well above the status of mere "accompaniment." We have the clear sense of two melodies proceeding at the same time. During the bridge, by contrast, a **homophonic** texture predominates, as the saxophones accompany Nance with sustained **chords** (**Track 6**).

The next part is a brief *transition,* or connecting passage, between Nance's two trumpet solos (**Track 7**). Here the whole orchestra plays *forte* (loud), providing

swing eighth notes   eighth notes that proceed in uneven (long-short / long-short) alternation, with accented upbeats.

chord   in its fundamental form, a harmonic unit composed of three to seven pitches, each spaced a third apart from the next one.

a refreshing contrast with the thinner solo textures before and after the transition. The transition supplies a good example of **modulation,** in which the music changes from one key to another. It also illustrates Strayhorn's imaginative rhythmic sense: here he switches briefly to triple **meter** to create instability and excitement. The transition consists of five bars—four in triple meter and the last one in quadruple meter:

1:37	ONE two three	bar 1
1:38	ONE two three	bar 2
1:39	ONE two three	bar 3
1:40	ONE two three	bar 4
1:41	ONE two THREE four	bar 5

In the next part—the third and final chorus—Nance plays his second solo and the piece builds to a climax. The texture now becomes more complicated: in a dialogue known as **call-and-response,** the saxophones "call" (four bars) and Nance "responds" (four bars), back and forth, for the first two A-sections. The saxophone "call" divides into two halves—a rising line and a shorter descending one (followed by a sustained note). The first half illustrates three principles: (1) the saxophones play in **chordal homophony;** (2) the line ascends in stuttering **syncopation;** and (3) the line consists of a complete **diatonic scale** (including the **octave**). The second half, a burst of rapidly descending notes, illustrates a **chromatic line** (proceeding, as it does, entirely by half-step) (**Track 8**).

This "call" is then followed by Nance's solo "response." In this solo he plays *open horn*—without a mute; his trumpet now sounds bold and expansive (**Track 9**). Then the trombones and saxophones provide *counterpoint* behind Nance's solo as the B-section builds to a climax.

The last part of the piece consists of a partial reprise of the main melody—the A-section—followed by a **coda** (or concluding section) (**Track 10**). In the coda the saxophones restate the A-section twice, playing softer each time in a long **decrescendo.** The piece ends with a variant of an old-fashioned vaudeville **cadence.**

Some Closing Thoughts

I hope by now that you have come to enjoy listening to "Take the 'A' Train." Perhaps you liked the piece the first time you heard it. Perhaps it will continue to grow on you. And perhaps, in spite of all your good faith efforts, you will *never* develop a real appreciation for the piece. There are some people out there, even musicians, for whom jazz never seems to "take," no matter how much they apparently give it a chance. I suspect, however, that like most things, jazz will become more interesting the more you learn about it.

If you are new to jazz, I have three pieces of advice as you begin to explore this music: first, remember that, like other complex art forms, jazz may become an acquired taste, one you appreciate only after lengthy exposure and contemplation. Second, you may prefer some styles, soloists, or bands over others, so keep your ears open! And third, don't ever suppose that because something falls into the stylistic category of "jazz," that it automatically merits your attention. There is some superb jazz and there is a great deal of very bad or mediocre jazz. Maintain a healthy curiosity and an open mind, and you will probably encounter some jazz that interests you. From time to time you may even find yourself swept into the realm of fascination inhabited by the Hans Klarers of the world.

call-and-response an alternating dialogue between individuals or groups common in much African American music, including jazz.

chordal homophony a texture in which each melody note is supported by an underlying chord. See homophony.

diatonic scale a scale having the following intervallic structure: whole-step / whole-step / half-step / whole-step / whole-step / whole-step / half-step.

coda a brief concluding section in a piece of music.

decrescendo gradually softer.

One

Origins

(c. 1900–1914)

Black Americans at the Turn of the Century

Chapter 1

BECAUSE EARLY JAZZ WAS RARELY NOTATED, IT IS IMPOSSIBLE TO SAY EXACTLY WHEN THE music came into being. The first recordings by a group that called itself a "jazz band" were made in 1917, but the stylistic consistency of those performances suggests they were already part of a tradition. Indeed, musicians from the period claimed that "jazz" (or something like it) was played in live settings long before it appeared on records—as early as the turn of the century, by many accounts. Scholars sometimes refer to the shadowy interval between the birth of jazz and its first recording as the **prehistory** of the music.

The testimony of eyewitnesses also makes clear that, although both black and white musicians performed early jazz, blacks took the lead in its development. They had strong incentives to do so. In post–Civil War America harsh discrimination often consigned blacks to menial labor or service occupations unless they showed talent for the lucrative fields of music, dance, and other forms of popular entertainment. Thus, early jazz served as a vehicle of upward mobility for blacks struggling to improve their lot. A brief survey of African American history in the late nineteenth century will lay the groundwork for a closer look at the origins of jazz.

c. 1830s–1910s	Age of minstrelsy
1861–1865	Civil War
1865–1877	Reconstruction
1865	Ku Klux Klan organized
1871–1878	Fisk Jubilee Singers tour
1892	John Philip Sousa organizes his professional band
c. 1890s–1930s	Age of vaudeville
1895	Booker T. Washington's Atlanta Compromise Speech
1895–1907	Buddy Bolden active musically
1896	*Plessy v. Ferguson*
1899	Scott Joplin publishes "Maple Leaf Rag"
1903	W. E. B. Du Bois's *Souls of Black Folk*
1909	NAACP organized
c. 1910	Charley Patton develops early blues songs
1911	Irving Berlin publishes "Alexander's Ragtime Band"
1910s	Bert Williams active in Ziegfeld's *Follies*

The Reconstruction Era

In some ways, the condition of blacks at the turn of the century was worse than it had been immediately after the Civil War. During the period of **Reconstruction** (1865–1877) the Republican-led federal government took dramatic steps to guarantee former slaves the full benefits of democratic citizenship and equal treatment under the law. With the Thirteenth, Fourteenth, and Fifteenth Amendments to the Constitution, Congress abolished slavery and gave blacks citizenship and the right to vote. For the first time, southern blacks could now legally marry, own property, and participate in the political process.

In order to rebuild the South and help blacks enter the mainstream of society, Congress sent northern officials to fill leadership positions in the southern states. Such federally sponsored Reconstruction governments made it possible for blacks to hold elected office and to help determine policy for their own constituencies. African Americans served as U.S. senators, members of the House of Representatives, and at the state level as lieutenant governors, speakers of the house, secretaries of state, and Supreme Court justices. With black political empowerment this period held out the prospect of a free and equal society.

Southern intransigence, however, blocked such aspirations. White southerners resented and feared black representation in government. They referred contemptuously to the visiting northern politicians as "carpetbaggers" (for the suitcases they carried), and called southern whites who supported Reconstruction "scalawags." To perpetuate the condition of black enslavement southern states enacted the so-called **black codes.** Modeled on the slave codes of the pre–Civil War period, the black codes limited the types of property blacks could own, excluded them from some professions, forbade interracial marriage, and prohibited the use of firearms. Taking advantage of freedmen's economic vulnerability, the black codes also permitted forced labor of one convicted of vagrancy—that is, of lacking a job and a home.

Racial Violence

When the black codes failed to achieve their repressive purpose, angry white southerners turned to violence. Some joined and many gave tacit support to white supremacist groups like the **Ku Klux Klan,** a grassroots terrorist organization formed immediately after the war. Apparently taking its name from a corruption of the Greek word *kyklos* (circle), the Klan sought to thwart the goals of Reconstruction by killing, beating, and otherwise intimidating black leaders and their white supporters. In 1871 several black officials in South Carolina received an ultimatum: resign or face "retributive justice." Blacks who insisted on exercising their right to vote were often driven from their communities or hanged. Laws passed by Congress in the early 1870s temporarily dispersed the Klan but not the hatred.

Mob violence against blacks increased after Reconstruction. In both North and South, bands of racial zealots performed illegal executions of blacks (and other minorities) suspected of wrongdoing. This type of summary justice by the rabble is known as **lynch law,** after Charles Lynch, an American vigilante during the Revolutionary War. Unlike the Ku Klux Klan, ad hoc lynch mobs did not always wear masks or wait until nightfall to carry out their sentences. In fact, many lynchings were highly publicized events to which morbidly fanatical white parents brought their children. Not content with simple execution, the vigilantes often inflicted torturous deaths such as burning at the stake and dismemberment. Between 1882 and 1951 over thirty-four hundred black Americans were killed by lynching.

The Segregationist Movement

Conscientious white citizens may have been horrified by such atrocities, but most Americans favored other forms of black disfranchisement, including discriminatory legislation. After federal officials withdrew from the South in 1877, white southern Democrats kept blacks from voting through violence, intimidation, and various types of procedural subterfuge, such as changing the polling areas without notice or imposing literacy requirements to exclude poorly educated former slaves. Having thus regained political power, Democrats began passing laws that segregated blacks in virtually every public space, including streetcars, schools, parks, cemeteries, theaters, and restaurants. The segregation laws came to be known colloquially as **Jim Crow laws,** in reference to a stock character from minstrel shows who parodied the illiterate plantation slave.

By the end of the century, the federal government had retreated from its earlier egalitarian ideals, even becoming complicit with southern legislation. In 1896, the U.S. Supreme Court reviewed the case of Homer Plessy, a light-skinned Negro who had been arrested for sitting in a "white" car of the East Louisiana Railroad. At the time, leading American scholars were trying to justify segregation on "scientific" grounds. They argued, among other things, that blacks were inherently inferior, that interracial marriage was biologically unhealthy, that blacks had retrogressed since emancipation, and that white supremacy was the natural and most beneficial order for human beings. Partly on the basis of such ideas, the Supreme Court ruled in ***Plessy v. Ferguson*** that state laws segregating the races were constitutional so long as public facilities were kept "separate but equal." This doctrine legalized racial discrimination for almost sixty years, until 1954 when the ruling was finally overturned.

Black Political Leaders

In spite of discouraging odds, a sizable minority of African Americans somehow managed to get a college education and enter the professional world. Virtually every northern city boasted an echelon of black leadership that included doctors, lawyers, businessmen, scholars, ministers, politicians, and newspaper editors.

The most influential black leader at the turn of the century was **Booker T. Washington** (1856–1915), a former slave and the first president of Tuskegee Institute, then an elementary and secondary school for blacks in Alabama. In appeals such as his so-called Atlanta Compromise Speech (1895), Washington argued that the surest way for blacks eventually to gain equal rights was to demonstrate patience, industry, thrift, and usefulness while temporarily accommodating segregation. Rather than advocating political power through higher education, Washington urged blacks to strive for economic independence by mastering a practical trade. Instead of agitating for social change, he admonished them to "cast down your bucket where you are" and make the best of the present situation. As blacks proved themselves over time to be faithful contributing citizens, he predicted, the pall of racism would dissipate and they would become fully accepted and integrated into society.

Most Americans—whether black or white, northern or southern—accepted Washington's arguments. White southerners, in particular, were delighted by his emphasis on service and vocational training, which they believed would strengthen the subordinate role of blacks and perpetuate segregation. Ironically, some black intellectuals agreed, and for that reason opposed Washington's agenda. **W. E. B. Du Bois** (1868–1963), a Harvard-educated sociologist, led the opposition. Through his study of social conditions of American blacks, Du Bois had become convinced that good will and productivity would never prevail in the face of white xenophobia and legalized segregation. Above all, he viewed segregation as fundamentally unjust and therefore unacceptable in a democratic society. In his most influential work, *The Souls of Black Folk* (1903), Du Bois articulated an activist stance foreshadowing that of Dr. Martin Luther King Jr., declaring that "by every civilized and peaceful method we must strive for the rights which the world accords to men."

Together with other like-minded people of both races, Du Bois cofounded in 1909 the **National Association for the Advancement of Colored People (NAACP),** an organization to combat segregation, disfranchisement, and mob violence against American blacks. The NAACP would play a crucial role in the struggle for racial equality throughout the century.

The Rank and File

Although perhaps sympathetic to the political aims of Du Bois and the NAACP, ordinary black citizens continued to seek the self-improvement and economic freedom advocated by Washington. Many southern blacks took up

Fisk Jubilee Singers.

share-cropping, an arrangement in which (usually) white farmers allowed them to work a portion of land in return for a share of the annual crop. This occupation supplied black families with a precarious living while keeping them under the power of white landowners.

Blacks in the North enjoyed greater independence, but racism crowded the path to financial security there as well. Although the uneducated found work in factories, stockyards, and shipping docks, blacks were the lowest paid and the first to be terminated. Many tried to enter the middle class by obtaining a service position, such as that of butler, waiter, bellman, driver, or Pullman porter. Few entertained hopes of a professional career.

The musically talented had more options. After the Civil War, black musicians first attracted widespread attention through the triumphant international tour of the **Fisk Jubilee Singers.** Named after the biblical year of Jubilee (marking the end of Hebrew enslavement), the group originated at Fisk University, a recently founded but struggling school for freed slaves in Nashville, Tennessee. To raise money for the university, a young white director organized the Jubilee Singers and began the tour in 1871. For the next seven years they performed for enthusiastic audiences throughout the United States and Europe, singing light classical numbers and songs of the African American vernacular. By the end of the tour the Jubilee Singers had raised $150,000 (more than $2.5 million in today's money)—enough to insure the continuance of Fisk University. Upon hearing the group, Mark Twain remarked: "Their music made all other vocal music cheap. . . . In the Jubilees and their songs, America has produced the perfectest flower of the ages."

The Entertainment Industry

The success of the Jubilee Singers and of similar groups that followed them built on one of the few positive racial biases of the period—namely, that blacks harbored special gifts in music, dance, and comedy. White fascination with such gifts is clear from the robust tradition of American **minstrelsy.** Peaking in the mid-nineteenth century but extending into the twentieth, the minstrel show featured white entertainers satirically impersonating African Americans joking, dancing, singing, and playing banjo, fiddle, and percussion instruments. To appear black in a stylized way, the actors darkened their faces with burnt cork and painted a thick white band around their lips. Stock characters included "Jim Crow," the naïve plantation slave (who became the symbol of segregation), and "Zip Coon" (or "Dandy Jim"), the exaggeratedly pretentious urban fop, dressed in top hat and tails. Post–Civil War minstrelsy opened the programs to include black performers, sometimes in blackface themselves. Despite the oddity of self-caricature, minstrel shows gave blacks their central route into show business.

Around the turn of the century the traditions of minstrelsy began giving way to **vaudeville.** From the 1890s to the 1930s, vaudeville troupes toured all over the country, giving theater performances in cities and small towns from New York to Los Angeles. Featuring songs, dances, jokes, juggling, magic tricks, acrobatic stunts, bathing beauties, trained animals, and the like, vaudeville anticipated the variety shows of American radio and television in the mid-twentieth century. Indeed, vaudeville represented the principal form of mass entertainment before the age of mass media. The list of film stars who began their careers in vaudeville includes some of the most celebrated Hollywood icons: Jack Benny, George Burns, W. C. Fields, and Will Rogers, to name a few.

For black performers vaudeville represented a step up from minstrelsy. To be sure, segregation prevailed in vaudeville as elsewhere, dividing the industry into separate black and white performing circuits. In addition, racist stereotypes and stock characters persisted, limiting the salaries and the kinds of roles open to black performers. (Blacks reread the acronym for the Theatre Owners Booking Agency—TOBA—to mean "Tough on Black Actors.") Still, vaudeville lacked minstrelsy's built-in racial theme and thus provided a somewhat more neutral performance setting. Vaudeville offered attractive financial rewards, in any case. Whereas black laborers earned an average of $7 to $9 a week, vaudeville principals made three times that much.

The greatest star of black vaudeville in the early century was **Bert Williams** (1876–1922). A high school graduate who read Nietzsche and Mark Twain in his spare time, Williams played a character foreign to his own nature: a slow-witted, shuffling Negro in ragged clothes forever concocting get-rich-quick schemes and spouting monologues in ungrammatical dialect. Brilliantly personalizing this stereotyped role, Williams won fame as a comedian, singer, and songwriter. He became one of the first to break the color barrier in show business; in the 1910s he even starred in Ziegfeld's *Follies,* the most successful stage show on Broadway. Yet possibly because of the demeaning nature of his act, Williams struggled constantly with despair. W. C. Fields, the famous white comedian, described him as "the funniest man I ever saw and the saddest man I ever knew." For millions of black Americans, however, Williams became a hero and a role model—a member of their race who had reached the summit in the world of entertainment.

Bert Williams, in private and in public.

As we shall see, early jazz musicians sought their own share of that success, also through minstrelsy and vaudeville. In these fields, blacks could take some comfort, knowing that for once white public opinion seemed to be on their side. As a 1906 editorial in the Chicago *Tribune* prophesied (with forgivable exaggeration): "The Negro has a future in music . . . there is no prejudice against the Negro in music."

Chapter 2 Sources of Jazz

Many historians characterize jazz as a descendent of African and European music but one whose immediate ancestors consisted of fully American idioms. When black slaves arrived in the American colonies in the early seventeenth century, they brought with them their West African musical philosophies and practices. Judging from notes taken at the time by white observers, West African cultures valued (1) a functional conception of music as an expression of worship, work, play, and virtually every other social activity; (2) an emphasis on collaborative, communal music-making in which everyone participated (often nullifying the distinction between performer and audience); and (3) a method of transmitting music by aural tradition. As practitioners, West Africans cultivated (4) a memorized or improvised performance practice; (5) a fluid pitch spectrum; and (6) a texture of exceedingly complex polyrhythms.

As Table 2.1 shows, by the nineteenth century these features contrasted with Western European aesthetics in nearly every way. Although European society required functional music, the most prestigious type was art music for the concert hall (i.e., classical music). This was a music composed and notated by creative individuals who dictated pitch, rhythm, and every other detail of a piece to those who would be performing it. Another authoritarian figure, the conductor, imposed a particular interpretation on the musicians. Then as now, the experience of hearing a symphony or opera in a European-style concert hall was a far cry from the informal democracy of West African musical events.

The two cultures also diverged in their employment of pitch and rhythm. As we have seen, European classical music was based on a discrete pitch spectrum that divided the octave into twelve equal units (a tuning system known as *equal temperament*). By contrast, West African musicians used a **pentatonic scale,** an asymmetrical five-note collection built on the 1st, 2nd, 3rd, 5th, and 6th degrees of the diatonic major scale (e.g., C, D, E, G, A, in the key of C). Equally important, they freely modified their pentatonic melodies through microtonal shadings. Similarly, Europeans explored the harmonic system of tonality to build elaborate formal structures but lacked the rhythmic subtlety of the West Africans, who favored multiple layers of rhythmic activity in irregular and unpredictable relationships by European standards. Despite the stark contrasts among them, all of the elements listed in Table 2.1 appear to a greater or lesser degree in jazz.

And yet jazz absorbed European and West African traits only after both had passed through a number of American genres in the nineteenth century. American composers of marches and hymns, for instance, grafted a New World

pentatonic scale an asymmetrical five-note collection built on the 1st, 2nd, 3rd, 5th, and 6th degrees of the diatonic major scale.

Table 2.1 A Comparison of West African and Nineteenth-Century European Music

West African	European
Functional	Art
Collaborative	Authoritarian
Aural tradition	Notated tradition
Memorized/improvised	Composed
Fluid pitch spectrum	Discrete pitch spectrum
Rhythmic sophistication	Harmonic sophistication

simplicity and pragmatism to a technical foundation of European melody, harmony, and meter. In the black community, Africanisms were preserved mainly in the southern states. Throughout most of the South, whites prevented slaves from practicing their African music and dances in the correct belief that the native customs nurtured black identity and solidarity. But they could not stop them from applying African mannerisms to the hymns and folk songs they learned from their white masters. In time, slaves produced their own hybrid genres. **Spirituals** and **slave songs** (or plantation songs), while employing European harmony and meter, retained the African elements of *pentatonic melodies* and *syncopation,* the latter representing a drastically reduced shorthand for the complex polyrhythms of authentic West African music. Spirituals, introduced to the world by the Fisk Jubilee Singers (see Chapter 1), were sacred songs emphasizing biblical themes of divine comfort and liberation. Slave songs formed the backbone of the minstrelsy repertoire, to which white composer **Stephen Foster** (1826–1864) made the most lasting contributions. After the Civil War, published spirituals sometimes called for the performance practice of *call-and-response,* another holdover from African music and one that would play an enormous role in jazz. One African element, however, defied notation: the fluid bending of pitches to achieve a multitude of expressive vocal effects. Although absent from published music, this feature was described in memoirs by many fascinated white listeners. It would become a defining characteristic of the blues.

By the late nineteenth century a great variety of popular genres—some African American, some European American—swirled in American musical life. Although details remain obscure, it seems clear that jazz arose from a syncretic mix of these vernacular traditions. Influential genres included hymns, spirituals, minstrel tunes, ballroom dances, and other musical types that evolved over the course of the nineteenth century. The most important sources of jazz, however, were *marches, ragtime, popular songs,* and *country blues.* All four genres originated or reached crucial points of development in the 1890s.

Marches

One of the most popular musical institutions in turn-of-the-century America was the touring **concert band.** Through U.S. victory in the Spanish-American War (1898) and associated imperialist moves in the Caribbean and Pacific islands, the country had begun to establish itself as a world power. On the domestic front, the reforms of the Progressive movement filled Americans with a sense of moral righteousness. As a result of these developments, the country grew in national pride and patriotism. Wind bands playing military marches and

spiritual a Negro sacred song emphasizing biblical themes of divine comfort and liberation.

slave song a pre–Civil War Negro secular song popular on minstrelsy circuits.

sentimental songs that glorified the Republic were enthusiastically received at outdoor concerts and parades throughout the land. Some of the bands came from the Armed Forces, others from the private sector; some were local, others nationally famous.

John Philip Sousa

The most successful band of the period was led by **John Philip Sousa** (1854–1932). Sousa began his adult career as bandmaster (conductor) of the U.S. Marine Band, which he raised to a high level of technical musicianship. In 1892 he left the Marines and organized his own professional band, consisting of forty-nine virtuoso musicians on flute, clarinet, saxophone, oboe, bassoon, cornet, trumpet, French horn, trombone, euphonium (an instrument like a small tuba), tuba, and percussion. Through annual tours both in the United States and abroad, Sousa and his band won a large international following.

Sousa exerted an even greater influence through his compositions. His 136 **marches**—band compositions for parades—earned him the popular title "The March King." Several of Sousa's marches have become beloved standards of American music, including *The Washington Post*, *Semper Fidelis*, *The Liberty Bell*, and *Stars and Stripes Forever*.

The principal features of the march are these:

- To support the left-right pattern of those marching in parades, marches were invariably written in a two-beat meter.
- Marches consisted of several repeating sections, as in the scheme AABBCCDD. This type of structure is called multistrain form, or, logically enough, **march form.**
- Sometimes march composers combined melodies to create polyphony. In such cases instruments were often assigned particular roles. One common arrangement gave the cornets the main melody, the high woodwinds faster embellishing melodies called *obbligatos*, and the low brass countermelodies in the low register.

JOHN PHILIP SOUSA, *Semper Fidelis* (1888)

All these features can be seen in Sousa's *Semper Fidelis*, a march widely admired for its musical excellence. The piece consists of four primary strains or melodies: A, B, C, and D. Each strain lasts for sixteen measures of two-beat meter. As often happened, Sousa added shorter subsidiary passages (an introduction, an interlude) to connect the main melodies. The high point arrives at the traditional moment of climax in pieces in march form: the C-section or *trio*. Here the music modulates to a new key, and the cornets play a fanfarelike melody while the tubas play a faster countermelody that rises in the low register. When C is repeated, the clarinets add still livelier descending flourishes in the upper register. At the third statement of C, the trombones add a jaunty countermelody that echoes the fanfarelike character of the cornet line. Throughout this passage the gradually thickening polyphony is accompanied by slowly increasing dynamics. By the end of the third C the music has reached a climax, which effectively serves to introduce the final triumphant strain, D.

march a military band composition for parades.

march form the musical form found in most marches, usually following the pattern AABBCCDD, etc. (aka *multistrain* form).

LISTENING CHART 2

John Philip Sousa, *Semper Fidelis* ("Ever Faithful") (Sousa)

CD 1 / Tracks 11–15

COMPOSED AND PUBLISHED IN 1888

Recorded by the Dallas Wind Symphony, 16 July 1998, Dallas, Texas, Reference Recordings

Genre: March			Form: March form

			Introduction
11	0:00	8 bars	Homophonic texture: full ensemble plays opening fanfare
			First strain
12	0:08	A (16 bars)	Homophonic texture: full ensemble plays bouncy first strain
	0:24	A (16)	*A-section repeated*
			Second strain
13	0:39	B (16)	Two-part polyphony: ensemble plays broad second strain while trumpets add percussive countermelody of rapidly reiterated notes
	0:55	B (16)	*B-section repeated*
			Interlude
	1:11	8 bars	Unaccompanied solo: snare drum
			Third strain: Trio
14	1:18	C (16)	*New key* (4th higher): Cornet melody plus low brass countermelody = two-part polyphony
	1:34	C′ (16)	*Repeated*, plus clarinet obbligato = three-part polyphony
	1:50	C″ (16)	*Repeated*, plus trombone countermelody = four-part polyphony
			Fourth strain
15	2:06	D (16)	Return to homophonic texture: ensemble plays triumphant closing strain of wide leaps and decisive phrase endings
	2:22	D (16)	*D-section repeated*

Ragtime

One might view **ragtime** as a rhythmically electrified march transferred to the medium of solo piano. Like marches, ragtime pieces employ a two-beat meter and unfold according to the contrasting sectional structure of march form. The primary difference lies in the rhythmic relationship between treble (the high notes) and bass (the low notes). In a march the high and low instruments reinforce the same downbeat patterns in the music. In piano ragtime, by comparison, the left hand (in the bass register) stresses downbeats, often through *"oom-pah" figures* that regularly alternate between a low note and a middle-register chord. At the same time, the right hand (in the treble register) plays syncopated melodies. The combination creates a rhythmic tension that early listeners described as "ragged time," thereby coining the idiom's ancestral name. The rhythmic "pulling" between registers accounts for the quality of insouciance and abandon that delighted and disturbed listeners. The rhythmic tension of ragtime is not, however, what we would ordinarily call swing. Ragtime employs *straight eighth notes* and the overall execution is almost classical in nature.

In summary, characteristic features of ragtime include the following:

- Composed, notated tradition
- Two-beat meter
- March form
- Syncopated right hand; downbeat-oriented left hand
- Straight eighth notes, semiclassical execution

Marketing and Distribution

Ragtime originated in the black community in the late nineteenth century. It developed for several years as an aural tradition before receiving broad public exposure during the World's Columbian Exposition in Chicago in 1893. Ragtime was cultivated primarily by itinerant pianists performing in brothels and saloons in Missouri cities such as St. Louis, Sedalia, and Carthage. As its popularity spread, ragtime invaded other genres besides piano music, including popular songs and concert band marches.

Industry executives marketed ragtime primarily through **sheet music** sales. Inexpensive and convenient, sheet music allowed amateur pianists to try their own hands at the lively new music. The economic vitality of sheet music distribution, combined with phonograph companies' reluctance as yet to record black music, virtually guaranteed that commercial ragtime would develop as a composed, notated tradition, notwithstanding its spontaneous origins.

Ragtime was also marketed through **piano rolls.** In the years before recording technology transformed the music industry, player pianos offered a novel and popular means of distributing musical performances on a wide scale. Fortuitously, the first ragtime publication appeared in the same year as the first player piano (1897), and the two novelties boosted each other's sales. Professional pianists made "recordings" on piano rolls—rolled strips of paper—which consumers then installed on the player pianos in their homes. Through a system of air pressure forced through punched holes in the piano roll, the keys on a player piano magically rose and fell in a ghostly reenactment of the live performance.

ragtime an African American piano style of lively melodies and syncopated rhythms popular in the early twentieth century.

Public Reception

From the beginning ragtime provoked debate. Critical descriptions of the music ranged from generous praise ("one of our most precious musical assets") to unrestrained scorn ("vicious trash"). As early as 1901 a leading music magazine announced with relief that "Rag-time has passed the zenith of its popularity, musicians say, and they are now anxious to lay out the corpse." That same year the American Federation of Musicians futilely declared a ban on the music. Despite such desperate measures, ragtime continued to sell briskly, in both sheet music and piano rolls. From the late 1890s to around 1917, it reigned as America's favorite and most notorious popular music.

Scott Joplin

Scott Joplin.

By general consent the greatest of the ragtime composers was a young African American from Texarkana (on the Texas-Arkansas border) named **Scott Joplin** (1868?–1917). Born the son of a former slave and a free black woman, Joplin grew up in a musical family. He became proficient on several instruments, but emphasized the piano. A local German immigrant kindly gave Joplin free lessons, instilling in him a love of classical music and an ambition to succeed not just as an entertainer but as an artist.

In the 1890s, Joplin performed in minstrelsy and vaudeville, attended an all-black college in Sedalia, and published his first compositions—a handful of popular songs, marches, and waltzes. Then, in 1899, he started publishing rag-time and his life changed. He sold his first ragtime piece for the standard rate: a one-time fee, probably of $25 or less. For his second piece, "Maple Leaf Rag," he wisely hired a lawyer and secured a contract that included royalties of one penny for each copy of sheet music sold. "Maple Leaf Rag" eventually sold a million copies, acquired for Joplin a modest financial independence, and established his reputation as "King of Ragtime."

SCOTT JOPLIN, *"Maple Leaf Rag"* (1899)

"Maple Leaf Rag" was named after the Maple Leaf Club, a Sedalia social club for black men where Joplin often played piano. This recording is taken from a piano roll that Joplin himself made in April 1916, a year before his death.

Like most rags, "Maple Leaf Rag" is in march form: AABBACCDD, with a brief return of the opening strain just before the trio. The A strain has three contrasting parts, labeled x, y, and z in the listening chart. The first and third parts (x and z) are in the major mode and sound cheerful and buoyant. The middle part (y), a transitional passage in the minor, sounds darker, more serious. The shifting moods create a sense of drama within this very brief opening strain.

The B strain provides further contrast through a change of texture: the left hand begins a lively oom-pah bass line. The oom-pahs generate energy, raising the overall level of tension. After the return of A the trio modulates, in typical march fashion, to a new key. Situated a fourth higher than the original key and presenting a rather aggressive melody, the trio raises the tension of the piece to a climax. Then the final strain (D) returns to the original key and a more carefree melody, resolving all previous tensions and bringing the piece to a close.

LISTENING CHART 3

Scott Joplin, "Maple Leaf Rag" (Joplin)

CD 1 / Tracks 16–19

COMPOSED AND PUBLISHED IN 1899

Piano roll recorded by Scott Joplin, April 1916/reissued in CD format on *The Smithsonian Collection of Classic Jazz,* vol. 1, RD 033-1, Smithsonian Institution, 1987

Genre: Ragtime				Form: March form

First strain

16	0:00	A (16)	x	*Major mode:* cheerful opening emphasizing syncopations
	0:06		y	*Minor mode:* darker, transitional passage leads from low register to high register
	0:11		z	Back to *major mode:* light bouncy closing material in upper register
	0:22	A (16)		*A-section repeated*

Second strain

17	0:44	B (16)		"Oom-pahs" in left hand create greater momentum, tension
	1:06	B (16)		*B-section repeated*

First strain returns

	1:28	A (16)		Mood relaxes somewhat

Third strain: Trio

18	1:50	C (16)		*Key change* (4th higher): Aggressive melody with stomping left hand; climax of the piece
	2:12	C (16)		*C-section repeated*

Fourth strain

19	2:34	D (16)		Return to *original key:* carefree final strain follows singsong contour, tension subsides
	2:56	D (16)		*D-section repeated*

Popular Songs

The last decade of the nineteenth century is sometimes referred to as the **Gay Nineties.** This term actually has limited application; it was coined during the Great Depression as a nostalgic tribute to the carefree world of the white middle and upper classes who dominated the economic and political life of the period. For this privileged minority it was an era of baseball, bicycles, barbershop quartets, and afternoon tea parties. The feminine ideal was the so-called Gibson Girl, illustrator Charles Gibson's pretty coquette with the hourglass figure corseted under petticoats. The Gay Nineties represented America's Victorian Age.

Victorian ideals found transparent expression in **popular songs.** The American popular song had been evolving since before the birth of minstrelsy, but only after the music industry became centralized in the 1880s and 1890s did popular songs generate big business. Two areas in New York City have come to symbolize this development: **Broadway** and **Tin Pan Alley.** A thoroughfare that bisects Manhattan diagonally, Broadway was home to most of the theaters that staged musical theater productions. Such Broadway shows introduced many of the finest popular songs in the American repertory, songs we sometimes call *show tunes.* Tin Pan Alley refers not to an actual street but to an area of town around 28th Street and 6th Avenue that supported the hub of the songwriting industry. In surrounding buildings dozens of songwriters and *songpluggers* (piano-playing salesmen) banged out new songs on upright pianos, creating a tinny clangor that may have given the district its name. By association, Tin Pan Alley has come to refer to the American songwriting and music publishing industry in general.

The potential for wealth in popular songs became clear when Charles K. Harris published his song-waltz "After the Ball" in 1892. Within a few years, it had sold over two million copies of sheet music and prompted numerous imitations. The most salient features of "After the Ball"—a lilting triple meter and sentimental lyrics—seemed perfectly to encapsulate the unruffled lifestyle of the Gay Nineties. The same features characterized the most beloved songs of the period, including many still well-known today: "Sidewalks of New York," "Take Me Out to the Ballgame," and "Daisy Bell" (better known as "A Bicycle Built for Two").

Popular Songs and Ragtime

Waltzes remained popular for several decades. But in the mid-1890s popular songs with ragtime elements and comic textual references to black culture began appearing in large numbers. Such songs came to be known as ragtime songs or—in the racist language of the period—**coon songs.** Far from being new to American music, coon songs were direct descendants of the slave songs that flourished in minstrelsy. Produced by both black and white songwriters, coon songs vastly outnumbered ragtime works for piano.

Coon songs evoked ragtime in various ways: through syncopated rhythms; more generally, through the overall spirit of the music; or through specific references in the lyrics. After the initial success of the piano version of "Maple Leaf Rag," Joplin published spinoffs for other media, including "The Maple Leaf Rag Song" (1903). The affectation of black folk dialect in the lyrics of this song, penned by Sidney Brown, might embarrass today's listeners. But Joplin probably

popular song a genre for solo voice and instrumental accompaniment aimed at a wide audience.

coon song a popular song containing elements of ragtime.

standard a popular song that remains familiar long after its initial success.

ABAC song form a 32-bar chorus structure governing the majority of popular songs written before 1930 or so; after that time, secondary in importance to AABA song form.

gave them little thought; they simply formed part of the coon song idiom, a part essential to commercial success. They also attest, even in hyperbole, to the perceived influence of ragtime:

> Oh go 'way man, I can hypnotize dis nation,
> I can shake de earth's foundation wid de Maple Leaf Rag!
> Oh go 'way man, just hold yo' breath a minit,
> For there's not a stunt that's in it, wid de Maple Leaf Rag!

Irving Berlin

The preeminent songwriter of the early twentieth century and perhaps in the history of American music was **Irving Berlin** (1888–1989). Born Israel Baline into a Russian Jewish household, Berlin immigrated with his family to the United States in 1893. After several years of limited success as a songwriter, his fortunes changed in 1911 when he published "Alexander's Ragtime Band," a coon song that became wildly popular, catapulting him to wealth and fame. The song sold a million copies in the first year, and shortly thereafter became an international juggernaut. *Variety* declared it "the musical sensation of the decade."

In 1914 Berlin expressed a desire shared by Scott Joplin: to compose a ragtime opera. Whether or not he succeeded is open to debate, given the porous definitions of both "ragtime" and "opera." But Berlin wrote all or part of the music for at least twenty Broadway or Hollywood musicals. During his long life, he produced many songs that because of their broad familiarity and continued performances have become American **standards,** including "Blue Skies," "All Alone," "God Bless America," and—his biggest hit—"White Christmas."

IRVING BERLIN, *"Alexander's Ragtime Band"* (1911)

CD 1 / Track 20

0:00	Introduction
0:07	Verse
	Chorus
0:34	A
0:47	B
1:00	A
1:13	C
1:26	Entire song repeated (with second verse)

Berlin's first hit song, "Alexander's Ragtime Band," actually has little if any ragtime syncopation. It does, however, employ a mild species of black folk dialect. And the song's melodic and rhythmic ebullience certainly conveys the spirit of ragtime. Otherwise, "Alexander's Ragtime Band" shares common features with many popular songs of the day, whether rags or not.

Like the vast majority of Tin Pan Alley and Broadway songs, "Alexander's Ragtime Band" follows what is called *verse-chorus form*. This design features a single, relatively non-descript verse followed by a catchy, tuneful chorus—the part of the song intended to remain in listeners' minds after the performance is over. Both verse and chorus in "Alexander's Ragtime Band" show Berlin's ability to write simple yet beguiling melodies. The form of the chorus is also conventional, having four sections—ABAC—of eight bars each. **ABAC song form** was the standard form of popular song choruses before World War I; later, as we will see, a different pattern (AABA) would predominate.

This recording, the first ever made of "Alexander's Ragtime Band," was produced less than three months after the song appeared in print. The performers, Arthur Collins and Byron G. Harlan, sang together in vaudeville and on many early popular song recordings. Harlan often sang the part of a woman, as he does here.

Great Debates

JOPLIN VERSUS BERLIN: A CASE OF PLAGIARISM?

The success of "Alexander's Ragtime Band" was almost immediately marred by rumors that Berlin had stolen material—if not the entire song—from a black composer. In later years, friends and relatives of Scott Joplin claimed that the theft came from *Treemonisha,* a ragtime opera that Joplin composed in 1910–1911. Subsequent research has shown that Joplin made the original accusation, that the two composers probably knew each other, and that Berlin had the opportunity, at least, to hear an unpublished version of *Treemonisha* before he copyrighted "Alexander's Ragtime Band." Moreover, there is a passing similarity between the song's verse and the opera's finale.

Was Berlin a plagiarist, then? It depends on whom you ask. In their book *The African-American Century,* the distinguished black intellectuals Henry Louis Gates Jr. and Cornell West accept Joplin's charges at face value as yet another example in a long and well-documented history of whites exploiting black musicians for commercial gain. Two leading music scholars—both of whom happen to be white—find the matter less conclusive. Edward A. Berlin (no relation), an authority on ragtime, states that "the resemblance [between the two pieces] is not close enough to charge Irving Berlin with plagiarism." And Charles Hamm, an expert on Berlin's music, argues that the appropriation, even if deliberate, was a routine aspect of Tin Pan Alley songwriting. The question of Berlin's plagiarism remains a matter of controversy, with opinion apparently dividing along racial lines. ■ ■ ■

Country Blues

Unlike marches, ragtime, and popular songs, the folk idiom of the **country blues** evolved almost independently of the financial power centers of American music. The original source of all other blues types, the country blues expressed the isolation and alienation of the lone individual from society at large. Sung primarily by black males to self-accompaniment on guitar, the country blues began as informal performances on front porches and in back bedrooms throughout the Deep South.

Although the origins of the blues are murky, historians generally believe blacks developed the idiom in the 1890s as a way of defining themselves in the face of rapidly proliferating segregation laws. The blues seems to have arisen from a fusion of work songs with British-style ballads about black folk heroes like John Henry and Stack O'Lee. **Work songs** were sung by groups of slaves and, later, sharecroppers, to help them work the fields spiritedly and efficiently. From work songs blues singers derived their characteristic manner of singing, a rich African-based style boasting a fluid pitch spectrum and a host of plaintive vocalisms: moans, cries, growls, and other raw expressions. From ballads the blues acquired the structure of multiple stanzas of text and, occasionally, the idea of telling a story of some kind.

The Mississippi Delta

Although important regional styles of country blues developed in Texas, Alabama, and other southern states, most experts agree that the blues

country blues the blues as it was originally performed by black male singers in the Mississippi Delta and other locations throughout the Deep South.

work song song sung by black field laborers to help them work spiritedly and efficiently.

Map 1. Mississippi Delta.

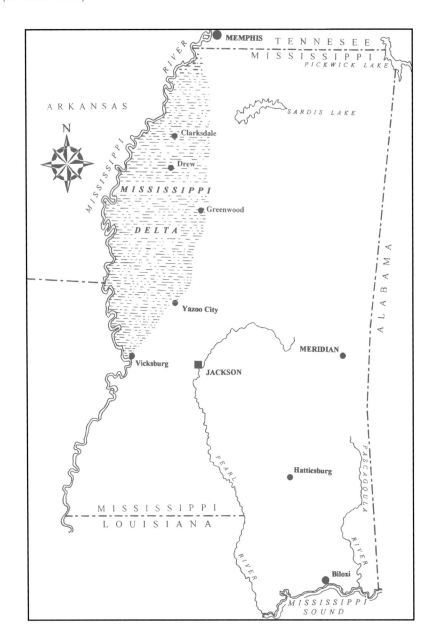

probably originated on the Mississippi Delta, or Alluvial Plain, in the northwest corner of the state of Mississippi (see Map 1). Silt deposits brought by annual flooding of the Mississippi River have made the soil in this region especially fertile. In the pre–Civil War period, mighty cotton plantations on the Delta produced much of the economic prosperity of the South. After the war the plantations continued under the system of sharecropping.

The earliest blues singers were sharecroppers on the Mississippi Delta. Living on plantations outside towns like Drew and Clarksdale, figures such as Charley Patton, Son House, and Robert Johnson developed a style featuring guttural, expressive singing and heavily accented accompaniment. As their music became known locally, they began playing for money in *juke joints*—rural black social halls for dancing, drinking, and gambling.

Blues Lyrics, Expression, and Form

Country bluesmen ordinarily sang of personal troubles. They lamented natural misfortunes such as floods, drought, or boll weevil damage to crops; they alluded to segregation and other forms of racism; they addressed crime, gambling, liquor, and prostitution. Many blues lyrics focused on sex and relationships with women, often in figurative language. A mood of alienation pervades the blues repertory, relieved only by images of escape through travel.

Among other expressive devices blues musicians employed **blue notes,** slightly lowered pitches of the diatonic scale (the 3rd, 5th, and 7th degrees), to convey stark emotions. Musicians often emphasized blue notes by distorting the pitch with "bends" and "smears" to increase the plaintive quality. Yet far from communicating self-pity, the music of the blues was intended to provide the means of exorcising the demons described in the lyrics.

Blues lyrics invariably have several stanzas, each of which is set to a *chorus* of music. The blues chorus would eventually become standardized as a twelve-bar structure in three phrases of four bars each. Strict **twelve-bar blues form,** however, applies to only a small percentage of country blues. Since singers accompanied themselves in informal settings, they felt free to linger or hasten at will, creating odd and constantly shifting chorus lengths. Still, most examples adhere to the pattern of three phrases, in which the first two present essentially the same melody and text while the third provides contrast and resolution. We will represent this pattern with the scheme AAB.

Charley Patton

Many historians consider **Charley Patton** (1891–1934) to be the father of the Delta blues, not because he invented the music but because he was among the first to record it. Patton grew up on the Will Dockery Plantation near Drew. His powerful performances gained him a minor following among other sharecroppers locally. By the 1920s, Patton's public appearances had become profitable enough for him to leave the Dockery Plantation.

A small and wiry man, Patton had a coarse, low voice and an aggressive singing style. As a guitarist he emphasized hard plucking, thumping on the body of the instrument, and other percussive effects. His volcanic musical personality reflected the roughness of his life. An alcoholic who was married eight times, Patton survived having his throat cut in a barroom brawl in 1933. He died of heart failure a year later.

The Urbanization of the Blues

In 1903, an itinerant black musician named **W. C. Handy** (1873–1958) assumed leadership of the Knights of Pythias band in Clarksdale, Mississippi. During the next several years, Handy traveled throughout the Delta, hearing many different performances of country blues. Later he moved to Memphis, Tennessee, where he published "Memphis Blues" for solo piano in 1912. Although technically not the first blues published, it quickly became so popular that Handy's promotional self-appellation "The Father of the Blues" was taken literally by much of the public. As blues publications multiplied in the next few years, the blues became a commercial, standardized, urban product played in vaudeville and cabarets throughout the North. We will discuss this phase of blues development in Chapter 4.

blue note in jazz and blues performances a slightly lowered pitch of the diatonic scale (usually the 3rd, 5th, or 7th) used to convey stark emotions.

twelve-bar blues form the most common blues form, consisting of twelve bars divided into three phrases of four bars each.

Charley Patton.

CHARLEY PATTON, *"Down the Dirt Road Blues"* (1929)

In 1929 a talent scout for Paramount records heard Patton and offered him the chance to record. In the next three years Patton made twenty-six 78 rpm discs under various names. Some of his recorded performances are thought to have been worked out before 1910, including "Pony Blues," "Banty Rooster Blues," and the present recording, "Down the Dirt Road Blues."

The text of "Down the Dirt Road Blues" exhibits several common themes of the blues repertory, including travel (first and sixth choruses), sex (second chorus), manual labor (third chorus), sadness (fourth chorus), oppression (fifth chorus), and intimations of death (first and sixth choruses). Patton's phrase "I've been to the Nation" in the third chorus refers to the so-called Indian Nation, or as it was formally known, Indian Territory—the region in Eastern Oklahoma populated primarily by Native Americans before Oklahoma became a state in 1907. The expression "oversea blues" in the fourth chorus may refer to the experience of World War I—the only opportunity men of Patton's social standing were likely to have had to go overseas. (If so, this stanza probably would have been a late addition to the text.)

Patton's raw vocal sonority heightens the disquieting mood of the text, and his percussive guitar playing generates momentum, causing the tempo to increase throughout. As accompanist he attacks the first two phrases of each chorus (AA) with special intensity, steadily playing a single guitar note or chord, tapping his foot, and occasionally thumping his guitar box. He often accentuates blue notes, some of which appear marked in bold in Listening Chart 4. After the third phrase of each chorus (B) he changes the texture, plucking a dancing guitar line that contrasts with the steady percussiveness of the chorus opening and lightens the mood momentarily. As in most country blues recordings, the phrases have irregular lengths and the choruses do not last exactly twelve bars.

The Rise of American Social Dances

In addition to enlivening the programs of minstrelsy and vaudeville, the four genres discussed in this chapter all played an important role in the rise of social dances indigenous to American culture. **Social dances** are dances performed by ordinary people for their own amusement rather than by professionals for the entertainment of others. Because early jazz was also used for dancing, it might be helpful to briefly review the history of American social dances before World War I.

The dance repertoire of nineteenth-century Americans consisted primarily of European imports: the waltz, galop, schottische, polka, and others. The waltz, once a scandalous interloper among established dances, by the late century out-ranked all others in respectability and prestige. Then in 1888 the "Washington Post," a march composed by John Philip Sousa, inspired a new dance called the *two-step*. Shortly thereafter, the *cakewalk* emerged as a ragtime dance. The cakewalk, a high-stepping dance, originated before the Civil War as a slave parody of the pretentious ballroom strutting of white masters. By the late 1890s, the cakewalk and the two-step competed with the waltz for the distinction of being the most popular dance in the country.

Under the influence of ragtime a series of new dances began evolving in black communities at the turn of the century. Embraced by large numbers of

LISTENING CHART 4

Charley Patton, "Down the Dirt Road Blues" (Patton)

CD 1 / Track 21

RECORDED 14 JUNE 1929, RICHMOND, INDIANA / PARAMOUNT 12854

Charley Patton (voice and guitar)

Genre: Country blues	Form: AAB / loose twelve-bar blues form

1st Chorus (after brief introduction)

21	0:00	A	*I'm goin' away to a **world un**known,*
		A	*I'm goin' away to a **world un**known,*
		B	*I'm worried now, but I won't be wor**ried** long* (dancing guitar line).

2nd Chorus

	0:33	A	*My rider [has] sumpin'—she try to **keep it** hid,*
		A	*My rider [has] sum**pin'**—she try to **keep it** hid,*
		B	*Lord, I got sumpn', mm, find that s**ome**thin' with* (dancing guitar line).

3rd Chorus

	1:01	A	*I feel like **choppin'*** (guitar echoes blue note) *chips flyin' **every**where.*
		A	*I feel like choppin'—chips flyin' **every**where,*
		B	*I've been to the Nation, mm Lord, but I couldn't **stay** there* (dancing guitar line).

4th Chorus

	1:29	A	*Some people say them oversea **blues ain't** bad,*
			(Spoken: *Why of course they are.*)
		A	*Some people say **them** oversea **blues ain't** bad,*
			(Spoken: *What is the matter with all of 'em?*)
		B	*It must not [have] been them oversea blues **I** had* (dancing guitar line).

5th Chorus

	1:56	A	*Every day seem like **murder** here,*
			(Spoken: unintelligible)

	A	*Every **day** seem like **murder** here,*
	B	*I'm gwine leave tomorrow, I know you don't [a] bit mo' care* (dancing guitar line).
		6th Chorus
2:23	A	*Can't go down any dark road **by my**self,*
	A	*Can't go down an**y** dark road by myself,*
		(Spoken: *My Lawd, who you gon' carry?*)
	B	*I don't carry my [rider], gonna carry me some**one** else* (dancing guitar line).
	Tag	Simple guitar cadence

white youth after around 1910, the new dances were called **animal dances** for their picturesque names: the Grizzly Bear, Turkey Trot, Bunny Hug, Camel Walk, and Lame Duck. The animal dances brought young dancers into closer physical proximity than before and encouraged ungraceful or provocative gestures. Not surprisingly, the dances—like the music that inspired them—provoked denunciations from arbiters of social behavior.

The Legitimization of Ragtime Dancing

By 1914 interest in American social dances had reached a critical mass. Of six books published on the subject that year, the most influential was a how-to manual by **Vernon and Irene Castle.** An expert dancing couple from vaudeville, the Castles undertook a nationwide campaign to focus and clarify the burgeoning dance craze. They completed a "whirlwind tour" of the country as a publicity stunt, visiting thirty-two cities in twenty-eight days.

Supremely elegant and graceful on the dance floor, the Castles aimed to elevate both the skill and propriety of amateur social dancers. In their book they condemned the more "vulgar" animal dances but defended ragtime itself as a wholesome music that cried out for appropriate dancing: "People can say what they like about rag-time. The Waltz is beautiful, the Tango is graceful, the Brazilian Maxixe is unique. One can sit quietly and listen with pleasure to them all; but when a good orchestra plays a 'rag' one has simply *got* to move." The Castles popularized the fox trot, the only ragtime dance still common today. Partly under their influence, Americans began viewing ragtime music and dance as respectable just as the Ragtime Era was yielding to another, even more shocking period—the Jazz Age.

A Transitional Figure: James Reese Europe

By the mid-1910s marches, ragtime, popular songs, and the blues had coalesced into a loosely organized and constantly shifting composite idiom with ragtime at its base. Ragtime pieces contained blues features, the blues incorporated ragtime or popular song structures, and marches combined elements of the other three genres.

The first recordings of this hybrid music were made in 1913 by the African American ensemble that accompanied the Castles in their dancing tours: **James Reese Europe** (1881–1919) and his Society Orchestra, a group of ten to sixteen pieces including cornet, clarinet, violins, cello, piano, banjo, and drums. A classically trained musician, Europe founded the first all-black musician's union in New York, and in 1912 introduced black music to Carnegie Hall with a historic "Symphony of Negro Music." Perhaps to distance himself from negative connotations, Europe disavowed the label "ragtime" as a "name given to Negro rhythm by our Caucasian brother musicians many years ago."

Somewhat squeamish about the term themselves (but for different reasons), historians have viewed Europe's recordings as inhabiting a sort of no-man's-land between ragtime and jazz. Nevertheless, his music is often referred to as **instrumental ragtime.** On recordings of "Castle House Rag" and "Castle Walk," Europe's band projects a pell-mell enthusiasm that almost warrants being called jazz—but not quite. The alchemy that produced the music upon which most commentators are willing to bestow the title of "jazz" took place in New Orleans.

instrumental ragtime ragtime music as played by a band or orchestra (as opposed to solo piano or voice and piano).

Chapter **3** New Orleans

During the first two decades of the century, many large American cities supported ensembles that played ragtime-based popular music similar to that of James Reese Europe and his Society Orchestra. And yet there was something special about the instrumental ragtime being produced in New Orleans. At least this seems evident from oral histories and early recordings from various regions around the country.

New Orleans musicians took a distinctive approach to rhythm, texture, and overall sonority that is hard to account for in historical terms. We can be confident only that the longstanding, unique blend of New Orleans culture—mingling French, German, Spanish, Italian, African, Caribbean, and other international elements—produced a musical fusion as well. In New Orleans the loose coalition of ragtime, blues, marches, and popular songs mingled with these ethnic strains to create a new type of music, first recognized publicly in the mid-1910s and variously spelled "jass," "jasz," "jaz," or "jazz."

An Urban Melting Pot

New Orleans was settled by France in 1718. But a combination of natural misfortunes and poor management made Louisiana unprofitable, and in 1762, during the French and Indian War, France ceded the colony to Spain. For the next thirty-eight years, Spanish administrators strengthened the city's commercial value and spread Spanish language and culture. Then as Napoleon overran Europe at the turn of the century, France wrested New Orleans back from Spain. Shortly thereafter, to avoid conflict with President Thomas Jefferson over control of the Mississippi river, Napoleon sold New Orleans along with the rest of Louisiana to the United States in 1803.

Americans governed New Orleans competently, soon building the most prosperous seaport in the country and attracting multitudes of European immigrants. In the 1840s large numbers of German and Irish immigrants arrived. Nearly half the population consisted of black slaves or free people of color. Despite a faltering economy after the Civil War, national and ethnic groups continued to pour into the city. In the 1880s and 1890s many Italians and Eastern European Jews arrived in New Orleans. With its French and Spanish heritage and its strong appeal to immigrants, New Orleans became the most cosmopolitan city in the United States.

Partly as a result of its unusually diverse population, New Orleans fostered more liberal attitudes toward race than did many other southern cities. The color line was softened partly by a long tradition of respect granted *Creoles of color* (hereafter referred to as "Creoles," a word taken from the Spanish "criollo," meaning "native to the place"). As citizens of mixed French African descent, Creoles derived a somewhat elevated social status from their European heritage. The division between white and black was also blurred by the common—and open—practice of white males taking black mistresses, over time producing children of increasingly ambiguous racial provenance, including the famously beautiful female "quadroons" (one quarter black) and "octoroons" (one eighth black) of New Orleans folklore.

A City of Celebration

Around the turn of the century jazz took nourishment from longstanding celebratory elements of New Orleans culture, including a musical omnipresence, a love of parades, a passion for dancing, and a residual commitment to African performing arts. From the beginning, music accompanied every conceivable social function in New Orleans, including ball games, balloon launchings, animal fights, and political events. Bands, orchestras, choirs, and various combinations of vocal and instrumental soloists resounded throughout the city. From the singing vendor on the street to the diva in the French Opera House, New Orleans was a city awash in music.

Parades have long captured the imagination of New Orleans citizens. By the early nineteenth century, parades celebrated Washington's Birthday, Independence Day, the Louisiana Purchase, the War of 1812, Mardi Gras and other holy days, elections, weddings, funerals—indeed, when it came right down to it, "good weather on a Sunday was the only excuse needed to turn out the bands of the militia companies." Parades could take place any time of the day or night, and military marching bands turned out by the dozens to participate. Although they included woodwinds, such bands were called **brass bands** because of their heavy emphasis on brass instruments.

Enthusiasm for parades ranked second only to a love of dancing. A visitor in the early nineteenth century called New Orleans "one vast waltzing and gallopading Hall." Another observer remarked that "neither the severity of the cold, nor the oppression of the heat, ever restrains [the people] from this amusement, which usually commences early in the evening, and is seldom suspended til late the next morning." Even children had their own balls; they usually danced from 3:00 P.M. until their bedtime at 8:00 P.M., at which point the adult balls began. The most famous (or infamous) of the adult dances were the **quadroon balls,** social gatherings begun in 1805 where white men came to select black mistresses.

The rage for dancing, together with openness about race, made possible the recurring public spectacles at **Congo Square.** Unlike their counterparts in other southern states, the New Orleans city fathers allowed slaves to revisit their African musical traditions on a limited basis: on Sundays and holy days in Congo Square, an open block behind the French Quarter once used for slave auctions (see Map 2). Using African drums and stringed instruments, hundreds of slaves would play, sing, and dance, while thousands of white citizens watched in amazement. As the music and dancing swelled to deafening peaks over the course of several hours, some dancers fainted to the ground in ecstasy as others took their place. The weekly performance-rituals at Congo Square lasted through the Civil War, and then died out sometime in the 1880s.

Map 2. New Orleans,
c. 1900.

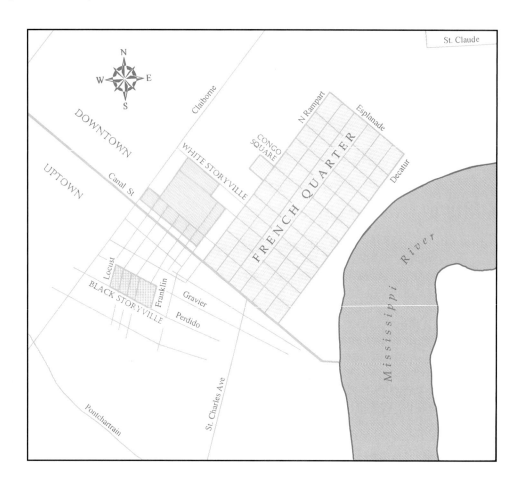

Uptown and Downtown

Despite comparatively relaxed racial codes, New Orleans blacks were divided into two communities. The older group, French-speaking Catholic Creoles, lived downtown, northeast of Canal Street. The newer group, English-speaking Protestants who had moved in from the country after the Louisiana Purchase, lived in the uptown "American" district southwest of Canal (see Map 2). The uptown-downtown division created both rivalry and synergy among black musicians. Indeed, it seems to have stoked—if not kindled—the flames of early jazz.

Speaking very generally, **downtown Creoles** had lighter skin, more education, and greater economic security than their uptown counterparts. Their French heritage gave Creole musicians access to European classical training and concerts; Creoles took pride in their polished instrumental skill and ability to read music. By contrast, **uptown blacks** were more likely to have descended from slaves. They enjoyed few opportunities to study music formally and thus relied on informal pedagogies and intuitive performance practices. Although some learned to read music, they excelled in an aural tradition emphasizing improvisation, memorization, and preset routines.

Before the Civil War, downtown Creoles and uptown blacks remained largely separate from one another, and for good reason: they spoke different languages. During Reconstruction various forces conspired to drive the two groups together. After emancipation large numbers of freed slaves moved to New Orleans and settled in uptown neighborhoods, greatly increasing the number of English speakers in the city. The weakened language barrier encouraged more interaction between uptown and downtown residents, including more mixed marriages. But the biggest reasons for change were economic. After the Civil War, railroads and canals elsewhere in the country sapped the potency of New Orleans trade. In the 1880s and 1890s, huge waves of immigration contributed to a glut of unskilled labor, forcing blacks both uptown and downtown to compete with one another for jobs.

In the scramble to make a living, uptown and downtown musicians gradually began performing together more frequently. Although intense rivalry persisted, over time the two groups came to respect each other's strengths. Creoles ultimately became fascinated with the originality, expressiveness, and spontaneity of uptown music, and uptown blacks coveted the classical training and literacy of the Creoles. The two elements—uptown imagination and downtown literacy—sowed an aesthetic tension in jazz that would periodically stimulate the music's growth for the next one hundred years.

Storyville and Its Environs

The melding of uptown and downtown musical cultures took place in and around **Storyville,** the notorious red-light district that flourished in the early twentieth century. Established in 1897, the district got its name from Sidney Story, a city councilman who originally proposed legalizing prostitution within a restricted area so as to discourage vice in other parts of the city. As America mobilized for World War I in 1917, the Navy issued a ban on prostitution within five miles of military sites, effectively closing Storyville.

There were actually two Storyvilles: one white and one black. White Storyville was the official red-light district covering twenty blocks on the downtown side of Canal Street, behind the French Quarter. Black Storyville, a four-block region located uptown between Perdido and Gravier streets, was designated for black patronage by the same 1897 city ordinance but did not receive legal status until briefly in 1917 (see Map 2). Even so, police officials generally ignored the prostitution going on in black Storyville as well.

Contrary to a widespread popular belief, jazz was not born in the brothels of either of the two Storyvilles. But the bawdy houses attracted a culture of nighttime entertainment and vice that supported early jazz bands. The two Storyvilles formed twin hubs of a broader pleasure district overlapping Canal Street and uniting uptown and downtown inhabitants. In the late 1890s, the creation of black Storyville began driving the more legitimate businesses out of the surrounding neighborhood. At the same time, the "sporting crowd" moved in, bringing so much crime and violence that the area became known as "the Battlefield."

It was in the **dance halls** and **honky tonks** (saloons) in this neighborhood that the first jazz bands played. Such establishments as Union Sons ("Funky Butt") Hall, Odd Fellows and Masonic Hall, and the Eagle Saloon, have become famous for the performers that held forth there in the early days. In white Storyville some of the more important venues included Globe Hall, Tom Anderson's Cabaret, and Pete Lala's Saloon.

The First Jazz Musician

The historical distinction of being the "first" jazz musician goes, fairly or unfairly, to an uptown black cornetist named **Buddy Bolden** (1877–1931). He was certainly the first legend of jazz history. Widely accepted claims that Bolden

Buddy Bolden and His Band, c. 1905. (Bolden stands in the back, second from the left.)

ran a barbershop and edited a scandal sheet called *The Cricket* have recently been disproved. Other colorful aspects of the Bolden story are apparently true: that a "harem" of female admirers accompanied him everywhere, carrying his hat, his jacket, his handkerchief; that he played a loud and raucous cornet that could be heard for miles around; and that he drank himself into depression and insanity and spent the last twenty-four years of his life in a mental institution.

Bolden began leading a string band (with himself on cornet) around 1895. By the turn of the century, he had done well enough to leave his day job as a plasterer and pursue music full-time. From then until his committal in 1907 Bolden reigned over black music in New Orleans, even acquiring a popular nickname: King Bolden. During this period he replaced strings with winds in his regular band, featuring what would become the standard instrumentation of New Orleans jazz bands: cornet, clarinet, trombone (Bolden's man actually played valve trombone), guitar, string bass, and drums.

Bolden's archrival was a Creole bandleader named **John Robichaux** (1866–1939). Whereas Bolden played mostly for rough crowds in the honky tonks and dance halls, Robichaux led a "sit-down" orchestra that played polite society music in white restaurants and ballrooms. Although Robichaux also performed occasionally in Bolden's venues (and vice versa), without question he consciously cultivated a more refined public image than Bolden. Whereas Bolden included waltzes, quadrilles, schottisches, and mazurkas in his dance sets, he became famous for his ragtime and blues playing. Robichaux, by contrast, built his reputation on a repertory of genteel popular songs and European dance music.

Despite his somewhat disreputable persona, Bolden earned more loyalty in the black community, especially among the young. Clarinetist George Baquet described the enthusiastic audience reaction the first night he heard Bolden's band at Odd Fellows Hall: "They played 'Make Me a Pallet.' Everybody rose and yelled out 'Oh, Mr. Bolden, play it for us, Buddy, play it!'" When Bolden's band played at Johnson Park opposite Robichaux's at Lincoln Park, Bolden used to point his cornet toward Lincoln and, as he put it, "call his children home." Like a New Orleans Pied Piper, Bolden drew Robichaux's patrons over to Johnson Park with the sheer sound of his horn—by all accounts loud, dark-tempered, and seductive.

Freddie Keppard.

The Post-Bolden Generation

After Bolden left the New Orleans musical world, his mantle fell on a downtown Creole cornetist named **Freddie Keppard** (1890–1933). When audiences in turn dubbed him "King Keppard," it became apparent that a dynasty of black New Orleans cornetists was in the making. The dynasty eventually extended to Joe ("King") Oliver and thence to his protégé, Louis Armstrong (aka "King Louie"). Keppard dominated New Orleans jazz until 1914, when he left the city to build a career in California and, later, Chicago.

As the passage of leadership from Bolden to Keppard symbolizes, it was evidently during this period—the decade before the war—that downtown and uptown musical cultures began to merge more fully. Bolden's popularity persuaded downtown musicians, in particular, to reevaluate their commercial prospects. As Creole violinist Paul Dominguez put it: "Us Downtown people, we didn't think so much of this rough Uptown jazz until we couldn't make a living otherwise. . . . If I wanted to make a living, I had to be rowdy like the other group. I had to jazz it or rag it or any other damn thing. Bolden cause all that. He cause these younger Creoles, men like [Sidney] Bechet and Keppard, to have a different style altogether from the old heads like [Lorenzo] Tio [Sr.] and [Manuel] Perez."

Brass Bands

As uptown and downtown musicians began collaborating more frequently, jazz itself underwent a transformation. Whereas Bolden had worked primarily within the string band tradition of providing indoor music for dances and parties, now outdoor brass bands increasingly played jazz as well. The marches played by these bands provided the instrumental roles (of cornet, clarinet, and trombone), metric disposition (a two-beat), and musical structures (blues and march form) favored by the earliest New Orleans jazz bands to record.

The brass band tradition in New Orleans, always vibrant, reached a peak during the nationwide craze for band music between 1880 and 1910. In these years black musicians established such distinguished organizations as the Onward, Excelsior, and Eureka brass bands. Those who had formal musical training—mostly Creoles—took great pride in the purity of their tone and in their ability to read and execute difficult passages without mistakes. But band music appealed to musicians throughout the black community, regardless of their conventional skill.

Brass bands and concert bands had been playing notated ragtime ever since the turn of the century. During his first international tour in 1900, John Philip Sousa introduced Europe to ragtime music. Thomas Preston Brooke, a lesser-known bandleader from Chicago, brought his concert band to New Orleans every winter season from 1900 to 1906. In New Orleans Brooke presented a series of immensely popular concerts devoted solely to instrumental ragtime, mostly in band arrangements of Tin Pan Alley songs.

With such examples before them it was only natural for uptown musicians to begin spontaneously "ragging" melodies in parades. This took place most conspicuously in **funeral parades,** one of the most important rituals of early jazz. While accompanying the casket to the cemetery the band would play a slow dirge, often on a hymn melody, out of respect for the dead. Then on the return trip the mood would brighten dramatically as the band launched into an exuberant jump tune to celebrate the deceased person's liberation from the troubles of mortality. As the parade gathered momentum, spectators would begin dancing to the music on the sidewalks and in the streets in what was called a **second line.** The steadily increasing excitement of the combined playing and dancing encouraged musicians to improvise, to reach beyond routines for suitably energetic embellishments. The dynamically escalating nature of the music cultivated a climactic or goal-oriented aesthetic in early jazz.

Cutting Contests

Another New Orleans social ritual that fostered improvisation and climax was a musical duel known as the cutting (or "carving" or "bucking") contest. New Orleans cutting contests, which often took place in the streets, could involve individual soloists or entire bands. In one common scenario, two bands advertising for furniture or some other commodity in horsedrawn wagons met at a street corner. Someone would chain the wagons' wheels together and force the musicians to do battle. Somewhat like the second-liners in funeral parades, large crowds would gather to cheer, applaud, and ultimately, name the winner. The need to outdo opponents impelled musicians to take spontaneous risks, and the heightened stakes with each turn to perform created a naturally intensifying musical trajectory.

Comedy Music

New Orleans jazz musicians before the war also nurtured a longstanding local penchant for unusual sounds. This inclination may have its roots in the nineteenth-century practice of **charivari,** a tradition (related to "shivaree") of harassing a newly married couple on their wedding night with loud cacophonous serenades. Connoting a bedlam of howling, screeching, and banging of metal objects, the word "charivari" may derive from the late Latin "caribaria," meaning "headache."

In the first decades of the twentieth century a possible descendent of charivari (minus the quasi-malicious intent) arose in the informal street ensembles known as **spasm bands.** Organized largely by children, the spasm bands performed on guitar, ukulele, and harmonica, but earned their oddball name and reputation for the players' skill on homemade or novelty instruments such as washboard, paper-and-comb, kazoo, and makeshift tambourines.

Motivated by a similar interest in unorthodox music, early jazz players found ways to modify the sounds of conventional instruments. Alphonse Picou used to play his clarinet with a kazoo in the end of it. Trombonists such as Kid Ory played *glissandos*—pitch "smears" that rise or fall continuously, like a siren. And cornetists developed a repertoire of muted effects to simulate talking, crying, animal sounds, and other noises from everyday life. The cornetist Mutt Carey described this music as "freak playing"; when New Orleans jazz bands first played in the North, audiences laughed and called it **comedy music.** Whatever the label, it was this eccentric manner of playing that won New Orleans jazz musicians a place in vaudeville. And it was vaudeville that introduced jazz to the world outside New Orleans.

PART **Two**

Early Jazz

(c. 1914–1929)

Historical Context: The Jazz Age

Chapter **4**

MANY HISTORIANS PLACE THE BEGINNING OF THE TWENTIETH CENTURY AS A historical period (as opposed to a chronological sequence) in 1914, at the outbreak of World War I. That gruesome, demoralizing conflict seemed to herald new ways of thinking and living, even in America where no blood was shed. Suddenly the world seemed colder, more efficient, and less predictable than before. The sense of entering a newly modern age grew in the 1920s, when scientific and technological advances, unraveling moral taboos, and a flourishing economy created a spirit of unprecedented excitement in daily life. This was the period that F. Scott Fitzgerald immortalized—somewhat sardonically—as the Jazz Age.

The year 1914 was as significant for jazz as it was for geopolitics. In or around that year James Reese Europe made his first proto-jazz records for the Victor Phonograph Company; social dance gurus Vernon and Irene Castle made their "whirlwind tour" of the United States; Henry Ford created innovations in automotive production that foreshadowed the twenties economy. And, most important, the first of several influential New Orleans jazz bands began their quest for professional fulfillment in West Coast and Northern cities. They very soon found audiences financially comfortable and looking for a good time.

Chronology

1914–1918	World War I
1914	Creole Band performs in Los Angeles
	Vernon and Irene Castle's "whirlwind tour"
1917	Original Dixieland Jazz Band makes first jazz records
1919	Eighteenth (Prohibition) Amendment
1920	Nineteenth (woman suffrage) Amendment
	Mamie Smith's "Crazy Blues" launches blues craze
1923	*Runnin' Wild* introduces the Charleston
	King Oliver makes his first records
1925	*The New Negro* published
	Louis Armstrong begins recording the Hot Fives and Hot Sevens
	Scopes Monkey Trial
1926	Jelly Roll Morton records with his Red Hot Peppers
1927	Charles Lindbergh crosses the Atlantic
	Duke Ellington opens at the Cotton Club
1929	Stock market crash

The Coolidge Prosperity

"The chief business of the American people is business," declared Republican president Calvin Coolidge, summing up the heady corporate spirit of the 1920s. The business ideas of automobile tycoon **Henry Ford** galvanized American industry. In 1914 Ford raised the minimum wage of his workers to $5 a day—more than double the industry average. He also began producing on an assembly line, thereby manufacturing Model T's seven times faster than before. These changes made it possible for Ford to charge much less for his cars, and Ford Motor Company soon dominated the market. Observing Ford's spectacular success, other industries quickly adopted similar techniques of **mass production.** By the 1920s new products like radios, refrigerators, and washing machines were made and sold by the millions. The stock market soared.

But the outward prosperity concealed economic weaknesses. To maximize profits, salesmen offered consumers a novel enticement: credit payment plans. Because of poor regulatory policies, banks made too many loans and became overextended. Farmers, one of the few groups that did *not* benefit from the strong economy, defaulted on loans and banks began to close. Seduced by the illusion of unending plenty, investors increasingly speculated on returns of the far future. Experienced traders became wary. When they finally began selling in large volume, a tidal wave of panicky investors followed their lead, precipitating the **stock market crash** of 1929. The ensuing depression, both economic and psychological, effectively ended the Jazz Age.

Fun and Nonsense

Up until that fateful point, however, the bull market encouraged people to enjoy themselves. A dramatic increase of Hollywood films, radio broadcasting, phonograph records, and new print media like *Time* magazine and *Reader's Digest* gave birth in the 1920s to modern popular culture. Americans especially enjoyed slapstick comedy routines in silent movies and vaudeville. During this period, Charlie Chaplin, Laurel and Hardy, and Harold Lloyd represented the first generation of film comedians to achieve international stardom.

Americans' love of comedy related closely to their obsession with **novelty.** For years, vaudeville had cultivated novelty almost as an institutional necessity. Writers in the trade press urged vaudeville performers to devise an original act (preferably with comic elements), whether they were singers, dancers, magicians, or performers with more unusual talents. One act showcased a team of "juggling dogs"; another featured a game of polo played on bicycles. Surely one of the most novel vaudeville performers was Hadji Ali, a "regurgitator" who closed his act by spitting up a pint of kerosene to ignite an object on stage, followed by a gallon of water to douse the flames.

Ordinary citizens partook directly of novelty through social fads. College students swallowed goldfish, sat at the tops of flagpoles, and rode pogo sticks. Otherwise respectable citizens gathered around darkened tables for séances. In 1923 the Chinese parlor game of Mah-Jongg became immensely popular; the next year it was crossword puzzles. Mass followings arose when in 1927 Charles Lindbergh flew across the Atlantic and Babe Ruth hit sixty home runs. Inspired by such professional record-breakers, everyday Americans subjected themselves to endurance contests. Marathon dancers staggered through the fox trot for days at a time, while amateur runners crossed the continent in a painful exercise known as the Bunion Derby.

It was in this context of comedy, novelty, and fads that jazz first came to national prominence. Indeed, jazz was first known as "novelty music" or "comedy music." The earliest jazz bands from New Orleans toured vaudeville circuits in the 1910s, capturing attention with the eccentric instrumental sounds they had developed in their hometown. A copycat New York band led by white drummer, Earl Fuller, incorporated vaudeville slapstick into its routine. The trombonist moved the slide with his foot, the clarinetist played with one hand while bouncing a hat on his free elbow, the cornetist fell off his chair, and Fuller himself pounded away on "sixty-four square feet of drums." Significantly, one New York jazz pianist went on to become a famous comedian—Jimmy Durante.

In addition to entertaining vaudeville audiences, jazz stimulated a new round of **fad dances.** By refining and popularizing the ragtime dances, Vernon and Irene Castle had helped launch a nationwide craze for social dancing in the 1910s. When the first jazz records began circulating at the

Dancers do the Charleston at a dance contest in St. Louis, 1925.

end of the decade, young people invented energetic dances to fit the new music. By the 1920s popular jazz dances included the shimmy, the toddle, the Chicago flop, and the black bottom, all of which originated in the black community. In 1923 a black musical introduced a dance that came to epitomize the entire era: the Charleston. Featuring opening and closing of the legs and jerky limb movements, the Charleston scandalized respectable citizens. But young people embraced the dance with vigor. In an attempt to stifle their exuberance, some ballrooms carried signs that read PCQ—"please Charleston quietly."

Postwar Morality

The fad dances reflected a new conception of morality in the years after the war. In the 1910s psychiatrist Sigmund Freud's unorthodox ideas about sexuality began infiltrating American sensibilities, eroding Victorian mores. The carnage and futility of World War I and the bungled peace accord bred cynicism toward traditional institutions. And in 1919 and 1920 Congress passed two constitutional amendments with far-reaching implications for the Jazz Age: the Eighteenth Amendment, prohibiting the manufacture, transportation, and sale of alcohol; and the Nineteenth, granting women the right to vote.

Prohibition accomplished its purpose of reducing drinking among the general population. But by placing the distribution of alcohol into the hands of criminals, the government unwittingly subsidized the expansion of organized crime. Gangsters built a multimillion-dollar industry selling bootleg liquor. In large cities they opened illegal bars called "speakeasies" where customers could enjoy live entertainment, including jazz, as well as alcohol. Competition over manufacture and distribution, however, led to bloody conflicts among bootleggers. Mob-owned speakeasies and nightclubs became dangerous and unstable places. Yet those very attributes made them romantically appealing to young people seeking adventure.

The right to vote, also known as **woman suffrage,** may seem unrelated to the world of nighttime entertainment. But as a huge and long-awaited victory for women's rights, the amendment emboldened women longing for greater social freedoms. In the 1920s women shortened their dresses, discarded corsets, wore cosmetics, started smoking and drinking in public, and became more open about sexuality. By mid-decade, newspapers and magazines had established a stereotyped image of the so-called *flapper:* bobbed hair, long pearl necklace, short skirt, rolled-down stockings, and rubber rain boots—all worn by a shockingly audacious, independent young woman.

Rising to defend traditional values, religious **fundamentalists** gained strength in the 1920s. The Scopes Monkey Trial of 1925, in which a Tennessee schoolteacher was convicted for teaching evolution, laid bare the division between literally minded religious believers and those who trusted in science. The power of radical fundamentalism became frighteningly clear in the nationwide resurgence of the Ku Klux Klan, which peaked at five million members before the end of the decade. Moderate and extreme fundamentalists alike waged a campaign against libertinism in society, denouncing the scandalous behavior as well as the freethinking that produced it.

Within this climate, jazz came under attack on several fronts. Editorials blamed the music for ills ranging from sexual promiscuity to cultural illiteracy to insanity. Classical musicians sneered at an idiom so evidently primitive and uncouth. Some even used jazz as an excuse to condemn the growing impact of blacks on American culture. But most commonly, critics assailed jazz for its morally pernicious influence. The title of an article published in *The Ladies' Home Journal* in 1921 framed the vital question: "Does Jazz Put the Sin in Syncopation?"

Taxonomies of Jazz

Not everyone opposed jazz, of course. Carl Engel, head of the Music Division of the Library of Congress, described good jazz as "recklessly fantastic and joyously grotesque" (see box—"Contemporary Voices: Music Historian Carl Engel Defends Jazz"). And John Philip Sousa mused that "there is no reason, with its exhilarating rhythm, its melodic ingenuities, why [jazz] should not become one of the accepted forms of composition." Then again, one wonders what *kind* of jazz these writers had in mind. As a new, rapidly evolving, and in some cases patently experimental music, jazz varied widely according to the race, class, social background, and intent of the performers.

Observers in the 1920s and 1930s spoke of two basic categories: hot jazz and sweet jazz. In reality these labels marked opposite ends of a broad continuum. And yet the two categories were not mere abstractions; some bands exemplified them in archetypal purity. **Hot jazz** (sometimes called "lowdown" or "gutbucket" music) was the original black idiom brought up from New Orleans, an animated, often blues-based, and rhythmically intense music that accompanied dancing in cabarets and speakeasies (see Chapter 5). The musicians themselves often touted their "hotness" through the names of their bands: Spike's Seven Pods of Pepper, Jelly Roll Morton's Red Hot Peppers, the Red Onion Jazz Babies, Louis Armstrong's Hot Five.

Sweet jazz (also known as "dicty" or "society" music) resulted from an effort by both black and white musicians to redeem jazz from its unsavory associations with crime and immorality. Following an impulse that would surface periodically throughout jazz history, bandleaders like Paul Whiteman and Fletcher Henderson attempted to fuse elements of jazz and classical music. The reformers especially wanted to orchestrate jazz more deliberately, thereby elevating the sense of refinement and decorum. Dance bands that aspired to these ideals played a music of lilting melodies, rich harmonies and orchestration, and serene rhythms (see Chapter 7).

Eventually, sweet jazz came to represent a compromise palatable to a large segment of the American public in the 1920s. Hot jazz, however, would more strongly influence succeeding generations. The hot style arrived in places like Chicago, New York, and Los Angeles as New Orleans blacks took part in a mass pilgrimage that has come to be known as the **Great Migration.**

The Great Migration

Ever since emancipation, southern blacks had ventured beyond the southern states in search of a better life. In the twentieth century, the black exodus from South to North (or West) and from country to city greatly increased, peaking twice: from 1910 to 1930 over one million blacks made the trek; from 1940 to 1960, over three million.

The first wave of migrants had strong incentives to leave. In 1915 the Ku Klux Klan reorganized for the first time since Reconstruction and began a campaign

hot jazz an early jazz style emphasizing bluesy effects, rhythmic intensity, and extroverted self-expression.

sweet jazz an early jazz style of lilting melodies, rich harmonies and orchestration, and serene rhythms.

MUSIC HISTORIAN CARL ENGEL

Defends Jazz—1922

Where did you hear, before jazz was invented, such multifarious stirring, heaving, wrestling of independent voices as there are in a jazz orchestra? The saxophone bleats a turgid song; the clarinets turn capers of their own; the violins come forward with an *obbligato;* a saucy flute darts up and down the scale, never missing the right note on the right chord; the trombone lumberingly slides off on a tangent; the drum and xylophone put rhythmic highlights into these kaleidoscopic shiftings; the cornet is suddenly heard above the turmoil, with good-natured brazenness. Chaos in order—orchestral technique of master craftsmen—music that is recklessly fantastic, joyously grotesque—such is good jazz. A superb, incomparable creation, inescapable yet elusive; something it is almost impossible to put in score upon a page of paper.

For jazz finds its last and supreme glory in the skill for improvisation exhibited by the performers. The deliberately scored jazz tunes are generally clumsy, pedestrian. It is not for the plodding, routine orchestrator to foresee the unexpected, to plan the improbable. Jazz is abandon, is whimsicality in music. A good jazz band should never play, and actually never does play, the same piece twice in the same manner. Each player must be a clever musician, an originator as well as an interpreter, a wheel that turns hither and thither on its own axis without disturbing the clockwork. . . . The playing and writing down of jazz are two different things. When a jazz tune is written on paper . . . it loses nine tenths of its flavor. . . . Jazz, fortunately, can be preserved on phonographic records for our descendents. They will form their own estimate of our enormities.

Carl Engel, "Jazz: A Musical Discussion," *Atlantic Monthly* (August 1922): 186–87.

of lynchings in the South. The election of Woodrow Wilson brought more southern Democrats into the White House, Congress, and Supreme Court than at any time since the Civil War. Under their influence, the federal government passed segregationist legislation that especially oppressed southern blacks. On the economic side, flooding and boll weevils destroyed southern crops in 1915–16. Meanwhile, employment beckoned in the North. After the war began, many white laborers moved into the newly formed war industries; at the same time war stanched the flow of immigration from Europe. These conditions created a demand for factory labor at relatively high wages. In sum, as Alain Locke put it in 1925, blacks were drawn north by "a new vision of opportunity, of social and economic freedom, of a spirit to seize, even in the face of an extortionate and heavy toll, a chance for the improvement of conditions."

The Harlem Renaissance

The 1920s was a time of great optimism for African Americans. Not only did upper- and middle-class blacks enjoy some of the prosperity of the period, but also they were beginning to win respect for their achievements and, in turn, see themselves in a different light. This new self-concept was articulated in a book of essays by black intellectuals published in 1925 under the title, *The New Negro.* The essays attested to an emerging black community populated by citizens who could match white Americans in education, cultural refinement, and artistic achievement. Because this activity was centered in the New York black neighborhood of Harlem, the movement became known as the **Harlem Renaissance.**

The Harlem Renaissance began as a literary movement. Such figures as James Weldon Johnson, Countee Cullen, and Langston Hughes wrote poetry, short stories, essays, and novels that sought to express the black experience in America. W. E. B. Du Bois, drawn to Harlem from his home in Atlanta, edited *Crisis,* the official publication of the NAACP. But the aims of the Harlem Renaissance were more artistic than political. Inspired by the writers, visual artists like Aaron Douglas and Archibald J. Motley Jr. tried to capture modern African American life in their paintings. And composers strove to wed black idioms with European classical practice in symphonies, concertos, string quartets, and sonatas.

Where did jazz fit into all of this? On the one hand, middle- and upper-class blacks tended to view jazz as immoral, unmusical, and, against the backdrop of cultural refinement posed by the Harlem Renaissance, a potential embarrassment. On the other hand, many black elites couldn't help feeling proud of the achievements of jazz musicians in show business. And the musicians themselves, aware of the negative stigma of their profession, sought to fashion a "high-class" image by incorporating sweet elements into their music and by wearing expensive clothing. In this effort they took inspiration from a new generation of black entertainers represented by people like tap-dancer and comedian, **Bill Bojangles Robinson** (1878–1949). Unlike his eminent predecessor, Bert Williams, Robinson eschewed blackface and other minstrelsy conventions in favor of a suave and sophisticated stage persona.

In retrospect, jazz musicians embodied the ideal of the New Negro more convincingly than many of their fellow artists. As one authority put it, "It is very ironic that a generation that was searching for a new Negro and his distinctive cultural expression would have passed up the only really creative thing that was going on. But then, it is not too surprising. The jazzmen were too busy creating a cultural renaissance to think about the implications of what they were doing."

The Blues Craze

The blues, rooted in semiliterate folk traditions, drew even more scorn among the socially ambitious in black society. Nevertheless, after the publication of W. C. Handy's "Memphis Blues" in 1912, the blues became increasingly popular in the North. Many of the most famous blues singers of the twenties got their start singing with minstrelsy and vaudeville troupes during the previous decade. Then in 1920 executives for OKeh Phonograph Company asked Mamie Smith to record a blues number—the first such recording—as a marketing experiment. The result, a record called "Crazy Blues," sold over a million copies in the first year, touching off a mania for the blues among black consumers that lasted until the end of the decade.

By the time it arrived in northern recording studios, the blues was a very different kind of music from the "country blues" of the rural South. Sometimes called **classic blues,** the northern variety was sung in the cities, mainly by

classic blues the blues as performed by black female singers in northern cities during the 1920s.

Bessie Smith.

women with piano or small band accompaniment. To coordinate the music among the members of such ensembles, classic blues performances generally adhered to a strict twelve-bar format, though they frequently incorporated popular song structures. Finally, the classic blues was an overtly commercial production, intended for vaudeville, cabaret, and record audiences.

By most reckonings the greatest of the classic blues singers, the "Empress of the Blues," was **Bessie Smith** (1894–1937). Born into wrenching poverty in Chattanooga, Tennessee, she left home as a teenager to sing with a minstrel company. In 1923 a talent scout for Columbia records brought her to New York, where she began her recording career. Smith quickly gained a reputation for mesmerizing her audiences during live performances. New Orleans guitarist Danny Barker compared her charisma with that of a black folk preacher: "If you had any church background, like people who came from the South as I did, you would recognize a similarity between what she was doing and what those preachers and evangelists from there did, and how they moved people. . . . Some would stand on corners and move the crowds from there. Bessie did the same thing on stage. . . . She could bring about mass hypnotism."

Recordings

Mamie Smith's recording of "Crazy Blues" inaugurated a new commercial category known as **race records**—records made by black musicians and marketed to a black audience. This was not just an industry term, but appeared on signs in the phonograph section of music stores similar to the various headings we encounter today when shopping for recorded music: classical, rock, jazz, blues, and so forth. The creation of a market niche for "race records" may seem to us like just another crude example of Jim Crow in the music industry, but without this category few if any black jazz musicians would have been recorded during this period.

Up until the mid-twenties, phonograph companies used a technology known as **acoustic recording.** In this process the musicians gathered around and played into a large funnel called a "horn." The sound vibrations passed through a membrane, then prodded a stylus which etched grooves in a wax cylinder. Because the balance among the instruments had to be achieved acoustically, the engineer typically placed the musicians at various distances

⊙ CD 1 / Track 22

0:00	Introduction
0:11	1st Chorus
0:44	2nd Chorus
1:16	3rd Chorus
0:25	4th Chorus
0:30	5th Chorus (climax)

BESSIE SMITH, *"Lost Your Head Blues"* (1926)

Although much of the electricity of her public performances is undoubtedly lost on records, one may nevertheless sense Smith's visceral power on songs like "Lost Your Head Blues." Accompanied by Joe Smith (no relation) on cornet and Fletcher Henderson on piano, Bessie generates tremendous energy and pathos over the course of five choruses. In the last chorus she produces an emotional climax by lengthening the notes to express the sense of loneliness and abandonment in the text. Notice, also, how Joe Smith improvises *fills* after each line of singing, as if "commenting" sympathetically on the sentiments in the lyrics. The fills create a pattern of *call-and-response* between the two Smiths, Joe and Bessie.

Record Labels

OKEH

A pioneering record label of early jazz, OKeh Records was started in 1918 by Otto Heinemann, the American manager of the German label Odeon. The small independent company sold ten-inch discs for 75¢ apiece and twelve-inch discs for $1.25. In 1920, OKeh discovered the vast economic potential of the African American market when it recorded Mamie Smith's "Crazy Blues" and the song became a hit. The following year, OKeh introduced "race records," transforming the record industry and indeed jazz itself. During the twenties, OKeh produced nearly all of Louis Armstrong's Hot Five and Hot Seven recordings, as well as the music of King Oliver, Sidney Bechet, Clarence Williams, and white jazz players Bix Beiderbecke and Frankie Trumbauer. Like many companies of the period, OKeh traveled throughout the country with mobile recording trucks capturing regional styles in cities like New Orleans, Atlanta, San Antonio, Kansas City, and Detroit. In addition to jazz and blues, OKeh recorded country music, calypso, Jewish music, Mexican music, and other ethnic specialties. In 1926 OKeh embraced electric recording technology and became a subsidiary of the major company, Columbia Records. Its influence as a jazz label declined in the mid-1930s, when it discontinued its race series. ■ ■ ■

from the horn. Around 1925 **electric recording** began replacing the acoustic method. In this process, the musicians played into microphones, which recorded the sound electronically. In addition to being more convenient, electric recording captured more details of a performance and eliminated much of the surface noise that marred acoustic recordings. Most records were 78 rpm discs, either ten or twelve inches in diameter, and contained approximately three minutes of music on each side. Recording musicians usually made around $30 per side for each record released.

Performance Venues

In most cases, this money supplemented a musician's steady job playing in theaters, dance halls, and nightclubs. In such live performance venues black musicians made anywhere from $45 to $75 per week, a salary that could double with tips. (Black hotel employees, by comparison, averaged about $20 per week plus tips.) When recordings were added to live engagements, a musician could live well indeed.

The two most important entertainment districts in the black community were New York's **Harlem** and the black neighborhood on the **South Side** of Chicago known as the "Black Belt" (later "Bronzeville"). Nightlife in black Chicago was concentrated along South State Street, in an area known as "The Stroll" (see Map 3). For South Side residents the Stroll provided relief from the daily strain of racism. There, as one writer noted in 1915, "for a minute or so one forgets the 'Problem.' It has no place here. It is crowded aside by an insistence of good cheer." It was in various venues on or around the Stroll that leading jazz musicians from New Orleans made their living in the 1920s.

Map 3. Chicago, c. 1920s.

The most prestigious and coveted jobs in black show business were in the **theaters.** Presenting vaudeville shows and movies, theaters carried an aura of respectability that distanced them from the seamy associations of cabarets and speakeasies. Classically trained musicians thrived in the theater pit orchestras, accompanying vaudeville acts and providing music for the silent films. To increase their earning power and versatility, jazz musicians worked to get theater orchestra jobs as well. Theaters exposed these musicians to classical repertories and helped them improve their sight-reading. In turn, the jazz players contributed exciting solos and novelty effects during the popular numbers.

Hot jazz was heard primarily in the dance halls and cabarets (either of which might have functioned as "speakeasies" by serving liquor). The most successful cabarets were the so-called **black and tans,** nightclubs that presented black

Carroll Dickerson Orchestra, Sunset Café, c. 1923.

entertainment to white or racially mixed audiences. In the late 1920s, Louis Armstrong at Chicago's Sunset Café and Duke Ellington at Harlem's Cotton Club broke down bourgeois prejudices toward jazz, drawing in enthusiastic white patrons in mink coats, top hats, and limousines on a nightly basis. This lavish attention by the elites of white society foreshadowed the mass embrace of black-influenced jazz by the entire country in the 1930s.

Chapter *5* New Orleans Jazz

During the Great Migration, a steady exodus of New Orleans musicians traveled north in search of better working conditions and more hospitable attitudes toward race. In most cases they headed for Chicago, arguably the most ambitious and progressive city in the North. Such figures as Jelly Roll Morton, King Oliver, Kid Ory, Sidney Bechet, and Louis Armstrong all undertook the journey hoping to "make good," and their now legendary status in the annals of jazz history shows that they succeeded, at least in the view of posterity.

The earliest New Orleans bands broke into the northern entertainment industry by playing "comedy music" with traveling vaudeville or minstrel troupes. Before long, however, many of them settled into various cabarets for extended engagements. While vaudeville continued to play an important role in cabaret entertainment, New Orleans musicians earned their northern reputations primarily by playing a hot, bluesy type of music that dancers loved. More important for future generations, they recorded their music extensively, exposing other musicians—from California to Europe—to New Orleans jazz.

The Pioneers

The first New Orleans band to win national recognition was organized in Los Angeles in 1914. Led by Freddie Keppard and a bass player named Bill Johnson, the group called itself the **Creole Band**—a name coupling New Orleans exoticism with lofty European sensibilities. The Creole Band first attracted attention playing at a prizefight in Los Angeles. The local press was divided, either praising the band's originality or denouncing its "vile imitation of music," as one writer put it. Nevertheless, the show business impresario Alexander Pantages immediately contracted the band to tour his vaudeville circuit. During a stopover in Chicago the Creole Band was described by one reporter as an "aggregation of comedy musicians" who knew "how to extract the most weird effects from their various instruments." In 1916 executives for the Victor Talking Machine Company offered the band the chance to record. Keppard allegedly rejected the offer, insisting that records would undercut the band's uniqueness: "We won't put our stuff on records for everybody to steal."

Thus the distinction of being the first jazz band to record went to the **Original Dixieland Jazz Band** (ODJB), a white New Orleans group that came north that same year. Performing at Reisenweber's Restaurant in New York, the ODJB initially bewildered and annoyed its listeners. Then someone tried dancing to the band's antic music, and the ODJB became an overnight sensation. When presented with the opportunity, the band seized the chance to record. On February 26, 1917, Victor recorded the ODJB's rendition of "Livery Stable Blues," a tune featuring barnyard effects that included a crowing clarinet, a whinnying cornet, and a mooing trombone. The record sold over a million copies in the first year, launching jazz as an international phenomenon.

Despite the fabulous success of the ODJB, the record industry was slow to capitalize on it. Over the next five years a few jazz recordings were made by other white bands, including the Louisiana Five and the Original Memphis Five. Then in 1922 a black band from New Orleans entered a Los Angeles recording studio and made six sides, the first records to document black New Orleans jazz. Led by trombonist Kid Ory and including cornetist Mutt Carey, the group was named **Spikes' Seven Pods of Pepper** after the Spikes Brothers, a vaudeville team that promoted the band. Ory's music differed dramatically from that of the white groups. The ODJB had presented a frenetic, madcap sort of jazz full of nervous energy and wild exuberance. By contrast, on tunes like "Ory's

Great Debates

Who "Invented" Jazz?

In the 1910s several New Orleans bands claimed to be the "original" creators of jazz. Twenty years later, in an attempt to trace the music's origins, jazz historians discovered the recently deceased Buddy Bolden. Fearful of losing credit for such an important contribution to American culture, some New Orleans veterans reasserted their claims of being there first. The most notorious assertions were Jelly Roll Morton's 1938 *Down Beat* article, "I Invented Jazz in the Year 1902," and the blustering protestations of Nick LaRocca, the cornetist and leader of the Original Dixieland Jazz Band. For decades LaRocca insisted not only that his band had created jazz, but more provocatively that black musicians had nothing to do with the origins of the music. As late as 1961 he published the ODJB's counterpart to Morton's manifesto entitled, "Jazz Started with Us."

Considering jazz to be the product of a collective, multiracial effort over the course of many years, most historians do not take seriously the claims of either man. But a debate still rages over the precise nature of their contributions. Whereas Morton's place in the pantheon of jazz pioneers is secure (some writers accept his boast as being true in spirit if not in letter), the question of the ODJB's role can scarcely be raised in some quarters without causing hard feelings. The ODJB was nothing more than a band of usurpers, it is often said, who profited from the unrecorded achievements of black musicians. And yet no less an authority on New Orleans music than Bruce Boyd Raeburn, curator of the Hogan Jazz Archive in New Orleans, has noted that "local reactions [in New Orleans] to the recordings of the ODJB tended to be enthusiastic," regardless of race. And the ODJB recorded almost ten years before the appearance of Morton's Red Hot Pepper recordings; is it not possible that Morton learned something from them? All the same, "inventing" jazz is another matter. That fictive honor may as well continue to rest on the music's patron saint, Buddy Bolden. ■ ■ ■

Creole Trombone" the Ory band sounded wonderfully relaxed and integrated; it generated a different kind of energy, one that created more momentum. In short, Ory's men swung "harder." The element of a finely calibrated swing is what most distinguished the jazz of black New Orleanians from that of white musicians.

King Oliver

In 1923 a New Orleans uptown cornetist named **Joe Oliver** (1885–1937) took his Creole Jazz Band into a tiny, sweltering studio in Richmond, Indiana, and made nine sides for Gennett Phonograph Company. During the next year or so, Oliver and his band produced the first large number of recordings by black New Orleanians. Performing nightly at Chicago's Lincoln Gardens, Oliver awakened an entire generation of white musicians to the wonders of black jazz.

Legend has it that Oliver rose to prominence in New Orleans after dethroning then-reigning cornetist Freddie Keppard. As pianist Richard M. Jones recalled the episode, "Keppard was playin' in a spot across the street and was drawin' all the crowds. I was sittin' at the piano, and Joe Oliver came over to me and commanded in a nervous harsh voice, 'Get in [the key of] B-flat.' . . . I did, and Joe walked out on the sidewalk, lifted his horn to his lips, and blew the most beautiful stuff I have ever heard. People started pouring out of the other spots along the street to see who was blowing all that horn. Before long, our place was full and Joe came in, smiling, and said, 'Now, that _____ won't bother me no more.'" Whatever the truth of this story, Oliver subsequently

King Oliver and His Creole Jazz Band, c. 1923. *Left to right:* Honore Dutrey, Baby Dodds, King Oliver, Louis Armstrong (kneeling), Lil Hardin, Bill Johnson, Johnny Dodds.

came to be known as "King" Oliver, after his predecessors King Bolden and King Keppard.

The Creole Jazz Band

At the height of its popularity, King Oliver's **Creole Jazz Band** was a septet consisting of Oliver (first cornet), Louis Armstrong (second cornet), Johnny Dodds (clarinet), Honore Dutrey (trombone), Lil Hardin (piano), Bill Johnson (formerly the leader of the Creole Band; bass and banjo), and Baby Dodds (drums). All the players came from New Orleans except Hardin, a young woman from Memphis. The band held forth at the **Lincoln Gardens,** a South Side dance hall for black youth, from 1922 through 1924 (see Map 3).

On a typical evening at the Lincoln Gardens dancers crowded the floor, drawn by the band's irresistible sense of swing, or "dance rhythm," as musicians in the 1920s would have called it. "When the Creole Jazz Band played," one admirer recalled, "every chorus seemed to swing more than the previous one until every bit of tension in you seemed to leave your body." As this comment suggests, Oliver's band generated tremendous rhythmic momentum which led finally to a powerful climax. The momentum derived from the complementary polyphonic interaction among the four horn players. Johnny Dodds and Armstrong, in particular, would play between Oliver's melodic phrases, spurring him on and enlivening the texture with more elaborate figures.

Vaudeville entertainment supplemented dancing at the Lincoln Gardens. Singers, dancers, and chorus girls put on elaborate floorshows between dancing sets, while King Jones, the diminutive master of ceremonies, shouted out introductions. Oliver's musicians often joined in the vaudeville spirit: Baby Dodds shimmied while playing drums; Johnson lay on the floor to play his bass; Armstrong performed a little comedy dance act; and Oliver himself drew upon the New Orleans freak tradition of muted techniques to talk, laugh, or cry with his cornet. Waving various hemispherical objects—cups, glasses, buckets, and bowls—at the end of his cornet bell, Oliver altered the timbre of his horn to create **"wah-wah" effects** and other clever or humorous sounds. In the North this unorthodox style was termed "novelty" or "trick" playing. In the summer of 1923 the *Talking Machine World* noted that "King Oliver is known to practically every musician in the country and is acknowledged to be the originator of the trick cornet playing in vogue to-day."

If listeners in the twenties interpreted Oliver's music primarily as dance and novelty music, for jazz historians the Creole Jazz Band records also reveal the hallmarks of traditional **New Orleans style.** Notice how many of these features stem from the concert band tradition:

- Polyphonic texture created by independent melodies in the cornets, clarinet, and trombone (cf. John Philip Sousa, *Semper Fidelis*, trio)
- Instrumental roles inherited from brass bands:
  - Cornet plays melody
  - Clarinet plays higher, faster obbligatos
  - Trombone plays lower countermelodies
- Ensemble-oriented texture, or at least a balance between solo and ensemble passages
- A two-beat metric feel (except on slow blues pieces)

wah-wah effects sounds produced by brass players waving hemispherical objects back and forth at the end of the bell of their instruments.

New Orleans style an early jazz style featuring such traits as swing feel, polyphonic ensemble textures, two-beat meters, solo breaks, and stop-time.

KING OLIVER'S CREOLE JAZZ BAND, *"Dippermouth Blues"* (1923)

Louis Armstrong, King Oliver's second cornetist, had a broad mouth that inspired many adolescent nicknames, including "Gatemouth," "Satchelmouth," and "Dippermouth." (It was a corruption of "Satchelmouth" that later produced his most famous nickname, "Satchmo.") "Dippermouth Blues," composed by Oliver and Armstrong, is apparently a tribute to Oliver's young protégé. It was Oliver's most famous recording in the 1920s and remains so today.

"Dippermouth Blues" is an *instrumental blues* on the standard twelve-bar structure. The piece illustrates many aspects of New Orleans style, including a powerful sense of swing, a two-beat metric feel, polyphonic ensemble texture (e.g., first two choruses), stop-time (third and fourth choruses), and breaks (one occurs just before the last chorus). It also showcases two of the great New Orleans soloists: clarinetist Johnny Dodds and Oliver himself.

Oliver's three-chorus solo—an unusually lengthy solo for the time—marks the high point of the piece. Most cornet solos during this period employed a technique called **melodic paraphrase,** in which the player would simply embellish the main melody. But in "Dippermouth Blues" Oliver creates an entirely new solo based on one or two blues ideas. The solo is notable, also, for Oliver's wailing *wah-wah effects* (typically on blue notes) and for its climactic structure: each chorus begins a little higher than the previous one, gradually increasing the intensity of sound. Oliver's solo ends with a happy accident: according to legend, Baby Dodds was supposed to play a drum break before the last chorus but was so nervous he missed his cue. Bill Johnson's spontaneous outburst, "Oh play that thing!" serves as a perfect entrée to the **outchorus,** or final polyphonic ensemble chorus meant to culminate the whole performance.

- Use of march forms, blues forms, and song forms
- Frequent use of **breaks,** brief (usually two-bar) openings for a soloist to perform unaccompanied by the rest of the band
- Use of **stop-time** accompaniment, in which the band plays a repeating rhythmic pattern, accenting certain beats of each measure while leaving other beats open for the soloist to fill alone.

melodic paraphrase an improvisational style in which the soloist embellishes the main melody of the piece being played.

outchorus in New Orleans style, a final polyphonic ensemble chorus intended to climax the performance.

break a brief (usually two-bar) solo unaccompanied by the rest of the ensemble.

stop-time a type of solo accompaniment in which the band plays a simple, repeating rhythmic pattern while leaving gaps for the soloist to fill alone.

Jelly Roll Morton

The pianist Ferdinand Joseph Lemothe, better known as **Jelly Roll Morton** (1890–1941), is one of the most colorful figures of jazz history. A notorious braggart, he famously claimed to have "invented" jazz in 1902 (that is, at the age of twelve). Although this claim may strain credulity, Morton evidently did know Buddy Bolden and performed with other jazz pioneers. Unfortunately, because he did not record with his own band until the twenties, it is difficult to assess his role in the development of New Orleans style. Still, Morton's compositions on these recordings unequivocally establish his preeminence as a master of the New Orleans tradition. He is sometimes regarded as the first great composer of jazz.

Morton grew up in a proud Haitian-Creole family in downtown New Orleans. (The name Morton was a version of his stepfather's French name, Mouton, anglicized for show business.) As a teenager he played ragtime piano in

LISTENING CHART 5

King Oliver's Creole Jazz Band, "Dippermouth Blues" (Oliver-Armstrong)   CD 1 / Tracks 23–26

RECORDED 6 APRIL 1923, RICHMOND, INDIANA / GENNETT 5132; MX 11389-B (ACOUSTIC RECORDING)

King Oliver (first cornet), Louis Armstrong (second cornet), Johnny Dodds (clarinet), Honore Dutrey (trombone), Lil Hardin (piano), Bill Johnson (banjo, vocal break), Baby Dodds (drums)

Style: New Orleans style			**Form: 12-bar blues**

			Introduction
23	0:00	4 bars	Homophonic cornet duet: King Oliver and Louis Armstrong
			Polyphonic ensemble
	0:05	*1st Chorus* (12)	The whole band plays together; Oliver plays the lead, while Johnny Dodds plays higher obbligatos and Armstrong and Honore Dutrey play countermelodies
	0:21	*2nd Chorus* (12)	
			Clarinet solo: Johnny Dodds
24	0:37	*3rd Chorus* (12)	Stop-time accompaniment: piano, banjo, and drums play on the first three beats of each measure
	0:53	*4th Chorus* (12)	
			Polyphonic ensemble
	1:10	*5th Chorus* (12)	Armstrong takes over the cornet lead here so Oliver can rest his lips right before his solo
			Wah-wah cornet solo: King Oliver
25	1:25	*6th Chorus* (12)	With polyphonic accompaniment: Johnny Dodds and Dutrey play discreet counterpoint, but Armstrong lays out
	1:41	*7th Chorus* (12)	Oliver continues his solo, starting this chorus a little higher than the last one . . .
	1:58	*8th Chorus* (10)	Climax: Oliver starts this chorus higher still . . .
	2:11	Spoken break (2)	Bill Johnson: "Oh play that thing!"
			Outchorus: polyphonic ensemble
26	2:13	*9th Chorus* (12)	The whole band plays together as at the beginning, but with greater intensity and rhythmic swing
	2:29	Tag (2)	This two-bar tag functions as a tiny coda

the brothels of white Storyville, an occupation that provoked stern disapproval from his great-grandmother, his principal guardian. At age seventeen he left New Orleans and embarked on a nomadic, multifaceted career as pimp, gambler, pool shark, and all-around vaudeville entertainer. In 1914 he settled in Chicago for three years, then moved to California where he stayed until the early twenties. He then returned to Chicago and began making the recordings upon which his musical reputation is largely based.

Morton's initial ambition was apparently to be a vaudeville comic. During the 1910s he often performed in blackface with a woman named Rosa. One colleague recalled that "Jelly wanted to be a comedian. He thought he was a funny man, [but] he was as funny as a sick baby. He never made nobody laugh." Although other accounts speak more favorably of Morton's comedy routines, one gets the impression that his piano playing is what really impressed people. A 1914 reviewer in the Indianapolis *Freeman* wrote, "Mr. Morton . . . does a pianologue in good style. He plays a good piano, classics and rags with equal ease. His one hand stunt, left hand alone, playing a classic selection, is a good one. . . . [He] composes most of his own songs and arranges his other work. As a comedian, Morton is grotesque in his makeup and sustains himself nicely through the work. [Morton and Rosa] are a clever pair, giving a pleasing show."

The Red Hot Peppers

When Morton arrived in Chicago in the summer of 1923, he cut a swaggering figure. Wearing a ten-gallon hat, a diamond in one of his front teeth, and expensive clothes, Morton still looked and acted the part of a vaudeville showstopper. But he had realized by this time that his greatest talents lay in the realm of music. In 1926 he organized a New Orleans septet called the Red Hot Peppers for the purpose of recording his recently published compositions.

Morton's approach to the New Orleans idiom differed from Oliver's. Whereas Oliver conjured an earthy, churning melange of sounds, Morton produced glossy and well-rehearsed music, full of snap and precision-timing. The polished (although not always flawless) performances of the Red Hot Peppers reflect Morton's fastidious direction of his musicians. Unlike the Creole Jazz Band, the Red Hot Peppers was not a regular working band but existed solely to record Morton's compositions. As clarinetist Omer Simeon recalled, "Walter Melrose brought all the music down from his music store. Morton was working for Melrose then and the pieces we played [in the recording studio] were mostly stock arrangements Jelly had . . . published with Melrose. . . . Jelly left our solos up to us but the backgrounds, harmony and licks were all in his arrangements." Morton took unusual pains, rehearsing for three or four days before recording, and—in a rare gesture—paying his men for their rehearsal time. On one occasion, the trombonist Zue Robertson refused to play a passage the way Morton wanted him to; frustrated, Morton pulled a gun from his pocket and laid it on the piano. Robertson complied with the composer's wishes!

Kid Ory

One of the most prominent sidemen in the Red Hot Peppers was Creole trombonist **Edward "Kid" Ory** (1890–1973). A veteran bandleader in his own right, Ory headed the most successful jazz band in New Orleans in the late 1910s,

Jelly Roll Morton and His Red Hot Peppers, c. 1926. (Kid Ory stands second from the right.)

Kid Ory's Brownskinned Babies. After an extended period in California he settled in Chicago in 1925, where he recorded with some of the most celebrated New Orleans bandleaders, including King Oliver and Louis Armstrong as well as Morton.

In the 1920s Ory's playing embodied the essence of New Orleans trombone style, an idiom commonly known as **tailgate trombone.** Featuring careening *glissandos,* explosive accents, and other boisterous effects, the tailgate style is associated with trombonists who played with advertising bands in New Orleans. As the bands rode around town in horsedrawn wagons, trombonists supposedly sat on the tailgate to insure free movement of the slide—hence the name. In the North, tailgate style became part of the growing repertoire of novelty devices, analogous in meaning to the wah-wah effects of the cornetists. In the hands of someone like Ory, however, the tailgate style produced energy and excitement as well, particularly during outchoruses.

Sidney Bechet

In the late twenties, jazz became far more solo-oriented than it had been under the stewardships of Oliver and Morton. The musicians most responsible for this change of style were two members of the rising generation: trumpeter Louis Armstrong—whom we will discuss in Chapter 6—and clarinetist **Sidney Bechet**

tailgate trombone a New Orleans trombone style featuring careening glissandos, explosive accents, and other boisterous effects.

JELLY ROLL MORTON, *"Black Bottom Stomp"* (1926)

Morton published the music for "Black Bottom Stomp" in 1925 under the original title, "Queen of Spades." While recording with the Red Hot Peppers the following year, he renamed the piece to capitalize on the popularity of the black bottom, a new fad dance introduced in the 1926 stage show, *Dinah.* Notice the sound difference between this recording, which took advantage of the new electric technology, and the old acoustic recording of "Dippermouth Blues."

"Black Bottom Stomp" is in march form with only two strains: A and B. After a fanfare-like introduction, the A-section appears three times—first as a homophonic ensemble passage, then as a call-and-response between trumpet (George Mitchell) and ensemble, and finally as a clarinet solo (Omer Simeon). Thus, the three statements show a gradual transition from an ensemble to a solo texture. Note that even in the last A, however, the clarinet solo still retains the basic pattern established in the first A—an alternation between a simple downbeat figure (x) and a more involved syncopated line (y).

Morton creates greater intensity during the repeating B-section (or trio) in several ways. First, the ensemble passages are polyphonic rather than homophonic. Second, a succession of solos builds momentum toward the final ensemble choruses. Third, Morton usually calls for a break at the end of each first phrase (z); as one writer put it, Morton's breaks serve as "subtle climaxes" in the musical flow, thereby anticipating the main climax of the polyphonic outchorus. The outchorus itself throbs with a strong **backbeat** (emphasis on beats 2 and 4) in the drums. Finally, by adding four bars to the end of each B-section, Morton creates a lopsided twenty-bar form. Because listeners expect the section to end after sixteen bars, the addition creates tension, delaying the resolution that comes with the end of the section. In his own solo, Morton exploits this tension by playing more fiercely, even speeding up the tempo slightly, during the last four bars.

(1897–1959). Bechet (pronounced buh-SHAY) grew up in a musical Creole family. Unlike most of the New Orleans pioneers, Bechet was a child prodigy on his instrument. By age eleven he was already playing professionally; by the mid-1910s, many musicians regarded him as the most impressive clarinetist in the city, even though he could not read music. Bechet's commanding virtuosity practically insured that, unlike Oliver and Morton, he would pursue his career primarily as a soloist, not as a bandleader.

Like others before him, Bechet performed initially with vaudeville companies. In addition to playing novelty clarinet (he clucked like a chicken), he acted in various comedy sketches and had his own feature stunt: while continuously playing the clarinet he gradually disassembled his instrument all the way down to the squawking mouthpiece. He also played wonderful solos. Reviewing a vaudeville performance at New Orleans's Lincoln Theater, the Chicago *Defender* praised Bechet while issuing a challenge on his behalf to "Big Eye" Louis Nelson, the clarinetist for the Creole Band: "Mr Basha [*sic*] is screaming 'em every night with his sensational playing. All send regards to the Creole Band. Basha says look out Louis Nelson I am coming."

In 1916 Bechet left New Orleans, beginning a restless, footloose existence that would characterize much of his life. In 1919 he traveled to Europe with Will

backbeat regular emphasis placed on beats two and four (in 4/4 time), especially in the drums.

LISTENING CHART 6

Jelly Roll Morton's Red Hot Peppers, "Black Bottom Stomp" (Morton)

CD 1 / Tracks 27–32

RECORDED 15 SEPTEMBER 1926, CHICAGO / VICTOR 20221; MX 142149-1 (ELECTRIC RECORDING)

Jelly Roll Morton (piano), George Mitchell (trumpet), Omer Simeon (clarinet), Kid Ory (trombone), Johnny St. Cyr (banjo), John Lindsay (bass), Andrew Hilaire (drums)

Style: New Orleans style				**Form: March form**

				Introduction
27	0:00	8 bars		Four-bar fanfare-like passage repeated once
		A (16)		**First strain**
	0:07		x (4)	Homophonic ensemble: sustained notes on the downbeats
	0:11		y (4)	Faster syncopated notes, then polyphony
	0:15		x (4)	*Repeated*
	0:18		y (4)	
		A (16)		**Call-and-response: trumpet versus ensemble**
28	0:22		x' (4)	Trumpet solo: George Mitchell
	0:26		y (4)	Ensemble
	0:29		x' (4)	Trumpet solo: Mitchell
	0:33		y (4)	Ensemble
		A (16)		**Clarinet solo: Omer Simeon**
29	0:37		x" (4)	Melodic paraphrase
	0:41		y' (4)	Improvises more freely
	0:44		x" (4)	Melodic paraphrase
	0:48		y' (4)	Improvises more freely
				Transition/modulation
30	0:51		4 bars	Call-and-response: trumpet versus ensemble
		B (20)		**Second strain: trio (new key)**
	0:56		z (6)	Polyphonic ensemble
	1:01		Break (2)	Trumpet, then trombone
	1:03		z' (12)	Polyphonic ensemble
		B (20)		**Clarinet solo: Omer Simeon**
	1:14		z (6)	The regularity of this elaborate solo suggests that it was written out, or at least well-rehearsed
	1:20		Break (2)	
	1:22		z' (12)	Solo becomes freer in this section, suggesting more improvisation at work

		B (20)		**Piano solo: Jelly Roll Morton**
31	1:33		z (8)	Unaccompanied, Morton shows off his virtuoso abilities here in classic *stride* style (see Chapter 9)
	1:40		z' (12)	
		B (20)		**Trumpet solo: George Mitchell**
	1:51		z (6)	Mitchell colors his tone subtly with a *wah-wah mute* while the band accompanies in *stop-time*
	1:57		Break (2)	
	1:59		z' (12)	
		B (20)		**Banjo solo: Johnny St. Cyr**
	2:10		z (6)	St. Cyr strums imaginatively on simple melodic ideas
	2:16		Break (2)	
	2:18		z' (12)	
		B (20)		**Polyphonic ensemble**
	2:29		z (6)	The entire band plays together polyphonically, building toward the climax of the piece: the outchorus
	2:35		Break (2)	Cymbals: Andrew Hilaire
	2:37		z' (12)	
		B (20)		**Outchorus: polyphonic ensemble**
32	2:48		z (6)	As the music intensifies in this final chorus notice the howling trombone and the *backbeat* in the drums
	2:54		Break (2)	Trombone: Kid Ory (tailgate style!)
	2:56		z' (12)	
	3:07		Tag (2)	

Further Listening from the *Prentice Hall Jazz Collection*
Track 1: Jelly Roll Morton, "Wolverine Blues" (1927)

Marion Cook's Southern Syncopated Orchestra, a note-reading organization that featured a large orchestra and chorus performing society dance music and light classics. In this context Bechet served as token jazz and blues soloist. In Europe Bechet's solos made a profound impression on a distinguished Swiss conductor named Ernest Ansermet. In a statement remarkable for its sensitivity and prescience, Ansermet described Bechet's improvisations as "extremely difficult, [and] equally admirable for their richness of invention, force of accent, and daring in novelty and the unexpected. . . . Their form was gripping, abrupt, harsh, with a brusque and pitiless ending like that of Bach's Second Brandenburg Concerto." Ansermet considered Bechet "an artist of genius" whose musical path might well be "the highway the whole world will swing along tomorrow." Ansermet's statement stands out for his willingness to consider jazz, a music of low comedy and dance halls, as an art form comparable to the great works of European classical music.

The Red Onion Jazz Babies

While in London Bechet bought a soprano saxophone, a straight lacquer-coated instrument in the shape of a clarinet. Despite the instrument's congenital reluctance to play in tune, Bechet fell in love with its penetrating and expressive sonority. The soprano saxophone soon became Bechet's main instrument, though he continued to play clarinet as well.

After returning to New York Bechet began making his first recordings. In 1924–1925 Clarence Williams contracted a recording band that included Bechet, Louis Armstrong, and Armstrong's new wife, Lil Hardin Armstrong. Called the Red Onion Jazz Babies (after a New Orleans nightclub named the Red Onion), the group presented an approach to New Orleans style that differed from both Oliver's and Morton's. Instead of suppressing individual personalities to create an integrated ensemble texture, the horn players in the Red Onion Jazz Babies frequently seem to be competing for

Sidney Bechet playing soprano saxophone, c. 1947.

RED ONION JAZZ BABIES, *"Cake Walking Babies from Home"* (1924)

Whereas the Oliver and Morton recordings in this chapter reveal blues and march forms respectively, "Cake Walking Babies from Home" is in popular song form. The verse-chorus form is sandwiched between instrumental choruses at the beginning and the end; the structure of the chorus itself resembles that of Irving Berlin's "Alexander's Ragtime Band" but with an added A: ABA'CA'. In this recording the lyrics are sung by one of the great blues singers of the twenties, Alberta Hunter, and her vaudeville partner, Clarence Todd. Known in show business as "Beatty and Todd," the two singers on this recording help us to better understand the role that jazz bands must have played when accompanying vocalists on a vaudeville stage.

The strong sense of individuality in the playing of Louis Armstrong and Sidney Bechet emerges at the very beginning. Yet, true rivalry becomes evident only during the third and fourth choruses. The third chorus features Armstrong in an eight-bar stop-time solo at C. Notice how lively and energetic Armstrong is compared with previous cornetists we have heard. In the fourth chorus it is Bechet's turn. Not content to wait for the stop-time opening at the end of the chorus, Bechet immediately launches into a series of surging *arpeggios* (chords played one note at a time) which transcend the subordinate role of obbligato to become primary material. After totally overwhelming the other players—including Armstrong—in the polyphonic section (ABA'), Bechet uses his stop-time solo as a "victory dance," so to speak, growling at his colleagues in a taunting manner and trading his onward rush for dainty falling gestures.

LISTENING CHART 7

Red Onion Jazz Babies, "Cake Walking Babies from Home"
(Williams-Smith-Troy)

CD 1 / Tracks 33–36

RECORDED 22 DECEMBER 1924, NEW YORK CITY / GENNETT 5627; MX 9248-A (ACOUSTIC RECORDING)

Louis Armstrong (cornet), Sidney Bechet (soprano saxophone), Charlie Irvis (trombone), Lil Hardin Armstrong (piano), Buddy Christian (banjo), Alberta Hunter and Clarence Todd (voice)

Style: New Orleans style	Form: Verse-chorus form with modified chorus: ABA′CA′

		1st Chorus	**Polyphonic ensemble**
33	0:00	A (8)	Louis Armstrong (cornet) plays an embellished version of the melody, while Sidney Bechet (soprano saxophone) plays equally ornate obbligatos and Charlie Irvis (trombone) adds counter-melodies. Notice how the horns don't blend into a larger ensemble texture as in the bands of King Oliver and Jelly Roll Morton, but stand out as individual voices.
	0:08	B (8)	
	0:17	A′ (8)	
	0:25	C (8)	
	0:33	A″ (8)	
		Verse	
	0:42	X (8)	*Continued*
	0:50	Y (8)	
		2nd Chorus	**Vocal duet: Alberta Hunter and Clarence Todd**
34	0:59	A (8)	*Here they come (Oh here we come)—those strutting syncopators,* *Go and come (Oh go and come), look at those demonstrators*
	1:07	B (8)	*Walk uptown, green and brown,* *Pickin' 'em up and layin' 'em down.*
	1:15	A′ (8)	*Prancin' fools (Oh prancin' fools), that's what I like to call 'em* *They're in a class all alone.*
	1:23	C (8)	*The only way for them to lose is to cheat 'em,* *You may tire 'em but you'll never beat 'em.*
	1:32	A″ (8)	*Strut their stuff, they don't do nothin' different,* *Cake-walking babies from home!*

		3rd Chorus	**Polyphonic ensemble / stop-time solo: Armstrong**
35	1:40	A (8)	The three horns improvise polyphonically again, but with greater intensity this time; both Armstrong and Bechet embellish more elaborately
	1:48	B (6)	
	1:54	2 bars	**Break: Sidney Bechet (soprano saxophone)**
	1:57	A' (8)	Polyphonic ensemble
	2:05	C (8)	**Stop-time solo: Louis Armstrong (cornet)**
	2:14	A" (8)	Polyphonic ensemble
		4th Chorus	**Polyphonic ensemble / stop-time solo: Bechet**
36	2:22	A (8)	Aware that it will be his turn to play the stop-time solo in this chorus, Bechet immediately casts aside his ensemble role and transforms his obbligatos into surging solo statements, leaving his bandmates in the background
	2:31	B (6)	
	2:37	2 bars	**Break: Charlie Irvis (trombone)**
	2:39	A' (8)	Polyphonic ensemble
	2:47	C (8)	**Stop-time solo: Sidney Bechet (soprano saxophone)**
			Bechet growls haughtily, plays dainty falling gestures, and resumes his driving arpeggiated lines
	2:56	A" (8)	Polyphonic ensemble: outchorus

the spotlight. Armstrong and Bechet, in particular, emerge as forceful opponents, struggling against one another for supremacy. Even in polyphonic ensemble passages they play like star soloists rather than team players bending for the greater good. Despite the damage this does to the unity of the ensemble, these recordings are widely regarded as among the most exciting in the New Orleans style. At the same time, they mark the beginning of a long decline for ensemble-based polyphonic jazz. After 1925, the soloist becomes increasingly preeminent.

Chapter *6* Louis Armstrong

After Louis Armstrong left King Oliver in 1924, his career followed an almost continuous upward path. In the twenties, he progressed from a relatively obscure soloist in Fletcher Henderson's dance band to an acknowledged master of the trumpet and a vocal artist of startling originality. In the process Armstrong helped to transform jazz into a soloist's art, established the rhythmic conventions of swing, and set a standard of virtuosity to which jazz musicians would aspire for years to come.

Armstrong's reputation as a pivotal figure in jazz history rests on a series of critically acclaimed recordings made with his Hot Five and Hot Seven between 1925 and 1928. But he became a hero to the black community for his expanding influence in the entertainment industry in general. Like Bert Williams and Bill Bojangles Robinson before him, Armstrong won larger audiences over time, eventually making a career in film. Some accused him of betraying the jazz tradition of artistry he had helped to found. Yet, to the end of his life, Armstrong remained committed to a crowd-pleasing musical ideal rooted in popular entertainment and comedy, an aesthetic he absorbed as a young man growing up in his hometown of New Orleans.

New Orleans

Louis Armstrong (1901–1971) was raised in the toughest section of New Orleans, in the area known as the **Battlefield** in the middle of black Storyville. His father abandoned the family shortly after Louis's birth, and his mother took work as a domestic and part-time prostitute in order to support the children. Young Louis and his sister scrounged for food in garbage bins, and Louis did odd jobs and sold newspapers. He also formed a children's barbershop quartet that sang and danced in the streets for pennies.

Armstrong's life changed dramatically on New Year's Eve 1912. In an act of celebration, Louis fired a pistol into the air. He was caught by a policeman and sentenced to a reform school called the **Colored Waifs' Home for Boys.** The Waifs' Home subjected Louis to an unaccustomed regimen of discipline in all aspects of life. But the music director of the Home also allowed Louis to play in the marching band, thus launching his musical career. In the band he moved up rapidly, from playing the tambourine to the snare drum to the bugle to the cornet; by the time of his discharge eighteen months later he was student director of the band.

For the next several years Armstrong scrambled to make a living, doing menial labor in the daytime and playing cornet in the honky tonks at night. He took informal music lessons from King Oliver in exchange for running errands. When Oliver went north in 1918 Armstrong replaced him in Kid Ory's Brown-Skinned Babies. The following year he took a job playing in **Fate Marable**'s Orchestra on the Mississippi riverboats, a job he kept for three summers. In 1921 he took pride in joining the Tuxedo Band, the premier brass band in the city. In the riverboat bands and the brass bands Armstrong worked hard to improve his limited ability to read music from a written score.

By this time Armstrong had developed a musical reputation of a peculiar kind. He was getting good jobs, certainly, but he also puzzled listeners. One old-timer recalled, "I didn't never understand Louis Armstrong, because that son-of-a-gun, he ... didn't care what you played. . . . He would play a obbligato all the time; be off [the melody], you understand." What he meant by this remark was that Armstrong spurned the traditional role of the cornet as bearer of the melody in favor of the embellishing role of the clarinet. His interest in clarinet style led him in the 1920s to explore faster, higher, and more complex figures than previous cornetists had done. It represents the first significant example of cross-instrumental influence in jazz.

Louis Armstrong, c. 1927.

Armstrong raised eyebrows for other reasons as well. Edmond Souchon, a local music contractor, said he refused to hire Armstrong for certain events because of his rough and raucous personality. A child raised on the Battlefield and befriended by gamblers, pimps, and prostitutes, lacked the social refinement Souchon was looking for in musicians for a "society" engagement. Indeed, as yet Armstrong had little desire to elevate his status. Baby Dodds recalled that in New Orleans Armstrong adopted the clothing styles of the pimps and gamblers, because "that's what Louis wanted to be in those days."

Chicago

Armstrong's sights rose in 1922 when Oliver invited him to join the Creole Jazz Band in Chicago. His economic status was the first thing to improve. Whereas in New Orleans he had made $1 to $2 per night, in Chicago his weekly salary soared to $52.50—an amount that could double with tips. Armstrong also found himself enjoying an unaccustomed level of prestige. Within Chicago's black community, he later recalled, "A musician . . . in the early twenties [was] treated and respected just like—some kind of a god."

At the Lincoln Gardens Oliver and Armstrong developed a system of harmonized **duet breaks.** A few measures before the break Oliver would cue Armstrong with the melody he was going to use for the break and, thinking fast, Armstrong would prepare a harmony line to accompany him. To visiting musicians, it seemed as though the two cornetists had a telepathic relationship: how did Armstrong know what Oliver was going to play at the break? Boasting at least as much novelty value as Oliver's trick cornet playing, the duet breaks did much to spread Armstrong's name throughout the musical community.

But Armstrong's role in the Creole Jazz Band was somewhat awkward. This became obvious at the band's first recording session in April 1923. In order to record as clearly as possible, the engineers deadened the studio by hanging thick draperies from the ceiling to the floor. As usual when making acoustic records, the engineers placed the musicians at various distances from the horn to get the proper ensemble balance. Armstrong's sound was so powerful, however, that they had to position him some twenty feet behind the rest of the band. It was this incident that caused Oliver's pianist **Lil Hardin** (1898–1971) to look at Armstrong in an admiring new light. In 1924 the two of them got married, and Lil began overhauling Armstrong's rough New Orleans persona and encouraging him to reach high for success. She also played an important role in the Hot Five series, playing piano on the recordings, notating Armstrong's melodies, and even composing some of her own.

New York

In 1924 Armstrong moved to New York to join the orchestra of **Fletcher Henderson,** the most successful black dance band in the country (see Chapter 8). The band performed nightly at the Roseland Ballroom on Broadway, an elegant dance hall catering strictly to white patrons. When Armstrong arrived wearing an old-fashioned box-back coat, long underwear, and policeman's shoes, Henderson's men initially mocked his provincial demeanor. But he soon won their friendship. At one early rehearsal Armstrong roared through a passage marked *pp*—the abbreviation for *pianissimo,* an Italian term meaning "very softly." Henderson stopped the band and asked Armstrong why he had not observed the dynamic marking. "Oh, I thought that meant 'pound plenty,'" he replied, to laughter all around.

The other musicians completely forgot about Armstrong's backward ways when they heard his solos. One of the trumpet players recalled that when Armstrong first soloed with the band at Roseland, people passing on the street outside would stop just to listen to him. Rex Stewart, a young cornetist who would later play with Duke Ellington, became one of many Armstrong idolators: "I tried to walk like him, talk like him, eat like him, sleep like him." After Armstrong's New York debut, Stewart recalled, "box-back coats was the latest style."

While in New York, Armstrong recorded many solos with Henderson's orchestra. He also made dozens of records accompanying blues and vaudeville singers, including Ma Rainey, Alberta Hunter, Sippie Wallace, Clara Smith, Trixie Smith, and, most notably, Bessie Smith. (It was at one of these sessions that he recorded "Cake Walking Babies from Home" with the Red Onion Jazz Babies.) He continued recording with singers throughout the decade, eventually completing more than eighty sides. This heavy involvement demonstrates the important role jazz musicians played in the blues craze during the 1920s.

Rising Star

In late 1925 Armstrong returned to Chicago and found himself a celebrity. Over the next few years he performed as featured soloist in the most exclusive nightclubs on the South Side, including the Dreamland Café, the **Sunset Café,** and the Savoy Ballroom (see Map 3). Joe Glaser, the owner of the Sunset (and Armstrong's future manager), proudly described his club: "Besides the band, we had twelve chorus girls, twelve show girls, and big-name acts. The place sat about six hundred people, and we had a high-class trade . . . the best people. There were lines for every show, and, mind you, we charged admission just to get in." Recognizing the talent he had in Armstrong, Glaser put a sign out front that read (in typically expansive promotional language): "Louis Armstrong, the World's Greatest Trumpet Player."

Each evening, before starting his cabaret sets, Armstrong performed with one of the most "high-class" musical organizations in black Chicago: **Erskine Tate's** "symphony orchestra." Tate's group provided background music for silent movies at the **Vendome Theater,** the leading movie house on the South Side. Armstrong soon became Tate's star performer, appearing as a soloist not only in novelty numbers and hot jazz arrangements, but also in classical transcriptions of Italian operas like Mascagni's *Cavalleria Rusticana* and Puccini's *Madame Butterfly.* Armstrong became so popular that the management asked him to come out of the orchestra pit and perform onstage. He developed two vaudeville-style routines: in one he put on a grass skirt and sang and played the popular song, "Heebie Jeebies"; in the other he donned a frock coat and spectacles and gave down-home country sermons as the "Reverend Satchelmouth." Yet it was his trumpet playing that produced the greatest audience enthusiasm. Trumpeter Adolphus "Doc" Cheatham recalled that when he once substituted for Armstrong at the Vendome the crowd noise was deafening as he stepped into the spotlight. Then when people realized it wasn't Armstrong playing, the screaming went "right down to nothing, and I'm up there playing like a fool."

Many young competitors tried to dethrone Armstrong in cutting contests. The most serious threat came from **Jabbo Smith** (1908–1991), an ingenious and nimble player from Charleston, South Carolina. On one occasion, Rex Stewart recalled, Smith threw down the gauntlet with an inspired performance. Then Armstrong stepped onto the stage, dressed in a white suit. "I've forgotten the tune," Stewart said, "but I'll never forget his first note. He blew a searing, soaring, altissimo, fantastic high note and held it long enough for every one of us musicians to grasp. Benny Carter, who has perfect pitch, said, 'Damn! That's high F!'" Armstrong's stunning command of the upper register allowed him to vanquish virtually all comers in the late twenties. It is no coincidence that during this period he switched permanently from cornet to trumpet; he surely wanted to take advantage of the latter instrument's natural brilliance and finesse in the high range.

The Hot Fives and Hot Sevens

In contrast to the classical music, stage accompaniments, and society jazz Armstrong was performing live, his recordings from the mid-twenties reflected his New Orleans musical roots. On November 12, 1925, Armstrong and four

Louis Armstrong and His Hot Five, c. 1925. *Left to right:* Louis Armstrong, Johnny St. Cyr, Johnny Dodds, Kid Ory, Lil Hardin Armstrong.

friends entered the OKeh studio to make Armstrong's first recordings as a leader. The records were credited to Louis Armstrong and his Hot Five, inaugurating the series of over sixty sides that would become known collectively as the **Hot Fives** and (with the addition of tuba and drums) the **Hot Sevens.** Like Morton's Red Hot Peppers, these were strictly recording bands that played few if any live engagements.

Armstrong's musicians included alumni from both Oliver's and Morton's bands—Johnny Dodds, clarinet; Kid Ory, trombone; Lil Hardin Armstrong, piano; Baby Dodds, drums—together with two newcomers: Johnny St. Cyr, banjo; and Pete Briggs, tuba. With these players Armstrong made several New Orleans–style records that have since become classics: "Muskrat Ramble," "Big Butter and Egg Man," "Potato Head Blues," "Struttin' with Some Barbecue." And yet the style of these performances is a far cry from that of Oliver or Morton. In the first place, Armstrong shifts the traditional New Orleans emphasis from the

LOUIS ARMSTRONG AND HIS HOT SEVEN, *"Potato Head Blues"* (1927)

One of Armstrong's great recordings from the 1920s, "Potato Head Blues" is *not* a blues, strictly speaking. During this period many songwriters put the word "blues" in their titles to capitalize on the blues craze, regardless of its appropriateness from a stylistic point of view. "Potato Head Blues," then, is in ABAC song form and displays few if any bluesy expressive devices. Armstrong made the recording with his Hot Seven, a fact evident in the rhythm section: Baby Dodds's drums defy audibility until the end, but you can hear tuba player Pete Briggs's "oom-pahs" marking the two-beat meter throughout.

"Potato Head Blues" reveals the power, virtuosity, and creativity of Armstrong's playing in the late twenties. By this time he had switched from cornet to trumpet, which allowed him greater brilliance of tone in the upper register. His first solo consists of a straightforward *melodic paraphrase* of the verse, but his second, after Johnny Dodds's clarinet solo, stands as a masterpiece of early recorded jazz. With the band providing *stop-time* accompaniment, Armstrong darts and soars imaginatively through the chord progression, relying on the chords themselves rather than the song's melody for his inspiration. At the beginning of the B-section, he uses *alternate fingering,* a tension-building ploy in which he switches rapidly between two fingerings for the same note. The fingerings produce slightly different shadings of pitch, creating a "mottled" or "shimmering" effect.

The stop-time setting makes it sound as though Armstrong is merely playing a series of breaks, but somehow he manages to connect them all into a larger shape. During the second half of the form (AC), he begins increasing the tension by reaching ever higher into the upper register. The climax comes at the very end, when he swoops up to the trumpet's high D (higher than most trumpet players could play at the time) and vaults back down two octaves with disarming grace and ease. In the outchorus he surges skyward again, dominating the ensemble as if his solo had never ended at all.

ensemble to the soloist. Continuing the individualistic bent so prominent in "Cake Walking Babies from Home," Armstrong solos extensively and utterly dominates the ensembles. His authority stems partly from his supreme virtuosity—which includes clarinet-like figurations and exuberant forays into the upper register—and partly from his dynamic sense of swing, for Armstrong swung harder than anyone of his generation. And it owes much to his golden tone, a richly beguiling sound that is impossible to ignore. Equally important, Armstrong crafted his solo lines into elegantly coherent structures, giving jazz a rhetorical force it had never had before.

For years critics assumed that Armstrong improvised virtually all of his Hot Five solos, but that no longer appears likely. We now know, for instance, that he wrote out his entire solo on "Cornet Chop Suey" (1926) fully two years before recording it. Scholars have compared **alternate takes** (multiple recordings of the same song on the same day or a few days apart) and found that many of Armstrong's solos with Henderson vary little from one take to the next. This indicates, of course, that on *these* recordings, at least, improvisation was minimal; perhaps the same was true of the Hot Fives. On the other hand, many anecdotes

LISTENING CHART 8

Louis Armstrong and His Hot Seven, "Potato Head Blues" (Armstrong)

CD 1 / Tracks 37–39

RECORDED 10 MAY 1927, CHICAGO / OKEH 8503; MX 80855-C (ELECTRIC RECORDING)

Louis Armstrong (trumpet), Johnny Dodds (clarinet), John Thomas (trombone), Lil Hardin Armstrong (piano), Johnny St. Cyr (banjo), Pete Briggs (tuba), Baby Dodds (drums)

Style: New Orleans style			Form: ABAC song form

		1st Chorus	**Polyphonic ensemble**
37	0:00	A (8 bars)	The full band plays together in typical New Orleans polyphonic fashion. Notice, however, how prominent Louis Armstrong's trumpet sounds amid the other horns. In this sense he continues the disintegration of classic New Orleans ensemble style begun with "Cake Walking Babies from Home."
	0:10	B (8)	
	0:21	A (8)	
	0:32	C (6)	
			Trumpet solo: Louis Armstrong
	0:40	Break (2)	Armstrong plays a dynamic break, then proceeds with . . .
		Verse	
	0:43	X (8)	. . . a straightforward paraphrase of the verse melody
	0:54	X' (8)	
		2nd Chorus	**Clarinet solo: Johnny Dodds**
38	1:05	A (8)	Johnny Dodds plays a solo that includes the figurations and *arpeggios* characteristic of New Orleans clarinet style
	1:16	B (6)	
	1:24	Break (2)	On the break he also shows his natural proclivity for the blues, with a sharply "bent" blue note in the middle register
	1:27	A (8)	
	1:38	C (8)	For the first half of the C-section the rhythm section accompanies in stop-time
	1:49	3 bars	**Banjo interlude: Johnny St. Cyr**
			Stop-time trumpet solo: Louis Armstrong
39	1:53	Break (1)	Armstrong begins with a one-measure break . . .

3rd Chorus		
1:54	A (8)	. . . then plays an imaginatively *arpeggiated* solo while the band accompanies with *stop-time* on the downbeat of every other measure
2:05	B (8)	At the beginning of the B-section Armstrong uses *alternate fingering*
2:16	A (8)	Here he begins reaching into the upper register, building toward the climactic high D at the end of the solo
2:27	C (8)	
4th Half-Chorus		**Polyphonic outchorus**
2:37	A (8)	The band plays polyphonically, but Armstrong continues playing in the upper register, dominating the ensemble
	C (8)	

tell of Armstrong's ability to perform lengthy, multichorus solos in a live setting. Such circumstances would almost certainly have involved extensive improvisation. Although many questions remain, it now appears that Armstrong and other jazz musicians of the 1920s favored deliberation over spontaneity in their recorded solos.

In the 1920s, Armstrong's best-known recording was "Heebie Jeebies" (1926), a novelty vocal number that fascinated musicians and laymen alike. "Heebie Jeebies" is significant for Armstrong's **scat singing** in the fourth chorus, the first lengthy recorded example of a vocal style based on improvised melodic lines and nonsense syllables. According to Armstrong himself, he began scatting on "Heebie Jeebies" to save the take when he dropped the lyric sheet in the middle of the recording. Be that as it may, the origins of scat hardly mattered to Armstrong's admiring contemporaries. Musicians recall Armstrong's followers sticking their wet heads out snowy windows in an attempt to catch cold so they could match his guttural vocalizing. The song became so popular that Armstrong, as we have seen, was compelled to perform it onstage at the Vendome as one of his regular featured acts.

Hot Meets Sweet

For his last edition of the Hot Five, assembled in June of 1928, Armstrong dramatically changed the band's personnel. Instead of hiring his old friends from New Orleans he used pianist **Earl Hines** (1903–1983), perhaps the only musician to equal him on the bandstand during this period, and other musicians Armstrong worked with every night at the Sunset and Savoy: Jimmy Strong (clarinet, tenor saxophone), Fred Robinson (trombone), Mancy Carr (banjo), and Zutty Singleton (drums). Apart from Singleton whom Armstrong had known in New Orleans, these were all northern players accustomed to performing a wide

scat singing a vocal style based on improvised melodic lines and nonsense syllables.

LOUIS ARMSTRONG AND HIS HOT FIVE, *"West End Blues"* (1928)

Armstrong's recording of "West End Blues," a composition by King Oliver, powerfully exemplifies the revolutionary character of his music during this period. The influential critic Gunther Schuller asserts that Armstrong's introduction to the piece not only "established the general stylistic direction of jazz for several decades to come" but also "served notice that jazz had the potential capacity to compete with the highest order of previously known musical expression."

More than on any other Hot Five recording, Armstrong dominates the proceedings of "West End Blues." Most strikingly, he begins the recording with an unaccompanied virtuoso solo—called a *cadenza*—that spans more than two octaves and alternates classical *arpeggios* with dancing blues figures, all in an elastic tempo that precludes (or makes irrelevant) any strict tally of measures. Armstrong continues at the forefront during the melody; note his characteristic use of *terminal vibrato* at the end of sustained notes. Then, after a trombone solo he participates (as scat vocalist) in a call-and-response duet with clarinetist Jimmy Strong. Earl Hines plays an exquisite piano solo (see Chapter 9), then Armstrong surges to the fore again—and into the high register—for the outchorus. Armstrong's three powerful entrances stand as structural pillars amid the contributions of his sidemen.

The performance blends New Orleans hot and northern sweet styles. The New Orleans sound can be heard in Armstrong's blues inflections, in the occasional polyphonic interactions among the horns, and, more mystically, in the spirit of King Oliver that seems to permeate the recording. Sweet elements include Armstrong's exceedingly suave singing, Hines's beautifully polished and urbane piano solo, and the generally high gloss of the performance as a whole. Such reductive analysis, however, does not do justice to the powerful emotional impact of this stylistic fusion.

variety of music ranging from light classics to hot jazz. Not surprisingly, their recordings with Armstrong represent a stylistic compromise, wedding hot and sweet idioms in roughly equal proportions. Among these recordings are some of the most acclaimed in the entire Hot Five series, including "Muggles," "Weatherbird" (a brilliant duet with Hines), "Beau Koo Jack," and above all, "West End Blues."

By the late twenties Armstrong had come a long way since Edmond Souchon refused to hire him for society gigs in New Orleans. At a banquet in 1929 a group of white musicians presented him with a watch inscribed, "To Louis Armstrong, World's Greatest Cornetist, from the Musicians of New York." Dave Peyton, the influential music critic for the black newspaper the Chicago *Defender*, began referring to him as "the Great King Menalick" after Menelik II, the late-nineteenth-century Ethiopian emperor who delivered his people from foreign rule. As Peyton's moniker suggests, Armstrong had won over even members of the black elite. By making jazz not only respectable but also praiseworthy, he represented the New Negro with special force. At the same time, thoughtful listeners were beginning to consider Armstrong's innovations not merely as clever vaudeville gimmicks but as the basis for a newly artistic approach to jazz.

LISTENING CHART 9

Louis Armstrong and His Hot Five, "West End Blues" (Oliver)

CD 1 / Tracks 40–44

RECORDED 28 JUNE 1928, CHICAGO / OKEH 8597; MX 400967-B (ELECTRIC RECORDING)

Louis Armstrong (trumpet, voice), Jimmy Strong (clarinet), Fred Robinson (trombone), Earl Hines (piano), Mancy Carr (banjo), Zutty Singleton (drums)

		Style: Modified New Orleans style	Form: 12-bar blues form

Introduction

40	0:00		**Opening trumpet cadenza: Louis Armstrong**

Armstrong plays with a power and facility unknown to this point in jazz recording, soaring into the upper register and alternating classical-sounding *arpeggios* with dancing blues figures

Melody

41	0:15	*1st Chorus* (12)	Armstrong plays the plaintive blues melody as the band accompanies; notice Fred Robinson's lazily swooping trombone lines—a sort of low-temperature tailgate

Trombone solo: Fred Robinson

	0:50	*2nd Chorus* (12)	Fred Robinson plays melancholy trombone solo to accompaniment of Earl Hines's shimmering *tremolos* (rapid oscillations between notes) on the piano and Zutty Singleton's clippety-clop "horse's hooves"

Call-and-response duet

42	1:24	*3rd Chorus* (12)	Jimmy Strong (clarinet) calls and Armstrong responds with exceedingly suave scat vocals

Piano solo: Earl Hines

43	1:59	*4th Chorus* (12)	Earl Hines shows his sophisticated blend of classical filigrees and hard-stomping jazz style, a style known as *Harlem stride* (see Chapter 9)

Outchorus (climax)

44	2:32	*5th Chorus* (8)	Armstrong transforms his lead here into an accompanied solo. He starts by holding a long high note for four measures, then breaks the suspense with falling blues figures which in turn yield to a debonair ascent back into the upper register

Tag

	2:56	6 bars	Earl Hines (piano) plays a delicate classically inspired interlude, after which the band joins together for a final cadence

Contemporary Voices

IRVING KOLODIN

*Describes an Armstrong
Performance at Harlem's
Lafayette Theater—1933*

A blast from the [Chick] Webb outfit, on the stage, and from the wings trots out a little brown man, gleaming like a new pair of shoes, in a tuxedo and a turn down collar, his face slit with a grin, dangling a handkerchief from his left hand, and from his right, a sleek, fabulously glittering trumpet. The applause, of course, is earshattering. . . . This audience knows what's coming. He sidles up to [the] microphone on the stage, and from a cluster of horns overhead, a froggy voice issues. . . . Armstrong fancies himself a vocalist and, leaning over the mike, he intones the first chorus [of "Ain't Misbehavin'"]. The tune eludes him, but what he does with the words and rhythm is audible joy. He surrounds the astonished microphone with his arms, pleading, cajoling, leering at it, pouring out the anthem in a voice that would melt an iceberg . . . when he doesn't like the words, he slides off into a guttural mouthing of syllables that is irresistible. Then he raises the trumpet to his lips and goes to town. . . . A tone of burnished brilliance, a rhythmic sense infinitely insinuating, descending and ascending *portamenti* that are absolutely a unique talent, high-flung Ds, Es, and a final preposterous F that is simply not [on] the instrument. . . .

He announces "When You're Smiling" and this time he has a new act. He backs off, downstage left, leans halfway over like a quarter-miler, begins to count, (swaying as he does) "one, two, three". . . he has already started racing toward the rear where the orchestra is ranged, and as he hits four, executes a slide and a pirouette; winds up facing his audience and blowing the first note as the orchestra swings into the tune. It's mad, it's meaningless, it's hokum of the first order, but the effect is electrifying. No shabby pretenses about this boy! He knows what his audience will take to their hearts, and how he gives it to them. His trumpeting virtuosity is endless . . . triplets, chromatic, accented, eerie counterpoints that turn the tune inside out, wild sorties into the giddy stratosphere where his tone sounds like a dozen flutes in unison, all executed with impeccable style and finish, exploits that make his contemporaries sound like so many Salvation Army cornetists. Alternately singing choruses and daubing with the handkerchief at throat, face, forehead (he perspires like a dying gladiator) the while a diamond bracelet twinkles from his wrist, he finally gets off the stage to rest.

Irving Kolodin, "All God's Chillun Got Fun," *Americana* (February 1933): 4.

White Jazz

Chapter 7

If you were to step into a time machine, go back to the 1920s, and ask a random person on the street—a white person—about jazz, what do you think you would hear? First of all, you probably wouldn't hear about any of the musicians we've been discussing thus far, except perhaps the ODJB. In *So This Is Jazz,* an introduction to the subject for general readers from 1926, Henry Osgood covers the music of Paul Whiteman, Vincent Lopez, Art Hickman, George Gershwin, Zez Confrey, and Ted Lewis. But no black soloists—including Oliver, Morton, Bechet, and Armstrong—appear in the book. They are simply not part of the world of jazz understood by Osgood and his readers—the likely cohort you would encounter on the street.

Nevertheless, if you persisted in your queries long enough you might eventually run across an Eddie Condon or a Jimmy McPartland, a Mezz Mezzrow or a Bix Beiderbecke—white musicians who knew the black New Orleanians just mentioned, and knew them well. In fact, if you took your sample from a pool of professional dance band musicians, your odds of hearing about Armstrong might have been rather good. For while the average white citizen knew virtually nothing about music in the South Side or Harlem, a select number of white pleasure-seekers and popular musicians were transfixed by that music. Their fascination led to the development of white jazz styles that proved historically significant in their own right.

Paul Whiteman

In the 1920s the nationally recognized "King of Jazz" was not King Oliver or Louis Armstrong, but a balding, portly white musician named **Paul Whiteman** (1890–1967). Whiteman was born and raised in a musical household in Denver, Colorado, the son of the music director for the city's public schools. Although he resisted his father's musical instruction (he tells of once smashing his violin against a sewing machine), Whiteman eventually became a proficient classical violist. In 1914 he moved to San Francisco and the following year got a job playing viola in the San Francisco Symphony. One evening on the town, Whiteman went to a cabaret with a friend and heard "jazz" for the first time. He later recalled it as a transforming experience: "My whole body began to sit up and take notice. It was like coming out of blackness into bright light. . . . My head was

Paul Whiteman and His Orchestra, 1929.

dizzy, but my feet seemed to understand that tune. They began to pat wildly. I wanted to whoop. I wanted to dance. I wanted to sing. I did them all. Raucous? Yes. Crude—undoubtedly. Unmusical—sure as you live. But rhythmic, catching as the small-pox and spirit-lifting."

In 1918, bored with classical music, Whiteman quit the symphony and took a job with a jazz band at Tait's restaurant. After only two days, though, the director fired him, explaining somewhat apologetically: "You can't jazz, that's all." Initially discouraged, he shortly determined to "learn to jazz," come what may. Whiteman began frequenting all the restaurants and saloons on the Barbary Coast, listening to as much jazz as he could. But, back at his apartment, he did not practice improvising on his viola; instead, he tried to "orchestrate"—that is, to notate in precise rhythms and tone colors for a large ensemble—the sounds he heard in the San Francisco night spots. In truth, the arrangements he developed represented greatly subdued versions of what was probably a rambunctious style of jazz based on New Orleans polyphonic models. His pieces generally favored sedate rhythms, graceful melodies, and homophonic textures, with a jazz spirit suggested by a bouncy beat and occasional brief passages of syncopated polyphony. Such jazzy notated dance music came to be known as "sweet music" among musicians and in the trade press. Although Whiteman was not the first to orchestrate jazz, as he claimed, he played a leading role in the rise of sweet music.

During the next couple of years Whiteman led several dance bands that performed in ballrooms from Hollywood to Atlantic City. Then in 1920 executives at the Victor Phonograph Company offered him a recording contract. "Whispering," one of the first records released, offers a good example of Whiteman's music at this time. The piece opens with the first verse and chorus stated homophonically by the ensemble, then continues with a solo chorus for musical saw followed by a reorchestrated ensemble version of the verse and chorus. The recording closes with a "sweet" answer to the New Orleans outchorus—a jazzed-up statement of the melody in a stiff, pseudo–New Orleans polyphonic style. "Whispering" eventually sold more than two million copies and Whiteman became a star.

Symphonic Jazz

After his first experiments with jazz, Whiteman faced criticism from old friends who lamented his defection from "real music" to pursue a bastard idiom. He wanted to prove that jazz could be presented in what he and others might view as musically respectable terms. With his strong background in classical symphonic music, Whiteman felt compelled to elevate jazz by fusing it with classical music, or—alternately—enliven the classics by jazzing them up. He hoped in the process to create a new genre, which he called **symphonic jazz.**

In the ideal, symphonic jazz would differ from sweet music in that it would be performed, not for dancing, but for respectful and attentive listening in a concert hall. In the early twenties Whiteman began assuming the role of impresario, commissioning talented and like-minded composers to produce the kind of lofty jazz-influenced music he envisioned in a concert setting. Whiteman officially introduced symphonic jazz to the world in a 1924 concert at New York's Aeolian Hall entitled, "An Experiment in Modern Music." The climax of the evening was the next to last selection, *Rhapsody in Blue,* composed by **George Gershwin** (1898–1937) and scored for orchestra by Ferde Grofé. Blending jazz expressive devices such as glissandos and blue notes with classical structural principles like thematic exposition and development, Gershwin showed the world what a true marriage of jazz and classical traditions might look like. Financially, the concert was a failure (Whiteman claimed to have lost $7,000), but critically and symbolically it was an overwhelming success.

After the Aeolian Hall concert Whiteman was credited with having "made a lady out of jazz." But he himself suffered no delusions about the music's authentic spirit or who produced it originally. In 1926 he suggested that "the chief contribution of the white American to jazz so far has been his recognition of it as legitimate music." Some listeners, it must be acknowledged, recognized its legitimacy even more fully than Whiteman did.

The Chicagoans

From the perspective of many liberal writers and social critics, the 1920s was a time of spectacular hypocrisy. Moralists decried drinking and other nocturnal vices; and yet Prohibition seemed a sham, encouraging rather than deterring criminal activity. The worst side of religious fundamentalism had to account for the revitalized Ku Klux Klan and other forms of racism. And polite society was becoming increasingly intoxicated with money and ephemeral social trends.

symphonic jazz in the 1920s a fusion of jazz and classical music intended, not for dancing, but for respectful listening in the concert hall.

Laissez-faire business policies seemingly gave government sponsorship to a lifestyle based on greed. To some observers, the unsavory alliance of religion, racism, politics, and money seemed far more sinful than bathtub gin.

For a group of young white musicians in Chicago later known as **the Chicagoans,** black jazz represented a rebuke of such middle-class hypocrisy. In their view, jazz was not only not sinful—it was sacred. Its expressive purity and honesty exposed the fraudulent morality of society. Clarinetist Mezz Mezzrow, a particularly devout jazz adherent, considered New Orleans music to be his own personal "millennium," something he had waited for all his life. Mezzrow's profound commitment to jazz included adopting the clothing styles, slang, leisure habits, and home neighborhood of South Side blacks—and if he could have dyed his skin he probably would have done so. Not all of Mezzrow's colleagues shared his all-encompassing intensity of feeling. But for most of them, to one degree or another, jazz was both a source of quasi-religious ecstasy and a means of rebelling against the complacent and corrupt values of the American establishment.

Far from being a coherent group, the Chicagoans were a loose, shifting network of friends and acquaintances of various ages and social backgrounds. Including, besides Mezzrow, Eddie Condon, Muggsy Spanier, Art Hodes, and numerous others, these musicians made nightly pilgrimages to the cabarets, especially the Lincoln Gardens. The doorman there would tease the young, self-conscious white boys about coming all the way down to the South Side to get their "music lessons." Once inside, the Chicagoans listened open-mouthed. On Eddie Condon's first visit, he recalled, "It was hypnosis at first hearing. Everyone [in the Creole Jazz Band] was playing what he wanted to play and it was all mixed together as if someone had planned it with a set of micrometer calipers. . . . [Bud] Freeman, [Jimmy] McPartland and I were immobilized; the music poured into us like daylight running down a dark hole."

The Austin High School Gang

One important subgroup of the Chicagoans was a handful of teenagers who later came to be known as the **Austin High School Gang.** Born and raised in the suburbs on the West Side, this group included Jimmy McPartland, his brother Richard, Frank Teschemacher, Bud Freeman, Jim Lannigan, and Dave North (only some of them actual students at Austin High). In the fall of 1922, every day after school this group of friends would congregate at a local ice cream parlor and listen to records on the phonograph provided there for customer entertainment. Initially the records were by Paul Whiteman, Art Hickman, and other sweet bandleaders. Then one day some new records appeared on the table by the **New Orleans Rhythm Kings.** This band was a group of white musicians from New Orleans who had learned to swing much harder than their famous predecessors, the ODJB. The Austin High kids put on the band's recently released "Farewell Blues" and listened spellbound. They played the new records over and over until the place closed at 8:00 P.M.; before leaving they had made up their minds to organize a band and learn to play like the New Orleans Rhythm Kings.

But first they had to buy instruments. Jimmy McPartland chose the cornet, Richard the guitar, Teschemacher the clarinet, Freeman the saxophone, Lannigan the tuba, and North the piano. They learned to play their instruments as they struggled to figure out jazz itself. Jimmy McPartland explained: "What we

Mezz Mezzrow

on the Austin High School Gang

There was a revolution simmering in Chicago, led by a gang of pink-cheeked high-school kids. These rebels in plus-fours, huddled on a bandstand instead of a soap-box, passed out riffs instead of handbills, but the effect was the same. Their jazz was only a musical version of the hard-cutting broadsides that . . . Mencken and Nathan were beginning to shoot at Joe Public in the pages of *The American Mercury*—a collectively improvised nose-thumbing at all pillars of all communities, one big syncopated Bronx cheer for the righteous squares everywhere. Jazz was the only language they could find to preach their fire-eating message.

These upstart small-fries were known as the Austin High Gang, and gumption was their middle name. It was on Chicago's West Side that they started hatching their plots, way out in Austin, a well-to-do suburb where all the days were Sabbaths, a sleepy-time neighborhood big as a yawn and just about as lively, loaded with shade-trees and clipped lawns and a groggy-eyed population that never came out of its coma except to turn over. In all their scheming these kids aimed to run out of town the sloppy, insipid, yes-we-have-no-bananas music of the day, which seemed to echo the knocked-out spirit of their sleepwalking neighbors. They wanted to blast every highminded citizen clear out of his easy chair with their yarddog growls and gully-low howls. . . . At night, instead of hugging the fireside and boning up on alge-bra and Louie the Fourteenth, they snuck out and beat it into town to tour the South Side, studying its flicker and frolic. There they got a liberal education that lowrated all the book-learning and Sunday-school sermons they had thrown at them out where the pretty lawns got a weekly finger-wave.

Mezz Mezzrow and Bernard Wolfe, *Really the Blues* (New York: Random House, 1946; reprint, Citadel Press, 1990), 103–04.

Contemporary Voices

used to do was put the record on . . . play a few bars, and then all get our notes. We'd have to tune our instruments up to the record machine, to the pitch, and go ahead with a few notes. Then stop! A few more bars of the record, each guy would pick out his notes and boom! we would go on and play it. Two bars, or four bars, or eight—we would get in on each phrase and then all play it. But you can imagine it was hard at first. Just starting, as most of us were, we'd make so many mistakes that it was horrible on people's ears. So . . . we had to move around [from house to house] because the neighbors couldn't stand it too long. It was a funny way to learn, but in three or four weeks we could finally play one tune all the way through—*Farewell Blues*. Boy, that was our tune."

Still in short pants, the Austin High School Gang began attending Friar's Inn, a downtown club where the New Orleans Rhythm Kings played (see Map 3). Then a college student offered to take them to the South Side to hear Oliver's band. Thus immersed in the Chicago jazz scene, the young musicians—and other Chicagoans—began building a jazz style based on the New Orleans idiom they loved. Both critics and the Chicagoans themselves have referred to their music variously as the **Chicago style,** the Chicago school, or Chicago jazz. Critics have never reached a consensus on the defining features of this music, and some have even rejected the idea of a distinct Chicago style. And yet it is hard to escape feeling that the music of the Chicagoans differs in some fundamental way from that of the black New Orleanians. The white players, for example, don't swing as hard in solo statements and generally adopt a more subdued ethos. Yet, in ensemble passages, they paradoxically generate a more intense physicality, an adamant, hellbent forward drive that contrasts with the more relaxed swing of Oliver and Armstrong. The music sounds "hot" and "cool" at the same time.

Bix Beiderbecke

The most illustrious musician to be associated with the Chicagoans (although he came from Iowa and spent much of his career in New York) was the influential cornetist, **Bix Beiderbecke** (1903–1931). Beiderbecke occupies a hallowed place in jazz mythology for his enigmatically beautiful solos, his tormented life, and his tragic early death from alcoholism. Two years younger than Louis Armstrong, Beiderbecke is often viewed as the great trumpet player's white counterpart. Together with Frankie Trumbauer, Jack Teagarden, and a few others, Beiderbecke offered convincing evidence that white musicians could make a real contribution to the unfolding language of jazz.

Bix Beiderbecke was born into a musical family in Davenport, Iowa, the son of a well-to-do businessman. In 1919 his older brother returned home from the military, bringing a Victrola and recordings of the Original Dixieland Jazz Band. Entranced with the music, fifteen-year-old Bix borrowed a cornet and spent hours painstakingly learning the parts on the recordings by ear. Though lovers of classical music, Beiderbecke's parents abhorred jazz and worried about its effect on his life. In 1921 they enrolled him at Lake Forest Academy, a prep school outside Chicago. In doing so, however, they unwittingly hastened his immersion in the world of jazz. At night Beiderbecke would sneak out of his dormitory and head into the city, where he heard Oliver's Creole Jazz Band at the Lincoln Gardens and the New Orleans Rhythm Kings at Friar's Inn.

In 1924, Beiderbecke joined a group inspired by the New Orleans Rhythm Kings called **the Wolverines,** with whom he made his first recordings. Widely popular in the Midwest, the Wolverines landed a job in the fall of that year at New York's Cinderella Ballroom. The publicity associated with this job brought Beiderbecke to the attention of **Jean Goldkette,** a sweet bandleader and the chief rival of Paul Whiteman. Goldkette impulsively hired Beiderbecke but then fired him when he discovered Beiderbecke could not read music well enough to handle Goldkette's elaborate arrangements. In 1925, hoping to remedy his musical deficiencies, Beiderbecke enrolled at the University of Iowa. Eighteen days later he was expelled for his participation in a drunken melee. As this incident suggests, drinking had by this time become a serious problem.

Frankie Trumbauer

Chicago style a term sometimes used to describe the New Orleans–inspired music of white jazz players of the 1920s.

In the summer of 1925 Beiderbecke joined the band of **Frankie Trumbauer** (1901–1956), under whose salutary influence he temporarily repaired his life. Beiderbecke and Trumbauer made records under the latter's name that have

The Wolverines in the Gennett recording studio in Richmond, Indiana, 1924. (Bix Beiderbecke sits second from the right.)

become landmark documents in the rise of white jazz: "I'm Coming, Virginia," "Clarinet Marmalade," "Singin' the Blues," "Riverboat Shuffle," among others. In these recordings one can hear elements of the newly emerging Chicago style. The music has a restraint, a transparency, and a sense of deliberation that one does not normally associate with black jazz of the period. Like other Chicagoans, Beiderbecke and Trumbauer follow Armstrong's example in emphasizing solos rather than ensembles.

The instrumental sounds of Beiderbecke and Trumbauer strongly influenced the "cool" affect of their music. Unlike many cornetists of his day, Beiderbecke refused to switch to the trumpet, insisting that it had "a 'pee-wee' tone" (an apparent reference to the more focused timbre of that instrument). Beiderbecke's desire to protect his sound is understandable; the pure tone of his cornet is often compared with a bell or a chime. Trumbauer, who played **C-melody saxophone** (a now defunct instrument pitched midway between an alto and a tenor saxophone), also had a distinctive tone. Whereas previous saxophonists sounded "like a buzz saw going through a pine knot," as one musician memorably put it, Trumbauer played with light, silky elegance. In addition to their shimmering tones, Beiderbecke and Trumbauer brought a pronounced lyricism to their solos; such elements created a "prettiness" of style new to hot jazz in the late twenties.

Both Beiderbecke and Trumbauer structured their solos carefully, a tendency that Beiderbecke evidently learned from Armstrong. In Armstrong's solos, Beiderbecke heard what he called "correlated choruses," solo choruses in which one phrase would echo a preceding phrase through melodic and rhythmic similarities. To achieve this level of organization, Beiderbecke would refine a solo over many performances. Paul Whiteman recalled that Beiderbecke "would never play a chorus the same way *until* he got just what he wanted. Then he'd stick to that chorus and play it that same way over and over again. Once in a while he'd try to improve on his finished product, but most of the time he didn't distort his new composition."

When Goldkette's band dispersed in late 1927, Beiderbecke and Trumbauer joined Paul Whiteman's orchestra, the best-paying and most prestigious organization in the country. The pressure of performing with Whiteman seems to have been too much for Beiderbecke. He became depressed, began drinking again, and his health declined rapidly. In 1928 he spent time in the Rivercrest Sanitarium on Long Island, then returned home to Davenport. In March 1929, he was back with Whiteman, but over the summer he started drinking again and by the fall was so ill he could not play. In October he checked himself into an alcoholism treatment center, just a few days before the stock market crash. But by this time intervention was futile. Within two years he died at age twenty-eight, a compelling human symbol of the Jazz Age and its deleterious aftermath.

FRANKIE TRUMBAUER AND HIS ORCHESTRA, *"Singin' the Blues"* (1927)

"Singin' the Blues" is one of those recordings—like "Dippermouth Blues" and "West End Blues"—that became an inspirational touchstone for other musicians. Trumbauer's solo demonstrated the solo possibilities of the saxophone, a relatively new instrument to jazz. African American tenor saxophonist Budd Johnson later remarked that "everyone memorized that solo. . . . At that time, Frankie Trumbauer was the baddest cat around." The solo was especially significant from a historical point of view for the influence it had on Lester Young, a dominant figure of the Swing Era. Beiderbecke's solo represents the cornetist's playing at its best and was also widely admired.

After a brief introduction, the recording shows its debt to Louis Armstrong by starting with solo statements rather than an ensemble exposition of the melody. Both solos manifest a strongly coherent structure. In the first A of Trumbauer's solo, for example, his closing four-bar phrase (x') resembles his first four-bar phrase (x) in melodic contour and binary subdivision. In a sense, the second phrase "rhymes" with the first one. Beiderbecke creates a similar relationship between y and y' in his opening A-section, but divides each phrase into three parts instead of two.

The final ensemble chorus lacks the pounding intensity of some of the group's other outchoruses, such as the one on "Riverboat Shuffle." After Beiderbecke's solo the ensemble enters sluggishly, as if struggling to rouse itself from sleep. This is not a criticism, but a neutral observation meant to highlight the "cool" approach here, which has a certain charm of its own. After Jimmy Dorsey's clarinet solo, however, the ensemble gathers itself somewhat for a more vigorous conclusion.

LISTENING CHART 10

Frankie Trumbauer and His Orchestra, "Singin' the Blues" (McHugh-Fields)

CD 1 / Tracks 45–47

RECORDED 4 FEBRUARY 1927 / OKEH 40772; MX 80393-B (ELECTRIC RECORDING)

Bix Beiderbecke (cornet), Frankie Trumbauer (C-melody saxophone), Bill Rank (trombone), Jimmy Dorsey (clarinet, alto saxophone), Paul Mertz (piano), Eddie Lang (guitar), Chauncey Morehouse (drums)

Style: Chicago style   **Form: ABA'C song form**

				Introduction
45	0:00			Ensemble: chordal homophony
		1st Chorus		**C-melody saxophone solo: Frankie Trumbauer**
	0:07	A (8)	x (4)	Phrase 1 (subdivided into two parts)
	0:13		x'(4)	Phrase 2 (subdivided into two parts)
	0:20	B (8)		Trumbauer continues his solo with remarkable lyricism and melodic sensitivity
	0:31		Break	
	0:34	A'(8)		
	0:48	C (8)		
	0:59		Break	
		2nd Chorus		**Cornet solo: Bix Beiderbecke**
46	1:03	A (8)	y (4)	Phrase 1 (subdivided into three parts)
	1:09		y'(4)	Phrase 2 (subdivided into three parts)
	1:17	B (8)		
	1:27		Break	Dramatic break divides between hectic opening and lackadaisical three-note close: daht, daht, dah.
	1:31	A'(8)		Beiderbecke "rips" with surprising force into the upper register to begin this section, then recedes back into his customary "cool" manner
	1:45	C(8)		
		3rd Chorus		**Outchorus**
47	2:00	A(8)		Modified New Orleans–style polyphony: much more subdued than comparable sections by King Oliver or Jelly Roll Morton
	2:14	B (8)		**Clarinet solo: Jimmy Dorsey**
	2:25		Break	
	2:29	A'(8)		Ensemble reenters polyphonically . . .
	2:43	C (8)		. . . and musters a more vigorous final statement

Chapter *8* New York Bands

T he most significant developments of early jazz took place in Chicago, primarily because New Orleans migrants tended to settle there. But New York musicians made important contributions to the music as well. The Harlem Renaissance provided a lively setting for cultural developments of all kinds, while Harlem itself boasted the largest and most vibrant black community in the country. It was here that pianists cultivated new keyboard styles and bandleaders coordinated large ensembles prefiguring the big bands of the 1930s.

Two Harlem bandleaders who would have a lasting impact on jazz were Fletcher Henderson and Duke Ellington. Henderson, known in the twenties as "The Colored King of Jazz," indeed tried to match Paul Whiteman in the "sweetness" of his music—at least at first. After Louis Armstrong's year with his band in 1924, Henderson retained the New Orleans–style swing Armstrong had brought to the band's repertory. Ellington fused hot and sweet styles even more compellingly. By the end of the decade he had created a jazz compound that could stand alongside Armstrong's own hybrid in musical originality, integrity, and force.

New York

Jazz in New York in the early 1920s had several manifestations. The earliest was initiated by the Original Dixieland Jazz Band, which won fame performing at Reisenweber's Restaurant in 1917 (see Map 4). Copycat white bands immediately sprouted up in the city, all bent on captivating their audiences with musical hilarity. Employing mostly slapstick effects, their music has sometimes been called **nut jazz.** Leading purveyors included the Frisco Jass Band, featuring xylophones for their novelty value, and Earl Fuller's Orchestra, a band dependent on physical humor and the leader's "sixty-four square feet of drums." The comedian Jimmy Durante got his start in show business playing piano for a nut jazz outfit; he used to stand while playing and shout comic insults at the drummer.

Another face of jazz was the sweet dance music pioneered by Paul Whiteman. On October 1, 1920, Whiteman's orchestra opened at the Palais Royal on Broadway. The following year he performed at the Palace Theater in Times Square, where his group made a "sensational hit," in the words of one reviewer. Whiteman soon opened a national booking agency. By 1922 he was rehearsing and sending

nut jazz in the late 1910s and early 1920s, a style of white jazz dependent on slapstick, novelty, and visual gags.

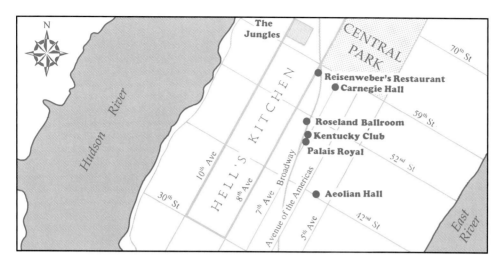

Map 4. Midtown Manhattan, c. 1910s–1920s.

out nineteen different orchestras to play dance pieces by Ferde Grofé and a staff of arrangers. When Whiteman returned from a trip to Europe in 1923, the music-publishing industry raised $7,000 for a homecoming reception in his honor. *Variety* explained that the munificence was "rightfully due a man [who has] done more for American jazz and dance music than any other individual."

In the New York black community jazz was represented by two main groups: bands that accompanied blues singers and large orchestras or military bands. In November 1920, as we have seen, **Mamie Smith's Jazz Hounds** launched the blues mania with "Crazy Blues." Smith's principal accompanist was a trumpet player named **Johnny Dunn** (1897–1937). Born and raised in Memphis, Tennessee, Dunn played with various novelty mutes, somewhat after the manner of King Oliver. One New York musician remembered that Dunn used to arrive at engagements with a valet, who brought "all sorts of trunks, and I used to wonder if they were all for one man. The valet would set them up against the wall, and in them would be all kinds of pots and pans, flowerpots, cans, anything to get a different sound out of his horn." Before Louis Armstrong arrived in 1924, Dunn was the single most important jazz soloist in New York.

Harlem promoters often used the word "jazz" to advertise musical extravaganzas by black performers. Because many people viewed "jazz" as a synonym for just about any kind of black popular music, we should not be surprised that James Reese Europe promoted his sixty-piece brass band as a "jazz outfit," or that the high-toned Clef Club Orchestra was billed on one occasion as "50 Joy Whooping Sultans of High-Speed Syncopation." Whatever their bonafide jazz content, these large black ensembles laid the foundation for future developments. Indeed, if he had not been fatally stabbed by a deranged drummer in 1919, Europe himself might have been the first to incorporate New Orleans hot style into arrangements for large dance band. In his absence, that task fell instead to a talented young pianist from Cuthbert, Georgia.

Fletcher Henderson

In the summer of 1920, **Fletcher Henderson** (1897–1952) arrived in New York with the intention of entering the graduate program in chemistry at Columbia

Fletcher Henderson and His Orchestra, c. 1924. *Second from left,* Coleman Hawkins; *third from left,* Louis Armstrong; *fifth from left,* Fletcher Henderson; *far right,* Don Redman.

University. While he ultimately chose to pursue a career in popular music instead of science, Henderson became a powerful example of what it meant to be a New Negro in the music industry. Surrounding himself with musicians of similar credentials, he played "high-class" music in "high-class" venues, for white audiences in the center of town.

A talented natural musician with perfect pitch, Henderson began his musical career in New York working as a song-plugger for the Pace and Handy Music Company, the first black-owned music publishing firm. As his industry contacts increased, Henderson gradually assembled a dance orchestra for recording only. From spring 1923 to late 1924 he and his band made over one hundred records. But unlike his blues recordings, these were not marketed as "race records"; they were sold as "general" records to white consumers. Henderson's orchestra played mostly sweet music, a repertory for which black journalists proudly awarded him the sobriquet, "the Paul Whiteman of the Race." Like Whiteman, Henderson had removed the negative stigma from jazz; even more important, he had exonerated black jazz musicians from charges of incompetence and poor taste. According to the Chicago *Defender,* Henderson's music was "soft, sweet, and perfect in dance rhythm."

The Roseland Ballroom

In the summer of 1924, Henderson and his orchestra took a steady job performing at the **Roseland Ballroom** (see Map 4), an elegant all-white dance hall known as "the 'class' dance place on Broadway." Roseland contracted at least two bands at any given time so that one could play for the dancers while the other rested. During Henderson's tenure at Roseland, which lasted until 1934, he shared the floor with the sweet bands of white musicians Jean Goldkette and Sam Lanin. Despite the difference of race, the musicians admired one another, and the bands often faced off in good-natured competition.

The Roseland promoted itself as "The Home of Refined Dancing." This meant that Henderson performed mostly fox trots and waltzes, not the music of rambunctious jazz dances like the Charleston, the shimmy, or the toddle. Henderson and **Don Redman** (1900–1964), his principal arranger, wrote dance arrangements of popular songs from Broadway and Tin Pan Alley. At the Roseland male patrons paid a cover charge, which entitled them to a given number of dances with a "hostess," or dance partner, provided by the establishment; extra dances could be bought for a nickel. The homebound participated vicariously by tuning in to radio station WHN, which regularly broadcast Henderson's music on location. After hearing one of these broadcasts, one writer declared in July 1924 that Henderson's band "is one of the best in the field, colored or white, and dishes up a corking brand of dance music."

The Armstrong Influence

When Louis Armstrong arrived that fall, his powerful example "changed our whole idea about the band musically," Redman recalled. Armstrong's solos brought a new excitement to the band and even to the dancers. One night at Roseland, "Fletcher Henderson's band was playing and there were thousands of dancers, all yelling and clapping. . . . The high spot came when Louis Armstrong began 'Shanghai Shuffle.' I think they made him play ten choruses. After that piece a dancer lifted Armstrong up onto his shoulders. . . . I stood silent, . . . asking myself if I would ever be able to attain a small part of Louis Armstrong's greatness." The abashed speaker here was a tenor saxophonist named **Coleman Hawkins** (1904–1969). Armstrong's style in 1924–1925 had a profound influence on Hawkins, who, as we shall see in Chapter 14, later went on to become a major figure in his own right.

By the time Armstrong left the band in late 1925, Henderson and Redman had begun to incorporate his stylistic ideals into the band's arrangements, and the players had begun to execute their phrases in a swinging manner resembling Armstrong's. Recordings from 1926 reveal the change in Henderson's approach. On pieces like "Stampede," the band demonstrates not only a new awareness of swing rhythm but also basic features of what would later be known as **big band jazz.** With as many as eleven musicians in the band by this time, it was not practical to adopt the free-wheeling polyphonic texture of the New Orleanians. Retaining instead the homophonic texture of sweet music, Henderson and Redman created interest by dividing the band into separate choirs of brass and reeds and pitting them against one another at close intervals.

Duke Ellington

A few weeks before Henderson made his first dance band recordings in 1923, a young pianist named **Edward Kennedy "Duke" Ellington** (1899–1974) arrived in New York. Raised in a middle-class family in Washington, DC, Ellington earned the nickname "Duke" for his stylish dress and natural aristocratic bearing. Even more than Armstrong and Henderson, perhaps, Ellington would attain a balance of sophistication and professional achievement that fulfilled the highest ideals of the Harlem Renaissance. More important for the history of jazz, he became known as the greatest composer that the music had produced—a view that prevails to this day.

big band jazz a style born during the 1920s and 1930s that emphasizes the power of large ensembles and their interaction with virtuoso soloists.

After a brief stint in New York vaudeville, Ellington joined a quartet of musicians he had known in Washington. At their first job in Harlem, the band played sweet and soft "under-conversation music." A few months later they got an unusual break when the offer came to serve as house band at the Hollywood Club—later named the **Kentucky Club** (a cabaret name with "southern" connotations)—in the middle of the white entertainment district in Times Square (see Map 4). At the Kentucky Club Ellington became the official leader, the group expanded to seven players, and the band acquired a new name: **the Washingtonians.** The musicians made radio broadcasts every Wednesday afternoon on WHN. At 9:00 P.M., they played for dancing. They also accompanied singers, dancers, and chorus girls in revues starting at midnight and 2:00 A.M. Sometime near dawn Ellington would send the band home and work the tables himself, coasting around with a little piano on wheels while drummer Sonny Greer sang requests. "Sometimes," Ellington recalled, "the customer would respond by throwing twenty-dollar bills away from him as though they were on fire."

Bubber Miley

At the Kentucky Club the Washingtonians changed their playing style from mostly sweet to mostly hot. As was the case with Henderson, this transformation took place through the catalyst of New Orleans style. In 1924 or 1925 Ellington briefly hired Sidney Bechet (see Chapter 5) to help with New Orleans pieces like "High Society." A stronger and more enduring influence was trumpeter **James "Bubber" Miley** (1903–1932). Miley was from South Carolina, not New Orleans, and he grew up in New York City. But he brought a New Orleans sensibility to the Washingtonians through his own deep absorption of King Oliver's music. Miley began his career imitating the wah-wah effects of local trumpet hero, Johnny Dunn. He also adopted a makeshift mute introduced by Dunn: the *plunger mute,* consisting of the rubber part of a household sink plunger. Within a few years the plunger mute became standard equipment among trumpet and trombone players specializing in wah-wah effects, which formed part of a more generalized **plunger style.**

In 1921 Miley substituted for Dunn on a midwestern tour with Mamie Smith's Jazz Hounds. During a stopover in Chicago Miley and clarinetist Garvin Bushell went every night to hear King Oliver, who at that time was playing at the Dreamland Café. Like many of Chicago's white musicians, Miley and Bushell were overwhelmed by Oliver's soulful, bluesy expressiveness. "Bubber and I sat there with our mouths open," Bushell recalled. After hearing Oliver, Miley enriched his own plunger style with similar bluesy inflections, including *growls* (raspy, guttural sounds produced in the throat), smears, and other plangent sounds. When he joined Ellington in late 1923 his effect on the band was akin to that of Armstrong on the Henderson orchestra. As Ellington explained, "Our band changed its character when Bubber came in. He used to growl all night long, playing gutbucket on his horn. That was when we decided to forget all about the sweet music."

As a slang word applied to jazz, **gutbucket** referred to a subcategory of hot style, one that emphasized poignant, expressive, earthy solo statements in a blues context. (Terms having a similar meaning included "lowdown," "barrelhouse," and "dirty.") According to jazz legend, Miley's gutbucket approach dispatched Johnny Dunn during a cutting contest from around 1924.

plunger style a brass solo style employing plunger mute, wah-wah effects, and growls.

gutbucket a subcategory of hot jazz emphasizing expressive, earthy solo statements in a blues context.

A *BILLBOARD* WRITER

Reports His Visit to the Kentucky Club—1925

I f you must stay up until sunrise, we can't think, offhand, of a better place to while away the small hours than at the Club Kentucky. Here no one wears a high hat— there is no bid for pretentiousness. Bert Lewis, master of "carah-moanies," would probably tell you that "this ain't the place for puttin' on the dawg—we leave that to Park avenoo." The place, appropriately, is in a cellar, with the music and show correspondingly low down. Lewis is an adept clown, politely offensive at times, and yet the kind one finds easy to forgive. His songs are strictly of the sawdust variety, with gestures equally "blue," but it is this very hotsy-totsiness of material that sells the pudgy little fat man. Peggy English warbles rag songs like few can. . . . Bernice Petkere, too, carols deliciously, while Jane Laurence, a hefty prima donna, is a good vocalist and an efficient check builder. Gypsy Byrne and Margaret Edwards are a pair of capable hoofers. . . .

And now for the band! If anybody can tell us where a hotter aggregation than Duke Ellington and His Club Kentucky Serenaders can be found we'll buy for the mob. Possessing a sense of rhythm that is almost uncanny, the boys in this dusky organization dispense a type of melody that stamps the outfit as the most torrid in town. Duke Ellington, director, pounds the baby grand, and while he chow-meins in an adjacent eatery Thomas "Fats" Waller understudies. Both lads are deserving of all the available superlatives in the English language, while it is necessary to borrow a few from the Latin to adequately extol the performance of the latter. Sunny [*sic*] Greer is the third best drum showman in the country. . . . Henry [Bass] Edwards' tuba is all bent from the heat its owner gives it and "Bub" Miley "kills" 'em with his trumpet. Fred Guy plays banjo, Charley Irvis trombones, and Otto Hardwick supervises the sax. section. The couvert at the Kentucky is $1.50, which is right for this place. Easily the best of the "kennel clubs" in town.

George D. Lottman, *Billboard* (December 5, 1925), 22; quoted in Mark Tucker, ed., *The Duke Ellington Reader* (New York: Oxford University Press, 1993), 23–24.

Contemporary Voices

The Cotton Club

In 1927 Ellington's fortunes began to soar when the Washingtonians moved to the **Cotton Club,** the most exclusive black-and-tan cabaret in Harlem (see Map 5).

The Cotton Club, owned by mob boss Owney Madden, was an expensive, "high-class" venue featuring black entertainment and service staff for strictly white customers. Despite the Deep South connotations of its name, the Cotton Club cultivated an "African" jungle ambiance to highlight the exoticism of its black music and dancing. Ellington's band was expected to provide musical atmosphere for the "primitive" stage presentations. Fortuitously, Ellington had been developing a musical style at the Kentucky Club that fit perfectly with the Cotton Club's "African" theme. Featuring throbbing tom-toms, minor keys, chromatic harmony, and above all, growling trumpets and trombones (simulating the roars of wild beasts), the style became known as **jungle style.** Such recordings from the Kentucky Club era as "East St. Louis Toodle-O" and "Black and Tan

jungle style a style, closely associated with Duke Ellington, featuring throbbing tom-toms, minor keys, chromatic harmony, and growling trumpets and trombones.

Map 5. Harlem,
c. 1920s–early 1940s.

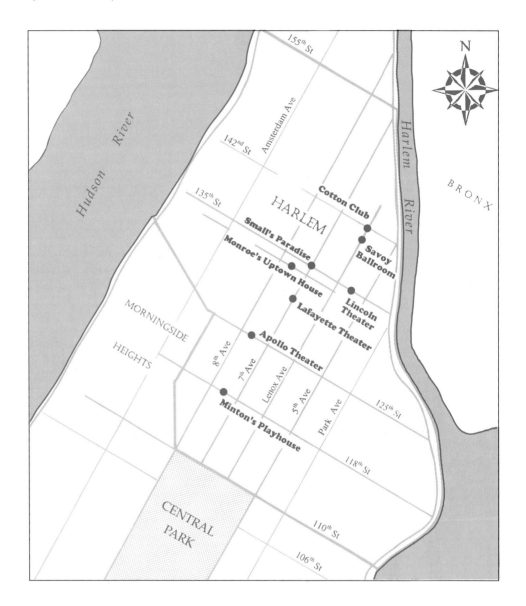

Fantasy" manifest these characteristics; at the Cotton Club Ellington added such pieces as "The Mooche" and "Jungle Nights in Harlem." The distinctiveness of Ellington's style captured the imagination of listeners across the country through regular NBC radio broadcasts from the Cotton Club. As Ellington recalled this period in 1962, "All the other bands in the country were trying to sound like Paul Whiteman, and naturally they were souped up with a lot of grandiose fanfares and all that sort of thing. But we had a very, very plaintive sort of style, and out of contrast alone we stuck out, and caught on."

Jazz and Art

Some listeners recognized that Ellington's music did more than simply evoke programmatic jungle themes in the comic tradition of jazz novelty playing. For R. D. Darrell, a classical music critic for the *Phonograph Monthly Review,* hearing

Duke Ellington and His Orchestra at the Cotton Club, c. 1929. *Top, left to right:* Tricky Sam Nanton, Harry White, Sonny Greer, Fred Guy, Wellman Braud; *bottom:* Freddie Jenkins, Cootie Williams, Artie Whetsol, Duke Ellington, Harry Carney, Johnny Hodges, Barney Bigard.

the record "Black and Tan Fantasy" marked a turning point in his opinion about the artistic worth of jazz. At first, he wrote in 1932, "I laughed like everyone else over its instrumental wa-waing and gargling and gobbling, the piteous whinny-ing of a very ancient horse, the lugubrious reminiscence of the Chopin funeral march. But as I continued to play the record for the amusement of my friends I laughed less heartily and with less zest. In my ears the whinnies and wa-was began to resolve into new tone colors, distorted and tortured, but agonizingly expressive. The piece took on a surprising individuality and entity as well as an intensity of feeling that was totally incongruous in popular dance music. Beneath all its oddity and perverseness there was a twisted beauty that grew on me more and more and could not be shaken off."

Much of the power of pieces like "Black and Tan Fantasy," of course, de-rived from the individual soloists who produced those haunting "whinnies and wa-was." First in importance was Miley, whose role had become so significant,

Venues

THE COTTON CLUB

The Cotton Club, located at 644 Lenox Avenue in Harlem, was founded in 1920 by former heavyweight champion Jack Johnson. Initially called the Club Deluxe, it became known as the Cotton Club in 1922, after mob boss Owney Madden bought the place. Thereafter, the Cotton Club became one of the most expensive and well-known clubs in New York City, catering primarily to wealthy white patrons.

In keeping with the club's "jungle" theme, the interior décor mingled synthetic palm trees with rich draperies and furnishings. The scantily clad chorus girls had to be "high yaller gals" (light-skinned Negroes), at least 5′6″, and no older than twenty-one. The tables were arranged in a horseshoe around the stage, and seated up to seven hundred people. Diners chose from a varied menu that included steak and lobster, Chinese food, Mexican food, and Harlem specialities like fried chicken and barbecued spare ribs. Like most speakeasies, the Cotton Club served beer primarily; customers who wanted something harder could buy champagne for $30 and a fifth of Scotch for $18.

After Duke Ellington's celebrated residency ended in 1931, the Cotton Club hosted swing-era icons Cab Calloway and Jimmie Lunceford. But in 1935 devastating race riots shattered Harlem's image as a safe playground for whites. The following year the Lenox Avenue Cotton Club was forced to close—although it reopened twice at other locations. ■ ■ ■

according to one musician, that Ellington "had the whole band built around Bubber Miley." Miley co-composed and played prominent solos in several of Ellington's early compositions, including "East St. Louis Toodle-O," "Black and Tan Fantasy," and "Creole Love Call." Miley's brass partner and friend was **Joe "Tricky Sam" Nanton** (1904–1946), who played plunger effects on trombone. Together, Miley and Nanton defined jungle style most audibly, with their animalistic growls and snarls. But, as Darrell realized, their plunger effects transcended the theatrical context to express a powerful artistic message on its own terms.

If so much credit goes to soloists for the strength of Ellington's compositions, what role did the Maestro himself play in their creation? Ellington was the irreplaceable alchemist who somehow brought all the elements together, fusing his own ideas and the contributions of his sidemen into something greater than the individual statements alone. We will further explore Ellington's mysterious creative processes in Chapter 12.

DUKE ELLINGTON AND HIS ORCHESTRA, *"Black and Tan Fantasy"* (1927)

CD 1 / Track 48

Recorded just two months before Ellington's band opened at the Cotton Club, this version of "Black and Tan Fantasy" projects the most striking aspects of jungle style: growling trumpets and trombones. The piece was a collaboration between Ellington and trumpeter Bubber Miley. The opening melody came from "The Holy City" (1892), by Stephen Adams, a sacred song Miley's mother used to sing. Miley placed the melody in the minor mode, contracted it to fit a twelve-bar blues progression, and added a harmony part for the trombonist Joe Nanton. The second theme, undoubtedly written by Ellington, provides an effective contrast with the severe opening. Assuming the guise of a show tune, this graceful, sensuous melody demonstrates that "sweet" style still had a role to play in Ellington's music.

The rest of the piece consists of a succession of blues solos (in major) by Miley, Nanton, and Ellington. The two "gutbucket" plunger solos by Miley are especially impressive—the first for its searing distortions of pitch and timbre, the second for the erratic stuttering quality of Miley's rhythms against the decisive punctuations of the ensemble behind him. The beginning of Miley's first solo—a high B-flat held softly for four measures—may have been a common opening among trumpet players; Louis Armstrong used it in the outchorus of "West End Blues." Miley's last chorus is cut short by a quotation of Chopin's "Funeral March" from Sonata No. 2, Opus 35, in B-flat minor. By the time the band reached the end of the arrangement and began the funeral march, Ellington said, "I used to see great, big ole tears running down people's faces."

Create your own listening chart (CD 1 / Track 48)

Chapter 9   Early Jazz Piano

Just as instrumental ragtime gradually evolved into small-group jazz, so ragtime piano gave birth to the first jazz piano styles. In Harlem such pianists as James P. Johnson, Willie the Lion Smith, and Fats Waller cultivated a newly virtuosic, improvisational, hard-swinging idiom. At the same time, a vigorous species of piano blues was evolving in Chicago under the leadership of Jimmy Yancey, Albert Ammons, and Meade Lux Lewis. These two styles, known as Harlem stride and boogie-woogie, dominated jazz piano of the 1920s and 1930s. Under the weight of these intense idioms ragtime quickly expired, to be revived only through the efforts of dedicated musical archaeologists later in the century.

East Coast Ragtime

Although we have come to associate "classic" ragtime with St. Louis, Sedalia, and other Missouri cities, Scott Joplin himself actually lived in New York from 1907 until his death in 1917. His change of residence mirrored a larger shift in the geographical center of ragtime from the Midwest to the East Coast in the first decades of the century. Baltimore, Washington, Philadelphia, and New York produced a generation of pianists that favored a style far removed from that of Joplin and his colleagues.

Dubbing themselves piano *ticklers,* eastern pianists belonged to an elite competitive fraternity with a flashy dress code, swaggering social etiquette, and, above all, brilliant pianistic technique. They worked out routines for their specialty pieces and developed a repertoire of "tricks"—such as registral leaps, sudden dynamic changes, or quirky melodic ideas—to distinguish themselves from other players. They also performed at the edge of their skill, emphasizing unpredictability and a certain amount of improvisation. To intimidate rivals and win the admiration of fans, the ticklers executed mind-bending feats of virtuosity often derived (directly or indirectly) from nineteenth-century classical piano literature. Many eastern pianists went unpublished and unrecorded, and the beginnings of this musical tradition remain as murky as those of New Orleans jazz.

The eastern players nurtured an emphatic approach to rhythm. During World War I ragtime rhythms underwent a nationwide change from straight eighth notes to the bouncier pattern of *dotted rhythms* (such as appear, for example, in the verse section of "The Battle Hymn of the Republic"). Eastern pianists evidently added elements of what we now call "swing feel"—accented upbeats, *legato* ("connected") phrasing, relaxed overall conception, and so forth. The precise impetus for this addition remains mysterious, but seems somehow related to the black church. The African ritual of the **ring shout**—which New Orleans slaves danced at Congo Square (see Chapter 3)—appears to have been influential. In the ring shout, some worshippers shuffled around in a circle while others sang and clapped. (In this context the word "shout" referred to the dance; "shouters" were thus dancers.) The ceremony would gradually build to a climax of musical and religious fervor. The eastern pianists believed their music shared a transcendent energy with the ritual. They even called their uptempo pieces "shouts."

The Jungles

In the 1910s eastern ragtime players began gravitating to New York City. James P. Johnson moved there from New Jersey in 1908, Luckey Roberts came from Philadelphia in 1911, Eubie Blake from Baltimore in 1915, and Willie the Lion Smith from the military in 1919. Before World War I, New York blacks did not concentrate in Harlem but lived in scattered pockets throughout the city. The black neighborhood that employed most of the ragtime pianists was **the Jungles,** a strip that ran from 60th to 63rd Streets in the northwest corner of Hell's Kitchen, the city's notorious vice district spanning forty blocks on the West Side (see Map 4).

Most of these pianists are known to us only by name (or nickname) and anecdotal reputation. Some of the more colorful, if now elusive, personalities were Jack the Bear, the Shadow, Fats Harris, Abba Labba, Willie Gant, and the Beetle. Abba Labba never took a steady job because he received full material support from female admirers. As one musician remembered, "he would come in and play for thirty minutes, cut everybody, and go out." We know more about Luckey Roberts, a Quaker by birth who started in show business as a child acrobat. Despite his rough professional environment, Roberts shunned liquor, tobacco, and drugs—although he was a master pool shark.

Harlem Stride

Harlem, located north of Central Park and south of 155th Street, began the twentieth century as the most exclusive white neighborhood in the city (see Map 5). Hoping to capitalize on improved transportation from Harlem to downtown, entrepreneurs built too many new dwellings too quickly. When demand fell short they sold the properties, out of desperation, to upper-class blacks. As blacks moved into Harlem, white residents began to move out. During the Great Migration Harlem attracted thousands of hopeful southern migrants; by the 1920s it had become the African American center of the city. Like most aspects of vernacular culture, the development of black music shifted from downtown to Harlem. And the continuously evolving eastern piano style came to be known as **Harlem stride.**

The word "stride" refers to the holdover from ragtime of the left-hand "striding" alternation between bass note and midregister chord. The resulting "oom-pahs" became a hallmark of stride style. Stride differs from classic ragtime in the following ways:

- Whereas ragtime grew into a composed, notated tradition, stride was a more spontaneous, improvisational idiom intended primarily for live performance or recording.

Harlem stride a virtuosic, swinging form of east coast ragtime that evolved in the 1920s.

- Stride pianists cultivated a more brilliant and virtuosic right-hand part.
- Stride pianists favored richer sonorities in the striding left hand, incorporating chromaticism, blue notes, and other forms of dissonance.
- Stride was potentially faster, particularly on shouts (although medium-tempo stride pieces are not uncommon).
- Most important, stride pianists played with a fiery sense of swing; for this reason, perhaps, stride represents the first generally recognized jazz piano style.

We have already encountered three examples of stride playing in the course of this book: Jelly Roll Morton's solo on "Black Bottom Stomp," Earl Hines's solo on "West End Blues," and Duke Ellington's solo on "Black and Tan Fantasy." As the Morton and Hines examples demonstrate, Harlem pianists were not the only ones playing Harlem stride.

Rent Parties

Knowing that black tenants could not easily move out of Harlem, predatory landlords charged them exorbitant rates. By 1927 black renters paid, on average, $10 more than other New Yorkers for a four-room apartment. The combination of high rents and low wages made it difficult for tenants to meet their rent payments. One solution they found was the **rent party.** For a nominal admission fee (from ten cents to a dollar), guests enjoyed live music, dancing, food, and bootleg liquor at the needy renter's apartment. On the night of the party, all nonessential furniture was moved into another apartment to make room for as many people as possible. As Willie the Lion Smith recalled, "They would crowd a hundred or more people into a seven-room railroad flat and the walls would bulge—some of the parties spread to the halls and all over the building." After covering expenses, the proceeds were used to pay the host's rent.

Held in many different residences every weekend, rent parties became an important incubator of Harlem stride. Often several pianists would arrive and hold cutting contests long into the night. They typically played on an upright piano with the front cover removed; sometimes they put newspapers behind the hammers and tin on the felts to get the sound of an old-fashioned player piano. Then they took turns jousting while onlookers gambled over the outcome. With the windows often wide open, the music attracted people to the party from throughout the neighborhood.

James P. Johnson

The acknowledged "father of stride piano" was **James P. Johnson** (1894–1955). Born and raised in New Brunswick, New Jersey, Johnson moved with his family to New York in 1908. There he discovered "real ragtime," as he put it. Over the next several years he met and shared ideas with Abba Labba, Luckey Roberts, Eubie Blake, and other fellow pianists. During this same period he studied classical piano, as well as harmony and counterpoint, with an Italian immigrant. This dual experience in ragtime and classical music came through in Johnson's live performances: "I used to like to rip off a ringing concert-style opening using Liszt's 'Rigoletto Paraphrase for Piano' that was full of fireworks in the classical manner and then abruptly slide into a solid, groovy stomp to wake up the audience and get a laugh."

After the war Johnson renewed his aquaintance with a young man who would become one of the greatest ticklers, **Willie "the Lion" Smith** (1897–1973),

WILLIE THE LION SMITH

Describes Harlem Rent Parties in the 1920s

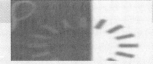

On occasions these sessions would start early in the afternoon and keep going until far into the next day. When I saw one of these long hauls coming up I'd eat ten eggs and a couple of steaks to get in shape. In addition to our fee we would get all the liquor we could drink and since I was drinking raw brandy with no chaser in those days I made it a point to be sure my stomach had a good firm lining before taking on all the fire water.

There were, of course, some of the chitterling struts [rent parties] where a bunch of pianists would be in competition. . . . Sometimes we got carving battles going that would last for four or five hours. Here's how these bashes worked: the Lion would pound out the keys for a mess of choruses and then shout to the next in line, "Well, all right, take it from there," and each tickler would take his turn, trying to improve on a melody. (There was actually more arguing going on between the listeners than there was jealousy between us. Hard cash was bet on the outcome and more than once they'd get ready to fight between them as to who had won.) We would embroider the melodies with our own original ideas and try to develop patterns that had more originality than those played before us. Sometimes it was just a question as to who could think up the most patterns within a given tune. It was pure improvisation.

You had to have your own original style and be able to play in all the keys. In those days we could all copy each other's shouts by learning them by ear. Sometimes in order to keep the others from picking up too much of my stuff I'd perform in the hard keys, B major and E major. I had my own attitude and way of working at the piano. My way was to get a cigar clenched between my teeth, my derby tilted back, knees crossed, and my back arched at a sharp angle against the back of the chair. I'd cuss at the keyboard and then caress it with endearing words; a pianist who growls, hums, and talks to the piano is a guy who is trying hard to create something for himself.

Willie the Lion Smith, with George Hoefer, *Music on My Mind: The Memoirs of An American Pianist* (New York: Doubleday, 1964), 154–55.

born William Henry Joseph Bonaparte Bertholoff Smith. Of mixed French, Jewish, Mohawk Indian, and African American blood, Smith may have earned his nickname "the Lion" for valiant action in World War I, for his commitment to Judaism, for his ferocious piano playing, or possibly for his crusty and imperious personality. Johnson and Smith became good friends and rivals, often playing together in cabarets and rent parties throughout the 1920s.

In 1921 Johnson recorded his most famous composition, "Carolina Shout," which cemented his reputation as New York's leading stride pianist. Ever since his first piano roll of this piece came out in 1918, it had gradually acquired the status of a "test piece" against which other pianists measured their skill. The young Duke Ellington learned "Carolina Shout" by slowing down the player piano and following the pattern of rising and falling keys with his fingers; when he came to New York a few years later, he got the chance to play the piece in front of Johnson himself. But the 1918 version still betrays rhythmic vestiges of ragtime; the performance from 1921 reveals stride style in its fully developed and swinging form.

Fats Waller

Sometime around 1920 Johnson walked into Leroy Wilkins' Club, at 135th Street and Fifth Avenue, where Willie the Lion Smith was playing. "Who the hell's the punk kid with you?" Smith demanded. "Fats Waller," Johnson replied. "He looks more like Filthy Waller," Smith shot back. "You can't bring no punk kid in here lookin' like that. Get his pants pressed and buy him a new shirt. This here's a high class joint." Johnson calmed his friend down and persuaded him to hear Waller play "Carolina Shout." The performance overcame Smith's sartorial objections and Waller soon began accompanying the two older men in their nocturnal forays through Harlem. Today, he is generally recognized as the greatest player of the Johnson-Smith-Waller triumvirate.

Thomas "Fats" Waller (1904–1943) grew up in Harlem, the son of a devout lay preacher. Because the family had little money for lessons, he learned to play the piano by ear. After quitting school at age fourteen, he went to the Lincoln Theater every day to watch the pianist and organist accompany the silent movies (see Map 5). His father did not approve of popular music and considered the movie house to be a sinful place. Hoping to redirect his musical interests, his father took him to see the concert pianist Ignace Paderewski at Carnegie Hall. Although enchanted by this experience, Waller continued to attend the Lincoln and within a year became the theater's regular organist. At night he roamed through Harlem soaking up the music of the cabarets.

In 1920 the conflict with his father came to a head, and, at the age of sixteen, Waller moved out. Shortly thereafter he was introduced to James P. Johnson, who became Waller's mentor and assisted him to find jobs. In 1923 Waller won a piano competition at the Roosevelt Theater for his version of "Carolina Shout." The following year he played as intermission pianist at the Kentucky Club, alternating with Duke Ellington. In 1925 he traveled with his new friend, Louis Armstrong, to Chicago, where he later performed with Erskine Tate at the

Fats Waller, 1938.

Vendome Theater. (While in Chicago, according to his son Maurice, Waller was once forced at gunpoint into a car by a group of white mobsters; when they arrived at their destination he discovered, to his relief, that he had been summoned to perform for Al Capone's birthday party.) Back in New York in 1928, Waller substituted for James P. Johnson at a concert of blues, spirituals, and jazz at Carnegie Hall.

Waller wholeheartedly embraced the "show-biz" aspects of his career. Later known as "The Clown Prince of Jazz," he leavened his performances with his abundant sense of humor. As a teenager he delighted audiences at the Lincoln Theater with his comic facial expressions and other visual shenanigans. At the Kentucky Club he put on a jeweled turban and portrayed "Ali Baba, the Egyptian Wonder." More important from a musical point of view, he wrote popular songs for the Broadway stage. In this respect he followed a pattern established by earlier stride players. In 1921 Eubie Blake collaborated on the hugely successful all-black Broadway show, *Shuffle Along*. Two years later James P. Johnson enjoyed similar success with his score to *Runnin' Wild* (the show that introduced the Charleston). Waller, in turn, composed two revues in 1926, collaborated with Johnson on another in 1928, and co-wrote the score to **Hot Chocolates** in 1929. The latter production, which featured Waller's now-classic song, "Ain't Misbehavin'," became a smash hit.

The year 1929 was equally significant for another reason: Waller made his first series of solo piano recordings. In these works one can hear all of his previous musical experiences coming together, fused by his impeccable technique

Fats Waller, *"Handful of Keys"* (1929)

In "Handful of Keys," Waller combines the structure of march form with two types of thirty-two-bar song form. The march aspect is evident in the multistrain progression from opening melody (A) through an interlude to a trio (B) positioned in a new key a fourth above the original. Inside these principal strains Waller has inserted song forms: aaba within A, and abac (here labeled cdce) within B. The second song form, abac, which we have already seen in "Alexander's Ragtime Band," "Cake Walking Babies from Home" (modified), "Potato Head Blues," and "Singin' the Blues," was most common early in the century. The first song form, **aaba,** appeared increasingly in 1920s show tunes and would become the favorite of songwriters—and jazz players who performed their works—in subsequent years.

Despite its tight stylistic integration, "Handful of Keys" reveals several distinct musical traditions. The exotic-sounding interval of the fourth in the introduction stems from the novelty piano idiom of players like Zez Confrey. At the end of the introduction (and the interlude) Waller plays a vaudeville cliché that served as "entry music" for stage acts. Then at A he settles into a rollicking stride in uptempo "shout" style, which prevails for the rest of the piece. For the final statement of A Waller marshalls a swirling right-hand figure of chromatic embellishments in various octaves that must have served as one of his signature "tricks" during cutting contests. In the bridge he uses Broadway orchestra-style *pyramids,* consisting of an ascending series of overlapping sustained notes. During the last eight bars, the intensity increases with sporadic syncopations in the manner of a white Chicago-style outchorus.

LISTENING CHART 11

Fats Waller, "Handful of Keys" (Waller)

CD 1 / Tracks 49–53

RECORDED 1 MARCH 1929, NEW YORK CITY / VICTOR V-38508; MX 49759-1

Fats Waller (solo piano)

Style: Harlem stride **Form: March form-song form hybrid**

				Introduction
49	0:00		(4)	Left hand: sustained chords; right hand: parallel fourths
	0:05		(4)	"Entry music" introduces the opening theme
				First strain: aaba song form
50	0:09	A	a (8)	Stride piano in uptempo "shout" style, which prevails throughout. The "a" theme elaborates an ascending scale
	0:17		a (8)	*a-section repeated*
	0:24		b (8)	Bridge: a brief, oscillating melody at various pitch levels
	0:32		a (8)	Return of the a-section
	0:39	A	a (8)	*First strain repeated (second chorus of aaba form):* right hand an octave higher this time
	0:46		a (8)	
	0:54		b (8)	Waller presents new bridge material—fluttering downward figures—at various pitch levels
	1:01		a (8)	
				Transition / modulation
51	1:08		(4)	Striding yields to fanfare, then "entry music"
				Second strain (trio): abac song form (shown as cdce)
	1:12	B	c (8)	New key (up a fourth); left-hand striding resumes, more intensely this time, engaging in rapid back-and-forth cross-rhythms with the right hand; the right hand dashes off bluesy figures
	1:20		d (8)	

	1:27		c (8)	Waller apparently "improvises" on the chords here . . .
	1:35		e (8)	
				Return of the first strain (aaba)
52	1:42	A	a (8)	Back in the original key; Waller plays "a" theme in middle octave, then restates it an octave higher, then restates it an octave higher still
	1:49		a (8)	Now he settles back into the second octave and stays there
	1:57		b (6)	"Improvises" on the bridge theme . . .
	2:02		(2)	Break!
	2:04		a (8)	"Improvises" on the "a" theme
53	2:12	A	a (8)	Final virtuoso routine: right hand plays chromatic embellishments in various octaves while left continues to stride
	2:19		a (8)	*Repeated,* with some variation
	2:26		b (2)	Bridge theme
	2:28		(2)	Broadway orchestra-style pyramids
	2:30		(2)	Bridge theme
	2:32		(2)	Pyramids
	2:34		a (6)	Wide syncopations in the manner of a Chicago-style outchorus
	2:39	Tag	(4)	Irregular, sputtering rhythms / dreamy closing pyramid

and refined musical judgment. One recording, "Handful of Keys," replaced "Carolina Shout" in the aspirations of young pianists, becoming a test piece for the next generation.

Earl Hines

Waller's contemporary and pianistic equal in Chicago was **Earl "Fatha" Hines,** whom we first encountered in Chapter 6. While growing up in Pittsburgh, Hines absorbed the eastern style of ragtime through the playing of locals and, later, Eubie Blake and Luckey Roberts. In the 1920s, he later acknowledged, Waller was his most important influence. But Hines was no mere imitator; he developed an inventive and entirely original approach to the piano.

Like most jazz pianists in the twenties, Hines used Harlem stride as the basis for his style. But he brought elements to stride that Waller had not. For instance, unlike Waller, Hines had received thorough classical training in his youth. Hines's rich classical background, which exceeded that of any of the Harlem players, may account for his subtlety of touch, careful use of dynamics, unpredictable rhythms, and general regard for textural variety. Although the Harlem pianists imaginatively varied the left-hand "oom-pah" patterns, Hines often broke with stride rhythm entirely to play a bass line or even a distinct melody that combined polyphonically with the right hand. As one critic observed, through his independent left-hand parts Hines created "conversational" textures in his music.

Hines also brought a fascinatingly quirky rhythmic sense to his playing. In his solo on "West End Blues," for example, he begins with rhythmically free, cascading scales and arpeggios in the right hand against a steady but unobtrusive stride in the left. Then in the middle of the chorus he abruptly shifts to a swinging *double-time feel* (the tempo *feels* twice as fast but the chords change at the same rate) in a brief evocation of a "shout." The chorus closes with an alternation between sturdy right-hand octaves, the previous cascading figures, and evanescent snatches of swing rhythms.

Critics have often noted Hines's development of **trumpet-style piano,** another example of cross-instrumental influence in early jazz. As defined by one authority, this style consists of (1) right-hand melody lines played in octaves to mimic the sonorous declamation of trumpet players; (2) phrase endings that correspond to the "breath points" of wind musicians; and (3) tremolos on sustained notes that echo the *terminal vibrato* of early jazz trumpet style. Having played the trumpet as a youngster, Hines understood the idiom he was borrowing. But it was only later, while playing with large ensembles in the early twenties, that he adopted the right-hand octaves simply as a way of making himself heard. His trumpet style developed further when he met and began playing with Louis Armstrong in 1925. As Hines later recalled, "We were very close and when we were playing we would steal ideas from each other. Or, rather, I'd borrow an idea from him, and say 'Thank you.' Then he'd hear me play something he liked, borrow it, and say, 'Thank you.'" In Armstrong-Hines collaborations from the late twenties—particularly in their spectacular duet on "Weatherbird" (1928)—one can hear not only Hines's trumpet-style piano playing but also the rare symbiosis generated by the two masters.

Boogie-Woogie

If stride developed out of ragtime, then **boogie-woogie** descended from the country blues. Unlike other vernacular idioms we have surveyed, boogie-woogie cannot be traced back to a single geographical center. Scholars believe that it arose around the turn of the century in lumber mills, turpentine camps, railroad construction sites, and mining towns in forested regions throughout the southern states. Witnesses recall hearing it in Memphis, St. Louis, Kansas City, New Orleans, Birmingham, and several Texas towns. Itinerant black pianists wended their way through this territory playing "piano blues" for the tough working crowd in *barrelhouses* (lowdown saloons that served alcohol straight from the "barrel"), honky tonks, and juke joints. These players were invariably self-taught,

boogie-woogie a type of piano blues from the early twentieth century featuring ostinato figures in the left hand, repeating riffs in the right, and a driving swing feel.

with little or no exposure to classical music and only rudimentary technical skills. To be heard above the noise in the places where they played, they pounded the keyboard violently. Eubie Blake recalled a boogie-woogie pioneer named William Turk (1866?–1911?), a huge man six feet in height and three hundred pounds in weight: "He had a left hand like God. He didn't even know what key he was playing in, but he played them all. He could play the ragtime stride bass, but it bothered him because his stomach got in the way of his arm, so he used a walking bass instead."

The Great Migration brought many of these players to Chicago in the 1920s. In this new urban environment they found work at rent parties and low dives on the South Side. A particularly frequent site of rent parties was **Mecca Flats,** an apartment complex at 34th and State Street in the center of the black neighborhood (see Map 3). Here, virtually all the important boogie-woogie pianists performed at some point during the twenties. Like their stride counterparts in New York, the boogie players honed their craft through cutting contests. But they never won significant respect among the stride pianists. Although Fats Waller occasionally evoked the boogie-woogie idiom in his solo recordings of pieces like "Alligator Crawl" (1934) and "I Ain't Got Nobody" (1937), he insisted that his contract clear him of any obligation to play boogie-woogie. The proud stride players considered this music to be lowbrow and simple-minded.

In the late 1920s, the first boogie-woogie recordings came out as race records, but they were not called "boogie-woogie" yet. In 1928 Clarence "Pinetop" Smith made a record called "Pinetop's Boogie-Woogie," which somehow gave the music its name. By the time of this recording, boogie-woogie had the following characteristics:

- Form based on the twelve-bar (or occasionally eight-bar) blues progression
- In the left hand, an *ostinato* (or repeating) bass figure in steady eighth notes (hence the term often applied to boogie-woogie: "eight-to-the-bar").
- In the right hand, a series of *riffs* (short, melodic ideas) that often conflict rhythmically with the left hand, thereby creating *cross-rhythms.*
- A propulsive sense of swing

Meade Lux Lewis

The major exponents of boogie-woogie in the twenties were **Jimmy Yancey** (1894–1951), **Albert Ammons** (1907–1949), and **Meade Lux Lewis** (1905–1964). Yancey, whose influence on younger players compares with that of James P. Johnson, served as mentor to Ammons and Lewis. Because their music was confined primarily to rent parties and similarly modest professional settings, they all had other sources of income: Yancey worked as a ballpark groundsman, and the other two drove taxis. Yet they each developed a distinct and compelling artistic style. One critic considers Yancey the most expressively soulful, Ammons the most viscerally powerful, and Lewis the most complex and inventive of the boogie-woogie pianists. For jazz historians, who have always placed a high value on originality of exposition, Lewis has seemed to outshine his contemporaries.

One year younger than Fats Waller, Lewis grew up in Chicago. In the early twenties, he spent a lot of time at the Lincoln Gardens listening to King Oliver's

Albert Ammons and Meade Lux Lewis, 1939.

band. Within a few years he was playing piano professionally, although not in the best venues. In 1927, for example, he played for several months in two brothels in South Bend, Indiana. At the end of the year, however, he got the opportunity to record his solo piano specialty, "Honky Tonk Train Blues." A honky tonk train was an excursion train provided by the railroad company for blacks in Chicago to return home to visit their families in the South. They traveled in the baggage car, equipped with a bar, a dance floor, and a boogie-woogie pianist. In "Honky Tonk Train Blues," Lewis explores a series of melodic ideas that change with each new chorus.

Neither Yancey nor Ammons nor Lewis achieved fame in the 1920s. But in the next decade a popular craze for boogie-woogie engulfed the nation as part of the traditionalist movement of the late Swing Era (see Chapter 10). Under the auspices of this movement, Yancey, Ammons, and Lewis became international celebrities. Although the ensuing market saturation and commercialization of boogie-woogie wound up killing the idiom in the 1940s, this revival of old-time "piano blues" did produce the most distinguished records ever made by the three Chicago masters.

PART

Swing

Three

(c. 1929–1945)

Historical Context: The Swing Era

Chapter **10**

T HE STOCK MARKET CRASH OF 1929 PLUNGED THE UNITED STATES INTO THE worst economic depression of its history. President Franklin D. Roosevelt sustained the country's morale through New Deal policies and dogged optimism. But, despite a plethora of government programs to create jobs and assist the poor, the economy would not fully revive until World War II began making demands on American manufacturing. For some people, the sacrifices of wartime were even more difficult to bear than material want.

Throughout this trying period Americans took comfort in popular entertainment, one of the few industries that flourished in the 1930s. Movies, radio, and music all emphasized romance and nostalgia, allowing consumers to fantasize the fulfillment of their dreams "somewhere over the rainbow," as Judy Garland sang in *The Wizard of Oz* (1939). Popular songs encouraged people to look on the bright side of life. Cheerful weather metaphors abounded in songs like "Singin' in the Rain" (1929), "On the Sunny Side of the Street" (1930), and "Pennies from Heaven" (1936).

For the first time in American history, a generation of teenagers and college students chose what would be the nation's favorite popular music. And for the only time, that choice was jazz. Consolidating earlier rhythmic practices, jazz

Chronology

1929	Stock market crash
1932	Election of Franklin D. Roosevelt
1934	*Let's Dance* NBC radio program
	First issue of *Down Beat* magazine
	Decca Records begins race series
1935	Benny Goodman's success at Palomar Ballroom
1936	Count Basie begins national career
1938	"Spirituals to Swing" concert at Carnegie Hall
1939	World War II begins in Europe
	Bunk Johnson revives musical career
	Jazzmen published
1941	America enters World War II
1942–1944	AFM recording ban
1943	Duke Ellington's debut at Carnegie Hall
1945	World War II ends
1947	Louis Armstrong organizes his All-Stars

bands in the thirties produced a cohesive, bouncy momentum that lured dancers irresistibly to the dance floor. The new style was called **swing,** a word by now familiar to us that jazz historians have applied to the period as a whole. In the Swing Era, which lasted until the end of World War II in 1945, Americans danced away their troubles to sentimental ballads and hot jazz.

The Great Depression

The ill effects of the stock market crash multiplied in the early thirties. President Herbert Hoover, a brilliant manager and unflinching optimist, kept insisting that an economic rebound was right around the corner. But almost every month new and ominous signs mocked Hoover's forecast. By the end of his presidency in 1933, about nine thousand banks had failed, the value of goods and services had fallen to half its 1929 level, one fourth of the country was unemployed, and more than twenty-five thousand families had become homeless wanderers.

African Americans bore the brunt of the crisis. Relief rolls of the period enlisted three to four times as many blacks as whites. With no jobs beckoning in the North, the Great Migration dried up. Leading representatives of the Harlem Renaissance scattered to other parts of the country or the world, or simply shelved their artistic ambitions to answer more basic needs. In the cities, white exploitation of black tenants and employees increased as jobs grew scarce. The resentment in Harlem, brewing since the 1920s, finally exploded in 1935 as blacks led a riot against white employers who refused to hire black workers. In the melee three blacks were killed and over two hundred stores vandalized; property damage exceeded $2 million.

Despite these problems, there were reasons to be hopeful in the early 1930s. The landslide election of **Franklin D. Roosevelt** expressed the hopes of a desperate country that the Democratic Party would do more than the Republicans had done to alleviate the suffering of its citizens. Roosevelt immediately enacted his promised **New Deal,** a vast array of government programs to provide employment and help the needy. Because many blacks benefited directly from these programs, African Americans began reconsidering their seventy-year-old allegiance to the Republican Party—the party of Lincoln.

The Music Industry

In the early years of the Depression, jazz suffered a heavy toll. As ordinary Americans were forced to curtail their entertainment spending, many nightclubs closed. Overall record sales plummeted from a high of 104 million in 1927 to 6 million in 1932. Because of the recent advent of "talkies" (films with pre-recorded soundtracks) and the increased popularity of Hollywood movies at the expense of vaudeville productions, theaters had less and less need for live musicians. In 1934 a new invention called the **jukebox,** a coin-operated record player, began taking the place of live music in restaurants and dance halls. One thriving medium that *did* employ musicians was radio. Many Americans owned a radio before the crash and, if not, were willing to sacrifice to possess this one link to the outside world of news and entertainment. Yet, the geographical breadth of the medium concentrated radio work in the hands of a few fortunate players.

With the notable exception of Louis Armstrong, most New Orleans musicians did not adapt well to these developments. Jelly Roll Morton managed to keep playing, but had to sell the diamond in his front tooth to get by. Sidney Bechet left music for a while to open a tailor shop, and Kid Ory ran a chicken ranch with his brother. Perhaps the saddest experience was King Oliver's. Cursed with a raging sweet tooth, Oliver developed pyorrhea of the gums—an affliction that loosened his teeth and severely weakened his trumpet embouchure. He spent the early thirties touring the southern states in a hopeless attempt to stay in the music business. By the middle of the decade he had become stranded in Savannah, Georgia, where he took work sweeping out a pool hall and selling fruit on the street. After writing a series of pathetic letters to his sister in New York vowing a comeback, Oliver died in 1938.

The New Orleans jazzmen were caught in the wheels of a historical transition: small jazz bands were yielding to **big bands,** and the music's creative center was shifting from Chicago to New York, where it has remained to this day. In hindsight, one can see why the New Orleanians faltered. They performed a high-spirited polyphonic music incomprehensible to much of the American public. When economic problems arose and the mood of celebration dissipated, New Orleans music lost much of its black working-class audience. The homophonic dance music played by large ensembles in New York, on the other hand, appealed to a broad range of listeners, both white and black. As a result, Paul Whiteman, Fletcher Henderson, Duke Ellington, and similar groups fared much better in the early years of the Depression. Not only did more people like their music, but harsh economic conditions actually promoted the survival of the big bands. Because musicians were willing to work for far less money, bandleaders could afford—and sometimes felt obliged—to maintain large orchestras.

big band a large performing group, usually of twelve to twenty players.

The Swing Craze

Three main types of big bands vied for popularity in the early 1930s. Sweet bands dominated the ballrooms and the airwaves. In 1930 Paul Whiteman's career climaxed with the production of his autobiographical Hollywood movie extravaganza, *King of Jazz*. But for smooth, serene dance music, no one could beat **Guy Lombardo** (1902–1977), who advertised "The Sweetest Music This Side of Heaven." Another popular type, which jazz musicians derisively called **mickey-mouse bands,** played in a rhythmically stiff, "corny" fashion and subordinated musical values to comedy and novelty stunts. Kay Kyser, for example, donned cap and gown to direct his "Kollege of Musical Knowledge," in which audience members received prizes for correctly answering musical questions while trumpeter Ishkabibble (aka Merwyn Bogue) performed comical antics in silly hats.

A third type of big band mixed hot and sweet styles in varying proportions. Duke Ellington and Fletcher Henderson spearheaded this development, but black bandleaders, being confined to race records, were not likely to win the attention of the broad American public. A few white bands, however, began to incorporate hot elements into their music. One especially influential group, the **Casa Loma Orchestra,** arose from the ashes of Jean Goldkette's defunct 1927 band. Based in Detroit, the Casa Loma Orchestra played college dances throughout the Midwest, building enthusiastic followings among students for its balanced mix of slow romantic ballads and uptempo jump tunes. The band's 1930 recording of "Casa Loma Stomp" provided the prototype for the big band *killer-diller* number, a headlong sprint executed with accuracy and élan.

If, as one writer has put it, the Casa Loma Orchestra "set the stage" for the swing craze, then **Benny Goodman** (1909–1986) performed the opening scene. Goodman, an outstanding clarinetist who as a teenager had spent countless nights listening to black jazz in Chicago, loved hot music. In 1933 a gifted young critic, producer, and talent scout named **John Hammond** (1910–1987) became Goodman's manager. The following year, Goodman organized his own band and got the break of his career: his band won an audition to play regularly on *Let's Dance,* a new NBC radio program sponsored by Nabisco. The program, broadcast to over fifty local stations across the country, would feature three different bands—a sweet band, a rhumba band, and a hot band. Goodman, who won the slot for the latter, now had to compile a book of original hot arrangements. The obvious course was to hire one of the leading black arrangers then working in New York. By a fortunate coincidence, Fletcher Henderson's Orchestra had recently disbanded after a ten-year stint at the Roseland Ballroom. Hammond, always well connected in the black musical community, invited Henderson to become Goodman's staff arranger at $37.50 per arrangement. Henderson accepted, and a historic partnership was forged.

For several months the Goodman band played to positive reviews on *Let's Dance.* But in the spring of 1935 a strike at Nabisco forced the company to cancel the program. Casting about for employment, Goodman accepted the offer from the Music Corporation of America (MCA) to play a month-long engagement at the **Palomar Ballroom** in Los Angeles. Since Goodman lacked the money for a bus, the musicians drove their own cars, playing one-nighters along the way. Lukewarm receptions during the cross-country trip put them on guard. But when they arrived for an extended stopover in Denver, the musicians were

Offstage Personalities

JOHN HAMMOND (1910–1987)

Critic, record producer, talent scout, and tireless advocate of civil rights for African Americans, John Hammond played an indispensible role in the rise of swing. He was born into a wealthy Manhattan family, a Vanderbilt on his mother's side. Trained on the violin as a child, he acquired a lifelong love of classical music. As a young teenager he began spending time in Harlem, where he also discovered black jazz and the blues— music he soon began writing about passionately in the trade press.

In 1931 he dropped out of Yale University and moved to Greenwich Village, whose open-minded bohemianism and left-wing politics suited him. He wrote confident and insightful articles for fledgling jazz magazines, including *Melody Maker* and *Down Beat,* and began producing his first recording sessions. From 1933 Hammond played a crucial role in the rise of swing itself through his influence as Benny Goodman's manager. A board member of the NAACP and a fierce opponent of racism, he "discovered" over the next few years many distinguished black jazz musicians, including Billie Holiday, Count Basie, Teddy Wilson, and Charlie Christian, as well as blues singer Robert Johnson and boogie-woogie pianist Meade Lux Lewis. In 1938 he organized the now-famous "Spirituals to Swing" concert in Carnegie Hall, featuring authentic performances of black vernacular traditions, an event that marked the climax of his early career.

Turned off by modern jazz, Hammond turned his attention after World War II to blues-based popular music such as rhythm-and-blues, rock 'n' roll, and gospel. After years of obscurity in the music industry he rejuvenated his influence as a talent scout and producer in the 1960s and 1970s, again discovering major new artists such as Bob Dylan, Aretha Franklin, Bruce Springsteen, George Benson, and Stevie Ray Vaughan. ■ ■ ■

unprepared for the local antipathy to Goodman's hot repertory. "What's the matter—can't you boys play any waltzes?" the ballroom manager demanded. Disheartened, Goodman quickly ordered one hundred *stock arrangements* (mass-produced orchestrations of popular songs) and began serving up mickey-mouse-style comedy routines. After an excruciating three weeks in Denver, the band continued on to the coast.

On August 21 the band opened at the Palomar. For the first set, Goodman played it safe with sweet numbers. Then, at the urging of his sidemen, who felt they had little to lose, he called up the Henderson arrangements. "To our complete amazement, half of the crowd stopped dancing and came surging around the stand," Goodman recalled. The kids yelled and screamed and applauded wildly. They had heard Goodman's broadcasts on *Let's Dance,* they knew the pieces, they knew the soloists, and they packed the Palomar every night. "After traveling three thousand miles, we finally found people who were . . . prepared to take our music the way we wanted to play it." This engagement placed a mainstream seal of approval on hot music, made Goodman's career, and launched the Swing Era as a cultural phenomenon.

Big Business

"Goodman Wakes Up West Coast with 'Swing' Style," declared the headline in *Down Beat* magazine. Since the twenties, black musicians had used the word "swing" to describe a rhythmic sensibility, but it had not been applied to an entire style before. As a gimmicky way of catching attention for his orchestra, Goodman had recently begun billing it as Benny Goodman and His Swing Band. After the ecstatic reception at the Palomar, *Down Beat* picked up on the term and before long "swing" stood for a new and exciting style in popular music. It also stood for big business.

In the next few years hundreds of "swing bands" sprouted up around the country. Several dozen became **name bands,** that is, bands that were recognized nationally. Name bands usually hired a manager associated with a national booking agency to plan their schedules, secure record contracts, and promote them to consumers. Unlike musicians in the twenties who spent large portions of the year ensconced at a particular urban venue, swing bands tried to boost their national profiles through frequent cross-country touring on buses and trains. Early in the Swing Era bandleaders recognized a proven formula for success: (1) land a location job at a prominent hotel or ballroom; (2) build a national audience through onsite radio broadcasts and/or recordings; (3) after enough (but not too much) of this kind of long-distance exposure, take the band on the road to meet the fans face-to-face and capitalize on the media publicity; (4) recoup money lost on the road with several weeks of a lucrative theater engagement; and (5) find another location job and start the cycle over again. Bands that did not balance airtime and recordings with touring (and vice versa) generally could not build up the momentum to flourish at the national level.

In a time of economic hardship, the most successful swing musicians made very comfortable livings. As the swing craze heated up in the late 1930s, record sales began climbing again, eventually reaching 140 million in 1942. Radio technology and increasingly sophisticated mass distribution of recordings made possible a level of celebrity undreamed of previously. Extended media exposure made superstars of the leading bandleaders, who projected a glamor rivaled only by movie actors and actresses. Indeed, swing music and Hollywood constituted closely related wings of the same entertainment industry. Swing musicians themselves often took cameo roles in movies. It is no coincidence that clarinetist Artie Shaw's eight wives included movie sex symbols Ava Gardner and Lana Turner.

Fans

The rise of swing was accompanied by another new phenomenon in popular music—the emergence of "fans." According to a 1938 feature in *Life* magazine, swing fans, also known as **jitterbugs,** were "the extreme swing addicts who get so excited by its music that they cannot stand or be still while it is being played. They must prance around in wild exhibitionist dances, or yell and scream loudly. In their quieter moments, they discuss Swing with weird words like *jive, gut-bucket, dog-house, push-pipe, agony-pipe.*" Fan magazines provided detailed stories about musicians' lives, and commentary on the history, culture, and meaning of the music. The jitterbugs' obsession, together with the provocative

Chic Young, *Blondie,* April 24, 1936.

rhythms of swing music, created a generation gap between the fans and their parents. Many older adults viewed swing with suspicion, if not outright contempt (see *Blondie* cartoon).

The musicians themselves held an ambivalent view of jitterbugs, whom they also called *ickies.* On the one hand, they felt grateful to the fans for their commercial and moral support. But on the other, they were repulsed by the jitterbugs' fawning demeanor and obnoxious ballroom behavior. As *Metronome* magazine disdainfully put it, the most objectionable kind of jitterbug "places himself in a conspicuous place and annoys the [band]leader by constantly shouting out his requests such as 'Dinah' and 'Tiger Rag,' etc. He claps his hands (usually rushing or dragging the tempo), dances a sort of mad dervish dance on one foot, or trucks, while his head is held to one side, eyes are rolled up in the corners, eyebrows raised so that the forehead is furrowed with premature wrinkles. This attitude alternates with a joyously painful expression induced by pushing the brows down formidably over the eyes, resulting in a squint. The teeth are bared in a violent smile, chin down, while the head is moving in a rhythmically negative shake. . . . These are his best 'sent' expressions."

Less moody jitterbugs tried new fad dances when the bands started playing. Swing dances, most of which originated in Harlem, included Truckin' (1933), the Suzy-Q (1936), and the Scronch (1937), but the most popular and exciting was the **Lindy Hop.** Developed in Harlem ballrooms in the mid-1920s, the Lindy Hop was named after Charles Lindbergh's celebrated "hop" across the Atlantic in 1927. At the **Savoy Ballroom,** an especially important location for this dance (see Map 5), Lindy Hoppers created a flowing, athletic style that perfectly suited the swing music of the 1930s. They developed two impressive virtuosic elements: the so-called *breakaway,* in which dancers would drop hands and improvise solo steps (often during improvised solos in the band); and *aerials,* high-flying movements in which the boy would toss the girl into the air. Soon hordes of young white kids began learning the Lindy Hop. To facilitate dancing, girls wore bobby socks and saddle shoes; to accentuate their flowing movements, they sported billowing skirts. In white circles, the Lindy Hop was typically called the Jitterbug. The dance became the fans' namesake—*and* their redemption with musicians. Benny Goodman, for one, greatly admired "the chandelier-kicking type of jitterbug dancing. It's rhythmic mathematics, sometimes as gifted as the music that inspires it."

Lindyhoppers at the Savoy Ballroom, c. 1930s.

Jazz and Respectability

As we have seen, in the 1920s polite society often viewed jazz as comical, simple-minded, or immoral. But the achievements of leading black players had persuaded a few white commentators to carefully examine the music on its merits. By the early thirties an underground cult of "hot record" collectors had grown up in Europe and America. For them, jazz was not novelty music or a menace; it was an art form, to be taken as seriously as any classical symphony. It should be said that at this point, jazz players themselves often viewed their music more modestly and pragmatically. Benny Goodman said that "swing isn't as important as the icky thinks it, and certainly not as unimportant as the long-haired classicist

Venues

THE SAVOY BALLROOM

Located at 596 Lenox Avenue in Harlem, the Savoy Ballroom opened in 1926. Fifteen years later Maurice Zolotow, a white reporter, gave this vivid (if typically patronizing) firsthand account of the place during the height of the Swing Era: "From the outside, the Savoy is a drab two-story building. You buy a ticket and check your coat in the basement. You walk up two flights of steel stairs, and then suddenly you are in a sort of machine-made African jungle. The ceiling is low. Opposite you is the bandstand, where sixteen feverish Negroes blow their brains out. The dance floor is only a hundred yards wide, thirty yards long. At one corner is a long bar, which serves beer at ten cents a glass and California wine out of gallon jugs at twenty cents a glass. In the back is a row of booths, on one side a section of tables. There are thick carpets, deeply upholstered chairs, chromium furniture, indirect lights exuding a pink ray supposed to flatter dark skins. The place is packed solid, and the whole room seems to be one vast drum that some huge ebony jinni is beating. Then the dancing ceases for a few moments, as one of their favorites, saxophonist Lester Young or trumpeter Erskine Hawkins, starts to take a chorus, and two thousand of them wedge in tightly in a solid phalanx in front of the bandstand, and they begin to sway slowly in time to the music, and then faster and faster as they become one with the rhythm, until suddenly you are conscious that the floor itself is perceptibly swaying, perhaps as much as three inches. Then the dancing begins again, and you wonder how the lean-limbed black boys and girls can find room on the dance floor to do the Lindy Hop." ■ ■ ■

Maurice Zolotow, "Harlem's Great White Father," *Saturday Evening Post,* September 27, 1941, 64.

thinks it." Nevertheless, the enthusiasm of hot record collectors fostered two developments that greatly enhanced the perceived respectability of jazz: the birth of jazz criticism and the emergence of jazz concerts.

The Birth of Jazz Criticism

The first periodicals devoted to jazz appeared in European journals like the French *Revue du jazz* (1929) and the Dutch *Der Jazzwereld* (1930). The most influential commentator was French writer **Hugues Panassié,** whose book *Le Jazz Hot* (1934) established the direction of much future criticism. Dedicating the book to "Louis Armstrong—the Real King of Jazz," Panassié argued for the preeminence of black musicians in the jazz tradition. His perspective, although more critical than historical, aimed to discredit the white-dominated introductions to jazz from the 1920s written by people like Paul Whiteman and Henry Osgood.

In the United States, the repeal of Prohibition in 1933 prepared the way for Americans to consider jazz more objectively, without the moral taint of gangland associations. Jazz criticism proper emerged the following year with the establishment of ***Down Beat*** magazine and the switch to jazz coverage of ***Metronome*** magazine in 1935. Writers for these magazines often attended Ivy League colleges on the East Coast and, like many intellectuals during the Depression, espoused left-wing politics. Their political views predisposed them to sympathize with black Americans, whom they saw as a downtrodden race exploited by a white capitalist system. They came to believe, somewhat fancifully, that jazz was originally a type of black folk music. In this view, improvisation represented the black soul spontaneously crying out against oppression. This attitude was romantic, to say the least: as we have seen, blacks played early jazz primarily to better their financial condition, not to make political or artistic statements. Even so, the recognition of black leadership was significant. In 1939 a team of devoted researchers published *Jazzmen,* a groundbreaking history based on dozens of interviews with early musicians including Louis Armstrong, Sidney Bechet, and Jelly Roll Morton. Together with critical works coming out of Europe, *Jazzmen* redressed serious distortions in jazz historiography.

The First Jazz Concerts

Most jazz in the twenties had been confined to a functional role accompanying dancing or sharing a varied entertainment program with other vaudeville acts. Audiences generally did not attend nightclubs or theaters to listen to jazz per se; they came to be entertained within a jazz-drenched ambiance. The hot record collectors in the thirties, however, wanted to listen to jazz for its own sake, without distractions. Their passion for the music gave rise to a new institution: public jazz concerts at which audiences were expected to give reverent, undivided attention to the musicians on stage.

The jazz concert has its roots in **jam sessions,** informal events in which players came together after hours to improvise lengthy solos, share musical ideas, experiment with new approaches, and compete in cutting contests. In the 1930s, to satisfy the desire of fans to hear such uninhibited and seemingly "authentic" jazz performances, various self-appointed impresarios began organizing jam sessions for public consumption. At the same time, several nightclubs on 52nd Street began providing jazz for listening only. One of them, the Onyx Club, sponsored an important early jazz concert at the Imperial Theater on May 24, 1936. The concert featured a smorgasbord of styles and players, including Louis Armstrong, Meade Lux Lewis, the Casa Loma Orchestra, and Artie Shaw. As Shaw recalled, "This was the first time such a concert had ever been given in New York City. The whole idea was brand new, since up to this time American dance music had always been regarded as a sort of bastard child of 'real' music. . . . Here, for the first time . . . 'swing' music . . . was something to be listened to for itself. Not the words, not the tune, not the popular melody—but the jazz idiom."

The small-group jam-session format inspired two important concert series that emerged in the next decade. In 1942 the guitarist Eddie Condon began a series of public jam sessions devoted to Chicago-style jazz in New York's Town Hall. Two years later, a young jazz aficionado named Norman Granz started a concert series presenting more recent styles at the Los Angeles Philharmonic Auditorium. In subsequent years Granz's productions continued to be billed as **Jazz at the Philharmonic (JATP),** even though the musicians actually performed in different cities and concert halls. Consistently staging performances by leading black musicians, Jazz at the Philharmonic became the most influential of the jam-session concerts (for more on Granz and JATP, see Chapter 16).

The Traditionalist Movement

In addition to writing criticism and promoting jazz concerts, hot record collectors spent a great deal of time compiling discographies of early jazz recordings. These labors prompted the rediscovery in the late 1930s of New Orleans–style music, alternately called the New Orleans revival, the Dixieland revival, or the **traditionalist movement.** In 1936 Louis Armstrong spurred this interest with the publication of his first autobiography, *Swing That Music.* Two years later, John Hammond produced a concert in Carnegie Hall entitled **"Spirituals to Swing,"** which consisted of an aural tour of black musical history. To meet the needs of a growing population of traditionalist fans, new record labels started rereleasing jazz records from the twenties, and magazines specializing in New Orleans music began circulation.

Around the same time, a number of white writers were trying to locate half-forgotten early jazz figures as part of the research efforts that went into the creation of *Jazzmen.* Their most significant discovery was **Bunk Johnson** (1889–1949), an old New Orleans trumpet player and contemporary of King Oliver who claimed (falsely) to have taught Louis Armstrong. Dogged researchers eventually found Johnson working in New Iberia, Louisiana, bought him new teeth and clothes, and brought him to New York, where he spent his remaining days performing and recording with other New Orleans veterans and basking in favorable publicity. In the next few years Sidney Bechet, Jelly Roll Morton, Kid Ory, and Johnny Dodds all emerged from obscurity and began revitalized careers as authentic representatives of New Orleans jazz—a music that traditionalist critics increasingly viewed as the original and "true" species of jazz, untainted by commercialism. Even Armstrong, who spent the Swing Era prosperously conducting big bands modeled on that of Guy Lombardo (and dodging charges of commercialism), switched in 1947 to a New Orleans small-group format with the creation of his All-Stars.

Inspired by these events, a group of young white musicians assumed the responsibility of inaugurating a new generation of New Orleans–style jazz. In memory of the Original Dixieland Jazz Band, they called their music **Dixieland** (a term sometimes applied retroactively to the music of King Oliver and other early New Orleans players as well). An important pioneer of white Dixieland was trumpeter Lu Watters, who organized his Yerba Buena Jazz Band near San Francisco in 1940. Under the influence of Watters, his protégé, trombonist Turk Murphy, and others, the traditionalist movement gained momentum after World War II and has continued into the twenty-first century. But New Orleans style is no longer equated, as in days of old, with sin and debauchery. Judging from its ubiquitous presence in political campaigns and car commercials, Dixieland jazz now appears to stand for all-American values and the joy of life.

Bunk Johnson.

Dixieland a term that refers to New Orleans style, and specifically to the music of white players who participated in the traditionalist movement of the 1940s and after.

Chapter *11* Black Bands

From the Jazz Age through the Swing Era, the paramount goal of black jazz musicians remained largely the same: to achieve commercial and popular success on a par with leading white players. In the 1930s for the first time that dream seemed within reach. Although white swing bands enjoyed greater fame and a multitude of advantages in ways large and small, a few black orchestras consistently ranked high in swing magazines' lists of the most popular bands. Through radio broadcasts the music of Fletcher Henderson, Jimmie Lunceford, Count Basie, and Duke Ellington became familiar not only to the black community but also to thousands of white households throughout the country.

These same individuals faced severe racial discrimination along the path to success. Yet for most jazz historians and critics they represent the most significant bandleaders of the Swing Era. Without denigrating the genuine artistic achievements of white leaders such as Benny Goodman and Tommy Dorsey, many writers consider the best work of Ellington and Basie to be the most original and inventive jazz of the period. Moreover, when one considers that Goodman and Dorsey hired blacks such as Henderson, Jimmy Mundy, Edgar Sampson, and Sy Oliver to arrange their music, it becomes clear that—as in the twenties—African Americans provided the aesthetic underpinnings for swing, despite the greater press coverage accorded whites.

Uncertain Fortunes

After Benny Goodman's spectacular success at the Palomar Ballroom, black musicians saw a chance to capitalize on the popularity of a musical style in which they particularly excelled. From 1935 to 1938, the market for swing heated up rapidly, leading to a proliferation of new bands across the country and bringing prosperity to black and white bands alike. But by 1939 the swing economy cooled as supply began to exceed demand. The most famous name bands continued to do well, but others felt the pinch of a saturated market. Not surprisingly, black bands suffered disproportionately. As *Down Beat* baldly acknowledged in 1940: "The truth is that the public will absorb only a very limited number of Negro bands."

When America entered World War II in 1941, the swing industry revived with the start of munitions manufacturing. Because the draft continuously drained bands of musicians, there were plenty of jobs for qualified players. But the rationing of gasoline and rubber led to a ban on "nonessential" automobile travel—including buses—for much of 1942–1943. This forced swing bands to tour the country by rail, a mode of transportation that served the main urban centers but not the usual rural stops. Sensing an opportunity created by this geographical concentration of talent, hotel managers in the big cities raised their entertainment fees to attract the leading white bands in the country. Black bands, by contrast, had to subsist on railroad tours of one-nighters, often in the South, where the threat of physical violence loomed constantly. In southern trains, black musicians were forced to sit in the **Jim Crow car,** a stuffy, soot-filled compartment located immediately behind the engine.

Worn down by the physical exhaustion of constant touring and the unremitting burden of racism, some black musicians gave up and returned home. The most gifted young players of the 1940s eventually forsook their careers as big band musicians to pursue small-group opportunities in nightclubs around New York City. Their explorations led to the rise of modern jazz, a development we shall survey in Chapter 17. But by and large, their elders in the swing industry stayed true to the music they had helped to found, leaving a cultural legacy all the richer for the sacrifices they endured.

Fletcher Henderson

Fletcher Henderson played a seminal role in the swing movement. In the mid-1920s, as we have seen, he had become the first to develop a swinging large ensemble (see Chapter 8). Ten years later, Benny Goodman rose to stardom on Henderson's music. At one time or another, dozens of other bands, both black and white, also used his arrangements. Partly through Goodman's prominence, Henderson's approach to the big band became the primary model for many other swing arrangers.

And yet his career as a bandleader during the Swing Era was rocky at best. Many of the problems stemmed from Henderson's own inability to effectively manage his band's business or impose discipline on his sidemen. In the twenties he had become leader of the Roseland orchestra almost by accident: the other musicians believed his education and handsome appearance would make him a good front man. In 1928 Henderson was seriously injured in a car accident; thereafter, his wife recalled, "He just changed. Everything would seem comical to him and he never [aspired] to go higher than he was. He never had much business qualities anyway, but after that accident, he had even less." With the onset of the Depression the band declined steadily, even as Henderson was producing some of his best arrangements—"King Porter Stomp," "Down South Camp Meeting," and "Wrappin' It Up," among others. In 1934 the band broke up.

At this point, John Hammond introduced Henderson's music to Goodman, who immediately liked it. "Fletcher's ideas were far ahead of anyone else's," Goodman later recalled. "After I heard one or two of his arrangements, I just couldn't get enough of them. Each one was a little classic." Some have accused Goodman of exploiting Henderson, and certainly he demanded a great deal, sometimes calling at 4:00 A.M. to request a new arrangement for a 10:00 A.M. recording session. Nevertheless, Goodman's patronage reinvigorated Henderson's career. After six months of arranging for *Let's Dance,* the new money and publicity allowed Henderson to organize his own band again. In early 1936, his band opened at the **Grand Terrace Ballroom** in Chicago. Henderson made frequent

Fletcher Henderson and His Orchestra, c. 1935.

radio broadcasts from the Grand Terrace, and he also made several recordings, one of which, "Christopher Columbus," became a big hit.

His career might have taken off then, if only he had followed up on his good fortune with an aggressive touring campaign. After the release of "Christopher Columbus," trumpeter Joe Thomas recalled, "Fletcher was hot. Everyone was asking for him. . . . Fletcher should have gone out on the road then, [but] by the time he got ready . . . somebody else had something big, and Fletcher couldn't get started." Another problem was Henderson's refusal to demand high performance standards from his musicians. As Garvin Bushell, one of his sidemen, admitted, Henderson's renditions of his own arrangements could not compete with Goodman's. Goodman—a notorious disciplinarian—rehearsed his band relentlessly, producing clean, exciting performances of Henderson's music. By comparison, Henderson's band appeared, ironically, to be a sloppy imitation of Goodman's.

Henderson's popularity declined each year, dropping from ninth place in the 1936 *Metronome* Readers' Poll to thirty-third place by the end of the decade. When the swing industry foundered in 1939, Henderson disbanded and sought refuge working as Goodman's full-time staff arranger. Within two years, though, the strain of constantly producing arrangements had eroded his health. With Goodman's blessing and financial backing, Henderson reorganized his own band again in 1941. Duplicating a by now familiar pattern, this band limped through two years of one-nighters before finally expiring. By 1945 Henderson was arranging for Goodman again. After suffering a debilitating stroke, he died in 1952.

Swing Style

Despite Henderson's administrative failures, his arrangements helped to establish conventions of swing style. The typical big band instrumentation from the mid-1930s consisted of three trumpets, two or three trombones, four saxophones (usually three altos and a tenor, two altos and two tenors, or two altos, a tenor, and a baritone), which also doubled on clarinet, and four accompanying instruments—piano, guitar, string bass, and drums. Swing arrangers organized these instruments into **sections** of trumpets, trombones, saxophones, and "rhythm." The more affluent bands sometimes included orchestral instruments like French horns, violins, and harp.

The swing rhythm section substituted guitar and string bass for the banjo and tuba combination of much earlier jazz. It also changed the rhythmic emphasis on tunes in medium or fast tempos. Whereas on 1920s pieces such as Louis Armstrong's "Potato Head Blues" or "Struttin' with Some Barbecue" the bass player marked out a two-beat feel, tunes in similar tempos during the Swing Era favored a **four-beat.** The rhythm section's emphasis on all four beats in each measure created a foot-tapping forward momentum that lay at the heart of the swing style.

The need to coordinate so many instruments insured that homophony would outweigh polyphony in most big band arrangements. In order to vary the predominantly homophonic texture, Henderson developed an influential approach to big band orchestration by pitting one section against another in alternating patterns—a technique known as **antiphonal voicing.** Antiphonal voicing sometimes takes the form of one section playing the melody while another echoes with background figures. In other cases the two sections will alternate passages of more or less equal importance. Henderson also pioneered the **saxophone soli** (SOE-lee), a passage featuring the entire saxophone section playing in harmony.

Henderson's most important contribution, perhaps, was his ability to transfer the jazz soloist's style of improvised melody and phrasing to the arranged portions of a piece. In 1939, Goodman acknowledged this gift: "What Fletcher really could do so wonderfully was to take a tune like 'Sometimes I'm Happy'

FLETCHER HENDERSON AND HIS ORCHESTRA, *"Wrappin' It Up"* (1934)

Fletcher Henderson's "Wrappin' It Up," in ABA′C song form, constitutes a catalogue of swing features. Notice, first of all, the smoothly pulsating *four-beat* laid down by the rhythm section—a far cry from the jerky, frenetic rhythmic textures of the 1920s. Now let's turn to the matter of *antiphonal voicing,* a most prominent feature. During the introduction the brass alternate punchy syncopations with a chugging line in the saxophones. The antiphony becomes progressively narrower: for the first four bars the choirs alternate at a distance of one measure; then they close the gap to half measures until finally the two groups play as one. A similar narrowing of antiphony takes place during the melody: in the first A-section the brass punctuate the saxophone melody at two-measure intervals; in the B-section they cut back to one measure. These textural compressions have the effect of building tension and excitement.

In the last chorus Henderson takes different approaches to orchestration: in the first A-section the trumpets trade one-bar segments with a *clarinet trio.* During the last A-section Henderson calls for a *saxophone soli,* featuring the entire section in four-part harmony. This is immediately followed by a **shout chorus,** a climactic section (not necessarily a complete chorus) for the full band. How does this sort of passage differ from a New Orleans outchorus? The *outchorus,* featuring fewer players, builds tension through polyphony, while the *shout chorus* exploits the strength of the big band through massed homophony, creating the combined effect of a "shout."

antiphonal voicing a big band arranging technique that pits one section against another (e.g., reeds vs. brass) in alternating patterns.

shout chorus in big band jazz, a loud, homophonic ensemble chorus intended to climax the performance.

LISTENING CHART 12

Fletcher Henderson and His Orchestra, "Wrappin' It Up" (Henderson)

CD 1 / Tracks 54–57

Recorded 12 September 1934, New York City / Decca 157; mx 38604-B

Henry "Red" Allen, Irving Randolph, Russell Smith (trumpet), Keg Johnson, Claude Jones (trombone), Buster Bailey, Hilton Jefferson, Russell Procope (alto saxophone, clarinet), Ben Webster (tenor saxophone), Horace Henderson (piano), Lawrence Lucie (guitar), Elmer James (bass), Walter Johnson (drums)

Style: Big band swing			**Form: ABA′C song form**

			Introduction
			Ensemble: *antiphonal voicing* between brass and saxophones gets progressively narrower:
54	0:00	4 bars	One measure each
	0:04	2 bars	Half-measures
	0:07	2 bars	Brass and saxophones play together
	1st Chorus		**Melody**
	0:09	A (8)	*Antiphonal voicing:* saxophones state the melody while the brass add punctuations every two measures
	0:19	B (8)	*Continued,* with antiphony narrowing to one measure
	0:28	A′ (8)	Now melody stated in varied form by the full ensemble (i.e., without the antiphony)
	0:37	C (8)	*Continued*
	2nd Chorus		**Alto saxophone solo: Hilton Jefferson**
	0:48	A (8)	Hilton Jefferson plays lyrical, wide-ranging solo based on the
	0:57	B (8)	harmony rather than the melody of the song, while trumpets
	1:07	A′ (8)	and trombones provide sustained background chords.
	1:16	C (8)	
	3rd Chorus		**Trumpet solo: Red Allen**
55	1:25	A (8)	Kicked off by the other trumpets, Red Allen at first continues their reiterated jabs, then plays a smoothly flowing solo. Behind him the saxophones play an active line of their own, creating a polyphonic texture with Allen.
	1:34	B (8)	Ensemble: brass play "breathless" rocking line in antiphony with saxophones

1:44	A′ (8)	*Allen resumes his solo:* Again building on his ensemble lead-in, Allen ascends for a dynamic opening
1:53	C (8)	
	4th Chorus	**Closing ensemble chorus**
2:02	One-bar lead-in	Ensemble
2:03	A (8)	Antiphonal voicing: trumpets vs. clarinet trio
2:13	B (8)	**Clarinet solo: Buster Bailey**
		Bailey plays with liquid fluency to the accompaniment of sustained chords in the brass
2:22	A′ (8)	**Saxophone soli**
		Saxophones play together in chordal homophony
2:32	C (8)	**Shout chorus**
		Full band plays high and loud to climax the piece

(Track markers: 56 at 2:02, 57 at 2:22)

Record Labels

DECCA

From small beginnings the Decca label rose to become one of the most prolific documenters of black swing, by the early 1940s taking its place alongside Victor and Columbia as one of the three "majors" (i.e., major record companies). Founded in Great Britain in 1929 by Edward Lewis, Decca opened an American branch in 1934 and began issuing race records. This opening serendipitously coincided with other signal events in the rise of swing, including Benny Goodman's appearance on the radio program *Let's Dance* and the establishment of *Down Beat* magazine. Under the direction of black producer and talent scout, J. Mayo Williams (one of the few in an industry dominated by whites), Decca recorded many now-classic discs, starting with a seminal batch by Fletcher Henderson that included "Wrappin' It Up" and "Down South Camp Meetin'" (1934), and continuing with long runs by Jimmie Lunceford (1934–1945), Count Basie (1937–1939), Louis Armstrong (1935–1954), Ella Fitzgerald (1935–1955), Andy Kirk (1936–1946), and Lionel Hampton (1941–1950), to name only a few of the most prominent. ■ ■ ■

and really improvise on it himself. . . . Even [during solos] the background [parts] for the rest of the band would be in the same consistent vein, so that the whole thing really hung together and sounded unified."

Jimmie Lunceford

The shrewd and elegant **Jimmie Lunceford** (1902–1947) manifested a leadership style that seems just the opposite of Henderson's laissez-faire approach. He grew up in Denver, Colorado, where he studied several musical instruments under the direction of Paul Whiteman's father, Wilberforce Whiteman. In 1926 he graduated from Fisk University with a music degree. After briefly teaching high school in Memphis, he organized a band and began performing professionally. In 1930 the band, which was then a cooperative venture, made its first recordings under the name, the Chickasaw Syncopators. For the next three years the band added important new members, most notably the gifted trumpeter and arranger, **Sy Oliver** (1910–1988). In 1933 Lunceford became the official leader and—with his manager, Harold F. Oxley—the sole owner of the band.

Like Goodman and Henderson, Lunceford got his big break in 1934, when his band secured a six-month engagement at the Cotton Club. Through regular on-site radio broadcasts and popular recordings like "White Heat" and "Jazznocracy," Lunceford soon developed a national reputation and began an endless series of road trips. He demanded near-perfection from his men in their music and comportment but paid them relatively low wages. Sy Oliver once said that "Jimmie was definitely a leader. He was a strict disciplinarian, like a teacher in a schoolroom, but he was consistent in everything he did, and that gave the fellows in the band a feeling of security." The band became renowned for its virtuosity, impeccable appearance, and flashy showmanship. The trumpets tossed their horns into the air in unison, the trombones executed similar choreography with their slides, and all the brass fanned their bells with derby hats. At a gargantuan "battle of the bands" held November 18, 1940, at New York's Manhattan Center, Lunceford's was the only organization forced to exceed its fifteen-minute allotment on stage because of hysterical ovations from the audience. His competitors, it should be noted, included Benny Goodman, Glenn Miller, Count Basie, Glen Gray, Les Brown, Guy Lombardo, and twenty-two other bands.

In the late 1930s, the Lunceford band developed a distinctive and well-integrated style, largely through the ingenious arrangements of Sy Oliver. Lunceford's music was ambitious, difficult, quirky, and emphasized brilliant ensemble passages rather than soloists. The band became famous for the so-called **Lunceford two-beat,** an easy groove in moderate tempo of which "Organ Grinder's Swing," one of Oliver's best pieces, offers a good example. It also demonstrates a characteristic mix of novelty and artistic subtlety that, oddly, does not sound incongruous. The piece begins with a children's street song ("I like coffee, I like tea . . .") played in harmony by muted trumpet, muted trombone, and clarinet, with wood-block accompaniment, to evoke the sound of an organ-grinder. This passage shifts abruptly to an eight-bar blues featuring growling trumpet and a boogie-woogie bass line played by two baritone saxophones.

Taking pride in his appetite for road work, Lunceford once boasted: "We do a couple of hundred one-nighters a year, fifteen to twenty weeks of theaters, maybe one four-week location [job] and two weeks of vacation. All in all, we cover about forty thousand miles a year!" His men, however, were less sanguine.

In 1942 they met with Lunceford at a YMCA in Harlem to protest the decrepit condition of their tour bus and ask for a pay raise. But Lunceford was unmoved. "He called it mutiny and everything else," Trummy Young recalled. "He said he couldn't do any better, and that was that. The trouble started there and the guys began leaving one by one." Although the band declined rapidly thereafter, Lunceford continued his spartan work regimen. In 1947 he died of a heart attack while on tour in Oregon.

Count Basie

One of Lunceford's biggest admirers was a young bandleader and pianist named **William "Count" Basie** (1904–1984). From modest beginnings, Basie built up a band full of dynamic, influential soloists and redefined the meaning of swing for many listeners. Together with Duke Ellington, Basie represents the apex of big band music in the Swing Era.

Born and raised in Red Bank, New Jersey, Basie moved to New York in the early twenties where he met James P. Johnson, Fats Waller, and other stride pianists. Every day he went to the Lincoln Theater to hear Waller, who became his mentor and chief influence. Basie also toured with several vaudeville companies. During a tour in 1927, Basie was hospitalized in Kansas City for spinal meningitis. He stayed in that city for the next eight years, absorbing local jazz traditions and developing a highly original piano style. The southwest bands that he heard and played with are sometimes called **territory bands** (i.e., bands in "the territories") to distinguish them from those active in the major jazz centers of New Orleans, Chicago, and New York.

Kansas City

In the 1920s and 1930s Kansas City was one of the fastest-living towns in America. A former police officer recalled that Kansas City "was wide open for everything. There was no control whatsoever. There was no law." The political boss Thomas J. Pendergast turned a blind eye to gambling and prostitution, and kept the liquor flowing freely during Prohibition. Jazz, blues, and boogie-woogie could be heard throughout the black entertainment district centered at 18th Street and Vine on the Missouri side of town (see Map 6). Even the Depression could not dent the economic base upon which Pendergast founded his nighttime playground.

In 1929 Basie joined the leading orchestra in Kansas City at the time, a band led by **Bennie Moten** (1894–1935). Mixing local jazz traditions, Moten and his sidemen achieved a blend that by the early thirties represented the principal alternative to the big band style coming out of New York. The so-called **Kansas City style** had several distinguishing features:

■ The music was based on **head arrangements**—informal structures simple enough for players to remember without notating. Often worked out collectively in rehearsal or even during a performance, head arrangements tended to originate spontaneously.

■ Kansas City jazz was *riff-based;* that is, the melodic content of arrangements was highly compact and repetitive to facilitate memorization and generate rhythmic intensity.

■ Kansas City jazz was *blues-based* in both form and expression. Tunes that did not adhere to the blues format usually followed AABA song form.

Kansas City style a 1930s big band style that featured head arrangements, riff-based melodies, and improvising soloists.

head arrangement an informal musical structure simple enough for players to remember without writing down.

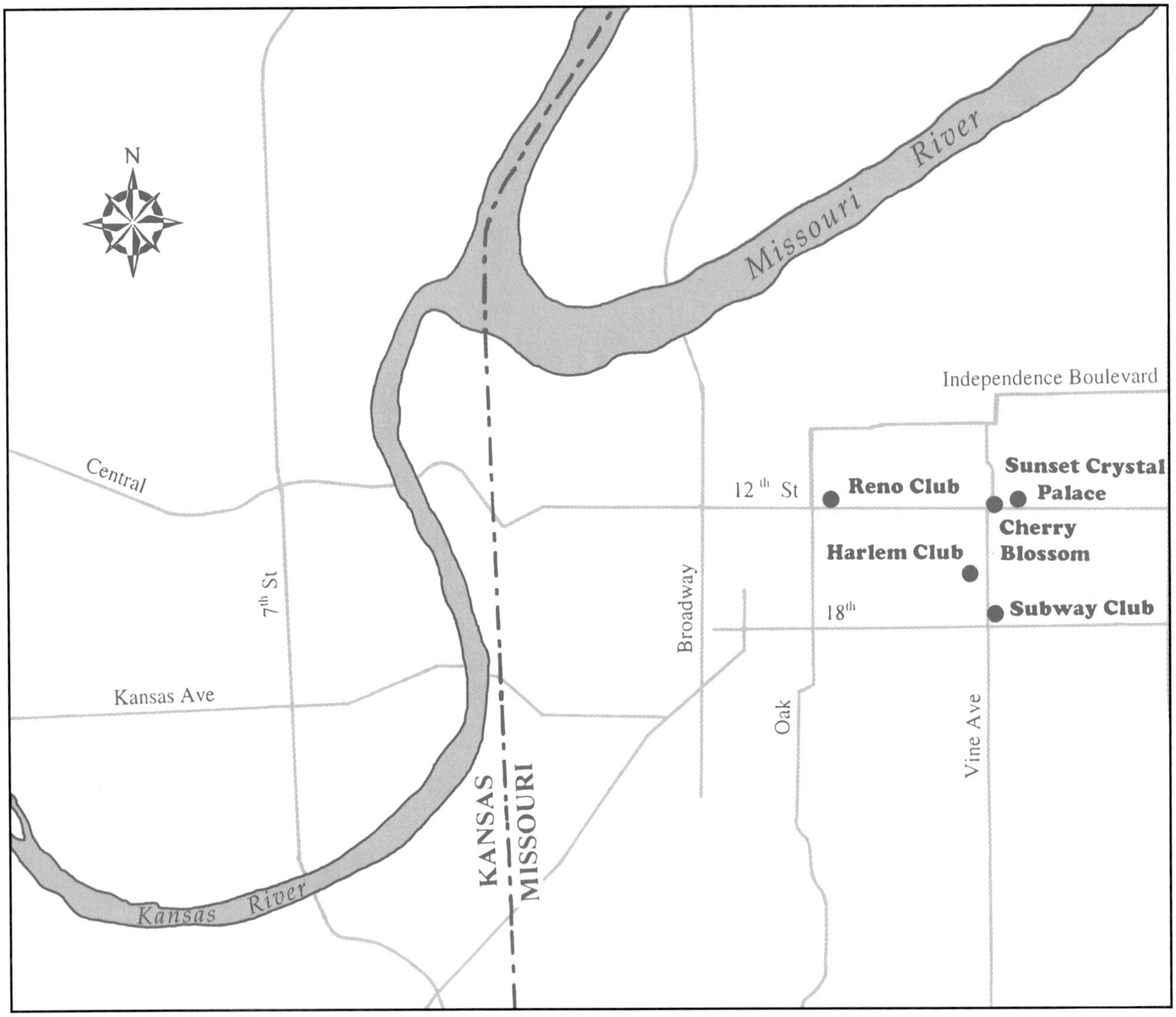

Map 6. Kansas City.

- Kansas City musicians played with a particularly buoyant and well-integrated sense of swing.
- All these features provided a loose, hospitable environment for improvising soloists, the primary focus of Kansas City jazz.
- More than other regional substyles, Kansas City jazz nurtured the development of the saxophone as a solo instrument. It is no coincidence that the two leading saxophone innovators of the 1930s and 1940s, Lester Young and Charlie Parker, entered the national arena from Kansas City.

The National Stage

When in 1935 Bennie Moten died suddenly on the operating table, Basie organized a nine-piece band using several of Moten's sidemen. Shortly thereafter, the band began a long engagement at the **Reno Club** (see Map 6). According to one

Count Basie and His Orchestra in the Columbia recording studio, 1940. *Far left,* Count Basie; *fourth from left,* Lester Young; *far right,* Harry "Sweets" Edison; *fifth from right,* Dicky Wells; *sixth from right,* Buck Clayton.

regular patron, "The Reno Club was a place that had nickel hot dogs and hamburgers, nickel beer, and whiskey for fifteen cents. It also had a floor show, complete with chorus line and three acts. The 'scale' of the musicians was $15 a week, and the hours were from eight 'til four, except on Saturday, when it was 12 solid hours from eight to eight. It was a seven-day week, naturally, and nobody got rich, least of all the club owner." From the Reno, Basie and his men made broadcasts every week on an obscure station called W9XBY.

In 1936 the ever-vigilant John Hammond discovered the Basie band on the radio one night while staying in Chicago with the Benny Goodman orchestra. Thrilled with Basie's music, Hammond flew to Kansas City and arranged contracts for the band with both MCA and Decca records. The three-year contract with Decca paid Basie a miserly $750 for twenty-four sides (twelve discs) with no royalties. The chagrined Hammond later said the contract "was typical of the underscale deals which record companies imposed on unsophisticated Negro and 'country' artists."

The year 1938 marked the beginning of Basie's rise to preeminence. In January, Basie and some of his leading soloists played during the jam-session segment of Benny Goodman's highly successful debut concert at Carnegie Hall. Later that same night the Basie band appeared at the Savoy Ballroom for a "battle of the bands" with the undefeated Chick Webb and his Orchestra. To universal surprise, Basie was named the winner of that contest by musicians and the press. Even more significant was the band's lengthy engagement at the

Famous Door on 52nd Street six months later. Critics and audiences responded to Basie's music with tremendous enthusiasm. As one commentator has noted, the Famous Door was "to Basie what the Cotton Club had been for Duke Ellington and the Palomar to Benny Goodman." In the late thirties Basie made a number of acclaimed recordings, including "One O'Clock Jump" (1937), "Jumpin' at the Woodside" (1938), and "Taxi War Dance" (1939).

Despite this success, Basie continued to face problems familiar to all black bandleaders. Basie's momentum flagged in 1939, when his business manager, Willard Alexander, left MCA to join the William Morris agency. Without Alexander's support, Basie found himself exploited by MCA. His road manager complained, "We haven't had a location job with air time in a year. Some weeks we work every night, jumping 500 miles a night. Other weeks we lay off." The overhead of constant touring had consumed Basie's profits. At the same time, MCA charged inordinately high fees; for example, in one year when Basie sustained a net loss of $11,000, the company took $19,000. Eventually, Basie paid a $10,000 penalty to break his contract with MCA so he could join Alexander at William Morris.

The Subtleties of Swing

In the late 1930s Basie won acclaim for his band's unparalleled unity of swing feel. Other bands, including white bands, were frequently described as "swinging." But swing rhythm was not a monolithic construct; it varied subtly in both form and feeling from one band to another. Basie opened people's ears to a refinement of rhythmic momentum that was genuinely new and wholly infectious.

Just as it is impossible to adequately define swing itself, so it is hard to describe the difference in Basie's approach. But it seems related to his rhythm section. Jo Jones, the drummer, created a light rhythmic accompaniment by transferring the four-beat emphasis from the bass drum to the **high-hat,** a tree of opposing cymbals operated with a foot pedal. Jones often played an

COUNT BASIE AND HIS ORCHESTRA, *"Taxi War Dance"* (1939)

The title of this recording, "Taxi War Dance," is a play on a common dance-hall expression, *taxi dance* (also known as a "dime-a-dance"). In a taxi dance, a male patron paid 10¢—the price of a taxi—to dance with a ballroom hostess for one tune. The piece features tenor saxophonist Lester Young. Or, in the inimitable words of Basie himself, "Lester had the meat on 'Taxi War Dance,' and it was a very big hit with his fans. . . . [Trombonist] Dicky Wells had himself a nice little helping [i.e., played a good solo] on that one, too, which has also been singled out by a few writers . . . as belonging with some of the best work he ever did with us."

This piece has all the features of a head arrangement, even if it was probably written down at some point. Notice that the first chorus does not start with a melody, but with a solo. When the full band does come in, in the third chorus, the horns play simple, repetitive riffs in call-and-response fashion. The band achieves textural variety by **trading fours**—that is, alternating four-bar phrases—with tenor saxophonist, Lester Young. (During the *coda*, soloists trade twos as well.) The *bridges* (B-sections) in the third and fourth choruses offer a good example of Basie's solo style.

trading fours when a soloist alternates four-bar phrases with another soloist or the ensemble; less common alternations include *trading twos, eights,* or *twelves.*

LISTENING CHART 13

Count Basie and His Orchestra, "Taxi War Dance"
(Basie-Young, arr. Clayton)

CD 1 / Tracks 58–61

RECORDED 19 MARCH 1939, NEW YORK CITY / VOCALION 4748; MX 24242-1

Buck Clayton, Shad Collins, Harry Edison, Ed Lewis (trumpet), Dan Minor, Benny Morton, Dicky Wells (trombone), Earle Warren, Jack Washington (alto saxophone), Buddy Tate, Lester Young (tenor saxophone), Count Basie (piano), Freddie Green (guitar), Walter Page (bass), Jo Jones (drums)

Style: Big band swing			**Form: AABA song form**

			Introduction
58	0:00	(4)	Piano solo: Count Basie plays boogie-woogie vamp figure in left hand
	0:04	(4)	Add trumpets and trombones
		1st Chorus	**Tenor saxophone solo: Lester Young**
	0:09	A (8)	Young begins his solo by quoting "Old Man River," then goes on to develop a series of ideas in turn
	0:18	A (8)	
	0:27	B (8)	Bridge in minor mode; Basie's *comping* especially noticeable here
	0:36	A (8)	
			Interlude
	0:45	(2)	Basie revives boogie-woogie vamp amid brass punches
		2nd Chorus	**Trombone solo: Dickie Wells**
59	0:47	A (8)	Wells swoops and swells in a manner that reflects his debt
	0:56	A (8)	to *tailgate* style, but with an urbanity and sophistication
	1:05	B (8)	appropriate for the more elegant swing idiom
	1:14	A (8)	
		3rd Chorus	**Trading fours: ensemble vs. Lester Young**
60	1:23	A (4)	Ensemble call-and-response: trombones vs. trumpets
	1:28	(4)	Tenor saxophone solo: Lester Young
	1:33	A (8)	Trading fours, *continued*
	1:42	B (8)	Piano solo: Basie
	1:51	A (8)	Trading fours, *continued*
		4th Chorus	
	2:00	A (8)	Trading fours, *continued*
			Ensemble: trombone line stays the same, but trumpets play continuously this time, eliminating sense of call-and-response; Basie adds boogie-woogie ostinato, further increasing the tension

	2:09	A (8)	Trading fours, *continued*
	2:19	B (8)	Piano solo: Basie
	2:28	A (8)	Trading fours, *continued*
			Notice Young's *alternate fingering* here

Coda: trading twos

61	2:37	(2)	Piano: Basie
	2:39	(2)	Tenor saxophone: Young
	2:42	(2)	Bass: Walter Page
	2:44	(2)	Drums: Jo Jones
	2:46	(2)	Ensemble

alternating open-closed pattern emphasizing beats two and four, creating a boom-CHICK-boom-CHICK effect. Walter Page was among the first bassists to develop a **walking bass** line—that is, playing on every beat in the measure—that sounded smooth and propulsive at the same time. Guitarist Freddie Green also reinforced the four-beat style, playing strummed chords in a continuous CHUNK-CHUNK-CHUNK-CHUNK pattern. Basie departed furthest from convention. Instead of providing yet another line of four-beat emphasis, he developed an accompaniment of sporadic, unpredictable, syncopated chords. This accompaniment, now called **comping** (a shorthand term for "accompanying"), greatly influenced modern jazz pianists of the 1940s.

As a soloist Basie replaced the verbose virtuosity of his stride heritage with a spare, repetitive style that was unique to him. In this style, the left hand is almost inactive, while the right plays short, simple, rhythmically precise riffs in the upper register. Basie's minimalism provides an ideal complement to the inexorable rhythms laid down by Jones, Page, and Green.

Basie's Saxophones

Basie furthered the Kansas City tradition of strong saxophones, especially tenor saxophones. "The band has always been built from the rhythm section to the tenors and then to the rest of the band," Basie once remarked. During all-night jam sessions and cutting contests in Kansas City, Basie's tenor players had often dominated the solo space in the band's performances. At the national level that role continued in the playing of master soloists **Lester Young** (1909–1959), Herschel Evans, and Buddy Tate. Young and Evans, in particular, enlivened performances by juxtaposing their contrasting styles on pieces like "Doggin' Around" (1938). We will examine Young's style more closely in Chapter 14.

walking bass a bass line consisting of one note for every beat in the measure.

comping a style of piano accompaniment emphasizing sporadic, syncopated chords.

Duke Ellington

Chapter 12

n some respects, Duke Ellington represents the oddball of the Swing Era. To be
sure, he anticipated the swing craze—at
least in spirit—with his 1932 recording, "It
Don't Mean a Thing If It Ain't Got That Swing."
Like the Henderson Orchestra, Ellington's band
was swinging long before Goodman shook the
Palomar to its moorings. And yet Ellington also seemed strangely outside the
whole swing movement. As Count Basie once remarked, "So far as this guy
Ellington is concerned, you can never tell what he's going to do. I mean, he'll
concert you all, and then he'll swing you all, too, you understand, when he's
ready to. He's not limited to anything."

Basie's comment identifies a central fact of Ellington's music: it did not fit
into conventional pigeonholes. Even his most "swinging" pieces often sounded
exotic, nonconformist, and somehow mysteriously constructed. Ellington himself detested labels, including "jazz" and "swing." Perhaps this explains why he
felt free to explore avenues normally reserved for classical composers—by writing extended works and performing in Carnegie Hall, for instance. For Ellington,
oppositions like "jazz" and "classical" made no sense; he aspired to create music,
as he put it, "beyond category." The recent tide of critics who consider Ellington
America's greatest composer, jazz or otherwise, suggests that he succeeded.

The Thirties

By the early 1930s Ellington had achieved a level of fame that insulated him from
many of the racial and economic problems faced by other bandleaders. At the
Cotton Club he won a national audience through NBC radio broadcasts and the
steady production of records (see Chapter 8). In 1930 his haunting "Mood
Indigo" became his first international hit and his band appeared in the Hollywood movie short *Check and Double Check*. The following year Ellington left the
Cotton Club and began touring the country under the management of **Irving
Mills,** a white businessman who had represented Ellington since 1926. Unlike
other bands that had to travel by bus or car, Ellington's men rode the rails in two
private Pullman sleeping cars. His stature was such that the Hoover administration invited Ellington, along with several other black dignitaries, to visit the
White House. In the summer of 1933 he made his first trip abroad, drawing
enthusiastic acclaim in England, France, and Holland. That year *Fortune* magazine disclosed that Ellington's band grossed $250,000 a year.

Duke Ellington, 1933.

During a time when concert hall composers were abandoning avant-garde techniques in an effort to reach a wider audience, Ellington was already popular enough to enjoy the luxury of writing frankly experimental music. In the early thirties, as we have seen, R. D. Darrell wrote a bold article praising the artistry of Ellington's Cotton Club pieces; in a similar vein the English critic Constant Lambert exclaimed: "I know of nothing in Ravel so dextrous in treatment as the varied solos in the middle of the ebullient 'Hot and Bothered,' and nothing in Stravinsky more dynamic than the final section." Emboldened by such highbrow recognition, perhaps, Ellington began writing **extended works,** pieces that exceeded the roughly three-minute standard of most dance music. Because of length restrictions imposed by 78 rpm recording technology, for years European symphonic works had been sliced up in the recording studio and distributed on multiple discs. Ellington now recorded his own longer pieces in the same manner. His "Creole Rhapsody" (1931) and "Diminuendo and Crescendo in Blue" (1937) each occupied two sides of a record, while the twelve-minute "Reminiscing in Tempo" (1935) required four sides on two complete discs.

The extended works, however, did not dim Ellington's popularity with ballroom and radio audiences. These listeners thrilled to his growing body of popular song hits, including "Rockin' in Rhythm" (1931), "Sophisticated Lady" (1933), "Solitude" (1934), and "In a Sentimental Mood" (1935). Ellington's music and his professional example especially inspired the black community. Ralph Ellison, the celebrated novelist who in the thirties was a young aspiring trumpet player growing up in Oklahoma City, recalled: "During the Depression whenever [Ellington's] theme song 'East St. Louis Toodle-oo' came on the air, our morale was lifted by something inescapably hopeful in the sound. Its style was so triumphant and the moody melody so successful in capturing the times yet so expressive of the faith that would see us through them."

Despite the publicity and perquisites that came with stardom, Ellington still had to face racial prejudice. He and his men were barred from most restaurants and hotels. Although he got considerable airtime, no business would sponsor him on the radio during the Swing Era. And there is evidence that his manager, Irving Mills, exploited him financially. In 1936 black political leader Adam Clayton Powell Jr. made several provocative allegations, which, though unproven, sound similar to MCA's abuses of Basie around the same time: "Duke Ellington is just a musical sharecropper. He has a drawing account which has been stated to run around $300 per week. At the end of the year when Massa Mills' cotton has been laid by, Duke is told he owes them several hundred or thousand dollars." However true this statement may have been, Ellington finally broke with Mills in 1939 and joined William Morris Corporation, where he hired Basie's manager, Willard Alexander, to represent him.

The Blanton-Webster Band

"Swing is stagnant," Ellington declared in 1939, accurately diagnosing the condition of his field. Swing may have been stagnant, but Ellington after twenty years in the band business was approaching the climax of his career. *Metronome* magazine, which previously focused on white bands, for the first time gave Ellington "top record honors" in 1939 and 1940. In his 1940 review of "fifty favorite sides," George T. Simon picked eight Ellington recordings, a two-to-one plurality over the next runner-up. What makes this review significant is how closely Simon's views accord with those of later critics, not only regarding the importance of the years around 1940 in Ellington's career but also in the recordings singled out for praise: "Conga Brava," "Cotton Tail," "In a Mellotone," among others. To this list the judgment of history has added several more titles, including "Ko-Ko," "Jack the Bear," "Concerto for Cootie," "Take the 'A' Train," "Blue Serge," and "Main Stem."

The ensemble that produced the music of 1939–1942 is sometimes called the **Blanton-Webster band** in recognition of bassist Jimmy Blanton and tenor saxophonist Ben Webster, two distinguished sidemen who came and left during this period. But the success of the band also depended on a core of musicians that had been with Ellington for up to ten years already. The stability of Ellington's personnel, which contrasted with the almost constant turnover in other organizations, allowed the band to reach a point of rare symbiosis and cohesion. Equally important, virtually all of Ellington's sidemen were soloists possessing strikingly original musical personalities. Let us consider a few of these remarkable individuals.

Cootie Williams

If Basie was known for strong saxophone soloists, then Ellington built a reputation for distinctive brass players, starting in the 1920s with Bubber Miley and Tricky Sam Nanton. After Miley left the band in 1929, trumpeter **Charles "Cootie" Williams** (1911–1985) developed plunger style to previously unknown levels of subtlety. In his renowned feature recording, "Concerto for Cootie" (1940), Williams masterfully demonstrates three different trumpet styles: the suave, tightly closed plunger of the beginning; the growling wah-wah effects of the blues section; and the soaring melody of the middle section, where Williams plays open horn in the 1930s style of Louis Armstrong (see Chapter 14). Shortly after "Concerto for Cootie" was recorded, Benny Goodman lured Williams away from Ellington with an offer too lucrative to pass up.

The Trombones: Lawrence Brown, Juan Tizol, and Tricky Sam Nanton

Ellington's son Mercer once said, "The trombones were always Pop's favorite section in the band." During the Blanton-Webster period his trombones were **Lawrence Brown** (1907–1988), **Juan Tizol** (1900–1984), and **Tricky Sam Nanton,** three players who could scarcely be more different. Nanton, as we have seen, specialized in gutbucket plunger effects. Tizol, a Puerto Rican who joined the band in 1929, played valve trombone in a refined, almost classical manner. And Brown, an addition from 1932, played with a rich, creamy tone and astounding technical assurance. Their differences became apparent whenever they played solos, but when they played as a section their styles miraculously blended into a single homogeneous voice.

Johnny Hodges

Although Ellington's brass were important, his most brilliant soloist, perhaps, was alto saxophonist **Johnny Hodges** (1907–1970). With his trademark scoops and his shimmering, sensuous tone, Hodges crafted a sound and style that were instantly recognizable. During the Swing Era many favored the tenor over the alto saxophone as a jazz instrument, believing that the latter "does not lend itself easily to hot intonation," as the critic Helen Oakley put it. But in Hodges's hands, the alto became a peerless vehicle for improvised expression, particularly on blues tunes and ballads. The blues as interpreted by Hodges, Oakley continued, "has in it something of religion, something not to be caught in words, something of the supernatural." On romantic ballads like "Warm Valley" (1940) and "Magenta Haze" (1946), Hodges alternates between sultry meditations on the melody and dazzling—but never tasteless—virtuoso passagework.

Ben Webster

Ellington hired **Ben Webster** (1909–1973) in 1939. One of the truly great tenor saxophonists of the Swing Era, Webster was a Kansas City player with a deep, full-throated sound, equally adept at fast numbers and romantic ballads. Webster left the band in 1943 to lead his own small group on 52nd Street. (For further information about his playing, see the discussion of "Cotton Tail" later in this chapter.)

Jimmy Blanton

Ellington also hired **Jimmy Blanton** (1918–1942) in 1939, after hearing him perform at a St. Louis nightclub. Greatly impressed, Ellington offered the unknown twenty-one-year-old a permanent position before leaving town. Blanton played the stringbass with unprecedented facility among jazz players. Ellington particularly admired his development of a horn-like solo style at a time when most bass players did little more than keep time. Ellington immediately found ways to showcase Blanton's solo abilities on pieces like "Pitter Panther Patter" and "Jack the Bear" (both 1940). Tragically, Blanton died of tuberculosis in 1942. His influence as father of the jazz bass solo, however, lived on.

Harry Carney

Baritone saxophonist **Harry Carney** (1910–1974) supplied an indispensible foundation for the Ellington ensemble sound. He also was one of Ellington's most loyal sidemen, remaining with the band from 1927 until his death in 1974, only five months after that of Ellington himself. As a soloist Carney did not attract as much attention as some of the other stars in the band, but he played with tremendous conviction and originality. He stood as the most distinguished player of the baritone saxophone before Gerry Mulligan came to prominence in the 1950s.

Billy Strayhorn

Ellington's most significant recruit in 1939 was pianist and arranger **Billy Strayhorn** (1915–1967). Strayhorn quickly progressed from writing lyrics to arranging for small groups to contributing to Ellington's big band repertory. Some of his most enduring compositions include "Chelsea Bridge," "Passion Flower," and "Rain Check" (all 1941). Ellington's respect for his protégé prompted him to make Strayhorn's most well-known piece today, "Take the 'A' Train" (1941), the band's new theme song, replacing Ellington's own "East St. Louis Toodle-Oo" (CD 1, Track 1).

Ellington and Strayhorn quickly developed a close personal and musical relationship. They frequently composed collaboratively, sometimes by phone. Acting as Duke's alter ego, Strayhorn would often finish pieces begun by Ellington and vice versa. Their musical personalities meshed so completely that in later years it sometimes became impossible to discern who had written what (and Ellington and Strayhorn coyly refused to admit the truth). But Strayhorn was

Duke Ellington and His Famous Orchestra, 1943. Production still from film *Reveille with Beverly*.

absorbed into the Ellington sound world, not the other way around. As Strayhorn later recalled his apprenticeship, "[Ellington's] first, last and only formal instruction for me was embodied in one word: observe. I did just that, and came to know one of the most fascinating and original minds in American music."

Compositional Method

Ellington brought together the individual strengths of his sidemen into a unified ensemble as original sounding as his most inimitable soloist. Perhaps the most mysterious figure in the band, Ellington was a paradox on many levels. He mingled devout religious faith with an idiosyncratic bundle of superstitions. A man of enormous appetites (he once consumed thirty-two sandwiches in a sitting), he maintained a relatively healthy lifestyle, receiving a complete medical exam every three months and upholding his debonair image as a consummate ladies' man. He governed his men so lightly that road manager Jack Boyd once complained, "Trouble with this band is it has no boss." And yet, unlike his similarly mild-mannered contemporary Fletcher Henderson, Ellington somehow inspired loyalty, enthusiasm, and commitment in his sidemen.

Ellington's complex character produced an unorthodox compositional method. Among other traits, he cultivated:

- A collaborative approach involving Strayhorn and other members of the band. This attitude inspired his young players with idealism. "In the beginning," Cootie Williams recalled, "The idea was . . . to suggest something good for the band to play. . . . It was exciting and we were young. 'Do it like this, Duke,' we'd say. . . . Everyone made suggestions, it was a family thing."

Great Debates

DUKE ELLINGTON, GREAT AMERICAN COMPOSER?

Although celebrated during his lifetime, Duke Ellington was not always taken seriously as a composer. For example, the 1965 Pulitzer Prize Committee peremptorily rejected his nomination. But as his posthumous cultural stock rose, it became fashionable to speculate on the ultimate worth of his compositions. Even before he died, Ralph Ellison referred to him as "our greatest composer." A few years later, Gunther Schuller dared "to include Ellington in the pantheon of musical greats—the Beethovens, the Monteverdis, the Schoenbergs, the prime movers, the inspired innovators." In the 1980s, more writers echoed Ellison in considering Ellington not only the greatest jazz composer but also, in the words of Francis Davis, America's "greatest composer, regardless of idiom." James Lincoln Collier countered with the startling proposal that, because many of Ellington's works were created through intense collaboration, "we are entitled to question not just whether Ellington was America's greatest composer but whether he was a composer at all."

But measuring Ellington against the outstanding composers of the European canon can be misleading. To be sure, Ellington himself seemed to encourage it by writing extended works in classical genres like "concerto" and "suite" to be performed in Carnegie Hall and other high art venues. When set against the backdrop of the European symphonic tradition, Ellington's concert hall pieces—such as *Black, Brown, and Beige,* and *Such Sweet Thunder*—did not always wear well. Many observers believed that he should have stuck to the "three-minute masterpieces" of his dance-band repertory, in which domain he reigned supreme. Others, notably Gary Giddins and Stanley Crouch, staunchly defended Ellington's extended works as among the greatest of his—or any other—career. In an attempt to cut this Gordian knot, Mark Tucker proposed evaluating Ellington on his own terms: "The challenge for historians of American music . . . is not to determine whether a figure like Ellington measures up to Beethoven, but to learn more about [black musical entertainers] Bert Williams and Florence Mills, and to understand why Ellington would be proud to be viewed in *their* company." ■ ■ ■

- An emphasis on writing for individuals rather than parts (for example, for "Johnny Hodges" instead of "first alto"). Strayhorn made a famous statement: "Ellington plays the piano, but his real instrument is his band. Each member of his band is to him a distinctive tone color and set of emotions."
- A passion for **mixed voicing** in addition to the antiphonal voicing common among swing bands. To produce mixed voicing Ellington combined players from different sections. In "Mood Indigo," for instance, he called for a trio of clarinet, muted trumpet, and muted trombone. The heterogeneous combination of instruments, together with the blending of musical personalities, created a unique sound which Strayhorn called **the Ellington effect.**
- An unusual complexity not just of orchestration, but of melody, harmony, rhythm, texture, and form. Ellington's music, for example, was far more *chromatic* than most swing. From the melody of "Sophisticated Lady" to the bass line of "In a Sentimental Mood," Ellington frequently favored half-step relationships.

mixed voicing a big band arranging technique that combines instruments from different sections.

DUKE ELLINGTON AND HIS FAMOUS ORCHESTRA, *"Cotton Tail"* (1940)

Duke Ellington's "Cotton Tail" (1940), an uptempo romp in AABA song form based on the chord progression to George Gershwin's "I Got Rhythm," was one of the most forward-looking recordings of the Swing Era. The bright tempo, nimble horn lines, and dissonant harmonies mirrored the radical experiments taking place in Harlem nightclubs at the time that would eventually lead to the birth of modern jazz (see Chapter 17). In fact, bebop pioneer Dizzy Gillespie borrowed part of the bridge melody in Ellington's saxophone soli (Track 65, 2:20) for the bridge of his own "Dizzy Atmosphere."

Ellington built instabilities into his arrangement in several ways. In the opening melody the two most prominent notes of the A-section—the first note of the first half and the first note of the second half—clash mildly with the underlying harmonies. But Ellington revels in the dissonant notes, repeating and sustaining them with mischievous single-mindedness. He also catches listeners offguard in the final A of the first chorus. This section, full of lurching brass lines in the high register, is unstable anyway, but Ellington increases the imbalance by truncating the section, cutting it back to four bars instead of eight. In the second half of the piece Ellington builds to a climax by presenting a half-chorus soli for trumpets and trombones, then a full chorus of saxophone soli, and finally a stomping shout chorus before dropping back suddenly to a hushed closing statement of the opening melody (A-section only).

"Cotton Tail" is perhaps most famous for Ben Webster's tour-de-force tenor saxophone solo. Webster begins his solo at a simmer, tossing off short phrases in the lower registers and playing almost in *subtone* (a quiet, breathy manner). Over the course of the solo he raises the temperature to a boil. At the beginning of his second chorus, Webster plays a jagged ascending pattern against a *pedal point* (repeated single note) in the bass. The combination creates a mood of suspense—how long can he continue this?—until Webster finally breaks the pattern and the chord progression resumes at the start of the second A-section.

- A lifelong interest in extended forms, of which more below.
- **Programmatic associations;** that is to say, Ellington often based his instrumental music on a picture, story, or mood. "In my writing," he once said, "there's always a mental picture. . . . In the old days, when a guy made a lick, he'd say what it reminded him of." Thus, "East St. Louis Toodle-Oo" is about an old man trudging home after work, "Daybreak Express" depicts a train ride, "Mood Indigo" suggests sadness or nostalgia, and so forth.

Black, Brown, and Beige

In 1931 Ellington wrote prophetically, "The music of my race is something which is going to live, something which posterity will honour in a higher sense than merely that of the music of the ballroom to-day." In the same article he announced his intention to compose a multimovement work portraying "the experiences of the coloured races in America in the syncopated idiom." In these statements Ellington revealed his highest lifelong ambition: to memorialize the black American experience through music. His most complete attempt to realize

LISTENING CHART 14

Duke Ellington and His Famous Orchestra, "Cotton Tail"

CD 1 / Tracks 62–66

RECORDED 4 MAY 1940, HOLLYWOOD / VICTOR 26610; MX 049655-1

Wallace Jones, Cootie Williams (trumpet), Rex Stewart (cornet), Lawrence Brown, Joe Nanton (trombone), Juan Tizol (valve trombone), Johnny Hodges, Otto Hardwick (alto saxophone), Barney Bigard (clarinet, tenor saxophone), Ben Webster (tenor saxophone), Harry Carney (baritone saxophone), Duke Ellington (piano), Fred Guy (guitar), Jimmy Blanton (bass), Sonny Greer (drums)

Style: Big band swing			Form: AABA song form (based on chord progression to Gershwin's "I Got Rhythm")

		1st Chorus	**Melody**
62	0:00	A (8)	Mildly dissonant melody played *in unison* by trumpet and tenor saxophone
	0:08	A (8)	*A-section repeated;* harmonized trombones added
	0:16	B (8)	Plunger trumpet solo: Cootie Williams; saxophones supply sustained chords as backgrounds
	0:25	A (4)	Ensemble plays lurching, unpredictable rhythms; length of A-section cut in half
		2nd Chorus	**Tenor saxophone solo: Ben Webster**
63	0:29	A (8)	Ben Webster begins his solo quietly and builds gradually to more elaborate and intense statements
	0:37	A (8)	
	0:45	B (8)	Call-and-response: trumpets and clarinets vs. Webster
	0:53	A (8)	
		3rd Chorus	
	1:01	A (8)	Webster builds tension by playing a jagged ascending pattern over a *pedal point* in the bass
	1:09	A (8)	Chord progression resumes; Webster plays a long note with wide, swaggering vibrato, one of his trademark effects
	1:17	B (8)	Webster plays syncopated pattern at various pitch levels while ensemble supports him with sustained chords
	1:25	A (8)	Webster opens this section with bluesy figures

		4th Chorus	Brass soli / piano and baritone saxophone solos
64	1:33	A (8)	Brass soli: in *chordal homophony* trumpets and trombones play agile, punchy melody in the style of an improvised solo
	1:41	A (8)	
	1:49	B (8)	Baritone saxophone solo: Harry Carney
	1:57	A (8)	Stride piano solo: Duke Ellington
		5th Chorus	Saxophone soli
65	2:04	A (8)	Playing in *chordal homophony* saxophones issue a dynamic joint statement, again in the style of an improvised solo
	2:12	A (8)	
	2:20	B (8)	
	2:28	A (8)	
		6th Chorus	Shout chorus
66	2:36	A (8)	Call-and-response: brass vs. saxophones
	2:44	A (8)	*Repeated,* with some variation in the saxophone parts
	2:51	B (8)	Trumpets play tightly voiced phrases in upper register
	2:59	A (8)	Melody: trumpet (muted this time) + tenor saxophone *in unison* and at a soft dynamic level

this goal was ***Black, Brown, and Beige,*** his three-movement, nearly forty-five-minute "Tone Parallel to the History of the Negro in America," premiered in New York's Carnegie Hall in 1943.

Stimulated by the artistic aspirations of the Harlem Renaissance, Ellington had determined by 1930 to compose a "History of the Negro" for performance in a concert hall. Over the course of the next decade, Ellington composed several preparatory works, including the historically oriented film short, *Symphony in Black* (1935), and the racially progressive musical, *Jump for Joy* (1941). But the most important forerunner to *Black, Brown, and Beige* was Ellington's projected opera, ***Boola.*** This work, named after a slave who in turn represented all African Americans in their symbolic collective journey from Africa to the Deep South to Harlem, was never completed. But it provided the programmatic outline for *Black, Brown, and Beige:* the first movement, *Black,* evokes Boola's slave labors and conversion to Christianity; the second, *Brown,* treats the struggle for freedom in the nineteenth century; and the third, *Beige,* represents the modern Harlemite in the twentieth century.

RICHARD O. BOYER

Witnesses a Composition Taking Shape in the Duke Ellington Orchestra—c. 1944

The band rarely works out an entire arrangement collectively, but when it does, the phenomenon is something that makes other musicians marvel. . . . It will usually be after a performance, at about three in the morning. Duke, sitting at his piano and facing his band, will play a new melody, perhaps, [and] say, "Now this is sad. It's about a guy sitting alone in his room in Harlem. He's waiting for his chick, but she doesn't show. He's got everything fixed for her." . . . The tired band begins to sympathize with the waiting man in Harlem. . . . Lawrence Brown rises with his trombone and gives out a compact, warm phrase. Duke shakes his head. "Lawrence, I want something like the treatment you gave in 'Awful Sad,'" he says. Brown amends his suggestion and in turn is amended by Tricky Sam Nanton, also a trombone who puts a smear and a wa-wa lament on the phrase suggested by Brown. . . . Then [Ellington will] say, "Come on, you guys. Get sincere. Come on down here, Floor Show"—he is addressing Ray Nance—"and talk to me with your trumpet." In a moment or so the air is hideous as trombone and clarinet, saxophone and trumpet clash, their players simultaneously trying variations on the theme. . . . "Come on, you guys. Let's play so far," Duke says. As the band plays . . . the players stimulate one another and new qualities appear. . . . Duke raises his hand and the band stops playing. "On that last part—" he says, "trumpets, put a little more top on it, will ya?" He turns to Junior Raglin, the scowling bass player, and says, "Tie it way down, Junior, tie it way down." Again they play, and now the bray of the trumpets becomes bolder and more sure, the trombones more liquid and clearer, the saxophones mellower, and at the bottom there is the steady beat, beat, beat, beat, four to the bar, of the drums, bass and guitar, and precise, silvery notes of Ellington on the piano . . . until Duke suddenly halts them by shouting, "Too much trombone!" Juan Tizol, a glum white man and the only player in the band who likes to play sweet, complains, "I think it's too gutbucket for this piece. I'd like it more legit." . . . "Well, maybe you're right," Duke says, "but I still think that when Sam gets into that plunger part, he should give it some smear." Again the band begins at the beginning, and as the boys play, Duke calls out directions. . . . He may lean forward and say to one man, "Like you did in 'The Mooche,'" or he may shout over to Carney, who doubles on the clarinet, "The clarinet is under Tricky too much!" As the music begins to move along, he shouts, "Get sincere! Give your heart! Let go your soul!" . . . Perhaps two hours have gone by. . . . Now Juan Tizol grabs a piece of paper and a pencil and begins to write down the orchestration, while the band is still playing it. Whenever the band stops for a breather, Duke experiments with rich new chords . . . while the brass and reeds talk back and forth. By the time Tizol has finished getting the orchestration down on paper, it is already out of date.

Richard O. Boyer, "The Hot Bach [parts 1–3]" *The New Yorker* (24 June–8 July 1944); reprinted in Mark Tucker, ed., *The Duke Ellington Reader* (New York: Oxford University Press, 1993), 226–27.

The premiere at Carnegie Hall succeeded financially, but proved disappointing from a critical perspective. The critics present that night, most of whom usually wrote on classical music, were bothered by Ellington's awkward formal procedures in *Black, Brown, and Beige*. But the musical substance of the jazz-flavored individual themes drew praise. One reviewer wrote, "If you ask me, Mr. Ellington can make some two dozen brief, air-tight compositions out of *Black, Brown, and Beige.* He should." Taking the spirit of this advice to heart, Ellington performed only popular excerpts of *Black, Brown, and Beige*—such as "Come Sunday"—after the premiere and a few immediately subsequent performances, never again the entire piece. But he did not abandon his aspirations to compose extended works. He unveiled a new one each year at Carnegie Hall until 1948, and continued producing them until his death. To mitigate the formal challenges, he adopted the structure of the baroque **suite**—a succession of short, self-contained pieces—for most of these works. Among the most admired are *Deep South Suite* (1946), of which only the rollicking "Happy-Go-Lucky Local" survives, and *The Tattooed Bride* (1950).

Despite its structural shortcomings, *Black, Brown, and Beige* has had a powerful influence on jazz. Its premiere in Carnegie Hall represented a gauntlet thrown before the feet of later jazz musicians, inspiring John Lewis, Gunther Schuller, Charles Mingus, Anthony Braxton, and Wynton Marsalis, among others, to wed the jazz idiom to classical dimensions and procedures. If the continued cross-breeding ever yields a truly integrated and self-sustaining hybrid, *Black, Brown, and Beige* may well turn out to be one of Ellington's most significant long-range contributions to the jazz language.

suite a succession of short, self-contained pieces that together form a larger work.

whole-tone scale a six-note scale built entirely of whole-steps.

DUKE ELLINGTON AND HIS FAMOUS ORCHESTRA, *"Ko-Ko"* (1940)

CD 1 / Track 67

"**N**ot up to the Ellington standard," Barrelhouse Dan wrote of "Ko-Ko" in the May 15, 1940, issue of *Down Beat*. He was particularly troubled by the lack of improvisation, an essential jazz ingredient for white critics of his generation. In 1943 John Hammond took a similarly negative view, insisting that "Ko-Ko" was "not distinguished jazz." To say the least, later writers have not upheld these verdicts. The French critic André Hodeir pronounced "Ko-Ko" "the most perfect example of Duke Ellington's language" and "one of the undisputed masterpieces of orchestral jazz." For James Lincoln Collier the piece shows "Ellington at his best," and Gunther Schuller deemed it "as perfect a 'composition' as the three-minute limitation of the 10-inch 78-RPM phonograph record would permit."

With its throbbing tom-toms, minor mode, and growling brass, "Ko-Ko" is a late manifestation of Ellington's jungle style. Indeed, Ellington said the piece was originally an excerpt from *Boola*, and represented the dancing of black slaves in New Orleans's Congo Square (see Chapter 3). A sense of orgiastic accumulation determines the musical shape of the piece. A quiet, brooding introduction yields to a succession of increasingly agitated blues choruses, culminating in an ecstatic shout chorus. Yet the mood remains heavily shaded by the minor mode, dark low-register sonorities, and dissonant harmonies. Examples of the latter include the chromatic brass voicings in the shout chorus and Ellington's use of the **whole-tone scale** (a six-note scale built entirely of *whole-steps*) in his background figuration in the fourth chorus. Although the piece features Juan Tizol on the melody and a solo by Tricky Sam Nanton in the second and third choruses, its effectiveness depends mostly on an accumulation of stark, soul-rending cries in the ensemble passages.

Create your own listening chart (CD 1 / Track 67)

Chapter *13* White Bands

Despite the artistic achievements of Ellington, Basie, and other black bands, the public face of swing was predominantly white. Bandleaders like Benny Goodman, Artie Shaw, Tommy Dorsey, Glenn Miller, Harry James, and Charlie Barnet became the biggest stars of swing. They appeared in Hollywood movies and their music dominated the country's airwaves and jukeboxes. When the government imposed travel restrictions during World War II, the top white bands monopolized location jobs, playing lengthy engagements at the finest hotel ballrooms of major cities. In short, Duke Ellington may have won admiration for the eccentric beauty of his music, but Benny Goodman was the acclaimed "King of Swing."

It is easy to view the white bandleaders as profiting from a vast system of racial exploitation. But, to their credit, many of them championed the contributions of black musicians. During an era of racially segregated bands, Goodman hired black sidemen Teddy Wilson, Lionel Hampton, Charlie Christian, and Cootie Williams. Shaw employed the great singer Billie Holiday and trumpet star Roy Eldridge. Although their enlightenment on racial issues may fall short of today's standards, Goodman, Shaw, Barnet, and others often promoted black soloists in full knowledge of a potential racist backlash. Their efforts paved the way for fuller bandstand integration after the war, when some jazz bands became models of equality for society at large.

White musicians made solid contributions to jazz on their own terms. After learning (directly or indirectly) from the New Orleans masters in the twenties, they had prepared themselves to complement the strengths of black musicians during the Swing Era. Artistically inspired white bandleaders and soloists may not have been as numerous or influential as their black counterparts, but the best of them—notably Goodman and Shaw—rank with the music's all-time leading exponents.

White Jazz Comes of Age

White swing took root when white jazz players from Chicago and other midwestern centers began filling spots in New York big bands. As we have seen, in 1926 Bix Beiderbecke and Frankie Trumbauer joined Jean Goldkette's Orchestra. Other Chicagoans soon followed Beiderbecke's eastward drift, and by the late twenties, Benny Goodman, Gene Krupa, Bud Freeman, Jimmy McPartland,

Eddie Condon, and Mezz Mezzrow had all moved to New York. So had two brothers from Pennsylvania, Jimmy and Tommy Dorsey, and a Colorado trombonist, Glenn Miller. Together with Artie Shaw, a native New Yorker, these musicians played for the leading dance bands of Goldkette, Ben Pollack, and Red Nichols, or scrambled for small-group work wherever they could get it.

When the Depression struck, the best-trained New York musicians found employment in studio orchestras making records on call or playing for radio broadcasts. Denied to black musicians, such work in **the studios** was abundant and lucrative. Studio musicians had to be able to produce a classical tone and attack and read music perfectly on sight. Despite the pressure, Goodman, Shaw, Miller, and the Dorsey brothers flourished in this environment. The music, however, was unsatisfying. "You'll never know some of the stuff we had to put up with on a regular basis, the garbage we had to play," Shaw remembered. "There were times when it was so unbearable that you wished you were anywhere else, doing anything else."

The studio background of many white swing musicians reveals ways in which they differed from their black contemporaries. First, because studio work brought excellent wages, they played "hot music" for their own pleasure, not out of financial need. Second, when studio players transferred their energies to swing, they brought European-based performance techniques with them. As a result, white swing musicians tended to prize executive polish, crisp articulation, coordinated phrasing, and tightly rehearsed ensembles more than black players did. Because of this focus on "packaging," critics sometimes faulted white bands for emotional sterility and unimaginativeness. Third, whereas bandleaders like Goodman and Shaw were virtuoso improvisers, their sidemen were often note-reading studio veterans with anonymous musical personalities. Thus, white bands did not produce as many distinguished jazz soloists as black bands did. Nevertheless, the white players' conventional mastery of their instruments created a competitive environment that raised the level of European-based virtuosity across the entire swing industry.

Benny Goodman

During the Swing Era Benny Goodman achieved a level of fame that he could never have imagined a few years previously. He grew up in a Jewish immigrant family in the Maxwell Street ghetto, just southwest of downtown Chicago. Sensing his obvious musical talent, his father sacrificed to pay for two years of classical clarinet lessons with German-born Franz Schoepp, a leading pedagogue in Chicago. By age fourteen, Goodman had dropped out of school and was playing professionally. In 1926 he moved to New York.

By the early thirties Goodman had become the first-call clarinetist for studio and Broadway pit orchestra work. He had also absorbed the best jazz in New York and Chicago. Before leaving Chicago he and the Austin High School Gang spent many nights in South Side clubs, hearing King Oliver at the Lincoln Gardens, Freddie Keppard at the Lorraine Gardens, and Bessie Smith at the Entertainer's Café. Smith was accompanied by **Jimmie Noone** (1895–1944), a leading New Orleans clarinetist who had been one of Goodman's fellow students with Schoepp. Together with Johnny Dodds, Noone profoundly influenced Goodman's conception of the clarinet as a jazz instrument. Goodman combined these jazz influences with his studio-bred discipline and classical

Benny Goodman, sheet music cover to "Don't Be That Way" (CD 1 / Tracks 68–71).

virtuosity to create a compelling hot style of his own. By the time of his success at the Palomar (see Chapter 10), he was prepared to lead a new generation of jazz musicians into the Swing Era.

Benny Goodman and His Swing Band

Goodman's band in 1935–1938, the most successful of his career, had three key ingredients: the arrangements of black musicians Fletcher Henderson, Jimmy Mundy, and Edgar Sampson; the extroverted, crowd-pleasing drumming of **Gene Krupa** (1909–1973); and a succession of outstanding trumpet players. Goodman's first sideman to become a star was **Bunny Berigan** (1908–1942), the most creative white trumpet soloist of the Swing Era. His inspired, swinging lyricism shines through on Goodman's recording of "King Porter" (1935). Widely viewed as Bix Beiderbecke's musical heir, Berigan unfortunately also repeated Beiderbecke's self-destructive course with alcohol. After Berigan left in 1936 Goodman assembled a trumpet section that Duke Ellington once called "the greatest trumpet section that ever was." Chris Griffin was the least flamboyant of the three players. **Ziggy Elman** (born Harry Finkelman, 1914–1968), a perpetual talker and cigar-smoker, played loud, dynamic trumpet. "When he was warming up, he could barely tongue," Griffin said. "Then he got out in the front. And when the time was with him, he could play as fast as anybody." The last to join was **Harry James** (1916–1983), the son of circus performers who possessed a prodigious virtuosity. One of Goodman's saxophonists recalled that James "could read all of the highly syncopated charts at sight, and he played fantastic jazz solos—different every time." When playing as a section, these players exuded fiery intensity; they even tuned up a bit *sharp* (higher in pitch than the rest of the band) to get a more brilliant sound. Their brassy roar can be heard on such *killer-diller* numbers as "Bugle Call Rag" (1936) and "Sing, Sing, Sing" (1937).

The chief asset in the band, of course, was Goodman himself. As a leader he demanded perfection from his musicians; errant sidemen got the infamous "Ray"—Goodman's cold, unnerving stare. But as many have noted, Goodman asked no more of his musicians than he did of himself. He belonged to that relatively small cadre of jazz musicians whose improvisations sound like well-rehearsed compositions, free of hesitation or obvious "mistakes." If Goodman's solos lacked an exploratory sense of "thinking out loud," they compensated with liquid fluency and inventive, soulful ideas.

Reaching the Summit

With this band Goodman dominated the swing industry in the late thirties. In 1937 swing fans began showing the first signs of unbridled hysteria when Goodman's band played a three-week stint of matinees (alternating with the movie, *Maid of Salem*) at New York's **Paramount Theater.** When the musicians arrived at 7:00 A.M. to warm up on opening day, they were surprised to see long lines of teenagers already waiting outside. Once the performance started, the audience screamed and—famously—began jitterbugging in the aisles. During the first week the band grossed $58,000. Following a similar engagement at Boston's Metropolitan Theater a few weeks later, the *Globe* reported that "Benny Goodman, King of Swing, is in town, which means that the youngsters of the city are in their seventh heaven of rapture. . . . What shrieks of joy as he played 'Alexander's Ragtime Band' in his own swingy rhythms! What yells and whistles and stampings followed Gene Krupa's exhibitions!"

Goodman stirred up controversy with his **Carnegie Hall Concert** in 1938. Unlike Ellington, Goodman did not unveil any new experimental art music at his debut. Instead, he offered his usual dance repertory as music for listening, along with a musical tour of jazz history and a jam session featuring soloists from the bands of Count Basie and Duke Ellington. *Metronome* pronounced the concert a "real howling success," but a negative review of the concert in the *New York Times* prompted a heated debate in the letters section. An editorial concluded, "There seems to be no middle group who likes swing music a little. One either loves it to the point of distraction or takes to the hills to get away from it. It is of no use to argue about it." It was not until a recording of the concert was released in the early fifties that, in hindsight, the event was seen as the climax of Goodman's career.

BENNY GOODMAN AND HIS ORCHESTRA, *"Don't Be That Way"* (1938)

The opening number on Goodman's Carnegie Hall program was "Don't Be That Way," an arrangement saxophonist **Edgar Sampson** (1907–1973) had made for Chick Webb while playing in his band in the early thirties. Within a couple of months after its release in February 1938, Goodman's "Don't Be That Way" became a hit—one of four best-selling Victor records in March and the ninth most frequently broadcast recording in April, according to *Metronome*.

"Don't Be That Way" has several features typical of swing arrangements of the period. The basic chorus structure is expanded by the addition of an introduction, transition/modulation, and coda. Solo spots, even for Goodman himself, are limited to brief eight- or sixteen-bar passages. Three key changes help the piece build climactically. The final climax is momentarily deferred by what is called a "fade-away" coda, in which the main A-section is repeated at progressively softer dynamics. This technique inspired many imitations, including on such warhorses as Glenn Miller's "In the Mood," Tommy Dorsey's "Opus No. One," and Duke Ellington's "Take the 'A' Train." In "Don't Be That Way" the fading dynamics ultimately reverse course with a rousing drum break by Gene Krupa and a final shout statement of A, complete with *shakes* (wide, ragged vibrato in the upper register) in the trumpet section.

The impeccable rendition reflects Goodman's exacting performance standards and painstaking rehearsal. The instrumental sections carefully balance tone and dynamics. The players begin and end phrases in strict uniformity. And *articulation* (patterns of tonguing and slurring) is closely coordinated. Notice, for example, the crisp brass punctuations behind the saxophone melody at the beginning.

LISTENING CHART 15

Benny Goodman and His Orchestra, "Don't Be That Way"

CD 1 / Tracks 68–71

RECORDED 16 FEBRUARY 1938, NEW YORK CITY / VICTOR 25792 A; MX BS 019831-1

Benny Goodman (clarinet, leader), Harry James, Ziggy Elman, Chris Griffin (trumpet), Red Ballard, Vernon Brown (trombone), Hymie Schertzer, George Koenig (alto saxophone), Art Rollini, Babe Russin (tenor saxophone), Jess Stacy (piano), Allan Reuss (guitar), Harry Goodman (bass), Gene Krupa (drums)

Style: Big band swing   Form: AABA song form

			Introduction
68	0:00	4 bars	Ensemble plays fanfare opening
		1st Chorus	**Melody**
	0:06	A (8)	Saxophones play angular melody in *unison;* trumpets add backgrounds, tightly punctuating the melody
	0:18	A (8)	*A-section repeated*
	0:29	B (8)	*Antiphonal voicing:* harmonized trumpets play melody vs. saxophone punctuations
	0:41	A (8)	*A-section repeated*
			Transition/modulation
	0:52	(4)	Full ensemble plays homophonically; changes key
		2nd Chorus	**Solos (for clarinet, trumpet, drums, & trombone)**
69	0:58	A (8) (new key)	**Clarinet solo: Benny Goodman**
			Benny Goodman plays a *melodic paraphrase* solo in call-and-response with saxophone backgrounds
	1:09	A (8)	Goodman leaves melody to improvise more freely
	1:21	B (8)	**Trumpet solo: Harry James**
			Harry James plays brash, good-natured solo with lots of wide intervals and decorative blips; saxophones supply backgrounds
	1:32	A (8)	**Clarinet solo: Goodman**
			Goodman opens with repeated bluesy figure; brass backgrounds get gradually louder

		3rd Chorus	
70	1:44	A (8) (new key)	**Trading twos: ensemble vs. drums (Gene Krupa)**
			Full ensemble plays *forte;* Gene Krupa answers discreetly
	1:56	A (8)	**Trombone solo: Vernon Brown**
			Vernon Brown plays *melodic paraphrase* solo against saxophone backgrounds
	2:07	B (8)	**Clarinet solo: Goodman**
			Goodman ranges freely and confidently through the chords, adeptly fitting his last phrase to the final modulation
71	2:19	A (8) (new key)	**Melody (last A)**
			Fade-away coda (with final build-up)
	2:31	A (8)	*Repeated:* soft
	2:42	A (8)	*Repeated:* softer
	2:54	A (6)	*Repeated:* softest
	3:03	(2)	Drum break: Gene Krupa plays loud, rapid-fire break
	3:06	A (8)	Saxophones play melody once more as brass shout new backgrounds (notice the *shakes* in the trumpet section at phrase-endings); dynamics reverse course: band starts *forte* and crescendos to *fortissimo* (double loud)

Further Listening from the *Prentice Hall Jazz Collection*
Track 2: Benny Goodman and Charlie Christian, "Seven Come Eleven" (1939)

Artie Shaw

Benny Goodman's chief rival as both clarinetist and bandleader was Artie Shaw (born Arthur Arshawsky, 1910). Shaw grew up in an impoverished Jewish-immigrant household in New York. To master the clarinet and saxophone he manifested what one writer has called "the principal ingredient of Shaw's disposition—a deadly, dogged, skull-cracking determination." Practicing until his lips bled and his teeth ached, Shaw qualified himself to play professionally by age fourteen. In 1929, while on the road with bandleader Irving Aaronson,

Shaw discovered black jazz in Chicago. Back in New York the following year, Shaw began spending weeks at a time in Harlem, where he cultivated a friendship-cum-apprenticeship with Willie the Lion Smith (see Chapter 9). "My boy Artie was a good student," the Lion noted wryly. By the early thirties, Shaw was working regularly in the studios, oftentimes alongside Benny Goodman.

The New King of Swing

Shaw embarked on his career as a bandleader somewhat by accident. Almost a year into the swing craze, as we have seen, the proprietor of the Onyx Club organized the first generally recognized jazz concert at the Imperial Theater on May 24, 1936. Shaw was invited to put a small group together for a two- or three-minute performance while the stagehands changed the ensemble setup behind the curtain. Having recently rehearsed Mozart and Brahms pieces for clarinet and string quartet, Shaw decided to present an original jazz piece using the same instrumentation, plus rhythm section. His modest *Interlude in B-flat* created a sensation; in the words of one critic, it "broke up the show."

Showered with encouragement from eager businessmen, Shaw organized his own swing band. His ambition was to produce a band that "thought as one man, not like a string of soloists." Unlike Ellington, Shaw viewed his musicians as mere interpreters of his own artistic vision: "If you're running a band and you have a strong idea . . . of what you're doing, you're going to try different things, and you *impose* that on the men, without killing them, without diminishing their egos." In 1938 he signed a contract with Victor Phonograph Company and began making records. His first was an arrangement of Cole Porter's **"Begin the Beguine,"** a perfect marriage of hot and sweet elements. Nothing could swing harder than the saxophone accompaniment at the beginning, but when the saxophones state the melody in the second A (of the AABA song form) their coordinated vibrato evokes Guy Lombardo.

In a single stroke "Begin the Beguine" catapulted Shaw to superstardom. At the end of 1938 the *Down Beat* Reader's Poll voted his orchestra the best all-around swing band and the magazine proclaimed him the "New King of Swing." Such publicity inevitably sparked heated debates between Shaw's supporters and those of Benny Goodman. Shaw, after all, had developed a virtuoso jazz clarinet style that offered a distinct alternative to Goodman's. Shaw's tone was sweeter, his phrases more graceful, and he played in the extreme upper register—beyond the natural range of the clarinet—with unmatched ease and fluency. Goodman fans argued that Shaw fell short of Goodman's standard in hot playing and blues feeling. But Shaw's solos on "One Stop Flight" and "Back Bay Shuffle" show him to be an outstanding hot player.

The culture of celebrity weighed heavily on Shaw. Some weeks he personally netted $30,000 and received up to twenty thousand fan letters. But he resented being made to feel like a "sideshow," as he put it. One evening in 1939, after playing a concert on Boston Commons, he stepped into the limousine to return to his hotel. But, according to a *New Yorker* profile, "the crowd, despite 40 policemen in attendance, declined to open a way. Chanting, it took to rocking the car, which finally turned turtle, with a crash of glass. When Shaw had regained a measure of composure and mobility, he fought a retreating action on foot, fending off grasping hands all the way back to the Ritz. His lapels were ripped off, his

Artie Shaw and His Orchestra, 1938. Production still from Vitaphone movie short.

jacket was split down the middle, [and] his face was badly scratched. . . . It required three hours of steady persuasion by the manager to coax him down to the ballroom that night." Later that year such incidents drove Shaw to disband voluntarily at the height of his success. Yet he formed and dissolved several more bands before retiring from music for good in 1954. Justifying this final move, Shaw likened his tempestuous career to a "gangrenous right arm that was going to kill you; you cut it off to save your life."

A Jazz Standard: "Cherokee"

Although popular in their day, few of the swing compositions we have examined thus far—whether white or black—were able to endure outside the context of the Swing Era. Ray Noble's "Cherokee," recorded by Charlie Barnet, was different. The scion of a New York railroad tycoon, **Charlie Barnet** (1913–1991) was economically secure before he went into music. He defied his parents, who wanted him to go to law school, by becoming a jazz tenor saxophonist. More than any other white bandleader, perhaps, Barnet admired the great black bands of Duke Ellington and Count Basie and aspired to play like them. He helped pioneer the integrated bandstand, hiring black soloists like Roy Eldridge, Benny Carter, Charlie Shavers, and vocalist Lena Horne. "Cherokee," released in 1939, propelled Barnet to national stardom. As we will see in Chapter 18, through the intermediary of Charlie Parker "Cherokee" outlived its role as a hit of the Swing Era, becoming an anthem of modern jazz and, ultimately, a jazz standard.

CHARLIE BARNET, *"Cherokee"* (1939)

CD 1 / Track 72

After an introductory *vamp*, "Cherokee" opens with a long-note *pentatonic* melody presumably intended (in the spirit of the title) to evoke Native American lyricism. The melody, played by Barnet himself on alto saxophone, follows conventional AABA form but with expanded dimensions: each phrase lasts sixteen bars rather than eight, making a total of sixty-four bars in a chorus. The expanded chorus length allows the band to play, at medium tempo, only a little more than one-and-a-half choruses within the roughly three minutes allotted for recording. The bridge (B-section) changes keys every four bars (and changes more quickly near the end), creating an involved harmonic path that especially appealed to later jazz musicians. In order to fit the harmonic progression, the bridge melody outlines a descending *sequence*—a technical term for a melody that is repeated at progressively higher or, in this case, lower pitch levels.

Amid the polished execution and carefully coordinated phrasing typical of white bands, the influence of black swing emerges in the opening vamp—in the sassy wah-wahs in the trombones and trumpets, especially—and continues throughout in the leader's own bluesy inflections on alto saxophone and the band's wonderfully dynamic swing feel. (For your trivia file: this recording must contain one of the earliest examples of the now common *fade ending* in which the fade is produced electronically—that is, by the recording engineer gradually turning down the microphone until the sound is inaudible.)

Create your own listening chart (CD 1 / Track 72)

Virtuoso Soloists   *Chapter* **14**

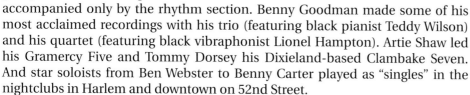

Sometimes the Swing Era is called the Big Band Era. But that can be misleading, since a great deal of outstanding small-group activity took place during this period as well. Duke Ellington and Count Basie both showcased "bands within a band," a select group of soloists that performed entire tunes accompanied only by the rhythm section. Benny Goodman made some of his most acclaimed recordings with his trio (featuring black pianist Teddy Wilson) and his quartet (featuring black vibraphonist Lionel Hampton). Artie Shaw led his Gramercy Five and Tommy Dorsey his Dixieland-based Clambake Seven. And star soloists from Ben Webster to Benny Carter played as "singles" in the nightclubs in Harlem and downtown on 52nd Street.

Whereas big band arrangements often limited soloists to brief statements, small groups or **combos** allowed them to improvise several choruses at a time. As a result, combos nurtured the development of improvisational style. By the 1930s this style no longer reflected the comedy and novelty values that had inspired soloists in the twenties. Nor was it yet the self-consciously artistic expression characteristic of modern jazz players after World War II. Soloists in the Swing Era aspired either to exhibit refined showmanship or, in private settings, to unspool a gripping musical narrative for their peers—to "tell a story," as the saying went. More than just playing a series of vivid ideas, **telling a story** meant presenting those ideas in a logical, linear succession.

The essentials of "storytelling" and other soloistic hallmarks had been established by Louis Armstrong. Although Armstrong's big bands were mediocre at best, his trumpet playing set a standard of inspired virtuosity that galvanized players of all instruments. Under his influence, unusual or previously under-used instruments emerged as jazz vehicles. The "hot" violin was introduced by French musician Stephane Grappelli; Lionel Hampton established the vibraphone as a solo instrument; the Belgian Django Reinhardt defined solo guitar style; and Jimmy Blanton emancipated the stringbass. Hot trombone style, already mature during the twenties, was further developed by Jack Teagarden and Dicky Wells.

The most significant stylistic advances of the Swing Era were made on tenor saxophone, trumpet, and piano. Tenor players Coleman Hawkins and Lester Young, trumpeter Roy Eldridge, and pianist Art Tatum, in particular, built upon Armstrong's virtuoso achievements. As Armstrong had been their

combo a small performing group, usually of three to seven players.

leading predecessor, so they would inspire the young radicals of the bebop generation.

52nd Street

New York's 52nd Street was to the Swing Era what Chicago's "Stroll" had been to the Jazz Age. From the mid-thirties to the mid-forties, the stretch of 52nd Street located primarily between 5th and 6th Avenues in midtown Manhattan hosted so much good music that it became known as "Swing Street," or simply, "the Street" (see Map 7). The nightclubs specialized in small-group jazz. Leading soloists held forth at venues like the Onyx Club, the Famous Door, Three Deuces, Jimmy Ryan's, the Spotlite, and Kelly's Stable. These were not glamorous places. One writer recalled that "all the [52nd Street] clubs were shaped like shoe boxes, and they had dingy canopies outside. The tables were three inches square and the chairs were hard wood. The drinks were probably watered."

Of course patrons went, not for drinks, but to hear the richest interaction of jazz talent then available on a single block. During intermission at their own gigs or after hours, star soloists would roam from club to club, socializing, listening to the music, sitting in with the band, and participating in jam sessions and cutting contests for hours on end. To facilitate improvisation, musicians played on chord progressions of well-known popular songs, often Broadway hits. Favorites included "Honeysuckle Rose," "How High the Moon," "What Is This Thing Called Love," and "Oh, Lady Be Good." But two progressions were worked over more than any other: the twelve-bar blues and George Gershwin's "I Got Rhythm."

52nd Street, 1948.

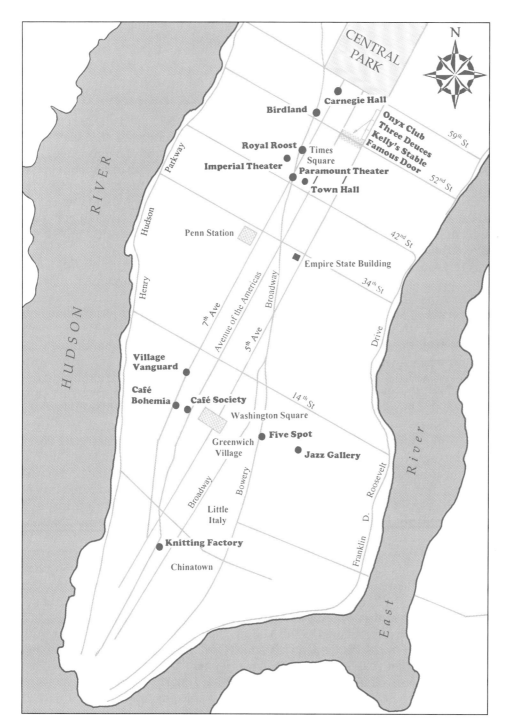

Map 7. Lower Manhattan, after c. 1935.

rhythm changes   the chord progression to George Gershwin's song "I Got Rhythm."

tempo rubato   a tempo that fluctuates freely, becoming slightly faster and slower in alternation.

Musicians used the latter so frequently that its chord progression (or chord *changes*) was referred to simply as **rhythm changes.**

Coleman Hawkins

If there was a single preeminent jazz soloist in the 1930s it must have been tenor saxophonist **Coleman Hawkins** (whom we first encountered in Chapter 8). Notwithstanding the publicity enjoyed by white clarinetists like Benny Goodman, Artie Shaw, and Woody Herman, the clarinet declined as a jazz instrument in the Swing Era. It had to make room for the powerful voice of the tenor saxophone pioneered by Hawkins, Lester Young, Ben Webster, and others. Most of these players shared a somewhat mysterious connection with Kansas City, and generally built their individual styles on some variation of the Hawkins sound. Only Young offered a distinct—and influential—alternative.

Hawkins grew up in St. Joseph, Missouri, about fifty miles north of Kansas City. His mother taught him music, but contrary to her wishes he chose to play the saxophone—then a disreputable instrument of the circus—rather than the impeccably pedigreed cello. At age seventeen he took his first professional job playing in the 12th Street Theater orchestra in Kansas City. That year Mamie Smith and Her Jazz Hounds came through town. Hawkins joined Smith's band and eventually returned with her to New York. In 1924 he joined Fletcher Henderson, with whom he stayed for the next ten years. During this period Hawkins almost single-handedly legitimized the tenor saxophone as a jazz solo instrument.

Hawkins's most significant influences in the twenties were not saxophonists or even clarinetists but players of other instruments: Louis Armstrong and Art Tatum. Armstrong, Hawkins's bandmate in 1924–1925, impressed Hawkins with his sheer rhetorical power, his instrumental command, and his driving swing feel. Shortly after hearing Armstrong, Hawkins abandoned his jerky "slap-tongued" articulation in favor of more graceful, swinging rhythms. Hawkins encountered Tatum in 1929 during a tour with the Henderson band through Ohio. Tatum inspired Hawkins to explore rhythmic complexities such as irregular phrasing and experimentations with **tempo rubato** (fluctuating tempo). Tatum also confirmed in Hawkins an intense harmonic adventurousness that he had already been pursuing. Yet, Hawkins did not appropriate "trumpet style" after hearing Armstrong, nor did he play "like a piano" after Tatum. Instead, Armstrong and Tatum showed Hawkins how jazz might sound as a serious, progressive art form rather than a musical expression of novelty.

By 1934 Hawkins reigned as the leading tenor saxophonist of the jazz world. Had he stayed in the United States he might well have profited from the swing craze. But in that year he decided to leave Henderson for a tour of Europe. The Europeans received him so enthusiastically that Hawkins stayed for five years, performing when and where he wanted to and enjoying all the attention of an operatic prima donna. In 1939 he returned to America and discovered, Rip Van Winkle–like, a world transformed. During his absence, several prominent tenor saxophonists had arisen, many of them determined to challenge his authority. But, despite his European interlude Hawkins was then playing at the height of his powers, a fact demonstrated repeatedly in jam sessions and cutting contests on 52nd Street. At the end of the year, *Down Beat* readers voted him "best tenor saxophonist."

Coleman Hawkins.

Musical Style

Hawkins had a dark, heavy tone and played with wide vibrato. Considering himself a forward-looking, progressive musician, he developed a highly intellectual approach to harmony. His intense harmonic interest, as well as the influence of Louis Armstrong, prompted him to depart from the solo convention of melodic paraphrase (variations of the melody) and instead pursue **harmonic improvisation,** a solo approach based entirely on the chord progression. To thoroughly address the harmonic nuances of a song, he manifested a "vertical" melodic conception, playing up and down the chords. He also substituted chromatically altered chords for the standard ones, creating higher levels of dissonance and daring harmonic colors. Rhythmically, Hawkins explored the use of rubato phrasing and **double-time,** playing eighth notes twice as fast as the tempo dictates. And structurally, he invested his solos with drama through climactic overall shapes.

COLEMAN HAWKINS AND HIS ORCHESTRA, *"Body and Soul"* (1939)

Coleman Hawkins recorded "Body and Soul" almost by accident. Although he had long favored the piece as an improvising vehicle, it was not on the initial list of selections for this recording session, and was apparently added as an afterthought. The recording consists of two choruses of Hawkins's improvisation, with the simplest of head arrangements—mostly sustained notes—supplied by the band in the second chorus. Not everyone reacted positively to "Body and Soul." A writer for *Jazz Information* complained in December that "Hawkins plays almost entirely without inspiration. His variations are mechanically constructed of clichés and are without much logic." *Down Beat*'s Barrelhouse Dan, however, commended Hawkins's "full, biting tone and fantastic ideas." Most listeners agreed with Barrelhouse Dan: the record sold one hundred thousand copies in the first six months and rapidly became a beloved classic among jazz musicians.

"Body and Soul" reveals Hawkins's mature solo style. The song may have appealed to him for its unusual harmonic trajectory, including multiple modulations in the B-section. Hawkins begins with an elegant melodic paraphrase, but by the second A he has already begun to explore the harmony of the song and by the bridge he has dropped the melody completely. Notice his harmonic substitutions and passing chords, especially at the ends of phrases. The first chorus presents languid rhythms shaded by subtle rubato effects. But double-time figures emerge early, intensifying the rhythmic content. In the second chorus Hawkins adopts a harder swing feel in the double-time figures, neutralizing the sense of rubato. The rhythmic intensification corresponds to a larger intensification of form, as the pitch and dynamics gradually rise to a peak in the final A. In addition to this broad unity of structure, the individual motives and phrases closely relate to one another, creating a logical discourse at the local level. Equally important, Hawkins plays throughout with intense romantic feeling; the balance of intellectual and emotional elements in the performance may account for its unusually broad-based positive reception.

harmonic improvisation an improvisational style especially common in postwar jazz, in which the soloist creates new melodies based on the chord progression of the piece being played.

double time when the tempo moves twice as fast as the original.

LISTENING CHART 16

Coleman Hawkins and His Orchestra, "Body and Soul"
(Green-Sauer-Heyman-Eyton)

CD 1 / Tracks 73–74

RECORDED 11 OCTOBER 1939 / BLUEBIRD B-10253; MX 042936-1

Coleman Hawkins (tenor saxophone), Joe Guy, Tommy Lindsay (trumpet), Earl Hardy (trombone), Jackie Fields, Eustis Moore (alto saxophone), Gene Rodgers (piano), William Oscar Smith (bass), Arthur Herbert (drums)

Style: Ballad			Form: AABA song form
			Introduction
73	0:00	(4)	Piano solo: Gene Rodgers
	1st Chorus		**Tenor Saxophone Solo: Coleman Hawkins**
	0:10	A (8)	Hawkins starts by paraphrasing the melody . . .
	0:30	A (8)	. . . then begins to drift from melodic paraphrase to harmonic improvisation; introduces double-time figures
	0:34		(Example of a chromatic passing chord)
	0:51	B (8)	Key change: Hawkins has completely abandoned melody by this time; continues playing in double-time
	1:01		Key changes again
	1:08		Modulates back to . . .
	1:11	A (8)	. . . the original key
	2nd Chorus		
74	1:31	A (8)	Hawkins continues soloing, now with band accompaniment on sustained notes; building intensity, he generates a harder swing feeling on double-time figures
	1:51	A (8)	
	2:12	B (8)	Key changes proceed as before; band drops out
	2:32	A (8)	Back to original key; band back in: Hawkins reaches climax of pitch, dynamics, and rhythmic intensity

Lester Young

The unorthodox playing of **Lester Young** (1909–1959) inevitably invited comparisons, both favorable and unfavorable, with Hawkins. He grew up just outside of New Orleans and spent his adolescence touring carnival circuits with the family band run by his father. Later, he performed as a freelance musician with various groups throughout the Midwest, finally settling in Kansas City in 1933. His main influence was not Hawkins but, perhaps surprisingly, the white saxophonists Frankie Trumbauer and Jimmy Dorsey. He especially admired Trumbauer, whose record, "Singin' the Blues," Young carried in his saxophone case. "Trumbauer was my idol," he recalled. "I used to buy all his records. I imagine I can still play all those solos off the record."

When Hawkins left for Europe in 1934, Henderson hired Young to replace him. But the Hawkins legacy was overpowering. Young had a light, airy tone, played with little vibrato, and favored a linear (instead of "vertical") melodic approach—characteristics inherited from the white players. In addition, Young's harmonic sophistication was of a different nature than Hawkins's. Young emphasized nonchord tones to add color to his lines, but eschewed Hawkins's ardent chromaticism and abstruse chord navigations. Henderson's musicians were dismayed that Young didn't play like Hawkins. Young recalled, "I was rooming at the Hendersons' house, and [Fletcher's wife] Leora Henderson would wake me early in the morning and play Hawkins's records for me so I could play like he did. I wanted to play my own way."

After six difficult months, Young returned to Kansas City. There in 1936 he joined the Count Basie band, an ensemble that provided the most successful big band home of his career. In that year he made his first recordings, including the small-group sides "Oh, Lady Be Good," and

Lester Young.

"Shoe Shine Boy," both of which reveal his mature style and rank with his most admired solos. The following year Basie hired singer Billie Holiday, who immediately struck up a close friendship with Young. Convinced that he was the best tenor soloist alive, Holiday coined his famous nickname, Prez. "The greatest man around then was Franklin D. Roosevelt and he was the President," she recalled. "So I started calling [Lester Young] the President. It got shortened to Prez." Young affectionately called Holiday "Lady Day."

In 1938 Young's reputation began growing as he soloed for Basie at the Famous Door on 52nd Street. But his role as the anti-Hawkins puzzled listeners. From 1938 to 1940 he never rose higher than fourth place in *Down Beat* polls. When Hawkins returned from Europe Young faced off with him in a now famous cutting contest in Harlem. *Down Beat* reported in September 1939 that the two tenors had "tangled for an hour in a carving contest, and according to members of Fats Waller's band it stopped when Lester said he'd had enough." Young's champion Billie Holiday immediately contacted the magazine to dispute this account, insisting that "Young really cut the Hawk, and most everyone there who saw them tangle agreed on that."

By 1940 Young had become frustrated playing with Basie. He later recalled that in a big band, "You don't get a chance to play. You walk to the mike for your eight bars or your sixteen bars and then you sit down. You're just sitting there and reading music. There are no kicks for me that way." Young's natural setting was in small-group jam sessions. He left Basie in December and shortly thereafter opened with his own small group at Kelly's Stable. Though he never achieved the recognition of Hawkins during this period, it was Young, not Hawkins, that most affected the young players of the forties.

Roy Eldridge

As Coleman Hawkins influenced tenor saxophonists during the Swing Era, so Louis Armstrong supplied the principal model for trumpet players. Far from merely recycling the innovations of his Hot Five records, Armstrong forged a new approach to jazz trumpet playing that perfectly fit the changing tastes of the 1930s. On records like "Sweethearts on Parade" (1930) and "I Gotta Right to Sing

COUNT BASIE'S KANSAS CITY SEVEN, *"Lester Leaps In"* (1939)

CD 1 / Track 75

Lester Young's most celebrated solo is the one he played on his own tune, "Lester Leaps In," during a recording session with Count Basie's small group, the Kansas City Seven. In its informality and flashes of inspiration, this performance projects the character of a jam session. The tune itself is slight, consisting of little more than a single repeated riff, thereby drawing attention to the solos. The chord progression is that of "I Got Rhythm."

A mistake in the performance reveals the spontaneous nature of this recording. In the third chorus Young continues his solo with stop-time accompaniment in the rhythm section—except for Basie, who prematurely begins a solo of his own! One gets the clear impression that Basie either forgot the stop-time or perhaps didn't know it was coming. In any case, Basie figures it out and aborts his solo by the start of the second A-section.

Young's solo is particularly inspired. One of his favorite devices was *alternate fingering,* a technique he uses in the last A-section of the third chorus. His solo also manifests a flowing articulation and rhetorical expansiveness absent in most saxophone solos of the period. One way to grasp the newness of Young's approach is to compare his solo on this recording with Ben Webster's on "Cotton Tail"—another piece in rhythm changes and at about the same tempo as "Lester Leaps In" (see CD 1/ Tracks 62–66). In his solo, Webster favors a riff-based approach; he tends to work over a few brief melodic ideas, which change from one section to another. Young, by contrast, plays relatively longer and more horizontally oriented lines. While he continues to use riff-based ideas, Young also presents lengthy phrases that do not easily subdivide into smaller units. In this regard he anticipated the protracted phraseology of modern jazz.

Create your own listening chart (CD 1 / Track 75)

REX STEWART

Recalls a Cutting Contest Between Coleman Hawkins and Lester Young

When Coleman Hawkins returned to his Harlem stomping grounds in 1939, after several years' absence in Europe, he was more than mildly concerned about whether the cats had caught up with him, as he put it. At that time, all the hippies hung out in former drummer Nightsie Johnson's joint, which I recall as on 131st Street near Saint Nicholas Avenue. . . . Hawk frequented the pad nightly for several weeks, and every time he was asked to play, he'd have another new excuse—he was resting from the constant grind of appearances in Europe, his horn was in pawn, he had a toothache, or he just couldn't bring himself to play in front of all these tenor giants. Fellows like Lester Young, Don Byas, Dick Wilson, Chu Berry, and many lesser talents were all itching to get a piece of the Hawk—especially Lester, whose staunchest fan was Billie Holiday. One night Billie brought the personal element into focus by "signifying," which in Harlemese means making a series of pointed but oblique remarks apparently addressed to no one in particular, but unmistakable in intention in such a close-knit circle. . . .

Hawk took Lady Day's caustic remarks as a big joke, but apparently he'd previously decided that this was the night to make his move. Up to the last minute, the old fox played it cool, waiting until Billie's juice told her it was time for her to sing some blues. Then, he slipped out, returning with his saxophone, and started to accompany Billie's blues, softly. Billie, hearing his sound, looked up, startled, and then motioned to Pres as if to say, "Take charge." So Lester began blowing the blues, and to give credit where credit is due, he really *played* the blues that night, chorus after chorus, until finally Hawk burst in on the end of one of his choruses, cascading a harmonic interruption, not unlike Mount Vesuvius erupting, virtually overpowering Lester's more haunting approach. When Hawk finished off the blues, soaring, searing, and lifting the entire house with his guttural, positive sonority, every tub began cheering, with the exception of Lady Day, Lester, and her pet boxer, Mister. They, like the Arabs, folded their tents and stole away.

Rex Stewart, "The Cutting Sessions," in *Reading Jazz,* ed. Robert Gottlieb (New York: Vintage Books, 1996), 391–92.

the Blues" (1933), Armstrong unveiled this style—a brawny, romantic idiom emphasizing soaring high-note melodies and such crowd-pleasing effects as **half-valve glissandos,** in which Armstrong depressed his valves halfway to produce a trombone-like sliding effect in the upper register. This kind of playing, sometimes called **majestic style,** can be heard in the work of black and white virtuosos alike, for example, on Bunny Berigan's "I Can't Get Started," Cootie Williams's open horn solo on "Concerto for Cootie," and Ray Nance's open horn solo on "Take the 'A' Train."

The greatest of the swing trumpeters, **Roy Eldridge** (1911–1989), wedded the high-note pyrotechnics of Armstrong's majestic style with unparalleled power, speed, and fluency on his instrument. Like Armstrong, Eldridge increased his agility on the trumpet by borrowing the idiom of woodwind players—in his case, both clarinetists and saxophonists. A Pittsburgh musician, Eldridge greatly admired Coleman Hawkins, whose solo on "Stampede" (1926)

Roy Eldridge, 1939.

Gene Krupa and His Orchestra, *"Rockin' Chair"* (1941)

One of Eldridge's most celebrated recordings is his showcase version of the ballad, "Rockin' Chair," accompanied by Gene Krupa's orchestra. The song is in ABCA song form, an occasional variant of the more common AABA. Following standard practice in the performance of ballads, Eldridge starts the last chorus from the bridge (C in this case), so that the slow tempo does not unduly lengthen the piece.

Eldridge begins with a virtuoso trumpet cadenza in the tradition of Louis Armstrong's "West End Blues" and—even more closely, given the sustained ensemble notes—Bunny Berigan's "I Can't Get Started" (1937). He then unleashes a highly intense performance, for a ballad. The energy of Eldridge's playing bursts through conventional boundaries in several ways—he frequently plays in double-time, he scarifies his tone with a raspy *buzz* (for example, in the first chorus, at the beginnings of C and the last A), and at the second half-chorus he roars into the upper register, searing the high F with an adamant *shake.* He concludes the solo with another cadenza, this time unaccompanied and out of tempo, that features more buzzing, a dainty classically oriented exchange with clarinetist Sam Musiker, and a final stepwise ascent to high F in pointed tribute to Louis Armstrong, who pioneered this very ending.

LISTENING CHART 17

Gene Krupa and His Orchestra, "Rockin' Chair" (Carmichael, arr. Carter)

CD 1 / Tracks 76–77

RECORDED 2 JULY 1941 / OKEH 6352; MX 30830-1

Roy Eldridge, Graham Young, Torg Halten, Norman Murphy (trumpet), Babe Wagner, Jay Kelliher, John Grassi (trombone), Mascagni Ruffo, Sam Listengart (alto saxophone), Sam Musiker (clarinet, tenor saxophone), Walter Bates (tenor saxophone), Milton Raskin (piano), Ray Biondi (guitar), Ed Mihelich (bass), Gene Krupa (drums)

Style: Ballad			Form: ABCA song form

			Introduction
76	0:00	8 bars	Opening trumpet cadenza: Roy Eldridge; band holds sustained notes; no rhythm section
		1st Chorus	**Solo melody: Roy Eldridge (trumpet)**
	0:21	A (8)	Eldridge plays free paraphrase of the melody; saxophones supply backgrounds; rhythm section accompanies in ballad tempo (note drummer Gene Krupa's use of *brushes*—splayed wires that he swishes across his snare drum in a gentle pulsating rhythm)
	0:42	B (8)	
	1:03	C (8)	Eldridge creates *buzz* at beginning of the phrase . . .
	1:25	A (8)	. . . again opens phrase with a *buzz*
		2nd Half-Chorus	
77	1:46	C (8)	Eldridge roars into the upper register, emphasizing his command of high F with a *shake*
	2:08	A (5)	
			Coda (tempo rubato)
	2:22		Closing trumpet cadenza: Eldridge plays brief classical-sounding call-and-response with clarinetist, Sam Musiker. Eldridge ends with stepwise ascent to high F

he learned note-for-note at age sixteen. Before moving to New York in 1930, he practiced for weeks from his brother Joe's clarinet manual in the hope of learning "to play fast like a clarinet." He also continued to absorb the idioms of Hawkins and saxophonist Benny Carter until, as he later put it, "I was playing fine saxophone on the trumpet." This meant, essentially, that he played lots of scales and arpeggios, and that he could negotiate chord changes in the harmonically astute manner of Hawkins.

In the early thirties Eldridge—nicknamed "Little Jazz" for his small stature and his devotion to playing—landed solo spots in the big bands of Teddy Hill and Fletcher Henderson. In the late thirties he led (or co-led with his brother, Joe Eldridge) his own small bands in Chicago and New York. He became famous when white drummer Gene Krupa hired him in 1941, marking one of the first instances of a black musician becoming a regular member of a white big band. With Krupa, Eldridge made several acclaimed recordings as a featured soloist, including "Rockin' Chair," "After You've Gone," and "Let Me Off Uptown." "They're all talking about him—now that he's with Gene Krupa's band," wrote a *Metronome* reporter. In 1944 he played as a featured soloist with Artie Shaw as well.

But Eldridge's stints with Krupa and Shaw were the most traumatic of his career. Touring the West Coast with Krupa, he repeatedly had to search for accommodations on the opposite side of town from the hotel occupied by the white players. With Shaw he faced similar indignities. At one engagement that featured his name on the marquee outside, Eldridge was initially barred from entrance for his skin color. "When I finally did get in," he recalled, "I played that first set, trying to keep from crying. By the time I got through the set, the tears were rolling down my cheeks." Reflecting on his experience with the white bands, he said, "Man, when you're on the stage, you're great, but as soon as you come off, you're nothing. It's not worth the glory, not worth the money, not worth anything. Never again!" To avoid Jim Crow, Eldridge in later years spent considerable time in Europe, where the appreciation was more generous and the racism less apparent.

Art Tatum

In terms of sheer instrumental skill, the greatest virtuoso of the Swing Era was undoubtedly the pianist **Art Tatum** (1909–1956). Tatum combined a mastery of Harlem stride with the classical technique of a concert pianist. Born and raised in Toledo, Ohio, Tatum lost the sight in one eye, retaining only partial vision in the other, at a young age (no one knows exactly how). Yet, he possessed a keen sense of hearing and an acute memory. From age three he was teaching himself hymns and popular melodies on the piano. He apparently received some musical training and, presumably, exposure to classical literature, as a teenager. But he learned to play primarily by listening to piano rolls, records, and radio, and by copying what he heard.

Art Tatum in a club on 52nd Street.

By the mid-twenties, he had already developed a local reputation for breath-taking keyboard technique. In 1932 singer Adelaide Hall hired him as her accompanist and brought him to New York, where he was met by the three kings of Harlem stride, James P. Johnson, Willie the Lion Smith, and—Tatum's main influence—Fats Waller. The cutting session they held in Harlem to test the newcomer's mettle has become part of jazz mythology. After hearing Tatum sail through his head-spinning rendition of "Tea for Two," his distinguished hosts each took their turns. Johnson played his specialty, "Carolina Shout," and Waller played "Handful of Keys," but both paled against Tatum's next number, "Tiger Rag," a hurricane treatment of the old ODJB standard. Johnson even tried upping the ante with a classical selection: Chopin's *Revolutionary Etude.* But such efforts were fruitless. Recalling that night, Waller said, "That Tatum, he was just

ART TATUM, *"Too Marvelous for Words"* (1955)

This performance was recorded at a private party at the home of Hollywood film composer Ray Heindorf one year before Tatum's death. In the words of critic Martin Williams, the recording suggests that Tatum "knew everything there is to know or could be discovered in jazz about the European harmonic system," and that "Too Marvelous" is "very likely . . . the greatest single Tatum performance we are fortunate to have."

Tatum's basic improvisational strategy in "Too Marvelous for Words" is one of elaborate melodic paraphrase. In the first chorus he states the melody fairly straightforwardly, allowing it to unravel into virtuoso digressions only in the last A-section. From the second chorus Tatum treats the melody more as a vehicle for improvisation, but never leaves it entirely. Like a porpoise diving in and out of the waves, Tatum often plunges below the line of melodic recognizability to explore abstract figurations only to reemerge moments later, rejoining the melody at exactly the right place (in "real time," so to speak), as if he had never left it.

Tatum takes a highly sophisticated—if occasionally tongue-in-cheek—approach to harmony in this recording. Examples include his distantly *chromatic* (out-of-key) reharmonizations of the melody in the bridge of the first chorus (0:19), his transitory surprise modulation in the second A of the second chorus (0:465), and his wacky "wrong-note" chords at the end of the second A of the third chorus (1:29). Sometimes Tatum combines unexpected harmonies with strange rhythms to momentarily obscure the form. For example, at the end of the bridge of the second chorus he lapses into a slowed-down, catawampus parody of stride style (1:03). As if stuck in a trance-like state, Tatum continues the parody past the end of the bridge and two measures into the final A-section, then "snaps out of it" and picks up the harmonic thread with disarming confidence, as if to wink at the listener: "Just putting you on!"

The climax of the performance begins during the bridge of the third chorus (1:39). Tatum plays increasingly florid virtuoso embellishments—a series of furious right-hand ascents, a longer and even more torrential descent, and finally a head-spinning, double-handed race down the keyboard (in parallel octaves) that seemingly brings the performance to the edge of chaos. Sensing the need to close soon after such an intense moment, Tatum begins the next chorus at the bridge rather than the A-section.

LISTENING CHART 18

Art Tatum, "Too Marvelous for Words" (Whiting-Mercer)

CD 1 / Tracks 78–81

RECORDED 3 JULY 1955, LIVE AT A PRIVATE PARTY IN BEVERLY HILLS / 20TH CENTURY FOX SFX 3029

Art Tatum (solo piano)

Style: Swing piano			Form: AABA song form

		1st Chorus	**Melody**
78	0:00	A (8)	Art Tatum plays melody fairly straightforwardly, in uptempo stride style (although the oom-pahs here are implied rather than explicitly stated)
	0:10	A (8)	
	0:19	B (8)	Tatum uses distantly *chromatic* (out-of-key) substitution chords to harmonize the melody
	0:28	A (8)	Melody begins to dissolve into increasingly elaborate running lines
		2nd Chorus	**"Solo" section**
79	0:37	A (8)	To open the "improvised solo" portion of the performance, Tatum plays fast runs in the right hand
	0:46	A (8)	Tatum returns to melody but in the wrong key . . .
	0:49		. . . then resumes the right key *here*
	0:55	B (8 + 2)	Tatum continues with the melody but at the end of the bridge lapses trancelike into . . .
	1:03		. . . a slowed-down parody of stride style that extends the section by two measures
	1:07	A (6)	Tatum picks up the chord progression two measures in and completes the chorus
		3rd Chorus	
80	1:15	A (8)	Tatum playfully stabs at the melody with his right hand while playing *trills* with his left, then . . .
	1:20		. . . launches a whirling cascade of runs into the upper register

	1:24	A (8)	Tatum resumes the melody, for the first time accompanying with the oom-pahs of classic stride
	1:29		. . . plays wacky "wrong-note" chords
	1:34	B (8)	Tatum opens the bridge with the melody, then . . .
	1:39		. . . begins a succession of increasingly florid embellishments that ascend inexorably . . .
	1:44	A (8)	. . . descend in a right-hand torrent, and finally CLIMAX with . . .
	1:49		. . . a head-spinning, double-handed race down the keyboard that seemingly brings the performance to the edge of chaos

4th Half-Chorus

81	1:54	B (8)	Tatum pulls back into the security of the melody (but begins the chorus half-way through, at the bridge)
	1:56		. . . plays strangely disorienting passage of surreal chord patterns and rhythmic dislocations

Rubato A-Section / Coda

	2:04	A (8 + 6)	Tatum closes in tempo rubato, whimsically restating the final A-section and expanding it into a coda

too good. . . . When that man turns on the powerhouse, don't no one play him down. He sounds like a brass band."

In 1933 Tatum made his first solo recordings, including "Tea for Two" and "Tiger Rag." During the next few years he played at the Onyx Club, the Three Deuces, the Famous Door, and other spots on 52nd Street and in Harlem. Through these engagements and the airtime that went with them Tatum developed a reputation of Herculean proportions. Larger-than-life stories circulated—about his fantastic speed and accuracy, his ability to play with his left hand what others could only play with their right, his superhuman endurance (he once reputedly battled a pianist for twenty-four hours straight), even his prodigious drinking capacity. But while musicians deified Tatum, the public was only dimly aware of him. That changed somewhat in 1943 when he organized his popular **Art Tatum Trio,** featuring Tiny Grimes on guitar and Slam Stewart on bass. But Tatum still ranked relatively low in the jazz polls. *Metronome* only named him the No. 1 pianist once, in 1945, while *Down Beat* never did.

The late forties and early fifties is now widely regarded as his finest period artistically. He performed a number of jazz concerts, including a very successful one in 1949 at the Shrine Auditorium in Los Angeles, which was later issued on record. In 1953 Norman Granz recruited Tatum to tour with Jazz at the Philharmonic. That same year Granz offered Tatum carte blanche in the recording studio: the chance to sit at the piano and play whatever he wanted. Granz

Great Debates

WHERE TO PUT ART TATUM?

Art Tatum is surely one of the most controversial figures in jazz history. Among musicians there is little argument: most consider him simply the greatest jazz pianist that ever lived. Legend has it that the great Fats Waller, upon seeing Tatum in the audience, announced from his piano bench: "God is in the house." Trumpeter Dizzy Gillespie remarked, "First you speak of Art Tatum, then take a long deep breath, and you speak of the other pianists." Pianist Mary Lou Williams said in a similar vein: "Tatum does everything the other pianists try to do and can't."

Critics have been far more reluctant canonizers. The three most influential critics of the postwar period, Gunther Schuller, Martin Williams, and Andre Hodeir, acknowledge Tatum's mind-boggling technique but question his long-term significance. In an article entitled (with sarcastic quotation marks), "The 'Genius' of Art Tatum," Hodeir argues that Tatum was no more than a suberbly gifted cocktail pianist who never achieved "true artistic creation" because of his faulty conception of jazz. In particular, Hodeir assails Tatum's unadventurous repertory, his penchant for ornamentation (as opposed to invention), his habit of performing preset routines rather than improvising, and his weakness for overt semi-classical references, which Hodeir views as in poor taste and antithetical to jazz. Schuller echoes these objections, asserting that "craft is perhaps a more apt term" than "art" when speaking of Tatum's music. For Schuller, Tatum ultimately failed to "channel his superior [technical] gifts into a more deeply expressive and creatively more original language."

Not all critics agree with these assessments. The distinguished British writer Leonard Feather, for instance, insists that Tatum "was the greatest soloist in jazz history, regardless of instrument." For Feather, Tatum's flowery style is not superficial. His greatness "was not due to the technique per se, but to the incredibly brilliant flow of ideas it enabled him to express." Pianist and educator Billy Taylor agrees. Whereas Schuller and Williams both claim that Tatum was harmonically inventive but melodically impoverished, Taylor states that "he was basically a melodic pianist; . . . his playing was always melodic, not just exercises." Despite such skirmishes over how to interpret Tatum's music, the real debate seems to hinge, as is so often the case, on the debaters' definition of jazz and what properly belongs in a jazz performance. In this regard, it may be helpful to remember what one of Tatum's friends said of him: "You could always get his goat by calling him a *jazz* piano player. He didn't like to be called that; said he was a *piano* player, a *musician*." ■ ■ ■

released the result—twelve long-playing records—under the promotional title *The Genius of Art Tatum.*

On these late recordings Tatum continued to play the same repertory he had played all his life—popular songs and light classics. As before, his technique was one of elaborate melodic paraphrase rather than harmonic improvisation. He worked up routines to the various items in his repertory, so that repeat performances would often follow similar contours. Yet despite all this, his best performances from this period do not sound stale; on the contrary, they give evidence of a depth and excitement in his playing, particularly through daring harmonic and rhythmic explorations, that are sometimes absent in his earlier recordings.

Female Singers   Chapter 15

Every name band during the Swing Era had singers—a "girl singer" or a "boy singer" (as the quaint language of the day had it) or both if the band was wealthy enough. Peggy Lee sang for Benny Goodman, Jimmy Rushing for Count Basie, Doris Day for Les Brown, Ivie Anderson for Duke Ellington, Frank Sinatra for Tommy Dorsey, and Anita O'Day for Gene Krupa. The top white bands could afford to hire complete vocal ensembles—trios and quartets for men's, women's, or mixed voices. The **Andrews Sisters** became famous for their hit recordings, "Boogie Woogie Bugle Boy" and "Don't Sit Under the Apple Tree," sung in swinging rhythms and close three-part harmony. Although less well known, the Boswell Sisters, the Mills Brothers, and the Sentimentalists also made outstanding recordings in this style.

Although both types of vocalist—the individual soloist and the harmonizing group singer—helped shape jazz history, the soloists had a far greater influence. Of special importance is the fact that for the first time in jazz, women dominated the field. Louis Armstrong laid the foundations for jazz singing in the twenties, and Jimmy Rushing and Billy Eckstine added to his legacy in the thirties and forties. But most other male singers, including Frank Sinatra and Bing Crosby, specialized in **crooning,** a soft, high-pitched vocal style for slow romantic ballads. The era of the male jazz singer would come later (see Chapter 25). In the meantime, female singers—known in the 1930s as "chirpers," "warblers," or "canaries"—overcame the staunch male exclusiveness among jazz musicians to make their own lasting contributions. No list of jazz legends would be complete without two names in particular: Billie Holiday and Ella Fitzgerald.

Women in Jazz

If you were to ask a male denizen of the Swing Era about the role of women in jazz, you might be as likely to hear about cheesecake photographs on the cover of *Down Beat* magazine as about any particular female musicians. It's not that women didn't play jazz; indeed, they had done so from the beginning. Female musicians performed on every jazz instrument throughout the twenties, thirties, and forties in **all-girl bands** like the black International Sweethearts of Rhythm and the white Darlings of Rhythm. But before the draft, very few female instrumentalists performed as "sidemen" with male swing bands. From the male perspective, women mostly added sex appeal to the swing movement. This

crooning a soft, high-pitched vocal style for slow, romantic ballads; usually associated with male singers.

Dick Haymes and the Andrews Sisters during a CBS radio broadcast.

attitude is clear in one critic's discussion of the male big band led by Ina Ray Hutton: "The band in which Ina Ray began waving her long baton in a languorous, seductive sort of way in 1940 was composed of several good jazz musicians. . . . It played well, if usually too loudly, but with Ina Ray weaving her torso in her magnificent, undulating manner, it managed to attract customers."

Widespread prejudices about the "femininity" of certain instruments hampered the progress of woman jazz musicians. Wind instruments and percussion were generally viewed as masculine; the spectacle of a straining trumpet player's red face and bulging veins, for instance, was considered unbecoming on a woman. But the piano allowed a woman to maintain graceful posture and perform "quiet" music that could be enjoyed in one's living room. The perceived "femininity" of the piano made it possible for female pianists to perform in male-dominated jazz bands from the music's earliest days. Pianist Lil Hardin Armstrong performed with the pioneering New Orleans Jazz Band, with King Oliver's Creole Jazz Band, and later with husband Louis Armstrong and her own groups. In the 1930s and 1940s **Mary Lou Williams** (1910–1981) and, later, **Marian McPartland** (b. 1920) made international names for themselves as leading jazz pianists. In the sixties and seventies, Toshiko Akiyoshi won broad critical acclaim for her big band compositions and piano playing (see Chapter 25). Still, an ingrained "boys' club" mentality among jazz musicians has always tended to favor male pianists over female.

It was only in the domain of singing that women surpassed men in stature and influence. During the Jazz Age the classic blues singers established unimpeachable authority as interpreters of the blues. Some of this authority was lost during the transition to the Swing Era. But in some ways sexist attitudes played to the advantage of female vocalists. Although "girl singers" were often viewed as glamorous ornaments to the big bands, sitting prettily and demurely until it was their turn to sing, this very role allowed them to participate unfettered by constant comparisons with men. Women could pursue careers as big band singers with the full expectation of reaching the top of their profession.

One might expect, in the aftermath of the 1970s feminist movement, that women today would have come a long way toward parity with men in jazz. It is true that a few woman horn players have earned reputations for inspired solo playing. But a glance at the most celebrated female jazz musicians of the early twenty-first century—people like the vocalist Cassandra Wilson and the pianist Geri Allen—indicates that the old instrumental stereotypes are probably still with us.

Jazz Singing and the Microphone

During the late 1920s popular singers in live settings usually sang into a small megaphone in order to be heard above the combined noise of the band and nightclub audience. In radio and recording studios, however, they used a new and entirely different technology to transmit their voices: a microphone. The microphone freed singers of the need to belt out songs in the manner of so many generations of vaudeville performers. They could, in fact, sing at the volume level of their speaking voices, creating a sound that was at once calm, casual, and intimate. By the early 1930s radio audiences preferred this more conversational singing style, with which crooners Rudy Vallee and Bing Crosby had won large (predominantly female) followings. Around the same time, technology had progressed to the point that singers began to replace megaphones with microphones and amplifiers in live performance.

This development crucially shaped jazz singing style. The live microphone allowed Louis Armstrong, Billie Holiday, Ella Fitzgerald, and others to explore the subtlest nuances of vocal expression, making complex and subjective emotional statements. Because the microphone "hears" so well, as one writer expressed it, "it is merciless in its exposure of blemishes. . . . But it can also detect and amplify virtues, delicate refinements of melodic line and vocal inflection, minute shadings and subtleties of enunciation and phrase, that would be inaudible without its electronic assistance." The intimacy of the microphone also permitted singers to connect more personally with their listeners, as if communicating with each of them one-on-one. These advantages especially played to the strengths of Billie Holiday, a weak singer in purely conventional terms who used the microphone as an indispensible part of her artistic expression.

Billie Holiday

Of the many sad biographies in jazz history, the story of **Billie Holiday** (1915–1959) is perhaps the most poignant. The details of her early life are uncertain. Originally named Eleanora Harris, she was born out of wedlock in Philadelphia and raised in Baltimore. Eleanora endured many traumatic experiences as a child. One day she awoke from a nap to find herself in the cold arms of her just deceased great-grandmother, one of the few nurturing adult figures in her life. Suffering abuse and scorn at the hands of relatives, she became a child of the streets and spent time in a reform school for truancy. After being left in the care of others at the age

Billie Holiday, 1943.

of ten or eleven she drifted into prostitution, in which environment she was repeatedly beaten and abused.

Around 1929 she moved with her mother to Harlem, where they lived in a tenement building that also housed a brothel. Eleanora ran errands for the Madam in return for being allowed to listen to the record player in the parlor. Her favorite records were those of Bessie Smith and Louis Armstrong—especially Armstrong's "West End Blues." Sometimes the music made her happy, she recalled, and "sometimes the record would make me so sad I'd cry up a storm." Drawing on her native pluck and charisma, Eleanora began singing in Harlem speakeasies as a teenager, bluffing her way past objections to her youth and lack of experience. At her audition at Smalls' Paradise, the pianist asked what key she wanted to sing in. "I don't know, man, you just play," she answered gamely. During this period she changed her name to Billie, after her film idol, Billie Dove. She took the last name of her father, successful dance band musician Clarence Holiday.

One evening in 1933 John Hammond by chance heard the eighteen-year-old Holiday sing at Monette's Supper Club at 133rd Street. He instantly decided that this unknown performer was the greatest jazz singer he had ever heard. "I couldn't believe it. In the first place, you couldn't have a microphone in a speakeasy because the noise might filter out to the street. So Billie was just singing . . . to customers at tables . . . she sang the same song at each table completely differently. I had never heard a really improvising singer until that time. So I knew that she was unique." Combining musical elements from Bessie Smith and Louis Armstrong, Holiday had developed a conversational singing style with acute rhythmic and tonal finesse. As Hammond recognized, Holiday—like a jazz instrumentalist—recomposed the melodies of the songs she sang, changing rhythms, dropping some pitches, adding others, gently stretching her material into vital new shapes. Like Armstrong, she liked to sing somewhat behind the beat, a technique jazz musicians call *laying back;* often she would sing a phrase late and then compress the melody to catch up with the chord progression. The color of her voice was haunting—fragile, bittersweet, with fast vibrato, yet curiously warm and full of emotion.

Teddy Wilson

In 1935, through the intervention of Hammond, pianist **Teddy Wilson** (1912–1986) hired Holiday to sing for his small-group recordings, inaugurating a now-classic series that would last for four years. Although Art Tatum was the most astounding pianist of the Swing Era, Wilson epitomized swing piano as practiced by mere mortals. This is not to slight Wilson, who matched Tatum in inspiration (and, some would say, exceeded him in subtlety). Raised in Tuskegee, Alabama, Wilson spent the 1920s playing in the Chicago cabarets with the likes of Louis Armstrong and Jimmie Noone. In 1933 he came to New York, where he developed a swing piano style of exceptional refinement and elegance. **Swing piano** retained the striding left hand of Harlem stride but freed the right hand to roam more freely—like an improvising horn player. In 1935 Benny Goodman broke the color barrier by hiring Wilson to play in his trio, along with drummer Gene Krupa. During the next four years Wilson played in Goodman's small groups while at the same time leading his own with Holiday.

Holiday's records with Wilson established her reputation as the country's premiere jazz singer. The records featured some of the finest jazz soloists of the day, including Roy Eldridge, Buck Clayton, Ben Webster, Lester Young, and

Benny Goodman. Holiday performed with many of these same figures in 52nd Street clubs like the Famous Door, the Onyx, and Kelly's Stable. By the end of the decade she had become, in the words of one biographer, "the biggest star" on 52nd Street. She also performed brief stints with the big bands of Count Basie (1937) and Artie Shaw (1938). With Shaw she became one of the first black singers to perform publicly with a white band. But Holiday was never comfortable with the conventional role assigned to her by the swing industry. In 1939 she even stopped recording under Wilson's name, declaring that she was no longer going to be someone else's "girl singer."

Solo Career

By this time Holiday was beginning to attract a broad popular audience. In 1939 she began an extended engagement at **Café Society** in Greenwich Village (see Map 7). The first New York nightclub with racially integrated clientele, Café Society strongly appealed to left-wing intellectuals. That same year, Holiday recorded a protest song called "Strange Fruit," with lyrics by the poet Lewis Allen. The song began:

> Southern trees bear a strange fruit,
> Blood on the leaves and blood at the root,
> Black bodies swaying in the Southern breeze,
> Strange fruit hanging from the poplar trees.

TEDDY WILSON AND HIS ORCHESTRA, *"I Wished on the Moon"* (1935)

CD 1 / Track 82

"I Wished on the Moon" was Billie Holiday's first recording with Teddy Wilson. Wilson recalled that he and Holiday would rehearse in his living room before going to the studio. Holiday would winnow a long list down to three or four songs, then they would work on each one: "And we rehearsed them until she had a very good idea of them in her mind, in her ear. . . . She would invent different little phrases—all great jazz singers do that, do variations on the melody, and they have to know the melody inside out in order to do that."

The lyrics for "I Wished on the Moon," written by Dorothy Parker, evoke a sadly sweet tale of love at its most innocent and trusting. Holiday brings to it her characteristic dead-on emotional interpretation. To emphasize the opening line she *lays back* dramatically, almost getting behind the rhythm section. When she casually wishes for "something I never knew," the authenticity of that sentiment echoes loudly, despite her gentle, understated expression. As she enumerates her wishes— "a sweeter rose, a softer sky," and so on—she sustains the syllables a little longer in each phrase, as if wanting to endow her dreams with permanence.

Holiday is accompanied here by (from our perspective) an all-star band, including Roy Eldridge on trumpet, Ben Webster on tenor saxophone, Benny Goodman on clarinet, and Cozy Cole on drums. Led by Teddy Wilson's superb piano playing, the rhythm section swings consummately. Notice also, the alternation of different improvisational styles between Goodman (melodic paraphrase) and Wilson (harmonic improvisation) in the first chorus, and the Chicago-style polyphony in the concluding half-chorus.

Create your own listening chart (CD 1 / Track 82)

As a powerful denunciation of lynching, "Strange Fruit" captured the imagination of socially conscious Americans, including most of Holiday's audience at Café Society. This recording marked her emergence as a *chanteuse*, a jazz-influenced pop singer of widespread appeal.

In the early forties Holiday specialized in dark, melancholy love ballads such as "Gloomy Sunday" and "Lover Man," songs that forecast multiplying troubles in her own life. Despite increasing financial success, Holiday began a long descent into misery and despair, which culminated in her premature death at age forty-four. She became addicted to alcohol and heroin, spent time in jail, and passed through several abusive relationships with men. Hackneyed as it might sound, the harrowing backdrop of her life experiences imparted an emotional potency to her music that no jazz singer has ever matched.

Ella Fitzgerald

In personality, singing style, and life experiences, **Ella Fitzgerald** (1917–1996) was in many ways Billie Holiday's polar opposite. Unlike the sensuous and worldly-wise Holiday, Fitzgerald came across, even in middle age, as naïve and childlike; an early reviewer wrote that her voice sounds like it "has peach fuzz on it." Plain and overweight, Fitzgerald never met the standard of jazz or pop singer as sex symbol. Despite her biography's lack of turbulent romance or scandal, Fitzgerald became one of the greatest jazz singers—some say the best ever.

Born in Newport News, Virginia, Ella moved with her family to Yonkers in the early twenties. Her favorite singers were Louis Armstrong and white singers Bing Crosby and **Connee Boswell** (1907–1976), one of the Boswell Sisters. This biracial listening diet helps to explain, perhaps, why in later years Fitzgerald could swing powerfully but, unlike many other black singers, felt out of place on the blues. When Ella was fifteen her mother died, leaving her an orphan. Sent to live with an aunt in Harlem, she began missing school and making money illegally, by running numbers for gangsters and serving as a "look-out" for prostitutes. At age seventeen Ella ran away and began a homeless life on the streets.

Her professional career began in 1934, when she performed in an amateur talent contest at Harlem's **Apollo Theater** (see Map 5). In the style of Connee Boswell she sang "Object of My Affection" and "Judy" to such tremendous applause that she won the contest. Yet bandleaders were slow to hire her. Not an attractive girl under the best of circumstances, as a street urchin Ella dressed poorly, smelled bad, wore disheveled hair, and was awkward socially. But in the spring of 1935 Chick Webb's male singer prevailed upon his boss to give her a chance. Drummer **Chick Webb** (1909–1939) was a leading bandleader in Harlem and a champion competitor at the Savoy Ballroom who in 1935 thirsted for a national reputation. Born with an affliction that left him short, crippled, and hunchbacked, Webb had his own physical challenges. But he didn't hire Fitzgerald out of sympathy. After giving her a trial period of a few weeks, he became convinced that she was just the "girl singer" he had been looking for.

Singing for Chick Webb, Fitzgerald offered a compelling alternative to Billie Holiday's style of jazz singing. "Her voice is seemingly tinged with honey," wrote one reporter, "and she sings with a rhythmic tempo that puts her over with a bang." Fitzgerald possessed a clear, girlish tone often mistaken for a white woman's voice. She had an unerring sense of pitch, meticulous diction, a wide range, virtuosic agility, and a rhythmic ebullience that often carried the entire

Ella Fitzgerald and Chick Webb at the Apollo Theater, 1939.

performance. Occasionally, especially in later years, she scatted with all the confidence and creativity of an improvising horn player. In short, she seemed the complete jazz singer. Her chief flaw was in emotional and psychological expression, the same area in which Billie Holiday excelled. Fitzgerald brought the same joyous exuberance to every song she sang, and sometimes sounded hollow on anything requiring more complex emotions.

Even so, in the mid-thirties she began to rival Holiday in popularity. She took first place in the 1937 *Down Beat* readers' poll for Best Female Vocalist. The rivalry peaked in early 1938 at the famous battle at the Savoy between Chick Webb and Count Basie, in which Fitzgerald sang for Webb and Holiday for Basie. Although most observers gave the overall night to Basie, Fitzgerald "was well out in front over Billie Holiday," reported *Down Beat.* "When Ella sang, she had the

ELLA FITZGERALD, *"A Fine Romance"* (1963)

CD 1 / Track 83

"A Fine Romance" formed part of the *Jerome Kern Songbook,* a collection that also included such evergreens as "All the Things You Are," "The Way You Look Tonight," and "Can't Help Lovin' Dat Man." The song first appeared in *Swing Time* (1936), a Hollywood film for which Kern wrote one of his best scores. Thus, while the vehicle comes from the Swing Era, Fitzgerald's performance here represents a much later, and somewhat evolved, manifestation of swing ideals. In this recording Nelson Riddle's Orchestra (which includes a full string section) accompanies Fitzgerald with a hard-swinging arrangement written by Riddle himself. (For more on big bands and singers after the Swing Era, see Chapter 25.)

Though not known for her deep emotional portrayals, Fitzgerald appears thoroughly at home with the mood of comic sarcasm and mock indignation of this lyric. Chiding her fictional boyfriend for their cold and boring relationship, Fitzgerald sings with wide-eyed exasperation: "I might as well play bridge with my old-maid aunts / I haven't got a chance / This is a fine romance!" Other references would have made sense to 1930s listeners (when the song was written), but probably not to today's. For example, the line, "But we just fizz like parts of a Seidlitz powder," refers to a popular cure for indigestion (which indeed had two "parts"—one in a blue wrapper and one in a white one). And the wonderful closing line, "You're just as hard to land as the Ile de France," suggests the struggle of maneuvering one of the largest luxury ocean liners of the day.

"A Fine Romance" showcases Fitzgerald's ability to build energy and excitement over the course of a performance. The recording lasts for three choruses in ABAC song form, each of which begins in a new key, starting a half-step higher than the previous one. Fitzgerald matches this natural intensification in two ways: by swinging harder with each new chorus, and by increasing the number of embellishments she adds to the basic melody. She (and the band) really shift into high gear at the end of the second chorus at the words, "I've never mussed the crease in your blue serge pants. . . ." Fitzgerald simultaneously stomps and floats through this transition to the third chorus with effortless aplomb. In the third chorus she swings fiercely (for instance, on "We two should be like clams in a dish of chowder"), while continuing to build toward the climax of the song—her final, rollicking "This is a fine ro-o-o-o-maaaaaaance," with the band wailing out a coda behind her.

Create your own listening chart (CD 1 / Track 83)

whole crowd rocking with her. . . . Handkerchiefs were waving, people were shouting and stomping, and the excitement was intense." Later that spring, Fitzgerald had her first number one hit with her own version of the nursery rhyme, **"A-Tisket, A-Tasket,"** arranged for Webb's band by Van Alexander. This recording made Fitzgerald a national celebrity and fulfilled Webb's dream of attaining name band status.

In 1939, the year of transition for so many swing bands, Webb died of tuberculosis of the spine. Fitzgerald led the band for three years, then disbanded and for the rest of her life worked as a single performing as a guest with other bands, with ad hoc ensembles on tour, or with hired orchestras in the studio. Like Holiday, she increasingly performed music from the pop repertory, a move that drew criticism from jazz purists. In the 1950s she toured with Jazz at the Philharmonic and Norman Granz became her manager. At Granz's urging she began, in 1956, an acclaimed series of albums called her ***Songbook*** **recordings.** On these records she sang standards from Broadway and Tin Pan Alley written by the great American songwriters—Cole Porter, Irving Berlin, George Gershwin, Richard Rodgers, and others. Writing in 1972, one critic summarized her achievement as follows: "Today Ella is firmly established within the jazz world as a great artist. . . . The arguments concerning her stature as a jazz singer have long since subsided. With the shrinking emphasis on categorization, the central fact has stood out in sharper perspective than ever: Ella Fitzgerald's is one of the most flexible, beautiful, and widely appreciated voices of this century."

Four

Bop
(c. 1945–1960)

Historical Context:
Postwar America

Chapter **16**

WHEN WORLD WAR II ENDED IN 1945, THE UNITED STATES ENTERED A PERIOD OF profound contradictions. Thousands of G.I.s came home from the war, got married, went to college, took executive jobs, bought houses in the suburbs, and in general enjoyed the postwar economic boom and immense prestige of the United States as "leader of the free world." But behind all this material satisfaction lurked more disturbing thoughts: the memory of a global war of unprecedented carnage, and a vague but real fear of sudden nuclear annihilation.

In the high art tradition in Europe and the United States, artists coped with these horrifying realities through a cerebral technical complexity, producing the theater of the absurd, abstract expressionism in the visual arts, and total serialism in music. American popular musicians, meanwhile, went in the opposite direction, drowning whatever anxieties they may have felt in the simple hedonism of sexually suggestive new dance idioms called rhythm-and-blues and rock 'n' roll. During this period the gulf between contemporary "art" and "popular" music widened to such a degree—with audiences generally fleeing the former and embracing the latter—that many questioned the future of modern music for the concert hall.

Chronology

early 1940s	Jam sessions at Minton's & Monroe's
1942–1944	AFM recording ban
1945	End of World War II
	Dizzy Gillespie and Charlie Parker make first records together
1948	Long-playing discs (LPs) introduced by Columbia records
1949	Birdland opens in New York City
1949–1950	Miles Davis makes *Birth of the Cool* recordings
1950s	Louis Armstrong tours internationally for U.S. State Department
1952	Modern Jazz Quartet organized
	Gerry Mulligan–Chet Baker Quartet organized
1954	*Brown v. Board of Education* Supreme Court decision
	Clifford Brown–Max Roach Quintet organized
	Dave Brubeck appears on cover of *Time* magazine
	First Newport Jazz Festival
1955	Miles Davis organizes his "first quintet"
1959	Miles Davis records *Kind of Blue*

People that grew up as teenagers during the Swing Era now had their own families to raise. Some continued to listen to jazz, but "jazz" no longer referred to a single type of music. One might have heard various species of swing, Dixieland, or a provocative new music played by black performers in New York City. Dubbed **bebop** by the press, the most recent style of jazz carried a modernist "edge" that affronted some audiences in the same way that avant-garde concert music did. Bebop changed and evolved throughout the fifties, eventually spawning two major substyles: **cool jazz** and **hard bop.** This Part (Chapters 16 through 21) treats these developments under the generic word "bop"—an umbrella term intended here to cover all three idioms.

That most of the bebop players were black is significant. Whereas black musicians previously saw jazz as a means to climb the social ladder, African Americans after World War II increasingly viewed their music as a channel for self-expression. This reflected a gradual shift in the black community from economic concerns to primarily political ones—from a mindset shaped by Booker T. Washington toward issues long advanced by W. E. B. Du Bois and the NAACP (see Chapter 1).

The Changing Status of Jazz

After the war, young Americans rejected big band jazz in favor of solo singers and other kinds of popular music. The decline of the big bands stemmed partly from the war itself. In clubs on 52nd Street and elsewhere, stiff wartime cabaret taxes motivated club owners to hire small groups instead of the more expensive big bands. In addition, the draft decimated the ranks of big bands, making it difficult to maintain a large ensemble during the war.

But perhaps the biggest reason for the big bands' loss of popularity was the **AFM recording ban.** Worried about musicians losing work due to the wide availability of records and radio broadcasts, the president of the American Federation of Musicians (AFM) wanted to force the "big three" record companies—Columbia, Victor, and Decca—to pay into a union fund for unemployed musicians each time a record was made. On August 1, 1942, he called a musicians' strike on all recording throughout the country. The ban lasted more than two years: Decca settled with the union in 1943, but Columbia and Victor held out until November, 1944.

During the recording ban most instrumental jazz recording came to a halt (with the notable exception of V-discs sponsored by the government for the sustaining of troop morale). The ban arrested the momentum of the big band movement. By the end of the war, even top bandleaders were forced to disband (sometimes temporarily) or scale back. In 1946 alone, the casualty list included Benny Goodman, Harry James, Woody Herman, Les Brown, Benny Carter, and Tommy Dorsey. Singers, by contrast, thrived. As members of the actors' rather than the musicians' union, singers had not been obligated to participate in the AFM strike. They continued to make records throughout the war, making do with *a cappella* vocal accompaniments (i.e., without instruments) during the recording ban. By the late 1940s, the biggest names in popular music were not Benny Goodman or Artie Shaw, but solo vocalists like Frank Sinatra, Doris Day, and Dinah Shore.

Where did this leave jazz? As we shall see in Chapter 25, some of the leading big bands limped along through the fifties and beyond, either on the strength of audience nostalgia or the bandleader's sheer will. But most musicians now turned to small-group jazz, with its emphasis on solo improvisation, as their principal mode of expression. During the war years, while the big bands had struggled, combos had flourished. Small groups—whether of the Dixieland, swing, or bebop varieties—weathered the recording ban by playing to enthusiastic audiences in nightclubs on 52nd Street and elsewhere. These audiences, however, did not represent the mass public; they were an elite cult of jazz fans who appreciated the music primarily for its listening, not dancing, pleasure. The jazz that emerged from World War II, then, was no longer America's favorite popular music; it was a chamber idiom of multiple styles valued for its artistic rather than its popular appeal. After a childhood in comedy and novelty, and an adolescence in glamorous swing showmanship, jazz had finally grown up as an art form—at least in the way it was perceived by the public.

The Prosperous Fifties

Despite their diminished economic status, postwar jazz musicians enjoyed the advantage of a prosperous society. After the war, as manufacturing shifted production from munitions to consumer products, the American economy boomed. In the 1950s the American dream was to own a house in the suburbs, where one could live close enough to a city to enjoy its cultural richness and economic strength but far enough away to escape its poverty, pollution, and—it must be acknowledged—ethnic diversity. American **suburbanization** thus manifested a strong element of "white flight." Yet, suburban life was glorified as a national aspiration in newspapers, magazines, and that all-important

$64,000 Jazz LP record jacket.

new medium, television. Popular TV programs such as *Father Knows Best* and *Leave It To Beaver* depicted the "ideal" American family happily ensconced in their suburban paradise.

Developed gradually over the previous two decades, television became as important to fifties culture as radio had been to the Swing Era. No longer at the center of popular culture, jazz played a supporting or a specialized role on TV. The most critically successful TV special on jazz was Robert Herridge's **The Sound of Jazz** (1957), an hourlong program featuring performances by such eminent figures as Count Basie, Billie Holiday, Roy Eldridge, Lester Young, Coleman Hawkins, Jimmy Rushing, Rex Stewart, and Thelonious Monk. In the late fifties, TV composers such as Henry Mancini and Pete Rugolo used jazz to evoke a tough, urban ambiance in the theme music for detective programs like *Peter Gunn, 77 Sunset Strip,* and *The Thin Man.*

One television show provided a barometer for the general popularity of jazz in the mid-fifties. In the summer of 1955 the first big money quiz show premiered under the name, *The $64,000 Question.* After the first celebrated contestants left with their winnings, the show's producers asked George Avakian of Columbia Records to put together a series of questions on jazz. Avakian eagerly accepted the assignment, hoping that if a contestant picked the "jazz" category, the show would help spur public interest in jazz, just as previous winning contestants had inspired widespread interest in Shakespeare or the Bible. When a minister from Oxford, Ohio, won the jackpot for his knowledge of jazz, Columbia released an album of jazz favorites called *$64,000 Jazz* to capitalize on his success. This incident reveals the predicament of jazz in the fifties: on the one hand, it drew respect culturally and intellectually but, on the other, it still needed promotional campaigns to increase its audience.

The Cold War

The happy lives portrayed on TV could not dispel the biggest cloud darkening 1950s society: the **Cold War** with the Soviet Union, a global struggle to determine which political system should rule the world—communism or democracy. The Korean War (1950–1953), fought to defend South Korea from the communist North, took the lives of over fifty thousand U.S. soldiers. Senator Joseph McCarthy and The House Un-American Activities Committee (HUAC) questioned the political loyalty of thousands of citizens, especially intellectuals, leading to destroyed reputations, blacklisting, and, for some, imprisonment. Awareness of the possibility of sudden nuclear attack produced widespread feelings of anxiety and alienation, driving multitudes of urban dwellers to undergo psychotherapy. To prepare for a surprise nuclear strike, public schoolteachers conducted bomb drills with their students.

Because the Cold War was essentially a war of ideologies, one of the most important weapons was propaganda. Among other tactics, the U.S. government presented jazz abroad as a powerful symbol of American freedom, creativity, and optimism. The government-sponsored radio program **Voice of America,** established in 1942 to broadcast American news and music to other countries during the Second World War, continued to be an important tool for disseminating American values during the fifties. Through Voice of America, disc jockey Willis Conover smuggled jazz into Eastern Europe, the Middle East, and other Soviet-controlled corners of the globe. In addition, the U.S. government commissioned prominent jazz artists such as Louis Armstrong, Duke Ellington, and Benny Goodman, to make "goodwill" **State Department tours** to other countries. Armstrong, with his joyous, upbeat stage presentation, became an especially popular emissary, even acquiring a new nickname: "Ambassador Satch." Commenting on the Cold War, a *New York Times* writer observed in 1955, "America's secret weapon is a blue note in a minor key. Right now its most effective ambassador is Louis (Satchmo) Armstrong. . . . American jazz has now become a universal language."

The Early Civil Rights Movement

In the black community the problem of racial injustice weighed as heavily as Cold War anxieties. During World War II blacks had continued to face segregation and other forms of discrimination even within the U.S. military. The NAACP newspaper, *Crisis,* pointed out the hypocrisy of being "*against* park benches marked 'Jude' [Jewish] in Berlin, but [being] *for* park benches marked 'colored' in Tallahassee, Florida." By the end of the war black Americans had reached a psychological turning point. It was time to demand fair treatment under the law for all citizens, regardless of race or color.

Armed with a firm belief in the righteousness of their cause, black leaders used the NAACP and the black church to challenge discriminatory legislation in court and organize nonviolent protests against unjust laws in the South. The most important early victory was the unanimous Supreme Court decision in ***Brown v. Board of Education*** (1954). Acknowledging that segregated educational facilities demeaned black students, this landmark decision demolished the doctrine of "separate but equal" enshrined sixty years previously in *Plessy v. Ferguson* (see Chapter 1). Now came the hard work of challenging segregation laws in all public places. In 1955 a seamstress named **Rosa Parks** was arrested for refusing to give her bus seat to a white passenger in Montgomery, Alabama. Under the leadership of **Dr. Martin Luther King Jr.,** a twenty-six-year-old Baptist preacher, the black citizens of the city organized the Montgomery bus boycott. As a divinity student, the young King had absorbed Mohandas Gandhi's teachings about nonviolent resistence. A trip to India in 1959 confirmed to him the necessity of taking "nonviolent direct action," as he put it, to achieve civil rights goals. By this time he had founded the **Southern Christian Leadership Conference (SCLC),** an organization that gave him national standing and influence.

Modern Jazz

The demand to be heard, to at last be taken seriously, that marked the early civil rights struggle also characterized the intellectual posture of the newest jazz styles—bebop, cool jazz, and hard bop. Young black exponents of these styles wanted to distance themselves from the dancing, joking, self-deprecating black

Louis Armstrong, c. 1956.

Miles Davis, *Round About Midnight* LP record jacket, 1956. Compare this image with Louis Armstrong's ingratiating demeanor.

entertainers of yore. They generally considered themselves artists, not entertainers, and self-consciously distinguished their music with the label **modern jazz,** a term which signaled their commitment to exploring the very latest musical developments. As Dixieland rose in popularity after the war, a prolonged debate ensued between its practitioners and those of modern jazz. The Dixielanders charged that bop musicians had forsaken jazz itself in their quest for expressive complexity. The boppers responded by branding the old-fashioned Dixieland players **moldy figs.**

The two camps were divided by generational as well as musical differences. Louis Armstrong (see Chapter 6), who in 1947 organized his own Dixieland group, the All-Stars, represented the old guard most prominently. In addition to performing hoary jazz tunes in an updated New Orleans style, Armstrong unabashedly sang, joked, and mugged in the tradition of his idols Bert Williams and Bill Bojangles Robinson. On the national and world stages, he enjoyed the greatest audience acceptance of his career, becoming a beloved icon of American popular culture. But in the emerging civil rights climate, young blacks felt embarrassed by Armstrong's obvious pandering to white tastes; they called him an Uncle Tom and rejected his music. For his part, Armstrong railed against bop and what he saw as the younger generation's shallow fixation on virtuosity and complexity for its own sake.

Armstrong's symbolic counterpart in modern jazz was undoubtedly trumpeter Miles Davis (see Chapter 21). Ever respectful of Armstrong's consummate musicianship, Davis resented his attacks on bop and his jolly, ingratiating stage persona. Embittered by racist incidents he had experienced growing up in East St. Louis, Davis took pride in being a *modern* jazz musician. This identity freed him from any obligation to please an audience; as a serious artist, he would

modern jazz general term covering several progressive jazz styles after World War II, including bebop, cool jazz, hard bop, and free jazz.

play music that he found meaningful, regardless of what others might think. As if to emphasize his role as the anti-Armstrong, Davis often turned his back on the audience and played toward his sidemen. For him, as for his slightly younger contemporary Martin Luther King, the time was long past for accommodating white preferences.

Armstrong and Davis, of course, did not represent all jazz in the postwar period. In the mid-1950s, British critic Stanley Dance coined the term **mainstream jazz** to describe the music of players who avoided the stylistic and ideological extremes of both Dixieland and modern jazz. By this definition, the large number of mainstream artists in the fifties included Billie Holiday, Ella Fitzgerald, Benny Goodman, Lester Young, Art Tatum, Roy Eldridge, Coleman Hawkins, and most of the other Swing-Era soloists that toured regularly with Norman Granz's popular concert series, Jazz at the Philharmonic (see "Offstage Personalities: Norman Granz"). As jazz continued to evolve and diversify in subsequent decades, however, the concept of a jazz "mainstream" would become increasingly difficult to rationalize.

Offstage Personalities

NORMAN GRANZ (1918–2001)

More than any other single person in the 1950s, perhaps, impresario and record producer Norman Granz fostered the public perception of jazz as art music. Born and raised in Los Angeles, Granz discovered jazz through the intermediary of Lester Young's younger brother, who invited him to attend jam sessions. Thrilled with what he heard, Granz determined to market jazz in its authentic, unvarnished, improvisational state. In 1944 he booked Billie Holiday, Lester Young, and pianist Nat Cole (better known today as Nat "King" Cole) for a concert at the Los Angeles Philharmonic Auditorium, thereby launching his concert series, Jazz at the Philharmonic (JATP). Until 1957, when he discontinued the concerts, Granz brought such figures as Duke Ellington, Count Basie, Billie Holiday, Ella Fitzgerald, Roy Eldridge, Coleman Hawkins, Dizzy Gillespie, and Charlie Parker to audiences all over the United States and abroad, sometimes touring over fifty cities a year.

Granz worked tirelessly to present jazz with dignity, demanding due respect for the performers. At first he had to ask that audiences listen quietly rather than dancing or talking—an odd request today, perhaps, but not in the mid-forties. During a time of increasing civil rights agitation, Granz also fought to break down racial prejudice, insisting that his concerts be open to blacks and that his artists be granted access to hotels and restaurants, even in the most segregated cities. Granz paid his performers well—Ella Fitzgerald, for instance, made $50,000 a year for her JATP performances. And Granz's musicians appreciated the safe haven he created for them. "The whole outfit [JATP] was like a big family," recalled bassist Ray Brown. "Black musicians couldn't stay in decent hotels until Norman came along. People forget about what he did." In addition to his concert series, Granz was an influential record producer, starting the Verve label in 1955 and Pablo in 1974. Yet despite his honest commitment to jazz, he was a practical businessman. "I've never tried to prove anything," he said in 1952, "except that good jazz, properly presented, could be commercially profitable." ■ ■ ■

mainstream jazz in the 1950s, the music performed by the large group of soloists outside the Dixieland and modern jazz camps, mostly Swing Era–holdovers, who enjoyed fairly broad public acceptance.

Modernism and the Cult of Spontaneity

In New York, modern jazz connected with other modernist developments in the arts. In his famous essay "The White Negro" (1957), Norman Mailer extolled the life of the **hipster,** an enlightened white person—typically a writer, painter, or intellectual—who had appropriated the bohemian worldview and lifestyle of black jazz musicians. Among literary hipsters, the beat poets deliberately infused their work with jazz ideals. Abstract expressionist painters, according to one art historian, also drew inspiration from jazz: "The daily music of gesture painters almost without exception was jazz, particularly bop, so much so that the famous jazz club, the Five Spot Café . . . was sustained initially by an artist clientele."

One aspect of modern jazz that especially attracted the hipster-artists was its emphasis on improvisation. This attraction reflected their embrace of **existentialism,** a thought-system developed by European philosophers Jean-Paul Sartre and Albert Camus. Given mankind's ominous future in the postwar world, existentialists argued, one should live in the moment and luxuriate in the freedom to do so. Together with **Freudianism,** an implicit confidence in the power of the subconscious mind, existentialism prompted New York painters, writers, and actors to pursue spontaneity in the creative act. Jackson Pollock and other abstract expressionists employed a technique known as *psychic automatism,* in which they sought to eliminate any barrier between primal inspiration and the application of paint to canvas. Beat writers such as Jack Kerouac and Allen Ginsberg sought a similar directness, writing down their thoughts in the brutal honesty of the moment. And actors like Marlon Brando adopted an approach called *method acting,* in which they identified so closely with their characters that their portrayals became intuitive.

Stirred by heightened political discourse in the black community, jazz soloists in the fifties likewise trusted spontaneous self-expression. In the 1920s and 1930s, soloists had often played the same solos over and over again, either to perfect them incrementally or to satisfy audiences who wanted to hear the recorded versions in a live setting. But, as left-wing critics began exalting improvisation as the crucial folk element in all "true" jazz, such rehearsed solos came under condemnation. At the same time, marathon jam sessions on 52nd Street and elsewhere made improvisation a practical necessity. By the 1950s it was expected—as part of the modern ethos—that most jazz solos would be fully improvised, with little material worked out in advance. The authenticity of the moment became such a paramount virtue that during his recorded solo on "Bag's Groove" (1954), Miles Davis audibly blew the water out of the spit valves of his trumpet without stopping the take.

Jazz and Drugs

A more sinister tendency uniting hipsters and jazz musicians was the widespread use of illicit drugs. This problem was not new, of course; musicians in the twenties drank bootleg liquor, and players from the Swing Era smoked marijuana. But with a few exceptions (notably Bix Beiderbecke and Bunny Berigan), these individuals did not squander their careers in pursuit of their next high. For members of the bop generation it was different; **heroin** was their drug of choice, and it almost always marred the lives and careers of those who used it.

When the government repealed Prohibition in 1933, illicit drugs replaced alcohol as an important source of revenue for organized crime. After World War II, the Mafia stepped up its heroin trade in U.S. ghetto communities. Black musicians who lived in these neighborhoods fell prey to narcotics, but they were not the only ones to do so. Largely because of Charlie Parker's charismatic but devastating example, nearly every major up-and-coming jazz player in the fifties used heroin, including Max Roach, Bud Powell, Fats Navarro, Miles Davis, Sonny Rollins, and John Coltrane, as well as white musicians like Red Rodney, Gerry Mulligan, Chet Baker, Art Pepper, Stan Getz, and Bill Evans. Almost all of these eminent figures eventually faced the brink of professional, and sometimes personal, destruction because of their addictions. Only a few—a Clifford Brown, a Dave Brubeck—managed to escape heroin's baleful influence.

Nightclubs and Festivals

The artistic agenda of postwar jazz musicians insured that their music would be heard primarily in nightclubs rather than in ballrooms. By the late 1940s, however, 52nd Street had lost its status as the jazz center of New York. Worn down by wartime cabaret taxes, an encroaching drug culture, and the demand for bawdy entertainment by roving servicemen, nightclub owners began substituting striptease shows for live jazz. The Onyx made this switch in 1949, and the Famous Door and the Three Deuces followed in 1950. As early as 1948 *Metronome* printed a story headlined: "Jazz is Dead on 52nd Street and Very Much Alive on B'Way [Broadway]."

The most important jazz clubs on Broadway were **Birdland,** which opened in 1949 in honor of Charlie "Bird" Parker (see Chapter 18), and the Royal Roost, a club that hosted a great deal of modern jazz beginning in the late 1940s. Other leading clubs—including Café Bohemia, the Five Spot, and Jazz Gallery—could be found scattered throughout the downtown area in the part of the city known as Greenwich Village. Perhaps the most influential of these venues over the long term was the **Village Vanguard,** a club that started as a place to hear beat poetry but by the late fifties specialized in jazz. Over the years the Vanguard hosted virtually every major figure in modern jazz. It is the oldest New York jazz club still in business. (For all these clubs, see Map 7.)

To perform at a New York club (or any venue that served liquor), a musician had to possess what was known as a **cabaret card.** The police used the cabaret card system to control a professional community (which included stand-up comedians as well as musicians) known to abuse drugs. To obtain a card, an applicant had to pay a $2 fee, then be photographed and fingerprinted at a licensing division of the police department. Many jazz musicians, including Charlie Parker, Miles Davis, Billie Holiday, and—most notoriously—Thelonious Monk (see Chapter 17), had their cards temporarily revoked for possession of drugs. Those guilty of cabaret card violations not only had to pay fines and serve jail sentences but also were prohibited from performing in clubs until their cards were renewed. In 1967 New York's mayor abolished the cabaret card system on grounds of unconstitutionality.

Although not a steady source of income, **jazz festivals** also played an important role in the lives of musicians. Jazz festivals were celebration-performances of several days' duration, often held outdoors, featuring a long and diverse roster of artists. The first international jazz festivals took place in France in the late

1940s. In the United States, major festivals of the fifties included the Newport Jazz Festival (from 1954) held annually at Newport, Rhode Island (later in New York City), and the Monterey Jazz Festival (from 1958) in California. Modeled to some extent on the public jam sessions sponsored by impresarios of the thirties and forties, jazz festival performances could sometimes degenerate into meandering group prattle or mindless one-upmanship between top soloists in the jazz equivalent of a cock fight. But because of their high publicity, jazz festivals also had the potential to inspire magnificent performances, sometimes dramatically altering a musician's career. At the 1955 Newport Festival Miles Davis delivered a solo that, for many critics, announced his "comeback" after a lengthy fallow period. And at Newport the following year, Duke Ellington's previously moribund career was jump-started with an electrifying twenty-seven-chorus solo by tenor saxophonist Paul Gonsalves on "Diminuendo and Crescendo in Blue."

Jazz Recording in the Fifties

Today we can relive some of the excitement of Ellington's rediscovery at Newport because Columbia subsequently released lengthy portions of the band's festival performance on a single record (*Ellington at Newport*), a feat of technology that would have been impossible during the Swing Era. In 1948 Columbia introduced the 12-inch, 33⅓ rpm **long-playing disc (LP),** which contained up to twenty-five minutes of music per side. Two related innovations increased the fidelity of these recordings: first, the LP was a *microgroove* disc (having roughly one hundred grooves per centimeter as opposed to the 78's forty grooves), allowing more details of a performance to be captured on recording; second, LPs were made from vinyl instead of shellac, decreasing surface noise considerably. Records now became collections of pieces called *albums.* Some musicians tried to unify their albums with a common theme: for instance, Duke Ellington recorded his suites, Ella Fitzgerald her songbooks, and Miles Davis collaborated with Gil Evans to record songs from Gershwin's *Porgy and Bess.* But the most significant legacy of the LP was the freedom it gave jazz musicians (such as Paul Gonsalves) to improvise for several choruses on a single recording, thereby nurturing the development of long-range solo improvisation.

Criticism and Historiography

As improvised solos became more lengthy and complex, a new generation of critics arose to meet the challenge of interpreting the music. The fifties inaugurated a golden age of jazz writing, producing such eminent critics as André Hodeir, Max Harrison, Gunther Schuller, Martin Williams, and Lawrence Gushee. These writers offered especially provocative insights on the music itself, insights that form the basis for many of our current critical perspectives. Landmark works included Hodeir's ***Jazz: Its Evolution and Essence*** (1956), a book that incisively analyzed the problem of stylistic diversity in jazz, and Nat Shapiro and Nat Hentoff's ***Hear Me Talkin' To Ya: The Story of Jazz As Told By the Men Who Made It*** (1955), a pioneering work of oral history culling the best interviews published in jazz magazines from the previous two decades.

The coexistence of multiple styles prompted a reassessment of jazz history. Like Western classical music, jazz appeared to have historical periods: New Orleans style, Chicago style, swing, bebop, cool jazz, and hard bop. Whether they personally preferred old or new idioms, most writers saw the historical succession of styles as evidence of the intellectual weight of jazz as an art form. Contrary to early predictions, jazz was not a fad; it was a robust, protean music that had not only survived but had grown and evolved with time. The story of jazz was a rich saga of progress and development, of musical and human achievement over several generations.

By the 1950s the history of jazz had taken on the fixed character of legend, with romanticized stock elements particularly relating to the music's origins and early flowering. According to the most naïve popular accounts, jazz was "born" in black New Orleans, then "traveled up the river" (through performances on Mississippi river boats) until it arrived in Chicago (see cartoon by Eldon Dedini), where it thrived as a collectively improvised folk music uncompromised by the marketplace. During the Swing Era the insidious influence of commercialism drained the music of its vital force. Disturbed by the commercialized and overrehearsed arrangements of swing music, the young beboppers rebelled, reclaiming jazz for themselves and reinstituting its essential features of artistic integrity and pure improvisation. Despite many grains of truth in this narrative, historians today tend to view it as fanciful and ideologically driven. But in the fifties it served the useful purpose of making the story of jazz appealing and comprehensible to the public. It represented the first stage in an ongoing public relations campaign to recognize jazz as a noble and inspiring chapter in the larger drama of American history and culture.

"Pop, tell me again how Jazz came up the river from New Orleans."

Eldon Dedini, *New Yorker,* October 19, 1957. This cartoon places jazz history in the same camp with fairy tales, thereby emphasizing the drama, romance, and historical dubiousness of some of the stories about the music that circulated in the 1950s.

Chapter 17 Bebop

In the early 1940s a musical revolution was brewing in Harlem nightclubs. That's how it looks in hindsight, at least. At the time, the young players sparring in late-night jam sessions at Minton's and Monroe's harbored no explicitly subversive intentions. They were mainly just having a good time and trying to prepare themselves for the next chance to play with a name big band. Their radical experimentation and electrifying virtuosity, they hoped, would help them succeed in an increasingly competitive swing industry.

But as even the most famous and established black musicians struggled to survive the setbacks of the war years, disillusionment gripped the younger generation. If Fletcher Henderson and Jimmie Lunceford couldn't make it economically, how would little-known journeymen succeed, even with extraordinary abilities? This sobering realization prompted the young experimentalists to search for ways to make a living *outside* the big band world. Fortunately, the 52nd Street club scene and a wave of newly formed record companies provided just the opportunities they needed. By 1945 their music—now called *bebop* (or *rebop* early on)—represented a commercially viable alternative to swing.

When it first became known to the public, bebop contrasted with big band swing in fundamental ways. Its main characteristics included the following:

- Combo instrumentation, often featuring two horns (usually trumpet and saxophone) and a rhythm section (usually piano, bass, and drums)
- Simple arrangements, usually following the jam-session format: a succession of improvised solos between opening and closing statements of the melody
- Intricate melodies played in unison or octaves by the front-line horn players
- Higher levels of dissonance than what would be found in standard swing pieces
- Extremely fast tempos, or extensive *double-time* playing during slow and medium tempos
- Dazzling virtuoso solos, featuring angular, disjunct lines with irregular accents
- Little vibrato in sound of horn players; musicians not concerned with "beauty" of tone in traditional sense

This combination of unstable features—so different from the tuneful and danceable strains of the big bands—initially alienated many swing veterans, critics, and listeners. But as its novelty wore off and musicians began exploring its rhetorical possibilities, bebop acquired a friendlier sound and reputation. It would become the lingua franca for nearly all subsequent jazz soloists.

Cradles of Modern Jazz

The heyday of Harlem nightlife died with the Jazz Age. The effects of the Depression crippled the Harlem community, leading to civil unrest that culminated in the devastating riot of 1935. Harlem no longer seemed as safe or inviting to the wealthy whites who in the twenties had patronized such venues as the Cotton Club. By the mid-1930s, as we have seen, the center of jazz activity had begun shifting to 52nd Street (see Chapter 14). But two Harlem clubs would make a final—and crucial—contribution to the music before it moved downtown. As hangouts for the young players developing the language of bebop, Minton's and Monroe's became the cradles of modern jazz.

Minton's Playhouse, located on 118th Street in Harlem, was opened by Henry Minton in 1938 (see Map 5). Intended as a gathering place for musicians (not the public), Minton's offered jazz players the chance to jam in a relaxed atmosphere without a formal audience. Members of the house band received a nominal wage; other musicians were paid with food and drink. After their regular engagements, leading swing players such as Count Basie, Benny Goodman, Coleman Hawkins, and Roy Eldridge came to Minton's to jam, listen to the music, and socialize. After Minton's closed at 4 A.M., the city's wartime curfew, the musicians would move several blocks north to **Monroe's Uptown House** on 134th Street. As a technically illegal after-hours club, Monroe's didn't have a sign outside, and patrons—including movie stars and other entertainment celebrities—learned of the place by word of mouth. The owner, Clark Monroe, offered casual entertainment in the form of singers and dancers, but also hired a house band, mostly of talented teenagers. Knowing that the best jazz players in the city would sit in for free, Monroe paid the house band very little—about $2 per night plus refreshments.

Bebop Takes Shape

In 1940 Henry Minton hired big band leader Teddy Hill to organize the music at Minton's. Hill hired a house band of youngsters that included bebop pioneers Kenny Clarke and Thelonious Monk. Drummer **Kenny Clarke** (1914–1985) cultivated a new drumming style that had already gotten him fired from one big band. Swing drummers would unobtrusively thump the bass drum on all four beats and close the high-hat on beats two and four, creating a chugging momentum suitable for dancing. But Clarke began breaking up this symmetrical rhythmic flow by reinforcing the band's rhythms at important places and playing fills in between ensemble phrases—devices that earned him the onomatopoeic nickname, "Klook-Mop." Two of his innovations figured prominently in the future of bebop: transferring the steady "ding-dinga-ding" right-hand pattern from the high-hat to the more richly resonant *ride cymbal,* and releasing sporadic, unpredictable pops on the snare or bass drum—a technique known by the war-inspired term **dropping bombs.**

dropping bombs the practice among bebop drummers of playing sporadic, unpredictable pops on the snare or bass drum.

Many of the young musicians hung out at Minton's only because they were between jobs with touring swing bands. But pianist **Thelonious Monk** (1917–1982), who enjoyed the financial security of living with his mother, did not aspire to the big time. He worked at Minton's so he could "play my own chords," as he put it. "I wanted to create and invent [new musical ideas] on little jobs." The chords that captured Monk's imagination were unusually dissonant. He especially favored chords containing the *tritone,* an interval separated by three whole-steps (e.g., C to F-sharp). When the tritone was built on the *root* of a chord (i.e., the pitch on which a chord is based), the beboppers called it a **flatted fifth.**

One of the most influential early participants in Minton's jam sessions was an electric guitarist named **Charlie Christian** (1916–1942). Born and raised in Oklahoma City, Christian gained a local reputation for his precocious playing. After Gibson made the electric guitar commercially available in 1936, Christian adopted that instrument in order to compete with the volume of horn players. In 1939, the indefatigable talent scout John Hammond introduced Christian to Benny Goodman, who began featuring him in his small groups. Widely viewed today as the father of modern jazz guitar, Christian anticipated bebop with his long, flowing lines and chromatically embellished melodies. These traits attracted much admiration during his brief moment of celebrity with the Goodman sextet and after hours at Minton's and Monroe's. Unfortunately, Christian succumbed to tuberculosis at age twenty-five.

Further Listening from the *Prentice Hall Jazz Collection*
Track 2: Benny Goodman and Charlie Christian, "Seven Come Eleven" (1939)

An Elite Music

Leading players at Minton's and Monroe's used the rhythmic, harmonic, and melodic novelties of Clarke, Monk, Christian, and others, to exclude the "no-talent guys," as trumpeter Dizzy Gillespie put it, who tried to join in the jam sessions. If the regular participants wanted to ostracize or simply evaluate an interloper they would call standard tunes in unfamiliar keys (usually with many sharps or flats) and at blisteringly fast tempos. Together with unusually high levels of dissonance and rhythmic disruption, such tactics vanquished all but the most proficient players. The jam sessions at Minton's and Monroe's thus produced an elite circle of musicians who delighted in virtuosity and intellectual musical devices.

Trumpet players reached especially startling new levels of virtuosity. Dizzy Gillespie, Fats Navarro, and Howard McGhee all played faster and higher than any previous trumpet players had done, partly because of cross-instrumental influences. Like Louis Armstrong before them, several of the leading bop trumpeters took inspiration from clarinet style—or, in some cases, saxophone style. As we have seen, Roy Eldridge practiced from his brother's clarinet book and memorized Coleman Hawkins solos. Earl Hines recalled that Gillespie and alto saxophonist Charlie Parker used to practice from one another's exercise books. Howard McGhee, who played clarinet as a child, acknowledged that instrument's influence on his trumpet playing: "I got so I could play as fast as Roy [Eldridge], and eventually even faster because I studied clarinet in school." And Clark Terry, one of the most impressive trumpet virtuosos of the postwar generation, used to spend hours practicing from a clarinet manual and learning Lester Young solos.

flatted fifth a tritone built on the *root* (fundamental pitch) of a chord.

Dizzy Gillespie

No one did more to advance the new idiom than trumpeter **John Birks "Dizzy" Gillespie** (1917–1993). As a sideman in swing bands, he pushed the boundaries of his own ability in his solos; after hours he constantly practiced and experimented with new chords and rhythms. His attempt to master unorthodox techniques soon earned him an agility and range matched by few other trumpet players of his day. Together with his equally brilliant counterpart, alto saxophonist **Charlie Parker** (see Chapter 18), Gillespie moved bebop style from its experimental stage into a fully coherent and mature musical conception.

A native of Cheraw, South Carolina, Gillespie moved with his family to Philadelphia in 1935, the year swing became a national craze. Mostly self-taught on the trumpet, Gillespie developed some bad habits by conventional standards: he puffed his cheeks, and his tone was thin—not the rich romantic tone of most swing trumpet soloists. Even so, he played well enough to get a job with a local big band in Philadelphia. During this period he absorbed Roy Eldridge's style, learning many of his solos note-for-note. He also acquired his lifelong nickname, "Dizzy," for his outrageous comic behavior. Although Gillespie became one of the founding fathers of modern jazz, he shared with his predecessor Louis Armstrong a love of vaudeville tomfoolery.

In 1937 Gillespie moved to New York. Over the next several years he played as a soloist with various leading black big bands, including those of Teddy Hill, Cab Calloway, Earl Hines, and Billy Eckstine. While with Calloway, Gillespie began frequenting Minton's and Monroe's. At Minton's, according to jazz folklore, he liked to challenge his idol, Roy Eldridge, in cutting contests. As Kenny

Charlie Parker and Dizzy Gillespie at Birdland, 1950. *Right:* A youthful John Coltrane (see Chapter 24).

Clarke recalled, "Dizzy could play and his ideas were new, but try as he would, Dizzy could never cut Roy. Roy had drive and execution, and he could keep going chorus after chorus. Every time Dizzy tried, Roy gave him a lesson, made him pack. But Dizzy never quit. Then one night Dizzy came in and started blowing. He got it altogether that night. He cut Roy to everyone's satisfaction and that night Roy packed his horn and never came back. Dizzy was the new king and the cats were already beginning to call [the music] bop."

In 1942, Gillespie and Charlie Parker, whom he had met two years previously, joined Earl Hines's big band. During their stint with Hines, Gillespie and Parker spent a great deal of time together on the road and in hotel rooms, jamming, experimenting, and forging a close personal and musical bond. Gillespie showed Parker his favorite **substitution chords** to the standard harmonies of popular songs. Substitution chords, often altered chromatically to higher levels of dissonance, made harmonic progressions more challenging for a soloist. The most common substitution chord was the *tritone substitution,* a chord located a tritone away from the second to last chord in a cadence. Parker, in turn, influenced Gillespie with a new kind of phrasing based on asymmetrical melodic patterns and an unpredictable series of accents.

In 1944 Hines's male singer, **Billy Eckstine** (1914–1993), organized his own big band—the "first bop big band," according to many historical accounts—in which he intended to showcase the new music being developed in Harlem nightclubs. Eckstine made Gillespie the band's musical director, charging him with recruiting, rehearsing, and writing arrangements. Gillespie formed a powerhouse ensemble that featured some of the hottest young players then available, including Fats Navarro, Dexter Gordon, Sarah Vaughan, Art Blakey, Howard McGhee, and Lucky Thompson. When the band came through St. Louis, an eighteen-year-old Miles Davis listened spellbound: "When I heard Diz and Bird in B's band, I said, 'What? What is this!?' . . . [That] music [was] all up in my body, and that's what I wanted to hear. The way that band was playing music—that was *all* I wanted to hear." Yet, both Gillespie and Parker felt stymied with Eckstine. Like most black organizations, the Eckstine band had to make lengthy and exhausting tours of the South, where their black dancing audiences primarily wanted to hear the blues. This was not what Gillespie and Parker had hoped for; by late 1944 both had returned to New York to cast their lot with small groups on 52nd Street.

The Move to 52nd Street

In March 1945, Gillespie opened at the **Three Deuces** with a quintet that included Charlie Parker, white pianist Al Haig, bassist Curly Russell, and Max Roach on drums. On the strength of its residency at the Three Deuces, the Gillespie-Parker quintet was booked for two successful concert performances at New York's Town Hall that summer. Reporting on the first concert in May, a *Metronome* critic wrote, "Dizzy was in magnificent form. I've never heard him play so well . . . and reach such inspired heights. Dizzy's boys played through the first half of the concert unrelieved [by other groups], and the effect was stunning." Despite the excitement generated by these performances, the combo disbanded in July, and thereafter Gillespie and Parker pursued their careers largely independent of one another. One conflict that led to the breakup was Gillespie's desire to form a bop big band; another was Parker's increasing irresponsibility due to his heroin addiction.

substitution chord an alternate chord substituted for the standard chord of a piece.

The First Recordings

Bebop sounded revolutionary, in part, because the first recordings seemed to come from nowhere. The AFM recording ban precluded any commercial recording of bebop during the crucial period from 1942 to 1943. But after Decca settled with the musicians' union in late 1943, a spate of new independent record labels sprang up and agreed to the same terms with the union that were accepted by Decca. In a frenzied effort to capture the market and build a name before Columbia and Victor became active again, such fledgling labels as Savoy, Apollo, Manor, and Guild took a chance on "alternative" repertories, including—for their "race record" series—the music that would soon be called bebop.

In 1944 Gillespie and Parker played on proto-bop recordings as sidemen for other musicians. Early in the year Coleman Hawkins made a series of records for Apollo with a twelve-piece swing band. Featuring Gillespie, Don Byas, Oscar Pettiford, and Max Roach, the **Apollo recordings** are sometimes considered the "first bop recordings." In the fall Parker played for Art Tatum's ex-guitarist, Tiny Grimes, on four cuts for Savoy records. But not until 1945 did Gillespie and Parker team up in the studio under Gillespie's nominal leadership. In February and April Gillespie's groups recorded such bebop classics as "Groovin' High," "Salt Peanuts," "Shaw 'Nuff," "Hot House," and the eponymous piece of the entire movement, "Be-Bop." In the **1945 Gillespie-Parker recordings,** we at last hear the new music in its prototypical form, in both horns and rhythm section, with few residual elements of swing style.

Many of the pieces recorded by Gillespie, Parker, and their associates combined new melodies (which the beboppers called **heads**) with familiar chord progressions. For instance, to create "Groovin' High," Gillespie composed a bebop-style melody using the chord progression of Paul Whiteman's "Whispering" (see Chapter 7). In a similar way, "Hot House" was based on the chords to "What Is This Thing Called Love?" and "Shaw 'Nuff" on rhythm changes. The new melodies announced the arrival of bebop but also allowed the musicians to improvise on the chord progressions to well-known standards without the record company having to pay royalties to the original songwriters.

The Reception of Bebop

Swing veterans and jazz traditionalists often responded to bebop with bewilderment or anger. When he first heard one of Gillespie's bands at the Onyx Club, drummer Dave Tough felt as though he were hearing a different language: "As we walked in, see, these cats snatched up their horns and blew crazy stuff. One would stop all of a sudden and another would start for no reason at all. We never could tell when a solo was supposed to begin or end. Then they all quit at once and walked off the stand. It scared us." Cab Calloway contemptuously dubbed bebop "Chinese music," while Louis Armstrong castigated the young players for replacing the melody with "fancy figurations." Critics were divided, with some hailing bebop as evidence of progress, while others denounced the music as a betrayal of jazz. In 1948 *Metronome* critic George T. Simon, an erstwhile bop admirer, confessed being dismayed by "the flagrant faults displayed by so many of bop's greats, by the constant repetition of the same overcute, multinote phrases and by the increasing deemphasis of certain basic factors . . . of good music" such as "blend, dynamics, shading, [and] intonation."

DIZZY GILLESPIE ALL STAR QUINTETTE, *"Shaw 'Nuff"* (1945)

In the December, 1945, *Down Beat* column, "Diggin' Discs with Don," the writer reviewed "Shaw 'Nuff" with a surprising jadedness given the still early stage of bebop's development. Wearily, he notes "the now familiar and rather over-exhibitionistic style" of the music. "There's a lot to this style," he admits, "yet for lasting worth it must rid itself of much that now clutters its true value. Dizzy's and Charlie's solos are both excellent in many ways, yet still too acrobatic and sensationalistic to be expressive in the true sense of good swing." Don's measuring rod of jazz excellence—"good swing"—betrays his inability to hear the music on its own terms. Writing about "Shaw 'Nuff" much later, Martin Williams voiced his own generation's hearty acceptance of bebop, praising the recording's "superb unison passages," its "leaping, ebullient, even humorous solos," and its full-blown revelation of "a new style of jazz."

"Shaw 'Nuff" was a tribute to Billy Shaw, Gillespie's manager with the William Morris Agency. It features virtually all of the key attributes of bebop as it would develop over the next few years. Like many bebop compositions, "Shaw 'Nuff" is in *rhythm changes;* it also adopts the jam session format of head-solos-head. One "arranged" feature is the carefully worked-out introduction, which also functions, at the end, as a coda. The signature harmonic interval of bebop, the *flatted fifth,* appears conspicuously throughout the introduction and closes the first two phrases of the bridge melody. The head itself is intricate, angular, and rhythmically unpredictable—qualities that Gillespie and Parker emphasize by playing in the stark scoring of unison or octaves. Gillespie and Parker play solos with similarly recondite traits, leaping and darting furiously in long, circuitous phrases. (You might compare Parker's solo with those of Ben Webster and Lester Young on the other two *rhythm changes* recordings we have looked at: "Cotton Tail" and "Lester Leaps In.") One can sense the importance these players placed on "shock value," for instance in Parker's dissonant arpeggios during the bridge of his solo and in Gillespie's semicomic roar into the upper register at the beginning of his.

Another thing that bothered Simon was the faddish cult that had grown up around the music. By 1948, in the popular imagination bebop comprised a hip cultural matrix of music, language, and clothing style. Musician and non-musician fans alike sported goatees, berets, and horn-rimmed glasses in imitation of Gillespie. A *Life* magazine feature article of that year showed a picture of Gillespie and Benny Carter sharing a "bebop greeting." Meanwhile, gifted musicians like Fats Navarro, Dexter Gordon, Miles Davis, and Lee Konitz were quietly building on the achievements of Gillespie and Parker, ultimately taking the music far beyond the noise generated by such publicity.

Bebop Piano

The bebop generation was the first to break with the Harlem stride tradition which had dominated jazz piano since the 1920s. Like bebop drummers, the pianists replaced the steady four-to-the-bar rhythm of swing (and stride) with sporadic rhythmic accents—that is, with the technique of "comping"

LISTENING CHART 19

Dizzy Gillespie All Star Quintette, "Shaw 'Nuff" (Gillespie-Parker)

CD 2 / Tracks 1–5

RECORDED 11 MAY 1945 / GUILD 1002; MX 566

Dizzy Gillespie (trumpet), Charlie Parker (alto saxophone), Al Haig (piano), Curly Russell (bass), Sidney Catlett (drums)

Style: Bebop			**Form: AABA song form (rhythm changes)**

				Introduction
1	0:00	Part 1 (8)		Rhythm section: lurching, syncopated rhythms
	0:06	Part 2 (16)		Minor mode: Dizzy Gillespie (trumpet) + Charlie Parker (alto saxophone) play fanfare-like call in harmony, then a boppish line in octaves
		1st Chorus		**Head**
2	0:19	A (8)		Major mode: Gillespie and Parker play the typically angular and erratic head in unison (or octaves)
	0:26	A (8)		*A-section repeated*
	0:33	B (8)		Bridge: first two phrases end on *flatted fifth* (the sustained notes)
	0:40	A (8)		*A-section repeated*
		2nd Chorus		**Alto saxophone solo: Charlie Parker**
3	0:46	A (8)		Parker plays effusive, intricate solo of mercurial contours and long lines
	0:53	A (8)		
	1:00	B (8)		Chromatic, dissonant arpeggios
	1:07	A (8)		
		3rd Chorus		**Trumpet solo: Dizzy Gillespie**
4	1:14	A (8)		Gillespie roars into the upper register, introducing a solo that fairly bursts with energy throughout
	1:20	A (8)		
	1:27	B (8)		

	1:34	A (8)	Gillespie opens this section with one of his signature riffs—a rapidly spinning figure in the low register that eventually extends upward before resolving
		4th Chorus	**Piano solo: Al Haig**
5	1:40	A (8)	One of the few white players in the inner bebop circle, Haig acquits himself well in this solo
	1:47	A (8)	
	1:54	B (8)	
	2:01	A (8)	
		5th Chorus	**Head**
	2:07	A (8)	Gillespie and Parker play head exactly as in the first chorus
	2:14	A (8)	*A-section repeated*
	2:21	B (8)	Bridge
	2:28	A (8)	*A-section repeated*
			Coda (Introduction)
	2:34	Part 1 (8)	Introduction material now presented as a coda
	2:41	Part 2 (16)	

Further Listening from the *Prentice Hall Jazz Collection*
Track 3: Dizzy Gillespie, "Groovin' High" (1947)

developed by Count Basie. Two pianists represented, in very different ways, the highest achievements in piano in the bebop era: Thelonious Monk and Bud Powell.

Thelonious Monk

Born in Rocky Mount, North Carolina, Thelonious Sphere Monk moved to New York City with his family at the age of four. His earliest musical experiences related to the black church; as a teenager he toured with a singing evangelist, playing piano and organ. Around the age of twenty he began working with jazz groups in New York. In early 1941 his friend Kenny Clarke got him the job as house pianist at Minton's. In 1944 Monk made his first recordings, as a sideman for Coleman Hawkins. That same year he played with Cootie Williams's big band, which recorded Monk's most famous composition, "'Round Midnight."

In the late forties Monk performed primarily at two 52nd Street clubs—the Downbeat and the Spotlite—and on Broadway at the Royal Roost. In addition, he recorded several original compositions for **Blue Note** records that have come to be regarded as masterpieces, including "Evidence," "Misterioso" (both 1948), and "Criss-Cross" (1951). These highly original pieces demonstrate Monk's characteristic delight in the enigmatic phrase, the unexpected gesture. They also reveal Monk's startling ability to craft unified structures in which important motives and themes are reworked and developed. This developmental aesthetic, rare for jazz musicians from this period, also appears in Monk's solos. On Miles Davis's recording of "Bag's Groove" (1954), for example, Monk develops a new idea in each of nine blues choruses while retaining continuity from one chorus to the next.

Minton's Playhouse. *Left to right:* Thelonious Monk, Howard McGhee, Roy Eldridge, Teddy Hill.

Despite his artistic successes, Monk faced opposition during this period. Having made his professional, pre-bebop, debut as a stride player, Monk did not lack for technique. But he deliberately compromised orthodox methods of execution, playing with hands flat on the keyboard and lurching through performances as if uncertain about his ideas or unable to carry them out. He favored dissonant harmonies, "wrong" notes (by conventional standards), and awkward pauses in the musical flow. When a critic complained about the pauses, Monk's manager answered plaintively, "Man, that's just it. It's not so much the notes he plays as the ones he leaves out that mean so much." Writers showed the same impatience with his compositions. Reviewing "Little Rootie Tootie" and "Trinkle Tinkle," a *Metronome* critic wrote in 1953 that "he's as monotonous a composer as ever . . . rooting, tooting, trinkling, tinkling and rarely emerging from a boppist, impressionist morass." As if to compound the problem of negative press coverage, Monk's nightclub career stalled in 1951 when the police found a small amount of heroin in his car. He spent sixty days in jail on a narcotics charge and lost his cabaret card for six years.

Even before regaining his cabaret card, however, Monk's career started to turn around. In 1955 one of his few staunch supporters, producer Orrin Keepnews, persuaded Monk to sign with the recently formed record label, **Riverside.** With Riverside Monk made several important albums, including *Brilliant Corners* (1957). Critics began to grasp Monk's musical aims, finally recognizing that his unusual technique actually produced a rare expressiveness. In a landmark piece of Monk criticism for the *New Yorker* (1958), Whitney Balliett reinterpreted Monk's perceived liabilities as strengths: "Monk is superb. In the first version [of "Bag's Groove"] his solo is broken by such long pauses that it appears he has left the studio; then he suddenly resumes with clumps of clattering, off-beat dissonances." Monk's public image as an incompetent or charlatan changed in the late fifties to that of visionary. His growing reputation as a major jazz figure climaxed in 1964, with his appearance on the cover of *Time* magazine.

Great Debates

BEBOP: EVOLUTION OR REVOLUTION?

Since its inception, bebop has provoked debate over its relationship with earlier styles and aesthetics of jazz. Was it a revolutionary break with the past? Its small-group emphasis on virtuoso improvisation seemed a far cry from the Swing Era's elaborate arrangements for big band. Moreover, bebop, with its "difficult" and complex material, seemed to repudiate the unabashed commercialism and occasional shallowness of swing. The revolutionary perspective even carried a racial component: whereas swing was dominated by white musicians, bebop was almost entirely an all-black creation. Leroi Jones (aka Amiri Baraka) thus interprets bebop as an expression of black political will, even militancy, which mirrored the emerging civil rights struggle.

Other critics have emphasized the continuity of bebop with the past. Pointing out that Dizzy Gillespie built upon the virtuosity of Roy Eldridge, that Charlie Parker elaborated Lester Young's linear conception, and that such swing arrangements as Duke Ellington's "Cotton Tail" foreshadowed many elements of bebop, the evolutionists made the case for incremental transformation from swing to modern jazz. They argued that the AFM recording ban exaggerated the sense of "revolution"; if we had a steady stream of recordings from 1940 to 1945, we would surely see that bebop emerged gradually and logically from swing traditions. David W. Stowe even suggests that bebop was really "swing redux"—the final flowering of the Swing Era.

The most dramatic departure from these perspectives appeared in Scott DeVeaux's landmark work, *The Birth of Bebop: A Social and Musical History* (1997). Rejecting the either-or dichotomies of the past, DeVeaux argues that the beboppers sought economic success every bit as much as any swing musician. They developed their radical virtuosic idiom in part to distinguish themselves in a tight market. But in the process they unwittingly set jazz on a new path, one that ultimately led away from the commercial entertainment traditions of previous decades. Thus, bebop was both evolutionary in its intent and goals and revolutionary in its consequences. ■ ■ ■

Bud Powell

Though vastly influential in the long run, Monk's idiosyncratic piano style attracted few imitators in the early years of bebop. **Earl "Bud" Powell** (1924–1966), widely regarded as the archetypal bebop pianist, offered a more comprehensible model for younger players. A native New Yorker, Powell studied classical piano from the age of six. As a teenager he began spending time at Minton's, where he became a close friend and protégé of Monk's. By the mid-forties, he possessed a piano technique rivaling that of Art Tatum—a technique, however, that he applied to the new bebop idiom. On solos he played long agile lines in the right hand in the manner of a bop horn player; in the left hand he played an irregular succession of dissonant chords, relying on the bass player to enunciate the defining pitches of the harmony.

While on tour with the Cootie Williams big band in Philadelphia in 1945, Powell sustained heavy blows to the head during a skirmish with the police. The details of this incident remain obscure, but according to the best-known account the police came into a Philadelphia nightclub where Monk had just

THELONIOUS MONK, *"I Should Care"* (1957)

"I Should Care" first appeared as a love ballad in the Hollywood musical, *Thrill of a Romance* (1945). Martin Williams considers Monk's 1957 version of this piece to be "his piano solo masterpiece." In this recording, Williams writes, "Monk has carried the jazzman's concept of individuality of sound further than any other player on his instrument; indeed, he has carried it almost as far as the hornmen." Monk's ability to draw a unique sound out of the piano, an instrument resistant to individual nuance, was one of his most remarkable traits. His thumpy attack and subtle use of the sustaining pedal impart great emotion to his performances. So, too, do his *chord clusters*—chords comprised of closely aligned pitches. One of Monk's signature devices was to play a dense chord cluster from which several pitches would "evaporate" (through Monk's deft use of the sustaining pedal), leaving a single note or group of notes still resonating. All of these features appear in "I Should Care."

There is a touch of schizophrenia in Monk's reading of this standard. In this performance—a single distended chorus in ABAC song form—we encounter by turns the virtuosic stride tradition, the quirky eccentricities of Monk's own language, and the soft nostalgia of the original song. Monk's distinctive personality dominates the performance through strange harmonizations, chord clusters, and the abruptly capricious tempo rubato (Monk's famous pauses). As decoration to this basic approach Monk periodically adds lavish arpeggiation in the upper register, flourishes that became the stock-in-trade of cocktail pianists. To provide contrast with the dissonant chords, Monk occasionally slips into a velvet harmonic world that conjures the romantic origins of his Hollywood vehicle.

finished playing and demanded to see his ID. When Monk refused, they began to drag him outside. Concerned about his friend, Powell adamantly protested Monk's innocence. At this point one of the officers took out his nightstick and cracked Powell on the skull, knocking him to the ground. Thereafter, Powell suffered a series of mental health problems, exacerbated by drinking and drugs, which kept him in and out of sanatoriums for most of his life and steadily eroded his ability to function as a professional musician.

Despite these challenges, Powell managed to gain recognition as the preeminent modern jazz pianist of the late forties and early fifties. He performed regularly with Dizzy Gillespie, Charlie Parker, Kenny Clarke, Oscar Pettiford, and other founders of bebop at such venues as the Three Deuces, the Spotlite, and the Royal Roost. In 1949 he began a series of acclaimed recordings with his **piano trio,** which included bop veterans Curly Russell on bass and Max Roach on drums. On such recordings as the live performance of "Night in Tunisia" (1951), Powell plays with fiery intensity, unleashing right-hand lines of tremendous power and intricacy while attacking the lower regions of the keyboard with spiky left-hand chords. At his best, Powell manifested a hungry creative thrust and a gift for melodic invention that place him within the top echelon of all jazz musicians.

In the mid-fifties, just as Monk's career began to rise, Powell's became more and more erratic. In 1959 he moved to Paris, where for the next five years he performed in trios (one of which included Kenny Clarke) to the adulation of European jazz fans. But by this time Powell's playing was falling prey to his

LISTENING CHART 20

Thelonious Monk, "I Should Care" (Weston-Stordahl-Cahn)

CD 2 / Tracks 6–7

RECORDED 12 APRIL 1957 / *THELONIOUS HIMSELF* RIVERSIDE RLP 12-235

Thelonious Monk (solo piano)

Style: Ballad			Form: ABAC song form
6	0:00	A	Opening melody played to dissonant clusters in upper register
	0:12		More conventional harmonies
	0:20		Virtuosic ("cocktail" style) arpeggiated ascent into high range
	0:32		Stabbing dissonant chords that immediately recede
	0:38	B	Melody continues, punctuated by stabbing chords
7	1:17	A	Octave *tremolando* (fast alternation between notes) in upper register, which yields to ascending flourish, then dissonant clusters of beginning
	1:26		Return to conventional harmonies again
	1:33		Two virtuosic arpeggiated ascents
	1:51	C	Stabbing dissonant chords, which "evaporate" leaving a single note
	2:28		Unharmonized swinging bebop line
	2:33		Descending *whole-tone scale* passagework
	2:44		Piece closes with "evaporating" clusters

Further Listening from the *Prentice Hall Jazz Collection*
Track 4: Thelonious Monk, "Misterioso" (1948)

increasing mental instability. After returning to the United States (in the same year that Monk's picture appeared on the cover of *Time*), he prepared for a solo concert at Carnegie Hall intended as a tribute to Charlie Parker. The concert, which took place in 1965, was a disaster. According to the *New York Times,* "Mr. Powell . . . was barely able to force out enough of the effort necessary to laboriously complete the three songs he had chosen." He died the following year.

Offstage Personalities

Baroness Pannonica de Königswarter (1914–1990)

One of the most mysterious offstage figures associated with modern jazz was the musicians' stalwart patron and supporter, the Baroness Pannonica de Königswarter. Born the daughter of a British banker, she was educated in France and worked for the French resistance during World War II. Her brother, a courier to Winston Churchill during the war, met swing pianist Teddy Wilson in the United States and took some lessons from him. Pannonica—or "Nica," as she was called—soon came to share her brother's fascination with jazz. After the war she married Baron Jules de Königswarter, and the couple moved to Mexico City, where Jules served as French Ambassador to Peru.

In 1951 she rented a luxury apartment at Manhattan's Stanhope Hotel on Fifth Avenue, and immediately began making acquaintances with her heroes in the bebop community, including Charlie Parker, Miles Davis, Horace Silver, Charles Mingus, and above all, Thelonious Monk. Recognizing their vulnerability—both to the police and to their own destructive habits—Nica offered them food, shelter, medicine, money, transportation, and moral support. "Monk was her immediate fascination," wrote *Time* in 1964, "and Monk, who only has eyes for [his wife] Nellie, cheerfully took her on as another mother. She gave him rides, rooms to compose and play in, and, in 1957, help in getting back the vital cabaret card." Some of Nica's beneficiaries showed their gratitude in perhaps the most meaningful way known to them, by dedicating compositions to her—for example, alto saxophonist Gigi Gryce's "Nica's Tempo" (1955), pianist Horace Silver's "Nica's Dream" (1956), and Monk's "Pannonica" (1956). Charlie Parker allegedly died while watching TV in her New York apartment, while Monk died nearly thirty years later, with Nellie by his side, at Nica's home in Weehawken, New Jersey. ■ ■ ■

Singing in the Bebop Era

The rise of modern jazz inspired important developments in jazz singing. The very word "bebop" was a fragment of scat, and the long nimble melodies of bebop enticed jazz singers like Ella Fitzgerald, Sarah Vaughan, and Betty Carter to develop scat more fully, along bop-oriented lines. Singers also developed a new device called **vocalese**—singing newly invented lyrics to the notes of a recorded instrumental solo, usually in the bebop idiom. But for some reason neither scat nor vocalese ever became the prevailing interest of jazz singers, as improvisation did among horn players. The abstraction of scatting continued to play a secondary role to the free interpretation of concrete melodies and lyrics. And vocalese, even today, sometimes suggests the fringe quality of a novelty effect rather than the status of a mainstream technique.

Sarah Vaughan

The most important jazz singer to emerge in the 1940s was **Sarah Vaughan** (1924–1990). Also known as "Sassy" or the "Divine One" for her temperament and her singing respectively, Vaughan came of age with bebop itself. She grew up in an impoverished household in Newark, New Jersey. At the First Mount Zion

CD 2 / Track 8

BUD POWELL TRIO, "Night in Tunisia" (1951)

On this live recording Bud Powell and his trio perform Dizzy Gillespie's bebop anthem "Night in Tunisia." This piece, composed in 1942, represents one of Gillespie's first attempts to fuse bebop and Afro-Cuban music, a blend sometimes called **Cubop** (see Chapter 26). Following conventional AABA song form, "Night in Tunisia" calls for an Afro-Cuban rhythmic groove during most of the A-sections and a swing feel during the bridge. In Gillespie's hands, this piece became especially famous for its relatively long (four-bar) break just before the first solo chorus, a break that he further dramatized with an introductory twelve-bar interlude. In this break Gillespie typically unleashed, in the words of one critic, "the musical equivalent of the aurora borealis."

In the present recording Powell emits similar fireworks at this break, then continues in the same explosive vein throughout his solo, favoring fast runs and long unbroken lines in the right hand. The bassist (Curly Russell) and drummer (Max Roach) replace the Afro-Cuban beat with a swing feel during Powell's solo: Russell *walks* and Roach, using brushes instead of sticks, does what drummers call *stirring soup*—he swishes the brushes in circles on the snare drum to establish the basic beat. One moment in Powell's solo illustrates a common occurrence among jazz musicians playing in AABA song form: in the third chorus Powell forgets the second A-section and goes straight to the bridge, making an ABA pattern for that chorus.

Create your own listening chart (CD 2 / Track 8)

Sarah Vaughan.

cubop a blend of bebop and the Cuban mambo.

Baptist Church she sang in the choir and learned to play the piano and organ well, which gave her a thorough understanding of harmony. Like Ella Fitzgerald, she won the amateur contest at Harlem's Apollo Theater in her late teens. In the spring of 1943 Billy Eckstine heard her again at the Apollo. At his enthusiastic recommendation, Earl Hines hired her to be second singer (after Eckstine) and second pianist (after Hines) in his big band.

On the road with Hines, Vaughan became friends with Dizzy Gillespie, Charlie Parker, and other progressive players then in the Hines band. Later, when many of these musicians reassembled in Billy Eckstine's band, Vaughan joined Eckstine as well. She shared a strong musical bond with the beboppers. "I thought Bird and Diz were the end," she recalled. "I think their playing influenced my singing. Horns always influenced me more than voices." According to Gillespie, Vaughan especially admired Parker: "She didn't want to know about nothing but Bird's music. She was a musician herself." As this last comment suggests, the respect ran both ways. Gillespie valued her piano-playing enough to use her in some of his early bop combos. But during the months with Eckstine, the members of the band provided an intimidating musical environment for the young vocalist. "They used to beat me to death if I got out of line," she said. "You had to sing within whatever the chords were they were playing. You had to know a little about music or have a hell of a good ear to stand before that band. I loved it, loved it!"

In the immediate postwar years Vaughan participated in some important early bebop recording sessions; her recording of "Lover Man" (1945) with Gillespie and Parker is especially admired. In the late forties she sought to capitalize on the commercial popularity of solo pop singers. From 1949 to 1954 she recorded easy listening songs for Columbia records and became a star. Thereafter she followed a dual career path, making records in both pop and jazz idioms. Some of her best jazz albums of the fifties include *Sarah Vaughan* (1954), a collaboration with trumpeter Clifford Brown and reedman Paul Quinichette; and two live records, *Live at Mr. Kelly's* (1957) and *After Hours at the London House* (1958).

Sarah Vaughan combined the expressive range of Billie Holiday with the dynamic execution of Ella Fitzgerald. To this mix she added a seemingly endless virtuoso technique that sounds almost operatic at times, though she never received classical training. She is sometimes criticized for using her voice as an end in itself, and ignoring the meaning of the lyrics. "I never think about singing," she once admitted. "It's just according to how I feel and it's never the same. . . . Sometimes I'm wondering if they fixed the fence, or I wonder if my dog got well. That's why I forget lyrics sometimes." Her indifference to lyrics partly explains why she absorbed bebop so readily. Vaughan's vocal style is essentially instrumental in nature; she excelled at scatting and often seemed more interested in what her voice could do than in any textual message she might convey.

Chapter 18 Charlie Parker

Although Dizzy Gillespie, Thelonious Monk, Kenny Clarke, and others made indispensable contributions to bebop, most writers consider the music's presiding genius to be alto saxophonist Charlie Parker. Parker's best solos have an inevitable rightness about them, a beauty and timelessness that somehow sets him apart from his contemporaries. He also contributed some of the most lyrical and memorable heads to the bebop repertory, including "Yardbird Suite," "Moose the Mooche," "Confirmation," and "Scrapple from the Apple." His role in the history of jazz is analogous to Louis Armstrong's: both musicians directly influenced an entire generation of soloists, regardless of the instruments they played. Parker's improvisational ideas, more than anyone else's, forged the lexicon of modern jazz.

Yet Parker left a mixed legacy. Every brilliant solo he recorded was matched by a self-destructive act, compelled by his insatiable need for heroin. Every kind gesture extended toward a fellow musician was balanced by an exploitative deed, a lie, a theft, in order to maintain his habit. Just as Parker influenced a multitude of musicians to adopt his improvisational language, so he also led them—ironically, by the power of his music—to take up heroin themselves, in the hope of emulating him in every respect. In many instances, fortunately, music proved more powerful than narcotics. This is especially clear in the case of Miles Davis, Parker's most significant heir, who in 1954 quit heroin cold turkey, freeing himself to break new paths in jazz for the next twenty years.

Kansas City

Charles Parker Jr. (1920–1955) grew up in Kansas City, Missouri, during the heyday of the Pendergast political machine (see Chapter 11). Reared by an indulgent but emotionally distant mother and an absent father, Parker sought excitement in the wild nightlife of Kansas City's vice district. As the pianist Mary Lou Williams recalled, "I found Kansas City to be a heavenly city—music everywhere in the Negro section of town, and fifty or more cabarets rocking on Twelfth and Eighteenth Streets." Kansas City was renowned for its jam sessions and cutting contests, especially those involving tenor saxophonists. One night in 1934 Coleman Hawkins came through town with Fletcher Henderson's band. After the dance Hawkins began jamming at the Cherry Blossom with local tenor players Lester Young, Ben Webster, Herschel Evans, and others. Around four in the morning, Mary Lou Williams awoke to a knock on her window. It was Ben Webster: "Get up, pussycat, we're jammin' and all the pianists are tired out now. Hawkins has got his shirt off and is still blowing. You got to come down."

It was into this high-stakes competitive milieu that Charlie Parker stepped as a young alto saxophonist. In 1935, while still a very naïve player, he tried to sit in with Jimmy Keith's band at the High Hat. Attempting to solo on "Body and Soul," he stumbled over the roving chord progression. As he later recalled, the other players "fell out laughing. I went home and cried and didn't play again for three months." The following year he had another humiliating encounter, this time with Count Basie's men at the Reno Club. A popular radio program at the time was the *Major Bowles Amateur Hour*, a talent contest in which the worst contestants were cut short by the sound of a gong. As Parker played his solo, Basie urged Jo Jones to "hit the cymbal on him!"—to give him the gong. Jones tossed one of his cymbals across the room, where it landed at Parker's feet with a crash. Furious, Parker said to one of his friends, "I'll get 'em! I'll get 'em! They rung that bell on me; I'll get 'em!"

During this same period, Parker became involved with drugs. As a young adolescent, he was already abusing alcohol, nutmeg, Benzedrine inhalers, and marijuana. Then at age fifteen someone gave him heroin. Recounting the excitement of this first experience with narcotics to a friend years later, Parker took money out of his pocket and exclaimed: "Do you mean there's something like this in this world? How much of it will this buy?" In a car accident in late 1936 he broke three ribs and fractured his spine; he may have increased his heroin use to kill the pain of his injuries. In any case, by this time he was an addict.

Charlie Parker, 1947.

Transformation in the Ozarks

Parker reached a turning point in his life in 1937. That summer he played in a dance band at a resort in the Ozarks near Eldon, Missouri. He brought several newly released Count Basie records with him. By tightening a screw on his portable phonograph player, he could slow the speed of the records enough to figure out the notes in Lester Young's solos. Over the course of the summer he practiced diligently, learning all of Young's solos note-for-note. He also learned about keys, scales, and other aspects of harmony from a guitarist at the resort. When he returned home at the end of the summer he was soon "the most popular musician in K.C.," according to one musician. "He had gone up into the mountains; and when he came back, only two or three months later, the difference was unbelievable." This breakthrough was dramatic, but Parker's practicing in the Ozarks was part of a larger effort to improve. He recalled that "the neighbors threatened to ask my mother to move once. . . . They said I was driving them crazy with the horn. I used to put in . . . eleven to fifteen hours a day." To master jazz harmony, Parker learned the blues, "I Got Rhythm," and Charlie Barnet's 1939 hit "Cherokee" in all twelve keys. "Then," he recalled, "I was ready."

New York

In the late thirties the federal government convicted Pendergast of income tax evasion, and Kansas City nightlife began to decline. In 1939 Parker moved to New York and began jamming at several Harlem venues, especially Monroe's Uptown House. One night Parker was practicing one of his favorite pieces,

Charlie Barnet's just released "Cherokee": "I'd been getting bored with the stereotyped changes that were being used at the time, and I kept thinking there's bound to be something else. I could hear it sometimes but I couldn't play it. Well, that night I was working over 'Cherokee,' and as I did I found that by using the higher intervals of a chord as a melody line and backing them with appropriately related changes, I could play the thing I'd been hearing. I came alive." By "higher intervals of a chord" Parker meant **triadic extensions**—the intervals of a seventh, ninth, eleventh, or thirteenth above the root. These were the "pretty notes" he once claimed to be searching for whenever he played a solo.

When his father died in 1940, Parker returned to Kansas City for the funeral. There, he joined the big band of a local boogie-woogie pianist, **Jay McShann** (b. 1916). In 1942, McShann opened at the Savoy Ballroom in New York, where Parker caused a stir among musicians. As the trumpeter Howard McGhee recalled, "We all stood there with our mouths open because we had never heard anyone play a horn like that." Parker's influence in the McShann band was highly volatile. On the one hand, his drug-induced erratic behavior created havoc; but, on the other, he inspired the musicians to excel, as one musician explained: "The Jay McShann band . . . was the only band I've ever known that seemed to spend all its spare time jamming or rehearsing. . . . All this was inspired by Bird, because the new ideas he was bringing to the band made everybody anxious to play." It was with McShann, according to one account, that Parker earned his famous nickname. One day the band's bus ran over a chicken. Parker asked the driver to stop so he could fetch that "yardbird," which he later asked his landlady to cook for him. Ever after, the musicians called him Yardbird—or, simply, **Bird.** (For information on Parker's career from 1942 to 1945, see Chapter 17.)

Musical Style

Parker played alto saxophone with little concern for the kind of romantically "beautiful" tone quality exemplified by such swing soloists as Johnny Hodges. Like Lester Young, Parker played with little or no vibrato (except on ballads). He also had the curious habit of playing sharp, perhaps to increase the edginess of his tone. He manifested outstanding technical facility and explored intricate melodic ideas. Yet, even on the fastest virtuoso steeplechases, Parker played with great lyricism, exuding tremendous warmth and lightness of spirit. As an improvising soloist he cultivated an approach sometimes called **formulaic improvisation.** He created his solos by combining previously learned melodic *formulas* or *licks* into new patterns. His solos thus resemble speech in that he arranged parts of a second-nature "vocabulary" into new "sentences" that fit the harmonic context at hand. Like many other jazz musicians, Parker also frequently employed a device called **quotation,** a reference to well-known melodies from the popular or classical repertories.

Los Angeles

In late 1945 Parker traveled to Los Angeles with Dizzy Gillespie, who had contracted to bring a quintet to **Billy Berg's** nightclub in Hollywood. Gillespie wanted Parker on the front line, but mindful of his unreliability brought along an

triadic extension   the interval of a 7th, 9th, 11th, or 13th above the *root* of a chord.

formulaic improvisation an approach to solo improvisation that involves combining previously learned melodic *formulas* (or *licks*) into new patterns.

quotation   in a solo, a reference to a well-known melody from the popular or classical repertories.

extra player, vibraphonist Milt Jackson, just in case. "When we got to Billy Berg's," recalled bassist Ray Brown, "The newspaper said after the first night: 'Men from Mars Playing at Billy Berg's!' They thought we were the most outrageous thing they had ever heard. They didn't understand a note of it. But all the musicians were in there every night, because they knew." Historians disagree as to the success of the engagement, but according to Brown, the club's manager eventually told Gillespie that if he wanted to finish out the booking he would have to "be more commercial, so Charlie Parker wrote out a couple of arrangements where we sang—the whole band [was] singing."

When the rest of Gillespie's band returned to New York in early February, Parker got a refund on his plane ticket—probably to buy drugs—and stayed in Los Angeles. Later that month he made his second recording session as a leader, for the newly founded Dial label run by record store owner (and future Parker biographer) **Ross Russell.** Parker could not easily locate a steady source of heroin in Los Angeles, but eventually found a dealer named Emery "Moose the Mooche" Byrd, whom he immortalized in his composition, "Moose the Mooche," recorded in March. A couple of months later Byrd was arrested, cutting off Parker's supply. This event sent Parker spiralling downward, as he

CHARLIE PARKER'S RE-BOPPERS, *"Koko"* (1945)

Parker recorded "Koko," an uptempo reinterpretation of "Cherokee," in late 1945 during his first recording session as a leader (see Charlie Barnet's "Cherokee," CD 1 / Track 72). He enlisted Gillespie to play on the torrential introduction and coda. The following May a trio of critics reviewed "Koko" for *Metronome*, revealing both incomprehension (particularly in their negative assessment of Max Roach) and stupefied wonder: "It's a series of mad improvisations by Parker's alto on the chords of 'Cherokee,' though the recording covers up the rhythm section's chords so completely that you'd hardly know it. With better discipline on the part of the men, and without that horrible, utterly beatless drum solo by Max Roach, this could have been a great side. Even as it is, it has some phenomenal illustrations of how Parker can run unusual chord changes at a fantastic tempo." Today, "Koko" (which is unrelated to Duke Ellington's "Ko-Ko") is regarded as one of Parker's greatest solos and, indeed, as a classic record of early bebop.

"Koko" does not have a melody in the usual sense. The closest thing to a head is the phrase (which we will call X) with which Parker opens the A-sections of the first chorus; the rest of the performance consists of Parker's free improvisations. "Cherokee" appealed to Parker partly for its harmonically adventurous bridge, which passes through five different keys. Notice the ease with which Parker negotiates these modulations, partly through the use of melodic *sequences*. Parker's favorite, or at least his most commonly played, lick or formula appears twice—once at the end of each bridge. He also uses quotation in his solo. To open the second chorus, he quotes the beginning of the clarinet obbligato from the old New Orleans tune, "High Society." At the beginning of the bridge in the second chorus, he quotes "Tea for Two" in a version heavily disguised by virtuosic arpeggiation. Contrary to what one might expect, the use of formulas and quotation do not produce a hodge-podge of unrelated ideas. Instead, Parker weaves together a coherent and compelling solo unmarred by the disparate origins of his materials.

LISTENING CHART 21

Charlie Parker's Re-Boppers, "Koko" (Parker)

CD 2 / Tracks 9–13

RECORDED 26 NOVEMBER 1945 / SAVOY 597; MX 5853-2

Charlie Parker (alto saxophone), Dizzy Gillespie (trumpet, piano), Curly Russell (bass), Max Roach (drums)

Style: Bebop			**Form: AABA song form (to the progression of "Cherokee")**

			Introduction
9	0:00	w (8)	Charlie Parker (alto saxophone) and Dizzy Gillespie (muted trumpet) play in octaves accompanied only by Max Roach (drums) using brushes
	0:06	x (8)	Muted trumpet solo: Gillespie
	0:12	y (8)	Alto saxophone solo: Parker
	0:18	z (8)	Parker and Gillespie (in harmony, then octaves): sporadic accents
		1st Chorus	**Alto saxophone solo: Charlie Parker**
10	0:25	A (16)	Parker opens his solo by playing X, a long, well-profiled phrase clearly worked out in advance (accompanied now by full rhythm section; Gillespie moves to piano; Roach switches to sticks)
	0:37	A (16)	Parker plays X again
	0:50	B (16)	Parker accommodates the descending key changes through the use of a *sequence*
11	0:59		Parker's "favorite" lick
	1:03	A (16)	
		2nd Chorus	
12	1:15	A (16)	Parker opens this chorus with a quotation from "High Society"
	1:28	A (16)	
	1:41	B (16)	Parker opens this bridge with a highly decorated quotation of "Tea for Two" (which also employs a *sequence*)
	1:51		Parker's "favorite" lick
	1:53	A (16)	

			Drum solo: Max Roach
13	2:06	(32)	(plays half chorus)
			Coda (introduction)
	2:29	w (8)	Parker, Gillespie, and Roach play as in the introduction, but with different solos
	2:35	x (8)	Muted trumpet solo: Gillespie
	2:41	y (8)	Alto saxophone solo: Parker
	2:47	z (8)	Parker and Gillespie (in harmony, then octaves): sporadic accents

drank vast amounts of alcohol to alleviate withdrawal symptoms. At a recording date on July 19 Parker played uncertainly despite being fortified with "a quart of whiskey," as he put it. When he returned to his hotel he was found wandering naked in the lobby and later set fire to his room. The police confined him in the psychopathic ward of the county jail; when Ross Russell and Howard McGhee finally found him, he was strapped in a straightjacket and handcuffed to his cot.

At the request of Russell, the judge sentenced Parker to six months at **Camarillo State Hospital.** Deprived of drugs and alcohol, he gradually recovered his health. He tended the hospital vegetable garden and played C-melody saxophone in the hospital band. Finally, in January of 1947, he was released into the custody of Russell. During the next few months he began performing again in public and made several more records for Dial, including a whimsical ode to his confinement, "Relaxin' at Camarillo."

Charlie Parker's Classic Quintet

Parker returned to New York in April 1947. According to the June issue of *Metronome,* "The night he arrived in town the word went around from one club to another, from one bar to another, 'Bird's back in town!', whispered in sepulchral tones, usually reserved for religious leaders and revolutionaries. Every session he appeared at for the next few weeks was ballyhooed days in advance among the beboppers as another Bird-letter day and attendance was compulsory for those who wished to continue in the bebop school." *Metronome* noted that Parker was "still a brilliant musical thinker, still the most influential bebopper of them all," but cautioned in a reactionary vein that he was "not yet in full possession of his technique, tone and taste."

For the next three years Parker would lead his most distinguished band, a group critics have dubbed his "classic quintet." Although the personnel shifted somewhat over time, in its definitive form the group included trumpeter

HOWARD MCGHEE

*on the Travails of Working with
Charlie Parker—1947*

We're supposed to be going to rehearsal . . . so I go to pick up Bird, blow on the [car] horn, sit out there waitin' . . . I said, "I gotta go see . . . " I don't like leavin' my car back there with my horns and everything . . . Los Angeles wasn't *that* safe, so I went to the front door and rang the bell . . . I called, "Hey, Bird!" I heard him say "Yeah!" I said, "Well, come on! We gotta go!" He said, "Yeah, you gotta come up here though!" So I go back to the car and get my horns and go in the house, and Bird's layin' in the tub, writin' music. [He's writing] "Relaxin' at Camarillo," right in the bathtub. An' he give me about twelve bars, an' he say, "You write this out for the band." So I said, "Well, come on, let's go, and I'll write it out when I get out there." So I finally got him dressed, and we went on out to rehearsal.

The following week, when I wrote out this thing, "Relaxin' at Camarillo," [none of the musicians] had an idea what that was 'cause the rhythmic thing was so different. I said, "What's the tempo, Bird?" He said, "'Bout like that [taps off]." I said, "O.K. Everybody get their parts ready. O.K. Let's go!" An' he kicked it off, an' wasn't nobody playin' but him! I said, "Jiminy!" I was lookin' at the part, too, an' I wrote it down for the guys. I said, "Wait a minute, we gotta get to this, we can't figure this out!" We took it real slow until we could play it. Boy, he had it. He said, "When you all get it, then call me." He went out, and got him a bottle of whiskey, and he was sittin' out in the car gettin' drunk, when we finally did get it together. So the next day we made [the record], and . . . he played the hell out of everything, he sounded so good. . . .

Man, it was such a pleasure to go to work with Bird, and such a horrible thought, too: After he gets through playin' what are *you* going to play? I used to be listenin' to him—he's havin' a ball—and all of a sudden that dawn on me, "Now you gotta follow him. What *you* gonna play?" Then you had to go in your brain, try to rack yourself. I couldn't wait to get to work, and I hated to be on the gig.

Ira Gitler, *Swing to Bop: An Oral History of the Transition in Jazz in the 1940s* (New York: Oxford University Press, 1985), 176–77. Italics added.

Miles Davis (see Chapter 21), pianist Duke Jordan, bassist Tommy Potter, and drummer Max Roach. The quintet performed on 52nd Street at the Three Deuces until the fall of 1948, when it opened at the Royal Roost on Broadway (see Map 7). On the Savoy and Dial labels, Parker made some of his most acclaimed recordings with this band. The **Savoy recordings,** a series initiated before the California period, boast such classic performances as "Koko," "Donna Lee," and "Parker's Mood." The **Dial recordings,** begun in Los Angeles, include "Embraceable You," "Klactoveedsedstene," and "Crazeology."

Unfortunately, during this period Parker began undoing all the progress he had made in managing his drug problem. During an engagement at Chicago's Argyle Show Bar in 1948, an inebriated Parker urinated in a telephone booth in the lobby, thinking he was in the men's room. One night at the Royal Roost, according to Miles Davis, he indulged in adolescent shenanigans like shooting the pianist with a toy cap gun and letting air out of a balloon into the

CHARLIE PARKER ALL STARS, *"Parker's Mood"* (1948)

CD 2 / Track 14

Many bebop musicians avoided playing the blues, believing it to be a primitive and simple-minded music unworthy of their attention. But Charlie Parker felt otherwise, and his many recorded blues solos—on "Now's the Time," "Billie's Bounce," and "Au Privave," for instance—amply justify his opinion. On these solos, as well as on the present recording, "Parker's Mood," Parker shows how it was possible to uphold the soulful and earthy tradition of great blues playing while at the same time retaining the virtuosic and intellectually complex rhetoric of modern jazz.

Parker recorded "Parker's Mood," not with his working band (Max Roach excepted), but with an "all-star" group that included highly busy studio sidemen pianist John Lewis and bassist Curly Russell. This arrangement of "Parker's Mood" includes the dual-purpose introduction/coda that we saw in "Shaw 'Nuff" and "Koko." The introduction is deceptive, leading the listener to expect a romantic ballad instead of a down-home blues. Parker begins his solo with a melody from deep in the vocal blues tradition (indeed, a jazz vocalist later set this melody to words). As his solo proceeds Parker alternates effortlessly between such highly vocal blues phrases (including frequently prominent *blue notes*) and the virtuosic figurations of bebop. Parker's solo also reveals his fecund melodic gift, particularly his fine instinct for *motivic development*—the elaboration of a simple motive through varied repetition. In the middle of the fourth chorus, for example, Parker develops a standard blues riff into a highly lyrical and harmonically graceful melody (see 2:26).

Create your own listening chart (CD 2 / Track 14)

microphone. Discouraged by his unpredictability and lack of commitment to the music, Davis and Roach left the band shortly thereafter. Ironically, Parker was just beginning to receive the greatest recognition of his career. In December 1949 the New York club **Birdland** was opened in his honor (see Map 7 and "Venues: Birdland"). And in 1950 *Down Beat* readers for the first time voted him best alto saxophonist, a judgment they would repeat annually until his death. Leading jazz impresario Norman Granz became his patron, organizing both his recordings and his live performances. Around this time Parker disbanded his quintet; in keeping with his celebrity status, he would work primarily as a single or as a guest artist with other groups in the fifties.

The Early 1950s: Classical Dreams

In 1949 Dizzy Gillespie was forced to disband his beloved but unprofitable bop big band. He immediately formed a rhythm-and-blues band, hoping to cash in on the current popular fad among black audiences. Parker faced a turning point that year as well, but his crisis was aesthetic not commercial. His trumpet player Red Rodney complained that Parker's band played the same tunes every night. According to the pianist Lennie Tristano, Parker knew he was becoming stagnant: "Bird told me that he had said as much as he could in this particular idiom.

Venues

BIRDLAND

Birdland, located on Broadway between 52nd and 53rd Streets, opened in 1949 in honor of Charlie "Bird" Parker. Promoted as "The Jazz Corner of the World," it rapidly became the best-known and most influential jazz club of the 1950s. It became a mecca of modern jazz in particular, hosting such figures as J. J. Johnson, Fats Navarro, Kenny Dorham, Miles Davis, Dizzy Gillespie, Lucky Thompson, Milt Jackson, and Sonny Stitt. Parker himself played there initially but was banished from the club in 1955 after causing a series of embarrassing public spectacles while under the influence of drugs. In the fifties Count Basie spent a long, celebrated residency at Birdland, and in the sixties John Coltrane did the same, recording at the club an acclaimed album, *Live at Birdland* (1963).

Birdland opened at 8:00 P.M. and closed at 4:00 A.M.; guests paid seventy-five cents for admission. The diminutive Pee Wee Marquette served as charismatic master of ceremonies, and disc jockey Symphony Sid Torin hosted regular live broadcasts from the club for radio station WJZ. Bassist Bill Crow left this recollection of the interior: "On the right side of the club were booths along the wall and tables directly in front of the bandstand. Along the left wall was the bar. Between the bar and the left side of the bandstand . . . was a section we called 'the bleachers,' with a long wooden bench at the rear and two or three rows of chairs in front of it. . . . Behind the bar were live birds in cages. The walls were covered with photo murals by Herman Leonard, done in the dramatic high-contrast style that was characteristic of his photography. Agaist jet black backgrounds, life-size action shots of Charlie Parker, Dizzy Gillespie, Lennie Tristano, and other modern jazzmen stood in sharp focus. . . . A sign near the door said that the maximum legal occupancy was 273 people, but on weekends the place was often so crowded that I could barely squeeze into it." ■ ■ ■

He wanted to develop something else in the way of playing or another style. He was tired of playing the same ideas."

Rather than tap black vernacular idioms, as Gillespie had done, Parker turned to the European classical tradition for inspiration. Parker had acquired a love of classical music in the mid-1940s. He was impressed with the melodic patterns of Johann Sebastian Bach, and remarked that the patterns in jazz "had already been put down [by Bach], and in most cases, a lot better." Parker especially admired the music of twentieth-century composers. During a "blindfold test" (a chance to identify and rate music aurally) given by *Metronome* in 1948, Parker heard Stravinsky's *The Song of the Nightingale,* and said, "Is it by Stravinsky? That's music at its best. I like all of Stravinsky—and Prokofiev, Hindemith, Ravel, Debussy . . . and of course Wagner and Bach. Give that all the stars you've got!"

In 1949 Parker traveled to Europe for the first time and performed at the **International Jazz Festival** in Paris. Upon returning to the United States Parker professed his desire to return to Europe to study classical composition under Nadia Boulanger, the famed mentor of Aaron Copland, Virgil Thomson, Walter Piston, and dozens of other American composers. Although Parker did not follow through with this plan, his European experience prompted a change in his music. In partnership with Norman Granz, Parker began performing and recording with a classical instrumentation including violins, viola, cellos, harp, oboe/English horn, together with jazz rhythm section accompaniment. In late

1949 he recorded several sides with this ensemble, which were later issued as the album, ***Charlie Parker with Strings.*** The repertory included popular songs like "Just Friends" and "April in Paris." As with similar experiments by previous jazz artists, Parker's shift ignited controversy, drawing praise from some critics and scorn from others.

According to Max Roach, Parker subsequently became more ambitious: "Bird had all sorts of musical combinations in mind. He wanted to make a record with [violinist] Yehudi Menuhin and, at least, a forty-piece orchestra." In an interview with Nat Hentoff in 1953, Parker said: "I'd like to do a session with five or six woodwinds, a harp, a choral group, and full rhythm section. Something on the line of Hindemith's *Kleine Kammermusik*." Parker did not intend to abandon jazz, only to bridge jazz and classical music. But Granz squelched his plans, according to Roach: "[Parker] mapped out things for woodwinds and voices, and Norman Granz would holler, 'What's this? You can't make money with this crazy combination. You can't sell this stuff!'" Undaunted, Parker went to avant-garde composer Edgard Varèse and pleaded for composition lessons. Although Varèse consented, Parker died before they had a chance to meet again.

Charlie Parker with Strings recording session, 1949. *Left to right:* Buddy Rich, Ray Brown, Charlie Parker, Max Hollander, Mitch Miller, Milton Lomask.

In view of Parker's genuine interest in exploring classical music, why—apart from Granz's opposition—did so few of his plans bear fruit? One reason may have been that he lacked confidence in his knowledge of conventional theory. A brilliant intuitive player, Parker made rudimentary mistakes in notation, once told a student there were thirteen (rather than twelve) keys, and on another occasion could not explain the chord progression of a certain bridge to his neophyte trumpeter Red Rodney. But the larger obstacle was his debilitating dependence on drugs and alcohol. By the mid-fifties his habits had alienated people to such an extent that in the end he found himself alone, abandoned by friends and family. For years no one could be sure about the exact cause and place of his death. The generally accepted account is that he died while watching Tommy Dorsey on television at the apartment of his friend and supporter, the Baroness Pannonica de Königswarter. He was thirty-four.

Chapter 19 Cool Jazz

I n 1949 *Variety* declared, "BOP IS A FLOP—COMMERCIALLY. The musical style is dying almost as fast as it began." That same year, as we have seen, a bored Charlie Parker began casting about for something new, and Dizzy Gillespie disbanded his bop big band and organized a rhythm-and-blues outfit. Swing bandleaders who had experimented with bebop, such as Benny Goodman, Woody Herman, and Charlie Barnet, gave it up (or disbanded temporarily) around the same time.

But although the bebop fad had ended, the music itself now underwent a lengthy process of refinement. Stung by the market failure of bebop, young players began smoothing the music's hard edges to appeal to a broader listening audience. Their labors produced a subspecies of bebop known in the press as cool jazz. Although some of this music's most distinguished representatives were black—notably Miles Davis and the Modern Jazz Quartet—cool jazz flourished primarily among white players in California. Emanating from bandstands and recording studios on the West Coast, it dominated the modern jazz horizon in the early 1950s.

The Cool Ethos

The old Jazz Age dichotomy of hot versus sweet remained current throughout the Swing Era. But when jazz entered its modern stage, this duality shifted: "sweet," as a foil to "hot," yielded to "cool." What was meant by cool jazz? Performances in this idiom drew from a common stock of the following characteristics:

- generally understated manner of expression or rhetorical stance
- subdued rhythms, soft articulations, muted accents
- lyrical melodies
- "pastel" ensemble sonorities achieved by combining mellow-sounding brass instruments, especially French horns, trumpets and trombones in bucket mutes, flugelhorns, and tuba
- soft dynamics (drummers often use brushes instead of sticks)
- a greater emphasis on arrangements than generally found in bebop
- exploratory musical forms and structures
- contrapuntal textures
- classically inspired clarity of tone and attack

Cool jazz was one manifestation of an emotional posture common to several artistic movements in the fifties. According to one cultural historian, "cool" connoted "an air of disengagement, of nonchalance"; to be cool supplied "an emotional mantle, sheltering the whole personality from embarrassing excess." Understood in this broad sense, cool sensibilities inspired the muted but powerful performances of such diverse artists as painter Mark Rothko, actor James Dean, writer Jack Kerouac, and singer Frank Sinatra. Like the work of these artists, cool jazz is often viewed as an expression of psychological tensions produced by the Cold War. Cool jazz manifested an urbane emotional restraint, a grace under pressure, so to speak, that seemed an apt response to the arms race. As one critic remarked in 1959, "Cool jazz . . . reflects the resignation of men who live well, yet know that H-bombs are being stockpiled."

Although cool jazz as a movement emerged in the fifties, the cool ethos was not new to jazz. As we have seen, Bix Beiderbecke and Frankie Trumbauer reinterpreted the New Orleans idiom in a subdued manner that is sometimes referred to as "cool." Trumbauer's most significant disciple, Lester Young, continued the cool impulse with his light, vibratoless tone, and nonchalantly swinging phrases. And Young's boss, Count Basie, explored a laconic and understated big band sound that directly influenced cool jazz ensembles of the fifties.

Guiding Spirits: Lennie Tristano and Claude Thornhill

European classical music, which had a negligible influence on bebop, played an important role in the rise of cool jazz. This role is apparent in the work of two pioneering figures, white bandleaders Lennie Tristano and Claude Thornhill. A native of Chicago, the blind pianist **Lennie Tristano** (1919–1978) moved to New York in 1946 where he began performing and recording with Dizzy Gillespie and Charlie Parker; the following year *Metronome* named him "musician of the year." An important teacher, Tristano attracted a circle of devoted pupils, some of whom—notably alto saxophonist **Lee Konitz** (b. 1927), tenor saxophonist Warne Marsh, and guitarist Billy Bauer—became his sidemen. Tristano's students studied works by J. S. Bach as well as solos by Louis Armstrong, Roy Eldridge, and Charlie Parker. In his own playing and that of his students, Tristano nurtured a conception of bebop based in part on the classical virtues of controlled execution, purity of tone, and subdued rhythmic accents.

If Lennie Tristano served as a mentor to young soloists, pianist **Claude Thornhill** (1909–1965) led an experimental big band that became a model for cool ensembles. A swing bandleader with an eccentric taste for sonority, Thornhill greatly admired Claude Debussy, a turn-of-the-century French composer known for the sensuous qualities of his textures and timbres. Thornhill dwelt upon similarly rich sonorities in his own music, producing an effect of stasis. **Gil Evans** (1912–1988), his principal staff arranger, recalled that "the sound of the band was almost a reduction to an inactivity of music, to a stillness. Everything, melody, harmony and rhythm was moving at a minimum speed. . . . The sound hung like a cloud." To produce arresting tone colors, Thornhill often mixed instruments from different sections in the manner of Duke Ellington; to create a softly blended "pastel" sonority, he combined French horns with the sound of trumpets and trombones playing into derby hats without vibrato.

Miles Davis and *Birth of the Cool*

Thornhill's music won admiration from the beboppers. In 1948 Thelonious Monk called Thornhill's band "the only good-sounding band I've heard in years." Miles Davis felt a special affinity for the Thornhill sound. As a young, inexperienced trumpeter in Charlie Parker's quintet, Davis initially struggled to keep up with Parker's breakneck tempos. He found it especially hard to fill the shoes of his virtuoso predecessor, Dizzy Gillespie: "Some things Dizzy played I could play, and other things he played, I couldn't. So, I just didn't play those licks that I knew I couldn't play, because I realized early on that I had to have my own voice—whatever that voice was—on the instrument."

Davis found his voice by wedding bebop with the quieter, more lyrical world of Thornhill. This pairing began when Gil Evans came into the Royal Roost to hear Parker. Wholly captivated by the music, Evans arranged Parker's compositions "Anthropology" and "Yardbird Suite" for Thornhill's band. As he later recalled, "Once this stationary effect, [the Thornhill] sound, was created, it was ready to have other things added to it. . . . You have to make personal use of harmonies. . . . There has to be more movement in the melody; more dynamics; more syncopation. . . . I did more or less match up with the [Thornhill] sound the different movements by people like Lester, Charlie, and Dizzy in which I was interested."

Within a short time, Evans's basement apartment, located close to 52nd Street behind a Chinese laundry, became a hangout for young jazz players of both races. Baritone saxophonist Gerry Mulligan, another Thornhill arranger who had experimented with bebop, was a ubiquitous presence; Parker himself, and his sidemen, pianist John Lewis and drummer Max Roach, also showed up frequently. The visitors had lengthy musical and philosophical discussions about the direction and purpose of modern jazz. Out of the intellectualizing, speculating, and brainstorming that took place, the material for the first generally recognized cool jazz recordings was created. Although the music resulted from intense collaboration, it was Davis, according to Mulligan, who "took the initiative and put the theories to work. He called the rehearsals, hired the halls, called the players, and generally cracked the whip."

In 1949 and 1950, Davis brought a *nonet* (a group of nine musicians) into the studio at Capitol Records and made a series of twelve records (six discs). The music called for unusual instrumentation: trumpet, alto saxophone, French horn, trombone, baritone saxophone, and tuba, plus rhythm section—piano, bass, and drums. The band's racially mixed character was striking as well: Thornhill alumni included Tristano's protégé Lee Konitz, French horn player Sandy Siegelstein, and tuba player Bill Barber; beboppers Lewis and (white musician) Al Haig played piano; Roach and Kenny Clarke played drums. Several musicians played solos, but the dominant voice was Davis's. Davis sounds far more at home in this context of subtly shifting textures and haunting melodies than in Parker's band. The arrangements were by Davis, Mulligan, Evans, Lewis, and John Carisi. These works seem to mark a reconciliation of swing and bebop, white and black, and in some respects, classical music and jazz.

Davis's nonet performed only a few times in public, mostly at the Royal Roost. For both the recordings and the live performances, reception was mixed. Some beboppers thought the music was too white; Count Basie considered it "slow and strange," but "good, real good." However listeners responded, the recordings announced the arrival of a new and soon-to-be influential style of jazz. Initially released as 78s, the records were rereleased in 1957 on an LP bearing the reverential title **Birth of the Cool.**

West Coast Jazz

Although the primary impetus for cool jazz started on the East Coast, the music never really took root there. In New York young black players continued to elaborate the hot side of bebop, eventually producing a fiery mutation that critics dubbed hard bop. Cool jazz, meanwhile, drifted to California, where (mostly) white players in Los Angeles and San Francisco developed it into a sophisticated, commercially successful, and highly controversial style.

In general, the critical establishment, which was centered in the East, favored East Coast players and condemned much of the music coming out of California. Not surprisingly, West Coast jazz strongly influenced television and film music being produced in Hollywood. Thus, while critics were ardently extolling the virtues of New York–based jazz, the average citizen was more likely to hear cool West Coast sounds on TV and in the movies. The debate between the coasts also became an implicit battle of art versus commerce, pitting "elite" eastern critics against the apparent populist preferences of California and the rest of the country.

This is not to say that jazz in California had the wide appeal of rock 'n' roll or other varieties of popular music in the fifties. Judging from marketing strategies evident from album covers and advertisements, West Coast jazz appealed primarily to economically comfortable white men in their twenties or thirties who wore dark suits, attended cocktail parties, and read *Esquire* or *Playboy* magazine. West Coast jazz suggested urbanity and sophistication, and as such, epitomized the postwar, self-consciously modern white male.

Gerry Mulligan (*right*) and Chet Baker at the Haig, 1952.

Gerry Mulligan

One of the earliest and most influential West Coast bands was led by *Birth of the Cool* veteran, **Gerry Mulligan** (1927–1996). A New Yorker by birth, Mulligan moved to Los Angeles after recording with Davis and began performing with ensembles of various sizes in two important L.A. venues: **The Haig** on Wilshire Boulevard and **The Lighthouse** in Hermosa Beach. Mulligan favored music for big band or at least the medium-sized chamber ensembles he had been involved with since the late forties. But for various reasons—partly economic, partly practical (since the Haig in particular had a very small bandstand)—Mulligan decided in the summer of 1952 to form his so-called **pianoless quartet,** a group featuring himself on baritone saxophone, Chet Baker on trumpet, Bob Whitlock on bass, and Chico Hamilton on drums. The band featured several novel aspects: the leader played baritone saxophone, an instrument previously neglected as a jazz solo instrument; the absence of a piano created a conspicuously spare texture in which the two horns frequently improvised contrapuntal duets; and the hard, lean sonority of the band, coupled with frequently soft dynamics, produced a cool sound of considerable freshness.

Mulligan's quartet became the first group to record for **Pacific Jazz,** a new label devoted to West Coast artists. The Mulligan records were immediately successful. In early 1953 *Time* magazine published a glowing article about Mulligan, hailing his music as an improvement on earlier modern jazz: "In comparison with the frantic extremes of bop, [Mulligan's] jazz is rich and even orderly, is marked by an almost Bach-like counterpoint." The writer took note of the earnest demeanor assumed by Mulligan on the bandstand, an attitude seemingly borrowed from classical musicians. He opens his eyes "only occasionally to glower at customers who are boorish enough to talk. . . . Mulligan is extremely serious about his music." In his earlier arrangements for Thornhill he looked "for ideas in his favorite composers—Stravinsky, Ravel, Prokofiev, and Bach."

Despite its broad appeal, Mulligan's pianoless quartet survived for less than a year. In 1953 Mulligan was convicted for heroin possession and spent six months in jail. Soon after his release, he met Chet Baker on Hollywood Boulevard one night. Baker, who had been making $125 per week with Mulligan, now asked for $300. He recalled that Mulligan "and this chick he was with, Arlene . . . for a minute they laughed in my face and said that's ridiculous, $300 a week; and that was the way the Gerry Mulligan Quartet ended."

GERRY MULLIGAN QUARTET, *"Bernie's Tune"* (1952)

CD 2 / Track 15

One of the first recordings made by the Gerry Mulligan Quartet, "Bernie's Tune," manifests many characteristics of cool jazz. The overall mood is subdued, with the horns playing softly and the drummer playing with brushes. The absence of piano leaves a sparse texture in the rhythm section. The medium tempo and the ambivalent, stop-and-start character of the head contrast strikingly with the pell-mell surge of "hot" bebop tunes like "Shaw 'Nuff" and "Koko." Unlike the beboppers, who typically played their heads in unison or octaves, Mulligan and Baker follow cool practice by playing "Bernie's Tune" in harmony. During the head the bassist and drummer play carefully worked-out accompaniments that are almost minimalist in their unobtrusiveness. The minor mode of the A-sections, while not necessarily a cool attribute, in this case enhances the starkness of texture and sonority already present.

The solos demonstrate the cool preference for transparency of musical structure. The first and last A-sections of Mulligan's solo, for example, each begin with a two-bar phrase that is immediately followed by a similar, though varied, corresponding phrase. When Baker begins his solo, Mulligan fades to a soft dynamic level and supplies discreet sustained notes and contrapuntal lines behind Baker. Baker shows a similar interest in logical exposition, beginning his second A-section, for instance, with a pair of balanced two-bar phrases in the manner of Mulligan. After Baker's solo the two horn players engage in improvised counterpoint, a conceptual throwback to the New Orleans period if rather different in its modern realization. Thematically, the starting point for the duet is a *downbeat* version of the stop-and-start opening motive of the head, which in the head begins on an *upbeat*.

Create your own listening chart (CD 2 / Track 15)

Chet Baker

Chet Baker (1929–1988) asked for the raise because he felt his dramatic rise in stature over the past year justified it. When Charlie Parker came to California in 1952 to play a three-week engagement, the slight, baby-faced Baker won the audition to be his trumpet player. Upon returning to New York, Parker warned Dizzy Gillespie and Miles Davis, "There's a little white cat in California who's going to eat you up." Baker rose in the readers' polls during his time with Mulligan, eventually taking first place for best trumpeter in *Down Beat* for his wistful 1953 ballad performance of "My Funny Valentine," beating out Gillespie, Davis, Clifford Brown, Clark Terry, and a host of other young trumpet stars both east and west.

After leaving Mulligan, Baker teamed up with pianist **Russ Freeman** (b. 1926) to form a standard quartet (the other instruments were bass and drums) with which Baker made the most acclaimed recordings of his career. Baker and Freeman developed the same sensitive contrapuntal relationship that Baker had pursued with Mulligan. Out of Mulligan's shadow, however, Baker played with greater energy and imagination. On pieces like "All the Things You Are" he proved himself to be a lyrical and inventive improviser with light, effortless articulation. With Freeman he began singing as well, quickly developing a completely individual vocal style—quiet, fragile, even more cool-sounding than his trumpet playing.

Dave Brubeck

While Mulligan and Baker were busy formulating a California cool sound in Los Angeles, pianist **Dave Brubeck** (b. 1920) was doing the same thing in San Francisco. Brubeck, a Bible-reading family man, did not fit the jazz musician stereotype. Raised on a forty-five-thousand-acre cattle ranch in northern California, he came of age in almost total isolation from the main currents of jazz.

To a greater degree than most of his jazz contemporaries, Brubeck was inspired by modernist composition in the European classical tradition. After serving in the military during the war, Brubeck studied with French émigré, Darius Milhaud, and the arch-modernist from Vienna, Arnold Schoenberg. In 1946 Brubeck and some of his fellow students organized, under Milhaud's supervision, an experimental octet. Named the Jazz Workshop Ensemble, the group performed pieces that brought together elements of jazz and classical music in various proportions.

Like Mulligan, Brubeck was forced by economic pressures to lead smaller groups in the early fifties. He began to achieve commercial success with his trio, which performed frequently at the **Blackhawk,** an important jazz club in San Francisco. He also recorded with **Fantasy,** a fledgling record label that succeeded largely on the basis of Brubeck's popularity. On these early recordings he reveals a piano style based on primal rhythmic accents, often involving two-hand chords, rather than on right-hand virtuosity. In 1951 he disbanded the trio and organized a quartet featuring alto saxophonist **Paul Desmond** (born Paul Breitenfeld, 1924–1977). Desmond is sometimes regarded as the paragon of cool on his instrument; he wanted a sound, as he put it, like "a dry martini." A supremely lyrical player whose gentle tone often dropped to a whisper, Desmond provided an apt foil to Brubeck's more percussive approach.

Brubeck's popularity rose dramatically, and in 1954 his picture appeared on the cover of *Time* magazine. But his success had not yet peaked. In 1957 he

third stream a hybrid style fusing improvised jazz with notated classical music; often associated with cool jazz.

formed his so-called **classic quartet,** featuring—besides Desmond—bassist Eugene Wright, and drummer Joe Morello. Despite controversy over Brubeck's hiring of Wright, a black player, this group attracted a wide following, toured internationally for the U.S. State Department, and stayed together until 1967. Brubeck's most important album from this period, *Time Out* (1959), experimented with unusual meters. The melody to "Blue Rondo a la Turk" proceeds in 9/8 time according to the beat pattern: 121212123/121212123, and so on. "Take Five," a piece written by Desmond in 5/4 time, became probably the most popular modern jazz piece ever recorded.

Further Listening from the *Prentice Hall Jazz Collection*
Track 6: Dave Brubeck, "Blue Rondo a la Turk" (1959)

The Modern Jazz Quartet

As we have seen, many cool and West Coast players enriched their music by borrowing elements from the European classical tradition. During a lecture at Brandeis University in 1957, composer, conductor, and critic Gunther Schuller coined a new term to describe the complete integration of improvised jazz and composed classical music: **third stream.** Third stream music was nothing new, of course; one can find the basic impulse in the work of Scott Joplin, Paul Whiteman, Artie Shaw, and Duke Ellington. In the fifties few ensembles realized third stream ideals more convincingly than the **Modern Jazz Quartet.**

The Modern Jazz Quartet (MJQ) began as members of the rhythm section in Dizzy Gillespie's big band in 1946. When it was organized formally in 1952, the band consisted of vibraphonist **Milt Jackson** (1923–1999), pianist **John Lewis**

Modern Jazz Quartet. *Left to right:* Percy Heath, Connie Kay, John Lewis, Milt Jackson.

(1920–2001), bassist **Percy Heath** (b. 1923), and drummer Kenny Clarke. As Lewis, the music director, later put it, "My ideals stem from . . . Count Basie's band of the '30s and '40s. This group produced an integration of ensemble playing which projected—and sounded like—the spontaneous playing of ideas which were the personal expression of each member of the band rather than the arrangers or composers." The members of the Modern Jazz Quartet achieved this kind of balanced interaction. This is especially clear in the playing of Jackson and Lewis, who—like Gerry Mulligan and Chet Baker—often played in counterpoint with each other. Jackson's extravagant blues-based improvisations perfectly complemented Lewis's spare, wry, aphoristic style.

In addition to fostering a collaborative music of greater structural variety, Lewis wanted to cultivate a public image far removed from the drug addiction and bohemianism so often associated with modern jazz. Part of the change in image stemmed from a quest for full acceptance within the rarified realm of European concert music. Wearing tuxedos, arriving on time, performing in concert halls as well as in nightclubs—such actions formed part of the players' concern with stage etiquette. But immaculate presentation also reflected their jazz roots. "We wanted to bring back a level of dignity that we all remembered from watching all those great big bands in the Swing Era," Jackson said. The fine clothes, Lewis agreed, were in "the Ellington-Lunceford tradition."

In 1953 the band took its first big engagement, at Birdland. "We had a hard time getting people to quiet down and listen," recalled Heath. So "we'd use reverse psychology and play softer. Suddenly, they knew we were up there and realized the conversation was louder than the music." Some listeners were put off by the band's emphasis on decorum and artistic seriousness, so uncharacteristic of most jazz performances. Ralph Ellison, for one, dismissed the MJQ's "funereal posturings." Others, however, found the band refreshing and even awe-inspiring. Ralph J. Gleason recalled the band's debut in San Francisco, so different from the Birdland reception: "When they opened at the Blackhawk, it was like a religious service. We were afraid to breathe for fear it would disturb them. And yet they had fire and a deeply swinging groove that was undeniable. And they always, in everything they ever did, have class."

In 1955 Clarke left the band and was replaced by **Connie Kay** (1927–1994), the band's drummer for the rest of its almost forty-year history. Kay's arrival marked a pivotal moment in the band's development. That year the MJQ performed at the Newport Festival and twice at New York's Town Hall. The following year, after previously recording for Prestige, the band switched to **Atlantic,** a label that produced most of its subsequent recordings. But it was during a European tour in 1957 that the MJQ became preeminent. "All the American critics were talking about Dave Brubeck and that kind of West Coast cool sound," said Heath, "and we came along with a sound that was also cool. But it wasn't until we made an impression on the European critics [in 1957]—they voted for the MJQ as the group of the year—that American critics jumped on the bandwagon."

Upon returning to the United States Lewis began collaborating with Gunther Schuller and others on third stream experiments at the **Lenox School of Jazz** in Massachusetts, where Lewis served as faculty director. In doing so he was continuing an interest that dated back to the beginnings of the MJQ. In 1952 Lewis wrote a jazz fugue called "Vendome." A **fugue,** a baroque genre epitomized by J. S. Bach in works like the *Well-Tempered Clavier,* presents a series of contrapuntal developments of a single short melody (called a *subject*). The defining

fugue a piece of imitation based on a single subject (main melody).

feature of fugal writing is *imitation,* the presentation of the subject in successive, overlapping voices, one after another (as in "Row, Row, Row Your Boat," for example). For his second fugue, "Concorde" (1955), Lewis organized the whole piece in a swinging jazz style, making seamless transitions between "composed" and "improvised" passages. "Concorde" was recorded at the first MJQ session to feature Connie Kay on the drums.

MODERN JAZZ QUARTET, *"Concorde"* (1955)

In "Concorde," John Lewis wedded the baroque fugue structure with jazz phrasing and style. The following list of definitions will clarify terms related to fugue that appear in Listening Chart 22:

Subject = a short melody upon which the piece is based
Countersubject = a secondary melody usually heard in juxtaposition with the subject
Exposition = an opening passage clearly stating the subject imitatively in all voices
Counterexposition = subsequent imitative statements of the subject in two or more voices
Episode = a discursive, exploratory passage, which, though often based on the subject, does not state it in its entirety. Episodes tend to be unstable, modulatory, and freely contrapuntal.
Free counterpoint = contrapuntal lines not based explicitly on the subject or the countersubject
Pedal point = a prolonged note, often in the low register, intended to generate tension before a final statement of the subject.
Stretto (Italian, "tight") = a counterexposition in which the subject entries overlap in close succession. Like a pedal point, passages of stretto are intended to create tension and often appear at the end of a fugue.

The exposition consists of Heath (bass), Lewis (piano), and Jackson (vibes) each presenting the subject in turn. Heath and Lewis play a countersubject behind Lewis and Jackson respectively. The rest of the piece presents an alternation of episodes and counterexpositions. In the first counterexposition Heath introduces a second countersubject which is then combined with the first one at Jackson's subject entry. The second counterexposition is longer than the first, involving three subject entries. The episodes consist of solos by the three melody instruments with various types of counterpoint added by the other players. The longest and most exciting solo is the last one, by Jackson. Whereas earlier it is sometimes difficult to know when the players are executing written lines, here it seems clear that Jackson is improvising. Notice Connie Kay's varied—but consistent—use of cymbals throughout. During the exposition and counterexpositions (including the stretto) he uses a high-pitched cymbal on a bell-tree; during the episodes he plays more conventionally on the ride cymbal. Thus he uses cymbal colors to delineate form. Similarly, Percy Heath plays written contrapuntal lines during the expositions but "walks" during the episodes (solos).

LISTENING CHART 22

Modern Jazz Quartet, "Concorde" (Lewis)

CD 2 / Tracks 16–23

RECORDED 2 JULY 1955 / *CONCORDE* PRESTIGE 7005

Milt Jackson (vibraphone), John Lewis (piano), Percy Heath (bass), Connie Kay (drums)

| Style: Cool jazz | | | | Form: Fugue |

Exposition

16	0:00	Subject		Percy Heath (bass) (Connie Kay accompanies on bell-tree)
	0:08	Subject		John Lewis (piano) (+ Heath on countersubject 1)
	0:18		Subject	Milt Jackson (vibes) (+ Lewis on countersubject 1) (Heath plays arranged bass line)
	0:26		Subject	Heath (bass) (+ Jackson on countersubject 1) (Lewis and Kay accompany)

Episode 1: Piano solo (John Lewis)

| 17 | 0:36 | | | (Jackson plays discreet counterpoint)
(Heath walks; Kay switches to ride cymbal) |

Counterexposition 1

| 18 | 1:19 | Subject | | Lewis (piano)
(+ Heath on countersubject 2)
(Kay switches back to bell-tree) |
| | 1:27 | | Subject | Jackson (vibes)
(+ Lewis on countersubject 1; Heath on countersubject 2) |

Episode 2: Bass solo (Percy Heath)

| 19 | 1:36 | | | (Lewis and Jackson play arranged backgrounds)
(Kay switches back to ride cymbal) |

Counterexposition 2

20	2:10	Subject		Jackson (vibes) (+ Lewis on free counterpoint)
	2:18	Subject		Lewis (piano) (+ Jackson on free counterpoint)
	2:28		Subject	Heath (bass) (+ Lewis and Jackson on new countermelody treated imitatively) (Kay switches back to bell-tree)

			Episode 3: Vibraphone solo (Milt Jackson)
21	2:38		Jackson's clearly improvising here!
			(Lewis plays free counterpoint based on subject)
			(Heath walks; Kay switches back to ride cymbal)
22	3:08	Pedal point	Heath repeats note in low register while Jackson plays bluesy riffs above him
			Stretto
23	3:21		Heath (bass), Lewis (piano), Jackson (vibes), in turn
			(Kay switches back to bell-tree)
		Final gong/chord	Kay (drums) + Jackson (vibes)

Hard Bop

Although cool jazz probably sold more records and soaked more deeply into the public consciousness, hard bop—its soulful and hard-swinging cousin—ultimately received greater critical acclaim. It is difficult to know how much of this critical bias reflected musical preferences and how much was based on race. Certainly, the spectacle of white players cashing in on black innovations was a familiar one by now; it had happened with ragtime in the 1910s, early jazz in the twenties, and swing in the thirties. Perhaps critics felt that cool jazz players—especially on the West Coast—simply homogenized bebop for lucrative mainstream consumption, and therefore should not be rewarded with critical accolades.

The players themselves generally did not think in terms of labels such as "cool jazz" or "hard bop." And yet there *was* a resurgence in black modern jazz in the mid-fifties that can rightly be viewed as a reaction against the popularity and publicity surrounding cool jazz. This resurgence corresponded with early civil rights triumphs and the crescendo of hope that attended them in the black community. In 1954, the year of the landmark Supreme Court decision *Brown v. Board of Education,* several events signaled the parallel advent of hard bop: Miles Davis recorded "Walkin'" and "Blue 'n' Boogie"; Art Blakey and Horace Silver formed the Jazz Messengers; and Clifford Brown joined Max Roach as co-leader of their short-lived but illustrious quintet. As the civil rights movement advanced and white southern reactionaries dug in, hard bop became more intense. At the end of the decade the music exploded in a metaphorical cry of impatience and frustration, producing yet another species in the evolution of jazz styles: free jazz.

Grass-Roots Influences

Whereas cool jazz musicians drew inspiration from European classical music, hard boppers tapped idioms of the black vernacular, especially gospel music and its secular counterpart, the blues. **Gospel** developed in "sanctified" Pentecostal churches around the turn of the century. Services in these churches emphasized intensely demonstrative modes of worship, including call-and-response singing, dancing, clapping, and shouting. During the 1920s gospel absorbed elements of the classic blues and, under the leadership of pianist

gospel a popular African American genre of sacred music emphasizing virtuosic vocal soloists and exuberant choral singing.

225

Thomas A. Dorsey, became a commercial product in the black community. One of Dorsey's protégés was a young woman from New Orleans named Mahalia Jackson. After a long period of dues-paying and false starts, Jackson recorded "Move On Up a Little Higher" for Apollo records in 1947. The song became a hit, launching Jackson's career. In 1954 she signed a contract with Columbia records, began hosting her own CBS radio program, and became an international star.

In secular music, various blues-based styles became popular with black consumers around the same time. **Rhythm-and-blues (R&B),** pioneered by Louis Jordan in the 1940s, applied boogie-woogie and swing rhythms to an instrumentation that featured electric guitars and honking saxophones. Little Richard's big hit of 1954, "Tutti Frutti," marked both the apotheosis of rhythm-and-blues and the birth of rock 'n' roll. Meanwhile, some gospel singers began converting their bluesy sacred hymns to love songs, thereby creating a new genre called **soul.** As with many of the developments treated in this chapter, soul emerged in 1954, with Ray Charles's recording of "I've Got a Woman," a secular lyric based on the gospel song, "I've Got a Savior." Sam Cooke, the popular lead singer for the gospel quartet, the Soul Stirrers, embraced soul two years later (to the dismay of his gospel fans). Cooke's record "You Send Me" (1957) sold over a million copies and stimulated a soul movement that would climax in the 1960s with the music of artists like Otis Redding, Wilson Pickett, and Aretha Franklin.

The popularity of gospel, rhythm-and-blues, and soul inevitably influenced black jazz musicians. These genres comforted and encouraged black listeners at the grass roots level, strengthening their sense of ethnic identity and political and economic power. Much of the jazz that came to be known as "hard bop" reflected a desire to participate somehow in the interrelated cultural developments in popular music and civil rights.

Characteristics of Hard Bop

In some ways "hard bop" is a more slippery term than "cool jazz." The "hardness" of hard bop usually refers to heavily accented rhythms and an overt bluesy expressiveness. Yet in the absence of clear gospel or R&B influences, some jazz seems to fall into the hard bop category almost by default: if it is clearly not "cool," it must be hard bop. Moreover, many hard bop recordings contain cool elements as well; the two styles are not mutually exclusive. Even so, hard bop performances usually contain one or more of the following characteristics:

- Generally aggressive manner of expression or rhetorical stance
- Emphatic rhythms, blunt articulations, strong accents among horn players; in rhythm section, percussive piano style, driving bass, explosive drums
- Hard-swinging rhythmic sense in both solos and rhythm section
- Drummers assume prominent role, both as players and as bandleaders
- Interaction between drummers (and other members of rhythm section) and soloists
- Bluesy expressiveness on both melody and chordal instruments
- Sometimes gospel-related chord progressions and stylistic gestures
- Catchier, more accessible heads than often found in bebop
- Renewed interest in arrangements and in balancing improvisation with composition

rhythm-and-blues (R&B) in the 1940s and 1950s a genre of black popular music applying boogie-woogie and swing rhythms to an instrumentation that featured electric guitars and honking saxophones.

soul a genre of black popular music from the 1950s and 1960s that fitted gospel music with secular lyrics.

East Coast Jazz

Just as cool jazz prevailed on the West Coast, so hard bop flourished in the East. Philadelphia and Detroit produced a disproportionate number of leading players. Out of Philadelphia came trumpeters Clifford Brown and Lee Morgan, tenor saxophonists John Coltrane and Benny Golson, and pianists McCoy Tyner and Bobby Timmons. Detroit musicians included bassists Paul Chambers and Doug Watkins, drummers Elvin Jones and Louis Hayes, and trombonists Curtis Fuller and Frank Rosolino. Virtually all of these players made their mark in New York City. Most of them recorded extensively for **Blue Note,** a record label that came to epitomize hard bop in the fifties and sixties (see "Record Labels: Blue Note"). As one authority has pointed out, the black-and-white, smoke-suffused interior photographs that appeared on the covers of Blue Note albums contrasted starkly with the open-air seaside images featured on records produced by West Coast labels such as Pacific Jazz and Fantasy. East Coast jazz, the Blue Note covers seemed to say, was hot, gritty, urban—the essence of soulfulness.

Record Labels

BLUE NOTE

Blue Note Records, now regarded as a bulwark of modern jazz, actually arose as part of the traditionalist movement of the late 1930s (see Chapter 10). The company was formed in 1939 by Alfred Lion and Francis Wolff, German refugees from the Nazi regime who had been friends since childhood. The impetus for the company came from Lion's experience of watching boogie-woogie pianists Albert Ammons and Meade Lux Lewis perform at John Hammond's famous "Spirituals to Swing" concert in 1938. Overwhelmed with what he heard, Lion took Ammons and Lewis into a New York studio and produced what would be the first Blue Note records. The label's introductory brochure stated the company's high-minded philosophy: "Blue Note Records are designed simply to serve the uncompromising expressions of hot jazz or swing. . . . Hot jazz is expression and communication, and Blue Note Records are concerned with identifying its impulse, not its sensational and commercial adornments."

   World War II disrupted the company's production, but in the late forties Blue Note revived its activities, now focusing on bebop. The company recorded Miles Davis, Tadd Dameron, Fats Navarro, Bud Powell, and especially championed Thelonious Monk at a time when Monk was not yet widely appreciated. When Blue Note began issuing LPs in 1951, the company reproduced Wolff's stunning black-and-white candid photographs of the musicians for the album covers. During the 1950s and 1960s, Blue Note played a direct role in the evolution of hard bop and soul jazz, helping to create the studio identities of Art Blakey's (and Horace Silver's) Jazz Messengers, bringing jazz organist Jimmy Smith to national prominence, and launching the careers of dozens of talented sidemen as leaders in their own right. More than most companies, Blue Note took pains to produce the best jazz recordings possible, preceding each session with extensive planning and consultation with the musicians and several days of paid rehearsal. ■ ■ ■

Miles Davis Changes Course

Miles Davis played a leading role in the emergence of hard bop. When Davis's nonet recordings came to nothing in the short run, he felt unclear about the direction he should go artistically. In 1949 he began taking heroin to soothe his despondency over leaving his Parisian girlfriend, existentialist actress and singer Juliette Greco. As his addiction grew stronger, his music stagnated and his poll numbers dropped. Determined to beat heroin once and for all, he returned to his father's farm outside East St. Louis and locked himself in a small guest house. "I laid down and stared at the ceiling for twelve days and cursed everybody I didn't like. . . . I lay in a cold sweat. My nose and eyes ran. . . . My pores opened up and I smelled like chicken soup. Then it was over."

When he returned to New York in the spring of 1954, Davis immediately began a series of recordings for Prestige that captured the attention of the jazz world. On **"Blue 'n' Boogie"** and **"Walkin',"** Davis seemed to be reconnecting with his bop roots ("Blue 'n' Boogie," an uptempo blues, was first recorded by Dizzy Gillespie and Charlie Parker in 1945). And yet it was a bop at once enriched by cool developments and bolstered by a new soulfulness. Cool traits include striking sonorities and Davis's clear determination to take his time, even on "Blue 'n' Boogie." But the soulful elements predominate. During the head of "Walkin'," Davis plays with an attitude that bespeaks musical strutting; the rhythm section responds with a down-home, hip-swinging groove. With Davis having apparently subordinated the impetus that spawned *Birth of the Cool,* later critics hailed this moment as a "return of the hot."

Founding Fathers: Art Blakey and Horace Silver

Davis's pianist on the record "Blue 'n' Boogie"/"Walkin'" was a young player named **Horace Silver** (b. 1928). Raised in Norwalk, Connecticut, within an immigrant family from Cape Verde, Silver developed a percussive, blues-inflected piano style. He secured a strong position on the New York jazz scene, serving as de facto house pianist at Birdland from 1951. Silver found an important ally in veteran bebopper, **Art Blakey** (1919–1990). Touring with Billy Eckstine's bop big band while Dizzy Gillespie and Charlie Parker were still in it, Blakey became an ardent modern jazz devotee. In 1948 he traveled to West Africa, where he spent two years studying Islam. He returned with a Muslim name and an African-inspired commitment to forceful, explosive drumming.

Over the next few years Blakey teamed up with Horace Silver in various contexts, both as sideman and leader. A turning point came in February 1954, when Blakey made a live recording for Blue Note released on two albums as *A Night at Birdland.* On the front line, the band featured young trumpet star Clifford Brown and alto saxophonist Lou Donaldson, with Silver and bassist Curly Russell in the rhythm section. On pieces such as "Wee Dot"

Art Blakey.

and "Quicksilver" the Blakey quintet offers a turbulent, percussive approach to jazz. The virtuosity of Brown and Donaldson hark back to bebop, but the overflowing energy of the band, sparked by Silver's bluesy comping and Blakey's churning polyrhythms, set it apart from earlier jazz.

The Jazz Messengers

Later that year Blakey and Silver assembled a new quintet featuring trumpeter **Kenny Dorham** (1924–1972), tenor saxophonist **Hank Mobley** (1930–1986), and bassist Doug Watkins. Adopting the evangelical-sounding name, **The Jazz Messengers,** the quintet recorded under Blakey's leadership on some sessions and Silver's on others. This band became an archetypal group in the early history of hard bop. The instrumentation, with trumpet and tenor saxophone on the front line, provided the basic model for future hard bop ensembles. For this group Silver composed pieces, such as "The Preacher" and "Doodlin'," in a gospel-influenced funky style. Consisting of simple, catchy melodies and foot-tapping rhythms, these tunes helped introduce modern jazz to a larger audience.

In 1956 the band broke up when Silver left to form his own group. Blakey kept the name, Jazz Messengers, which would thereafter be associated almost exclusively with him. Between numbers at the Birdland session in 1954, he had introduced his youthful sidemen, and then told the audience: "Yes sir, I'm going to stay with the youngsters. When these get too old, I'm going to get some younger ones. . . . Keeps the mind active." These words aptly predicted the remaining thirty-six years of his career. Art Blakey and the Jazz Messengers became a revolving conservatory for young players, helping to launch the careers of many eminent soloists, including Lee Morgan and Donald Byrd in the fifties, Freddie Hubbard and Wayne Shorter in the sixties, Woody Shaw and JoAnne Brackeen in the seventies, and Wynton and Branford Marsalis in the eighties.

Horace Silver and "Funky" Jazz

"I loved bebop for taking jazz further along," Silver once recalled. "But as hip and as great as it was, there was a period when musicians had [almost] eliminated the blues, you know? They got so sophisticated that it seemed like they were afraid to play the blues, like it was demeaning to be funky. And I tried to bring that [back]." Silver pursued **funky,** or gospel- and blues-soaked, styles of jazz for much of his career.

After making the split with Blakey, Silver also led a series of influential hard bop combos. But he earned his reputation more for his compositions than for his bands. Many of his pieces have become jazz standards, including "The Preacher," "Opus de Funk," "Sister Sadie," "Nica's Dream," and—his most popular piece—"Song for My Father." A deeply spiritual person, Silver assembled his music from disparate sources ranging from bebop, gospel, and the blues, to Latin dance music and the folk traditions of his native Cape Verde. In 1959 he organized the quintet for which he is best known. This band, which remained intact for five years, featured Blue Mitchell on trumpet, Junior Cook on tenor saxophone, Gene Taylor on bass, and Louis Hayes on drums. In 1964 he recorded ***Song for My Father,*** which now stands as Silver's most significant album, both in critical and commercial terms.

Further Listening from the *Prentice Hall Jazz Collection*
Track 7: Horace Silver, "Señor Blues" (1956)

The Clifford Brown-Max Roach Quintet

Less than a month after Art Blakey recorded *A Night at Birdland,* **Clifford Brown** (1930–1956), Blakey's prodigious twenty-three-year-old trumpet player, received a phone call from Los Angeles. The caller was **Max Roach,** who had just finished a six-month engagement at the Lighthouse Club. He had heard Brown on a J. J. Johnson record and "fell in love" with his playing. Now he invited Brown to join forces with him in a new quintet.

Perhaps because he possessed such extravagant talent and died young in a car accident, Brown's reputation has long assumed a mythic character. He was raised in Wilmington, Delaware, but spent much time in Philadelphia, twenty-seven miles away. In Philadelphia he met and jammed with **Fats Navarro** (1923–1950), a lyrical, big-toned trumpet player who became Brown's mentor and chief influence. (Navarro died in 1950 from the combined effects of tuberculosis and heroin addiction.) A series of recordings in the early fifties—first with an R&B group, then with jazz mainstays Tadd Dameron, Lou Donaldson, J. J. Johnson, and Lionel Hampton—introduced Brown to the jazz world. In a record review one critic wrote that "Clifford's melodic contours at times are reminiscent of Miles Davis, yet his tone and attack are blunter, more emphatic." The year 1954 was pivotal for Brown: in February, he recorded with Blakey; in March, Roach called him; in April, he was interviewed for *Down Beat,* which hailed him as "the New Dizzy"; in August he won *Down Beat*'s New Star Award.

Brown was a breath of fresh air in more ways than one. In the *Down Beat* interview, he obliquely denounced drug abuse: "[For] a long time you weren't anywhere if you weren't hung on something, but now the younger guys frown on anyone who goofs. There's a different feeling now. You can notice how things are cleaning up." Brown himself avoided drugs and alcohol. Rejecting the carefree, footloose lifestyle of many jazz musicians, Brown was a family man devoted to his wife and infant son. Like members of the Modern Jazz Quartet, he wanted to bring a new sense of social responsibility and intellectual seriousness to jazz. He studied mathematics at Delaware State College and played a cutthroat game of chess. These cerebral interests shaped his solos, which—despite breath-taking virtuosic intricacies—manifest a high degree of logical construction. Yet, by all accounts, Brown was also warm-hearted and generous. These emotional attributes come through in his playing as well—in his Navarro-inspired effulgent tone, his fiery uptempo performances, and his poignant ballad renditions.

The Clifford Brown-Max Roach Quintet included **Harold Land** (1928–2001) on tenor saxophone, Richie Powell (Bud Powell's younger brother) on piano, and George Morrow on bass. The quintet featured inventive arrangements by Powell, dramatic risk-taking solos by the horn players, and a relentless drive from Roach and Morrow. Unlike Blakey, who played heavy rhythmic accents, Roach boasted an agile "melodic" style that brought out the varied pitches and tone colors available to him on the drum kit. The band achieved an unusually cohesive sound. In a *Down Beat* feature of the

Clifford Brown.

quintet from 1955, Brown said that the band aimed "for the musical extremes of excitement and subtle softness whenever each is necessary, but with a lot of feeling in everything. . . . And we have a definitely organized sound because organization is the trend in all modern jazz groups today. We're trying more and more to have our solos built into each arrangement so that it all forms a whole and creates emotional and intellectual tension."

The Brown-Roach Quintet ended late on the night of June 26, 1956, after a gig in Philadelphia. Brown, Richie Powell, and Powell's wife Nancy drove off toward Indiana, with Nancy, an inexperienced driver, at the wheel. As Clifford and Richie slept, it began to rain. Caught off guard by the slick pavement, Nancy crashed the car into an embankment on the Pennsylvania turnpike. All three passengers were killed instantly.

Sonny Rollins

Six months before the accident, Harold Land had left the quintet to tend his ailing grandmother in San Diego. His replacement was **Theodore "Sonny" Rollins** (b. 1930), one of the hottest young tenor players in the business. A Harlemite by birth and upbringing, Rollins rose rapidly to prominence as a jazz soloist, recording in the early fifties with Charlie Parker, Fats Navarro, Bud Powell, and especially Miles Davis. But, like all of these figures, Rollins became entangled with heroin. It was shortly after tentatively overcoming his addiction in late 1955 that Rollins joined the Brown-Roach Quintet, where Brown provided a stabilizing influence. "Clifford was a profound influence on my life," he recalled. "He showed me that it was possible to lead a good, clean life and still be a good jazz musician."

With Rollins, it is often said, Brown found his true equal on the front line. While Rollins's somewhat rough, angular style contrasted with Brown's more mellifluous approach, they both shared an interest in structural coherence when soloing. Indeed, after Brown's death Rollins contributed to a breakthrough in improvisational architecture, according to Gunther Schuller in a 1958 article for *Jazz Review*. Noting that "there is now a tendency among a number of jazz musicians to bring thematic (or motivic) and structural unity into improvisation," Schuller offered Rollins's "Blue Seven" as a prime example of the practice. On "Blue Seven" Rollins uses his opening *motive* as the basis for his subsequent improvisations, developing it into longer and more elaborate structures. This technique, known as **motivic improvisation** (or more generically as *motivic development*), was not new; we encountered a similar process at work in Charlie Parker's solo on "Parker's Mood," and Thelonious Monk's on "Bag's Groove." But motivic improvisation would play an increasingly important role in jazz, particularly as soloists began expanding their statements to unprecedented lengths in the 1960s.

Widely viewed as the leading tenor saxophonist in jazz, Rollins used his stature as a celebrity to make a statement about the current political climate. For his album *Freedom Suite* (1958) he wrote in the liner notes that "America is deeply rooted in Negro culture: its colloquialisms, its humour, its music. How ironic that the Negro . . . who has exemplified the humanities in his very existence, is being rewarded with inhumanity." But Rollins—besieged by self-doubts, sorrow over a failed marriage, and drinking problems—shortly thereafter withdrew from music and public life. The only playing he did was at night on New York's Williamsburg Bridge. He resumed his career in 1961 playing as well as ever, but by this time the momentum had been irrevocably seized by another rising tenor star, John Coltrane (see Chapter 24).

motivic improvisation
an approach to solo improvisation that involves developing a motive or group of motives into a larger statement.

CD 2 / Track 24

CLIFFORD BROWN-MAX ROACH QUINTET, *"Gertrude's Bounce"* (1956)

Although the Clifford Brown-Max Roach Quintet is widely regarded as an archetypal hard bop ensemble, West Coast—if not outright cool—elements often appear in the music. This should not be surprising. Harold Land and George Morrow were both Californians. While in California, Brown made several records in frankly West Coast style for Pacific Jazz. Roach himself played at the Lighthouse for six months before forming the quintet, and, of course, the band made its debut in Los Angeles.

The West Coast sound permeates the first and last few bars of "Gertrude's Bounce." This piece, according to composer Richie Powell, was written for Gertrude Abercrombie, an artist he met in Chicago. She walks "just like the rhythm sounds in the introduction," Powell said. That introduction is indeed striking—for its lack of earthiness. One might compare it with fifties TV music; the chord progression, melody, and general spirit seem something like a cross between "Santa Claus Is Coming to Town" and the theme music of *Leave It To Beaver.* This white-sounding introduction might be intended as a tongue-in-cheek parody to contrast with the hard-swinging head. The Brown-Roach Quintet often juxtaposed "corny" and "hip" elements in their heads; some other examples include "Love Is A Many-Splendored Thing" and "I Get A Kick Out of You."

After the introduction the band surges forward with new energy, demonstrating many of the characteristic traits of hard bop. Clifford Brown and Sonny Rollins swing hard on the unison head, dramatizing its syncopations with thick articulation and heavy accents. Max Roach, playing with sticks, drives the band aggressively. The head itself, although active, is more tuneful and less angular than many of the classic bebop melodies. The solos of Brown and Rollins demonstrate their ability to "play the changes"—that is, to fit every improvised phrase with the appropriate underlying harmony—while constructing long and interesting lines. Brown plays a characteristically graceful and mellifluous solo, sailing effortlessly through lengthy and complex figures (his expansive first phrase lasts the entire A-section). Such abstract nonrepetitive passages alternate periodically with the sort of repetitive, developmental sections we observed in Charlie Parker's solo on "Parker's Mood." Roach's drum solo grows in intensity, beginning with snare and bass drums, then moving to include cymbals and tom-toms in the last half, thus showing his concern for developmental techniques.

Create your own listening chart (CD 2 / Track 24)

Charles Mingus

The case of composer, bass player, and bandleader, **Charles Mingus** (1922–1979), contradicts the common assumption that "West Coast" and "cool" jazz are synonymous. Though born in Arizona, Mingus grew up in Watts, the black ghetto of Los Angeles. Drawing from a wide range of sources including the blues, gospel, Dixieland, swing, bebop, Latin, and modern classical music, Mingus does not fit neatly into any single category. With regard to general aesthetic leanings, however, much of his mature music contains such ecstatic expressiveness, such emphatic emotion, as to seem the antithesis of cool and the essence of hot.

Mingus the man was as complex as his music. He could be gregarious, hospitable, even gentle. Yet, afflicted with psychological problems, he was prone to violent outbursts. As a bandleader he was a notorious tyrant, berating sidemen and audiences alike for stupidity, bad taste, and other perceived offenses. On one occasion he accosted his alto saxophonist Jackie McLean; on another he punched his white trombonist, Jimmy Knepper, in the mouth, knocking out his teeth and ruining his embouchure. The wonder is that both McLean and Knepper worked for Mingus again. They were willing to endure his outrageous behavior for the privilege of helping him realize his musical vision.

Mingus began his career with the ambition of becoming, as one of his teachers recalled, "the world's greatest bass player." He studied both jazz and classical bass, and took composition lessons during which he discovered Stravinsky, Debussy, Bach, and Beethoven. He rose to fame in 1950–1951 playing in white vibraphonist Red Norvo's trio, a cool jazz group, but left when Norvo bowed to demands that a white player replace Mingus for a television program. Mingus recorded with virtually all the leading black players of his day, including, in an all-star session at Toronto's Massey Hall, Dizzy Gillespie, Charlie Parker, Bud Powell, and Max Roach.

Charles Mingus.

In the fall of 1955 Mingus organized a band that he called his **Jazz Workshop** and changed his entire approach to rehearsal. He had become dissatisfied with the results he was getting with conventional notation. Revitalizing the aural roots of jazz, Mingus began teaching his sidemen his compositions entirely by ear. He also wanted his players, like Ellington's, to participate fully in the creative process. As he explained in 1959, "My present working methods use very little written material. I 'write' compositions on mental score paper, then I lay out the composition part by part to the musicians. I play them the 'framework' on piano so that they are all familiar with my interpretation and feeling and with the scale and chord progressions to be used. . . . [For solos] they are given different rows of notes to use against each chord but they choose their own notes and

CHARLES MINGUS, *"Boogie Stop Shuffle"* (1959)

"Boogie Stop Shuffle," from Mingus's famous album, *Mingus Ah Um,* reveals several hard bop traits. The minor blues was a favorite among East Coast players. And the bluesy expressiveness, percussive attacks, and barely contained energy certainly mark this as a record in the hard bop tradition. Beyond such general traits, the piece shows characteristics of Mingus's style. Like many of his uptempo compositions, the head unfolds in stages, with various layers being added or subtracted from one chorus to the next. One can perceive Mingus's link with the jazz heritage in several ways. His use of an eight-to-the-bar boogie-woogie-style bass line (Stage 1: [a]) connects him with jazz almost twenty years out of date by 1959. And his resurrecting of wah-wahs and other plunger effects in the horns serves as a tribute to Duke Ellington. Yet no one would mistake this piece for a composition by Meade Lux Lewis or Ellington. In Mingus's hands, these traditional materials form part of an eclectic vision that anticipates jazz of the future at the same time that it recapitulates past achievements.

LISTENING CHART 23

Charles Mingus, "Boogie Stop Shuffle" (Mingus)

CD 2 / Tracks 25–30

RECORDED 12 MAY 1959, NEW YORK CITY / *MINGUS AH UM* COLUMBIA CK 65512

John Handy (alto saxophone), Booker Ervin (tenor saxophone), Shafi Hadi (tenor saxophone), Willie Dennis (trombone), Horace Parlan (piano), Charles Mingus (bass), Dannie Richmond (drums)

Style: Hard bop			**Form: 12-bar (minor) blues**

Head (in five stages)

25	0:00	*1st Chorus* (12)	Stage 1: (a) Tenor saxophone, trombone, piano, bass, play low boogie-woogie figure in unison
	0:12	*2nd Chorus* (12)	Stage 2: (a + b) Piano and bass continue boogie figure; horns add harmonized wails and wah-wahs in the background
	0:23	*3rd Chorus* (12)	Stage 3: (a + b′) Piano and bass continue boogie figure; horn backgrounds become more substantial
	0:34	*4th Chorus* (12)	Stage 4: (a + c) Piano and bass continue boogie figure; saxophones and trombone play boppish melody in unison
	0:45	*5th Chorus* (12)	Stage 5: (c) piano and bass drop boogie figure, comp and walk respectively behind restatement of boppish melody

Tenor saxophone solo: Booker Ervin

26	0:56	*6th Chorus* (12)	(a) returns; Booker Ervin plays largely *motivic solo,* dwelling on a few striking blues phrases
	1:07	*7th Chorus* (12)	
	1:18	*8th Chorus* (12)	(a) dropped, piano and bass comp and walk; horns add riff-based backgrounds
	1:29	*9th Chorus* (12)	

Piano solo: Horace Parlan

27	1:40	*10th Chorus* (12)	(a) resumed by horns, bass; Horace Parlan begins solo by constantly repeating brief rising and falling riff
	1:51	*11th Chorus* (12)	(a) continued; Parlan adopts new repeating riff
	2:03	*12th Chorus* (12)	(a) dropped, horns out, bass walks; Parlan becomes more mobile but retains riff-based approach
	2:14	*13th Chorus* (12)	

			Alto saxophone solo: John Handy
28	2:25	*14th Chorus* (12)	(a) resumed in piano, bass; John Handy plays soulful solo on alto saxophone
	2:36	*15th Chorus* (12)	
	2:47	*16th Chorus* (12)	(a) dropped, piano comps, bass walks; horns add riff-based backgrounds first heard in eighth chorus
	2:58	*17th Chorus* (12)	

Head

29	3:09	*18th Chorus* (12)	Stage 1: (a) horns, piano, and bass play boogie figure as in beginning
	3:20	*19th Chorus* (12)	*Stage 1, repeated:* (a) this time, John Handy (alto) and Dannie Richmond (drums) play sporadic solo lines over top . . . head interrupted by drum solo

Drum solo: Dannie Richmond

30	3:31	*20th Chorus* (12)	Richmond plays fiery solo using entire drum kit
	3:42	*21st Chorus* (12)	

Head, continued

	3:53	*22nd Chorus* (12)	Stage 2: (a + b)
	4:04	*23rd Chorus* (12)	Stage 3: (a + b')
	4:15	*24th Chorus* (12)	Stage 4: (a + c)
	4:26	*25th Chorus* (12)	Stage 5: (c)
			Last note sustained, then eclipsed by solo "noodling"; brief drum solo closes performance

Further Listening from the *Prentice Hall Jazz Collection*
Track 8: Charles Mingus, "Fables of Faubus" (1959)

play them in their own style . . . except where a particular mood is indicated." His first album to exploit this new approach was ***Pithecanthropus Erectus*** (1956), a recording that marked his arrival as a major jazz composer.

Like Rollins, Mingus recorded pieces that addressed race politics. In 1957 Arkansas Governor Orval E. Faubus sent in the National Guard to prevent federally mandated integration in Little Rock. In protest, Mingus wrote a satirical piece called "Fables of Faubus," complete with taunting lyrics (expunged from the recording by Columbia executives) and square melody obviously referring to Faubus. Of the incendiary "Haitian Fight Song" (1957), a piece commemorating the Haitian slave revolt of 1801, Mingus said, "I can't play it right unless I'm thinking about prejudice and hate and persecution and how unfair it is." In a more positive vein, Mingus expressed his race pride through a number of exuberant gospel-jazz pieces, including "Wednesday Night Prayer Meeting" and "Better Git It In Your Soul." Both "Fables of Faubus" and "Better Git It In Your Soul" appeared on Columbia's ***Mingus Ah Um*** (1959), the most popular album of Mingus's career. Such impassioned music helped inspire developments in free jazz during the next decade.

Miles Davis

Chapter 21

T he one figure who helped pioneer all the modern jazz substyles we have discussed thus far—bebop, cool jazz, and hard bop—was Miles Davis. Unlike other legendary figures such as Louis Armstrong, Benny Goodman, Art Tatum, or Dizzy Gillespie, Davis changed the sound of his music frequently throughout his career. For a while, he made landmark recordings every ten years—*Birth of the Cool* in 1949, *Kind of Blue* in 1959, and *Bitches Brew* in 1969—in each case launching a new stylistic movement. During this period he also organized his celebrated "first" and "second" quintets, sending only slightly smaller reverberations through the jazz community.

Perhaps even more than his trumpet playing, Davis's various bands transformed the jazz landscape. Davis shared Duke Ellington's gift as a talent scout, discovering or bringing to prominence such players as John Coltrane, Bill Evans, Wayne Shorter, Tony Williams, Chick Corea, and Keith Jarrett. But more than simply finding brilliant young players, Davis knew—again, like Ellington—how to combine musical personalities to create a unique and compelling group sound. When Davis added his own authoritative voice to that of his sidemen, the results were often magical. Over the course of his forty-year career, he exerted the most dynamic and far-reaching influence on modern jazz of any musician except Charlie Parker.

East St. Louis to New York

Unlike most black jazz musicians, Miles Davis (1926–1991) grew up in a privileged environment. His father was a successful dentist with a home in East St. Louis and a two-hundred-acre farm outside town. When Miles was a child his family moved into a white neighborhood, where he endured taunts and intimidation. One of his earliest memories is of a white man chasing him down the street, yelling racial epithets. Such experiences planted deep resentment in him, but also prompted a (selective) color-blindness on matters of race. In later years Davis sometimes made withering comments about whites in general, but was notably egalitarian in the choosing of his sidemen.

As a young player Davis did not adopt the prevailing "hot" style of Louis Armstrong and Roy Eldridge, but instead absorbed two regional trumpet traditions: the restrained approach of fellow midwesterner Bix Beiderbecke and the sweet, lyrical bent of the so-called **St. Louis trumpet style.** Davis's teacher,

Elwood Buchanan, recommended that he listen to Bobby Hackett, a white disciple of Beiderbecke's, and Harold "Shorty" Baker, a local trumpet star who later played with Duke Ellington. Buchanan turned Davis away from the common practice of playing with vibrato, observing that "you're gonna get old anyway and start shaking." So "that's how I tried to play," Davis said. "Fast and light—and no vibrato."

Accounts of Davis's entrée into the professional world present a puzzling picture. Some sources depict him as precocious; others disparage his abilities. He began playing professionally at age sixteen, with Eddie Randle's Blue Devils at the Rhumboogie Club. When Billy Eckstine's band stopped in St. Louis, Davis substituted for three weeks for Buddy Anderson, who was sick with tuberculosis. Shortly after moving to New York in the fall of 1944, at age eighteen, Davis began playing with leading figures, including Dizzy Gillespie, Charlie Parker, Coleman Hawkins, and Benny Carter.

This meteoric rise to prominence, though a matter of record, is strangely belied by eyewitness testimony and, to some extent, the evidence of recordings. Billy Eckstine said that "Miles used to follow us around in St. Louis. He used to ask to sit in with the band. I'd let him so as not to hurt his feelings, because, then, Miles was awful. He sounded terrible, he couldn't play at all." Davis admitted feeling utterly inadequate playing in Parker's quintet. He refused to play the breakneck trumpet part on the recording of "Koko," requiring Gillespie to step in and do the job. Rather than take the voluble Gillespie as his model, Davis looked to **Freddie Webster** (1916–1947), a Cleveland player whose economical style and beautiful tone Davis could better comprehend. Despite his startling early successes, including his *Birth of the Cool* recordings, Davis was a late-bloomer who struggled to find his niche within the modern jazz idiom. Most critics feel he did not attain his definitive solo voice until the Prestige recordings of 1954.

Miles Davis as Soloist

"I never considered Miles a great *trumpet* player," Art Blakey once remarked. "I considered him a stylist. He wasn't my idea of a trumpet player like Clifford or Fats or Dizzy, not that kind of power. But, whatever he had, he sure used it all. Miles could take a bazooka, he'd *still* sound the same."

Unlike many of his competitors, Davis wanted to slow the music down, to emphasize tone, lyricism, even silence (a value jazz musicians call "space"). These characteristics appear in his music regardless of whether the context suggests a "cool" or "hard bop" approach. By the mid-fifties he had developed an instantly recognizable sound, a stark "eggshell tone" (in the words of one critic), which some listeners heard as the embodiment of existential loneliness. Davis defined his sound partly by expressive valving (pressing the valves only halfway, for instance) and partly through an updated conception of swing that evoked insistence and nonchalance simultaneously. His exploration of harmonic color—the "pretty" notes of the chords (i.e., triadic extensions or chromatically altered tones)—also became a salient feature of his approach.

The First Quintet

The "Blue 'n' Boogie"/"Walkin'" recording represented a breakthrough for Davis in hindsight, but at the time not everyone noticed the new vitality of his music. The moment of Davis's true resurgence came the following summer, at the **1955**

Miles Davis.

Newport Jazz Festival. Although left off the original program, Davis was belatedly invited to participate in the all-star jam session on the final concert. To everyone's surprise he stole the show with a taut, moody performance of Thelonious Monk's "'Round Midnight." He played with a **stemless Harmon mute,** a squat metal device with a hole in the center. The hollow buzzing sound of stemless Harmon soon became Davis's trademark, especially on ballads. Hearing it at Newport, a *Metronome* editor effused that "Miles was superb, brilliantly absorbing, as if he were both the moth and the probing, savage light on which an immolation was to take place."

Immediately after the performance, **George Avakian** rushed forward to talk to Davis about signing an exclusive contract with Columbia, the most coveted record company at that time. Clearly eager to have Davis on its roster, Columbia gave him a $4,000 advance, guaranteed in the contract a $300,000 annual fee (according to one source), and endured a costly negotiation with Prestige, Davis's then-current recording company, to win exclusive rights to his music. The Newport success also netted Davis a contract with the booking agency, Shaw Artists Corporation.

Though interested in Davis, Avakian made the contract conditional upon his organizing a band that would stay together more or less permanently, playing nightclubs and touring as well as recording. In fact, Davis had already assembled a rhythm section that would become legendary in jazz history: pianist **Red Garland** (1923–1984), bassist **Paul Chambers** (1935–1969), and drummer **Philly Joe Jones** (1923–1985) (whose hometown nickname distinguished him from Basie's famous drummer, Jo Jones). Davis hired tenorman Sonny Rollins, his first choice to complete the lineup, but within a month or so Rollins fled to Chicago to try to end his heroin habit. (Later in the year he would join the Clifford Brown-Max Roach Quintet.) In desperation, Davis turned to an unproven and initially unpromising tenor saxophonist from Philadelphia named **John Coltrane** (see Chapter 24) to make the club dates booked for September. With Coltrane in the band, Davis had what later critics would call his **first quintet** (so-called to distinguish it from his "second" great quintet of the 1960s).

Coltrane, an obsessive, analytical perfectionist, initially annoyed Davis with his constant questions about what to play and how. Davis favored minimal discussion during rehearsal, trusting his players to respond spontaneously to the right musical environment. But after a shaky beginning, Davis and Coltrane developed a close musical relationship. The laconic Davis and the loquacious Coltrane complemented each others' solo styles just as other frontline duos—such as Gerry Mulligan and Chet Baker, Milt Jackson and John Lewis, Clifford Brown and Sonny Rollins—had done. Critics and fans questioned Davis's judgment in hiring Coltrane, who manifested a searching, agonized, and uncertain manner. "People used to tell me to fire him," Davis said. "They said he wasn't playing anything. . . . I know what I want though." Where others heard restless redundancy in Coltrane's playing, Davis heard exploration: "What he does, for example, is to play five notes of a chord and then keep changing it around, trying to see how many different ways it can sound. It's like explaining something five different ways."

In 1956 the Miles Davis Quintet toured the country to great acclaim. Early in the year the band debuted at Jazz City, a nightclub in Los Angeles. One observer recalled that "nobody knew what to expect. [The band] literally blew everybody out of the water. It destroyed West Coast jazz overnight." Back in New York the band played regularly at the **Café Bohemia,** Davis's location job until mid-1958 (see Map 7). Davis closed out his contract with Prestige in a single marathon recording session, producing enough music for four similarly titled albums: *Cookin', Relaxin', Workin',* and *Steamin'*. Of *Cookin',* a *Down Beat* reviewer wrote: "All the tremendous cohesion, the wild, driving swing, and the all-out excitement and controlled emotion that was present at the best moments of the Davis quintet has been captured on this record." With Avakian as producer, the band also made its debut record with Columbia, a now-celebrated album called *'Round About Midnight.*

The Davis Mystique

In early winter 1956, Davis underwent an operation to have a growth removed from his larynx. The doctor told him to avoid speaking for ten days. But on the second day he got into a shouting match with a music executive, permanently damaging his vocal chords. For the rest of his life he would speak in a raspy whisper.

His ghostly voice reinforced a "bad boy" image he was acquiring on the bandstand. White critics noted with disapproval that Davis seemed distant in live performances—that he dispensed with spoken introductions, that he walked off the bandstand when his sidemen were soloing, even that he sometimes turned his back on the audience to play toward his sidemen. These infractions broke with long-established stage etiquette, adhered to even by the beboppers, which required jazz musicians to court the audience. Davis protested the criticism like a true artist by saying he did not want to detract from the music. But he was also reacting, subconsciously perhaps, against the grinning and mugging stage persona that Louis Armstrong, for one, still manifested in all his concerts. During the age of Martin Luther King and Rosa Parks, Davis's bandstand demeanor came across to young black observers as noble, dignified—and the ultimate in *cool*. Davis not only showed independence on the bandstand, he wore ultra-stylish clothes, sported dark glasses, and drove a Mercedes and a Ferrari. As comedian Bill Cosby recalled: "In the fifties, the status symbol in North Philadelphia for certain groups of teenagers was to be into Miles Davis. I mean, if you said 'Miles Davis' you were cool, if you had Miles Davis albums you were on top of things, so the man was more than just a musician."

The Collaborations with Gil Evans

Although Davis's personal life was clean at this time, his sidemen struggled constantly with drug addiction. Coltrane and Jones, in particular, became so irresponsible that in the spring of 1957 Davis angrily fired them both. For a few months Sonny Rollins and Art Taylor took their places in the quintet. But Davis was turning his attention elsewhere anyway. For the past year he had participated peripherally in various third-stream projects with Gunther Schuller, John Lewis, and Gil Evans. With Avakian's encouragement, Davis now teamed up with Evans for an expanded excursus into the kind of music featured on *Birth of the Cool*. Drawing upon nineteen musicians instead of nine, the music would explore the same pastel sonorities of the earlier recordings but with a greater range of timbral possibilities.

In May Davis entered the studio and made his second album for Columbia, *Miles Ahead,* a series of solo pieces composed and arranged by Evans. The orchestra included five trumpets, three trombones and one bass trombone, two French horns, tuba, alto saxophone, bass clarinet, two flutes (that doubled on clarinet), plus jazz rhythm section of piano, bass, and drums. Davis himself played flugelhorn, a deep, mellow brass instrument pitched and valved exactly like a trumpet. The ten pieces on the album flow directly, without a break, from one to the next, constituting, in the words of one critic, "a continuous aural fresco whose connective resonance and authority gain strength with each addition." The performances are extraordinarily well integrated, with a perfect alignment in style and attitude between Davis's semi-improvised solo voice and Evans's composed lines. According to Davis, the musical compatibility directly reflected their high personal regard for one another: "I wouldn't have no other arranger but Gil Evans—we couldn't be much closer if he was my brother."

On the basis of the excellent sales of *Miles Ahead,* Davis and Evans reconvened in the Columbia studio the following summer for a second collaborative

Great Debates

THE DAVIS-EVANS COLLABORATIONS: A RANGE OF OPINIONS

Despite positive reviews and commercial success, Davis's three main albums with Gil Evans have not escaped controversy. Reviewing *Miles Ahead* for the *New Yorker,* Whitney Balliett noted that while the playing throughout was "impeccable," the music lacked substance. "All the solos are by Davis, whose instrument sounds fogbound. . . . Buried in all this port and velvet is Evans's revolutionary use, for such a large group, of structure, dynamics and harmony. There is, in fact, too much port and velvet, and Davis, a discreet, glancing performer, backslides in these surroundings into a moony, saccharine, and—in *My Ship*—downright dirge-like approach." Max Harrison disagreed with this assessment, and with those who found the album rhythmically inert: "Complaints that these Davis/Evans collaborations produced unrhythmic music were due to faulty hearing, and the widely quoted metaphorical description of the textures as 'port and velvet' is inept. Despite its richness, the orchestral fabric is constantly on the move, horizontally and vertically; it is unfortunate that some listeners cannot hear a music's pulse unless it is stated as a series of loud bangs."

Perhaps the most original attitude toward the Davis-Evans collaborations was expressed by the influential black critic, Stanley Crouch, in his essay, "On the Corner: The Sellout of Miles Davis." For Crouch, these albums continued a misguided line of development begun with the *Birth of the Cool* recordings, a series that, fatally, "had little to do with blues and almost nothing to do with swing." The nonet recordings, ultimately "little more than primers for television writing," show that Davis "was not above the academic temptation of Western [classical] music." Crouch seems to view the later Davis-Evans projects more favorably, but thinks they also demonstrate that Davis "could be taken in by pastel versions of European colors." The albums "are given what value they have . . . by the Afro-American dimensions" of Davis's own playing. Setting Davis's contribution aside, Crouch dismisses most of Evans's celebrated arrangements, again, as "high-level television music." This characterization subtly marks the Davis-Evans albums as one step along the path to the total artistic "sellout" of Davis's popular recordings of the early seventies and eighties. ■ ■ ■

CD 2 / Track 31

MILES DAVIS, *"The Meaning of the Blues/Lament"* (1957)

It is impossible to fully understand Miles Davis's music in the 1950s without hearing at least one example of his ballad playing. "The Meaning of the Blues" was composed by songwriter Bobby Troup in 1956; bebop trombone master J. J. Johnson wrote the equally beautiful "Lament" in 1954. When Gil Evans was choosing the sequence of pieces to be stitched together into a larger compositional mosaic for the Miles Davis album, *Miles Ahead,* he paired "The Meaning of the Blues" with "Lament," placing them one after the other, without a break. The pairing works so well that during a casual listening one might easily miss the seam binding together the two pieces. Indeed, Davis later performed them as a two-part medley on his live album *Miles Davis at Carnegie Hall* (1961).

"The Meaning of the Blues" (0:20) is in ABAC song form. Davis plays the melody on flugelhorn in the brooding, introspective manner of his ballad style. During the second A-section he gently embellishes the melody, but otherwise neither this piece nor "Lament" contains much improvisation; Davis simply states the melodies in his plaintive, understated way. The performance thus stands as an eloquent rebuttal to those who insist that *real* jazz must be improvised.

"Lament" (2:49) is in ABA′B′ song form, a variant of ABAC song form. In "Lament" Evans sometimes gives phrases of the melody to the ensemble. The second half of A and A′, for instance, features a French horn–heavy cluster of brass—rather than Davis—on the melody. Similarly, Evans disguises the return of A (that is, A′) by changing the harmony and by giving the first two measures to the full ensemble—measures that in this context have the effect of climaxing a phrase begun in the previous section rather than restating the main theme after a departure from it. Throughout, Davis is accompanied by Evans's characteristic "pastel" orchestral sound—that heterogeneous, constantly shifting coalition of tuba, trombones, French horns, trumpets, and woodwinds (including flutes) that he made famous almost ten years earlier in the *Birth of the Cool* recordings.

Create your own listening chart (CD 2 / Track 31)

album: **Porgy and Bess.** *Porgy and Bess* (1935), the well-known American "folk opera" written for the stage by George Gershwin, was in 1958 being produced as a movie under the directorship of Otto Preminger. In part to capitalize on the publicity surrounding its premiere, Avakian encouraged Davis and Evans to produce an album of songs from the opera. The resulting recording, featuring essentially the same structure and instrumentation as *Miles Ahead,* became Davis's best-selling album for the next ten years. Subsequent collaborations between Davis and Evans include the much-admired *Sketches of Spain* (1960) and others far less successful.

The Sextet

In September 1957, Sonny Rollins left the quintet to form his own band. Davis replaced him with alto saxophonist, **Julian "Cannonball" Adderley** (1928–1975). Davis had had his eye on Adderley ever since the latter made his stunning New York debut at the Café Bohemia two years previously. Adderley combined

Charlie Parker's fluent bebop style with a buoyant sound and bluesy inflections that fit well within the funky side of hard bop. Davis was delighted finally to have Adderley in his band, but by the end of the year he longed for the special rapport of the original quintet. In December he called Coltrane and Jones back to the fold, but kept Adderley as well.

Through a profound religious conversion Coltrane had finally conquered heroin, but Jones was as "strung out" as ever. Nevertheless, in April of 1958 the newly constituted Miles Davis Sextet made its first album, *Milestones*. The title track, by Davis, was an early example of what is now called **modal jazz**. Instead of presenting his sidemen with chord progressions, Davis indicated a series of scales, or *modes*. The emphasis on a single mode for an extended period encouraged the soloists to think "horizontally" rather than "vertically," as Davis explained to Nat Hentoff in October: "When you go this way, you can go on forever. You don't have to worry about [chord] changes and you can do more with the line. It becomes a challenge to see how melodically inventive you are."

Despite the success of *Milestones*, the drug-induced erratic behavior of both Garland and Jones made clear it was time to get a new pianist and a new drummer. To the surprise of many, Davis hired white pianist **Bill Evans** (1929–1980). Yet Evans was an obvious choice, given Davis's interest in modal playing. Evans had been a protégé of jazz composer George Russell, who had been exploring modes for several years. To fill the drum spot, Davis hired **Jimmy Cobb** (b. 1929), a Philadelphia musician who modeled his playing on that of Philly Joe Jones. Although it only stayed together for a little more than six months, the group featuring Evans and Cobb is often regarded as the definitive Miles Davis Sextet.

As Davis later recalled, "Bill had this quiet fire that I loved on the piano. . . . The sound he got was like crystal notes or sparkling water cascading down from some clear waterfall." For his part, Evans was intimidated by the opportunity to

modal jazz a style of improvisation based on a series of modes (scales) rather than on a chord progression.

The Miles Davis Sextet during the recording of *Kind of Blue,* 1959 (see CD 2 / Track 32). *Left to right:* John Coltrane, Cannonball Adderley, Miles Davis, Bill Evans (Paul Chambers and Jimmy Cobb not shown).

play in a group that seemed, in his words, "to be composed of superhumans." In addition, he was painfully aware of being the only white musician in the group. Davis teased him by calling him "whitey," but his race only really mattered to audiences, Evans recalled. "The guys in the band defended me staunchly. We were playing black clubs, and guys would come up and say, 'What's that white guy doing there?' They said, 'Miles *wants* him there—he's *supposed* to be there.'" The pressures of performing with Davis were exacerbated by Evans's own heroin problem, which sapped his energy. Evans finally quit the band in November. A shy, somewhat delicate individual, Evans "felt exhausted in every way—physically, mentally and spiritually."

Kind of Blue

Evans had left before Davis got the chance to fulfill his modal aspirations. So in the spring of 1959 Davis called Evans and asked him to make two studio dates. Of the resulting sides, "So What" and "Flamenco Sketches" are modal, "Freddie Freeloader" and "All Blues" are twelve-bar blues (the latter in 6/8), and "Blue in

CD 2 / Track 32

MILES DAVIS SEXTET, *"So What"* (1959)

The first tune on *Kind of Blue,* and the most famous, is "So What." The title came from one of Davis's favorite wise-guy expressions. But the impetus behind the music itself was quite different. One source of inspiration came from a performance Davis witnessed of a kalimba (finger piano) player with an African dance troupe. Another was a sound he remembered "from being back in Arkansas [as a child], when we were walking home from church and they were playing these bad gospels. That feeling is what I was trying to get close to [in "So What"] . . . six years old, walking with my cousin along that dark Arkansas road."

The piece begins with a dark, gentle duet in tempo rubato for piano and bass, probably composed by Gil Evans. The head is played by bassist Paul Chambers with the piano and horns punctuating the bouncy minor bass line in call-and-response fashion. In light of the gospel influence suggested by Davis, one might hear Chambers playing the role of preacher (the call) and the horns representing the congregation with a minor "Amen" cadence (the response). The harmonic structure of the piece is modal. The AABA chorus form consists of *D Dorian mode* (the white keys on the piano from D to D) for sixteen bars, then *E-flat Dorian* (up a half-step) for the bridge, then back to D Dorian for the final eight bars.

Writers have often commented on how well the four soloists complement one another on this recording. Davis's pretty notes, open tone, and liberal use of space, contrast with Coltrane's immediately subsequent solo, with its torrent of anguished scales and his abrasive, searching tone. Adderley's bobbing fluency and bluesy licks introduce still another mood, while Evans's spare textures recall Davis's minimalism, bringing the music full circle. (Evans's practice of developing a new idea every eight measures sets him apart, however.) The rhythm section players enhance the solos with special nuances; note, for instance, Chambers's use of an ostinato to break up the walking line behind Davis and Coltrane, and Evans's similar recourse to a sharply accented repeating rhythm in Coltrane's first chorus.

Create your own listening chart (CD 2 / Track 32)

Green" is a ballad with a ten-bar chorus form. Despite this structural variety, the album coheres remarkably in mood and improvisational approach, which is primarily melodic rather than harmonic. Davis called the album ***Kind of Blue*** to suggest the generic ambiguity of the music. It remains one of the most popular jazz albums ever made.

The End of an Era

Perhaps the most enigmatic piece on *Kind of Blue* is Evans's haunting ballad, "Blue in Green." The unusual ten-bar chorus structure undermines any sense of symmetrical phrasing. The harmonies do not cadence clearly at the end of a chorus but, instead, reach into the next chorus making it difficult to tell where a new chorus begins. The resulting circular motion has a gentle hypnotic effect. Davis plays exquisitely in stemless Harmon and Coltrane cries out in deeply lyrical tones. The piece concludes with Evans accompanied only by Chambers, whose subtle bowing imparts a vaguely orchestral sound. "Blue in Green" conveys an autumnal mood, a faint nostalgia for the decade just past, in which one could still play a ballad without feeling the least bit anachronistic.

One night, four months after the *Kind of Blue* sessions, Davis escorted a young white woman out of Birdland and hailed her a taxi. He was between sets, so he lingered in the night air to relax and smoke a cigarette. "No loitering—move along," a policeman said. Davis explained that he was just taking a break from his work at Birdland, but the policeman was adamant. Feeling unjustly treated because of his race—and because he had been seen with a white woman—Davis refused. The confrontation intensified, a crowd gathered, and suddenly a plainclothes policeman jumped in and struck Davis on the head with a nightstick, spilling blood down his white sport coat. The police arrested him on charges of disorderly conduct and assault and revoked his cabaret card. The following day Davis's lawyer announced that he would sue the city of New York for illegal arrest. **The Birdland incident,** as it came to be known among Milesophiles, made the front pages and provoked dismay in the jazz magazines. But in 1959 such police behavior toward blacks was not especially scandalous. Davis was persuaded to drop his suit, and two months after the beating a review panel pronounced the arrest illegal and dismissed the charges.

The Birdland incident left emotional scars from which Davis never fully recovered. The racially charged incident foreshadowed the explosive sixties, a period in which Davis's own demeanor hardened. After a certain point he stopped playing ballads; his music moved into a brooding, unstable realm of experimentation. His forbidding persona, coupled with his relentless dominance in jazz, gave rise to a new, somewhat melodramatic, nickname: "The Prince of Darkness." But Davis's music remained vital. During the sixties, he continued his progressive pattern, breaking new ground twice more before withdrawing completely in retirement.

PART **Five**

Free Jazz to Fusion
(c. 1960–1975)

Historical Context: The Sixties

Chapter **22**

THE YEAR 1960 MARKED A TURNING POINT IN THE BLACK QUEST FOR FREEDOM AND equality. Nearly one hundred years had passed since the outbreak of the Civil War, and still legalized segregation prevailed in large parts of the country. Yet the charismatic leadership of Martin Luther King was attracting positive press to the black cause. John F. Kennedy, a Democratic politician especially attuned to civil rights issues, was elected president. And most significantly, in the early part of the year black and white college students began to risk their lives in nonviolent demonstrations throughout the South, initiating a process that would shortly culminate in sweeping and unequivocal civil rights legislation. As one historian noted, the students' courageous actions supplied "the introduction to a decade of political turbulence."

The turbulence ranged broadly across American society, encompassing racially motivated terrorism, political assassinations, the Vietnam War, the youth-based counterculture, and corruption in the federal government. Opposing responses to these upheavals created a divisive generation gap between children and parents, and more generally, between young people and "the establishment." The turmoil crested in the late sixties, overflowing into the next decade. Indeed, many historians consider "the sixties" as a cultural period to last

Chronology

1959	Ornette Coleman opens at the Five Spot
	French and Brazilian film *Black Orpheus* introduces bossa nova
1960	Student sit-ins in the South
1963	March on Washington
	John F. Kennedy assassinated
1964	Beatles tour the United States
	Miles Davis organizes his second quintet
	John Coltrane records *A Love Supreme*
1965	First U.S. combat troops sent to Vietnam
	AACM organized
	Thad Jones-Mel Lewis Big Band organized
1968	Martin Luther King and Robert Kennedy assassinated
1969	Woodstock concert
	Miles Davis records *Bitches Brew*
1974	Richard Nixon resigns over Watergate scandal
1975	Vietnam war ends with fall of Saigon

until 1974–1975, when Richard Nixon resigned the presidency over the Watergate scandal and the Vietnam War finally came to an end.

For jazz this was a similarly volatile period, one that opened with the subversive music of Ornette Coleman in 1959–1960, saw the development of an eclectic array of new styles—including free jazz, bossa nova, soul jazz, and fusion—and began fading with the sudden mysterious retirement of Miles Davis in 1975. Free jazz, in particular, served as a lightning rod of the period. Like rock music, its popular antithesis, free jazz reflected the tumult in society, dividing the jazz community and sparking bitter controversies over the nature of jazz itself. For this reason we must first address that tumult before we can understand the course of jazz in the sixties.

Civil Rights Triumphs

Southern resistance to desegregation intensified after *Brown v. Board of Education.* In 1956 101 members of Congress signed the so-called **Southern Manifesto,** asserting the constitutional right of states to refuse to integrate their schools. In the same year, the southern white power structure began an official campaign to destroy the NAACP. By 1960 black frustration reached a tipping point. On February 1, four black college students entered Woolworth's in Greensboro, North Carolina, ordered coffee, and waited to be served, in vain, until the store closed. In the months that followed, hundreds of black and white college students organized similar **sit-ins** throughout the South. White locals taunted the demonstrators, pouring ketchup, sugar, and other substances on them while they sat quietly. Thousands of demonstrators were arrested. But the sit-ins brought enough pressure on many stores—especially national chains—to compel them voluntarily to integrate their lunch counters. The sit-ins led directly to the formation of the

Martin Luther King Jr. speaking at the March on Washington, 1963.

Student Nonviolent Coordinating Committee (SNCC), one of the most effective civil rights groups of the decade.

In 1961 another important organization, the **Congress of Racial Equality (CORE),** launched a campaign to challenge segregation in the nation's public transportation system. In May two buses carrying black and white passengers seated side by side left Washington, DC, in the first of many **freedom rides** through the South. Bound for New Orleans, they traveled without incident until they reached Alabama. But, in Anniston, Birmingham, and Montgomery, angry mobs attacked the freedom riders. In Montgomery, Martin Luther King placed an emergency phone call to Robert Kennedy, the Attorney General, who dispatched four hundred federal marshals to keep the mob in check. Although none of the freedom riders ever made it to New Orleans, the freedom rides were effective. On September 22, the Interstate Commerce Commission prohibited segregation in buses, trains, and waiting rooms.

The civil rights movement climaxed on August 28, 1963, the centennial year of the Emancipation Proclamation. On that day Martin Luther King and other civil rights leaders led a **March on Washington** to compel Congress to address the issue of racial injustice. At the foot of the Lincoln Memorial, King spoke before two hundred and fifty thousand peaceful marchers, using the now well-known refrain "I Have a Dream" to conjure his vision of a racially just and harmonious society. The televised event prompted an outpouring of sympathy around the country, creating a politically favorable climate for legislation. The following summer Congress passed the **Civil Rights Act of 1964,** a landmark piece of legislation banning discrimination and segregation in virtually all public places, including places of employment.

Black Power

Racial violence grew along with civil rights gains. A couple of months before the March on Washington a sniper shot and killed NAACP chapter secretary Medgar Evers outside his home in Jackson, Mississippi. Four young black girls were killed in September, when the Ku Klux Klan detonated a bomb in a Birmingham church. Many blacks considered the assassination of President Kennedy in November to be a grievous strike against the cause of freedom. In the face of such hatred, some wondered if civil rights legislation would have any real effect.

During this troubled period a powerful voice arose in the black community to challenge the philosophy and methods of Martin Luther King. As a child **Malcolm X** (born Malcolm Little, 1925–1965) saw his home burned down by white supremacists. Two years later his father, an outspoken minister, was murdered. Driven mad by these events, his mother was committed to a mental institution. When he grew up, Malcolm converted to the Nation of Islam, a religion teaching black supremacy and the evil of the white race. He became a spellbinding speaker in Harlem, advocating racial separatism and independence rather than integration. Malcolm rejected nonviolent resistance, insisting that blacks defend themselves when attacked. His influence became so great, especially among urban youth, that the Black Muslim leadership began to fear the loss of their own political power. In 1965, during one of his speeches in Harlem, Malcolm X was shot and killed by Black Muslims. His assassination galvanized his followers and helped legitimize his radical teachings.

By this time, many in the mainstream civil rights movement had also begun to question nonviolent resistance. A pivotal moment came in 1966, when black activist James Meredith was shot and severely wounded during a solo march through Mississippi to encourage black citizens to register to vote. Outraged by this event, the new president of SNCC, **Stokeley Carmichael** (1941–1998), went to Mississippi to complete Meredith's march. To rally his followers, Carmichael shouted "Black power!" With this watchcry, Carmichael distanced himself and the SNCC from Martin Luther King and the SCLC. The SNCC no longer solicited white support but instead emphasized the values of separatism, self-sufficiency, and self-defense preached by Malcolm X. Rejecting American democracy as a failed system, Carmichael and others embraced Marxist ideology and pan-African cultural values. The assassinations of Martin Luther King in 1969 a long-time civil rights advocate and presidential candidate Robert Kennedy seemed proof enough that white supremacists would stop at nothing to preserve the old ways.

The Vietnam War

The struggle for civil rights was inextricably linked to another national trauma, the **Vietnam War.** As part of the Cold War policy of "containment," the United States wanted to defend South Vietnam against the communist North, or Viet Cong. From 1961 President Kennedy sent large numbers of military advisors to the southern capitol of Saigon; Kennedy's successor, Lyndon B. Johnson, sent the first combat troops in 1965. Though lacking an official declaration of war, Johnson gradually escalated America's involvement to include over five hundred thousand U.S. troops. In 1968 American delusions of early victory were shattered by the Tet Offensive, a ferocious Viet Cong assault on South Vietnam. Fearing the

Rescuing a wounded comrade in Vietnam.

war was a failure, Johnson did not seek reelection. The next president, Richard M. Nixon, began withdrawing troops in 1969, but simultaneously launched new offensives in the hope of saving face. The war dragged on for another six years, when Saigon fell to the Viet Cong. Nearly sixty thousand U.S. troops died.

The black community bore a disproportionate burden of sacrifice in Vietnam. While only 18 percent of eligible whites were drafted, the draft rate was 30 percent among blacks. Not surprisingly, many black activists opposed the war. Martin Luther King said that President Johnson's Great Society (his program to help the poor) "has been shot down on the battlefields of Vietnam." Others resented being sent to liberate a distant ally when their own freedom was in doubt. Heavyweight champion and devout Muslim Muhammad Ali (aka Cassius Clay) was stripped of his title in 1967 when he refused, on religious grounds, to be drafted. Black power adherents, many of whom sympathized with communism, viewed the U.S. campaign in Vietnam as evil.

The New Left

The civil rights struggle and the Vietnam War produced a radical political movement among America's youth. The movement, which came to be known as the **New Left,** began in 1960 as white students at the University of Michigan watched the Greensboro sit-ins. As one of them recalled, "Here were four students from Greensboro who were suddenly all over *Life* magazine. There was a feeling that they were us and we were them, and a recognition that they were expressing something we were feeling as well." Inspired by the civil rights workers, the

Michigan students organized the Students for a Democratic Society (SDS), which became the dominant voice of the New Left.

Beginning in 1964 New Left student activists staged campus demonstrations throughout the country, protesting against racism, poverty, paternalism, and various forms of official corruption. Because these demonstrations were initially suppressed by the police, they came to be known as the **Free Speech Movement.** In the first half of 1968 almost forty thousand students participated in over two hundred demonstrations at more than one hundred educational institutions. As students embraced Marxist ideals and U.S. casualties of the Vietnam War increased, the war became a favored target of protest. Some students publicly burned their draft cards in defiance of stiff jail terms. Three protesters made the ultimate principled statement: they poured kerosene on their bodies and lit a match, killing themselves in the flames. Violent clashes with the police became increasingly frequent. The campus demonstrations ended shortly after the tragedy at Kent State in 1970, in which four students were shot to death by members of the National Guard.

Rock and the Counterculture

"The Times They Are A-Changing," Bob Dylan sang in 1964. With these prophetic words Dylan hailed the advent of the sixties counterculture, a broad youth movement of which the New Left was merely an intellectual subgroup. The music of rock and folk musicians like Dylan was the glue that bound together all the disparate ideals of the rising generation. In addition to protesting injustice, hypocrisy, and corruption in "the establishment," these ideals eventually embraced freedom in all its forms: free love, free experimentation with drugs, freedom from societal norms in hair and beard length, clothing style, and personal hygiene. Older Americans often viewed these freedoms—hallmarks of the "hippie" lifestyle—as renouncing civilization itself. But for those who had ears to hear, rock music powerfully validated the countercultural message.

Rock—as distinct from fifties rock 'n' roll—seemed to burst onto Americans' consciousness suddenly, with the arrival of the **Beatles** in the United States in February 1964. In previous years Frank Sinatra and Elvis Presley had inspired mass adulation from fans. But no one expected the unbounded youthful hysteria that greeted the Beatles as they made their first tour of the United States. That month over seventy million Americans watched the Beatles on the Ed Sullivan Show, and in April Beatles songs occupied the top five slots on *Billboard*'s hit list. Other British rock groups such as the Rolling Stones and the Kinks soon became popular in the U.S. as well. This so-called **British invasion** transformed the pop cultural landscape with exciting, propulsive music and lyrics advocating enlightenment through drug use and the questioning of authority.

American rock musicians, meanwhile, cultivated two main traditions. In San Francisco's Haight-Ashbury district, the center of hippie culture, groups like Jefferson Airplane and the Grateful Dead developed **psychedelic rock,** a music intended to simulate the mind-altering experience of taking LSD. During the Summer of Love in 1967, thousands of hippies gathered in the streets around Haight-Ashbury to celebrate the experiences of free love, LSD trips, and psychedelic music while busloads of tourists gawked at them through the windows. In the urban black community, Motown, soul, and funk musicians built huge followings.

psychedelic rock a style of 1960s rock intended to simulate the mind-altering experience of taking LSD.

Soul queen Aretha Franklin asserted both racial dignity and feminine independence in her number one hit, "Respect" (1967), while her male counterpart James Brown aligned himself with the black power movement in songs like "Say It Loud, I'm Black and I'm Proud" (1968).

The two traditions came together in an event that climaxed the youth movement: the three-day Music and Art Fair at **Woodstock,** New York, in 1969. Before almost five hundred thousand people, white groups like the Grateful Dead and Joan Baez performed alongside black artists such as Sly and the Family Stone and Jimi Hendrix. The festival concluded with Hendrix playing a feedback-laced version of "Star Spangled Banner" on electric guitar, an eloquent commentary on Vietnam and the unstable meaning of patriotism.

Jazz in the Sixties

In a culture saturated by the din of political protest and electrified rock music, jazz had difficulty making itself heard. This is not to imply that it had nothing to say. Simultaneous with the rise of the civil rights movement, a new form of black jazz emerged—an intense, caustic idiom of unprecedented dissonance and complexity. Known popularly as **free jazz** (or "free-form" or "the new thing" or "the avant garde"), this music seemed a faithful reflection of the militant drive for freedom in society. Many free jazz players saw a direct tie between their music and black politics. Tenor saxophonist Archie Shepp, a particularly vocal figure, said, "We are not angry men. We are enraged. . . . I can't see any separation between my music and my life. I play pretty much race music; it's about what happened to my father, to me, and what can happen to my kids."

The uncompromising harshness of free jazz made bebop sound downright populist by comparison. Only a small cadre of devoted critics, fans, and colleagues showed any interest in the music. Few clubs were willing to support it; even its leading practitioners often went unemployed. Like the civil rights cause itself, free jazz was widely seen as a nuisance, even by those who sympathized with its goals. Yet, in keeping with the principled, antimaterialistic, anti-establishment spirit of the times, free jazz musicians continued to play the music they believed in. They found solidarity in cooperative ventures such as the Chicago-based Association for the Advancement of Creative Musicians (AACM) and the Black Artists Group (BAG) in St. Louis. And they asserted their independence from the musical centers of power by organizing their own concerts, often in spacious lofts in south Manhattan rented from apartment or warehouse owners. The **loft scene** served as an alternative to the traditional nightclub milieu until the late seventies. Though controversial, free jazz was the most vital and influential legacy of the sixties. We will examine this music more closely in Chapter 23.

Jimi Hendrix at Woodstock, 1969.

free jazz a style of jazz in the 1960s that abandons previous hallmarks of the music such as traditional melody, chord progressions, swing feel, tonality, and meter.

Jazz Criticism

The rise of black nationalism fostered new literary voices, including the first significant black jazz critics. **Ralph Ellison** (1914–1994), who in 1952 dazzled the literary community with his first novel, *Invisible Man,* published a collection of essays in 1964 entitled *Shadow and Act,* many of which discussed the role and meaning of jazz in American culture. Whereas Ellison mostly hailed the achievements of Duke Ellington, Charlie Parker, and other early figures, poet, playwright, and essayist **LeRoi Jones (aka Amiri Baraka)** (b. 1934) allied himself with black power and the avant garde. In two influential books, *Blues People* (1963) and *Black Music* (1967), Jones asserted the essential black identity of jazz, and rightly questioned why interpretation of the music had been forfeited to white

LeRoi Jones

on New York Loft Jazz—1963

Another manifestation of New York's messed-up jazz scene was the beginning of loft jazz, i.e., not just sessions, but formally arranged concerts in lofts featuring some of the very best young New York–based musicians. For the concerts, very little advertising is used due to the extremely limited finances at the sponsors' disposal (and the sponsors are in a great many instances the musicians themselves); one small ad is placed in the *Village Voice,* and a few hand-lettered signs are posted in important places all over the downtown area. But there are almost always very enthusiastic and empathetic, if not crushingly huge, audiences who respond. And they are usually treated to very exciting jazz. A kind of jazz that is getting increasingly more difficult to find in any regular jazz club in New York. As critic [Martin] Williams said, what these club owners don't realize is that audiences change, and now, certainly in New York, there is a growing younger jazz audience who doesn't especially want to spend any money to hear the tired sounds the clubs are sponsoring.

Of the loft concerts, two of the most recent, and undoubtedly the best, I've heard have featured the same group: a "pick-up" trio composed of Don Cherry, Wilbur Ware, and drummer, Billy Higgins. Hearing this group, one could only wish that they could somehow remain together. The music they made was simply beautiful. Each man is a very singular stylist and each is deeply intent on a great measure of extremely personal expression, but they played together as if they had to. It was extraordinary jazz. At the first concert featuring this group, which was held in a large loft on Great Jones Street, with people sitting in wooden folding chairs or squatting on the floor, the music was so lovely, there was almost no sound from the surprisingly large audience. But each solo was wildly applauded, and I'm sure the musicians could feel how direct an impact their music was making. . . .

Flasks (either formal or informal) seemed the most ubiquitous collation at the lofts, even though the Clinton Street people served free coffee and even some sandwiches. The admission this time was $1.50, which was money well spent. And many serious young jazz listeners now seem more willing to go sit on the floor in a loft and hear good music than go to the formal clubs downtown and hear well-known chumps. . . .

LeRoi Jones, "New York Loft and Coffee Shop Jazz," in *Black Music* (New York: William Morrow, 1967; reprint, Westport, CT: Greenwood Press, 1980), 96–98.

writers. ("Most jazz critics have been white Americans, but most important jazz musicians have not been," he began one famous essay.) But the validity of this complaint could not nullify the continuing importance of white writers. In 1968 **Gunther Schuller** (b. 1925) made this clear by publishing *Early Jazz,* a landmark book in critical and analytical acuity.

Mainstream Jazz

As in previous years, new jazz styles in the sixties did not replace old ones but coexisted alongside them. Louis Armstrong released a number one hit record with "Hello, Dolly!" (momentarily displacing the Beatles from the top slot in the summer of 1964), Duke Ellington launched his series of Sacred Concerts, swing veterans like Roy Eldridge and Coleman Hawkins attained the status of elder statesmen, and in 1961 Preservation Hall opened in New Orleans for partisans of Dixieland. At the same time, hard bop lived on in such bands as Art Blakey and the Jazz Messengers, bringing new stars to prominence like trumpeters Lee Morgan and Freddie Hubbard and tenor saxophonists Wayne Shorter and Joe Henderson. The emergence of free jazz redefined the meaning of "mainstream jazz." Whereas in the fifties the word "mainstream" referred mostly to popular swing holdovers like Benny Goodman, Ella Fitzgerald, or Coleman Hawkins, in the sixties bop-affiliated artists, no longer viewed as modernists, were absorbed into the mainstream concept as well.

Beleaguered by the negative publicity surrounding free jazz on the one hand and the suffocating popularity of rock on the other, many mainstream players struggled to find work. Jazz audiences declined, nightclubs went out of business. In San Francisco, the Blackhawk closed; in New York, Jazz Gallery and others did the same. In 1965, even Birdland shut its doors. A few leading players faced adversities recalling those of New Orleanians during the Depression (see Chapter 10). Charles Mingus suffered a series of reversals culminating in his eviction from his apartment in 1966. Chet Baker, who admittedly brought many troubles upon himself through drug addiction, was reduced to pumping gas after having his teeth knocked out by a gang of thugs in 1968. As in the 1930s, some jazz players fled to Europe, including Dexter Gordon, Bud Powell, Donald Byrd, George Russell, and Lester Bowie. Others took refuge in Las Vegas, a city that arose after World War II to become a party town in the wide-open tradition of Prohibition-era New Orleans, Chicago, and Kansas City.

Some top jazz musicians—notably Miles Davis and John Coltrane—actually prospered by exploring aspects of free jazz. The mid-sixties recordings of Davis and Coltrane stand among their most challenging and important works. Many other players, though, felt compelled to make concessions to the market, with mixed musical results. Artificial hybrids like Duke Ellington's cover of the Beatles' hit "I Want To Hold Your Hand" are not generally regarded as an advance for the art. But the best performances in the genuinely new genres of bossa nova, soul jazz, and fusion managed to strike an effective balance between commercial and artistic values. They also departed far enough from the traditional elements of swing, improvisation, and the blues, to cause some critics to wonder whether the long and robust evolution of jazz had finally reached a dead end.

Chapter *23* Free Jazz

The upheaval that created free jazz differed in important ways from the bebop revolution. Unlike bebop, free jazz had no Minton's or Monroe's—no central hub from which the music emanated across the country and the world. The key figures in the music's rise, Ornette Coleman and Cecil Taylor, made their discoveries entirely independent of one another. Furthermore, unlike the early beboppers who worked initially as loyal swing sidemen, Coleman and Taylor did not try to change the system from within. They worked on the margins of the jazz tradition, attacking conventions without having first apprenticed for any length of time with established figures. They and many of their followers were like guerilla warriors who ambushed the jazz establishment from the sidelines and tried to overthrow it.

The coup was only partly successful. Again, unlike bebop, free jazz never lost its radical image and never became the new mainstream. Even today, free jazz sounds as prickly as ever, and its audiences—while devoted—remain small. And yet the influence of free jazz on other substyles is pervasive. Though resistant to the new music at first, Miles Davis and John Coltrane eventually embraced free elements to varying degrees. As the functional equivalents of president and vice-president of the jazz establishment in the sixties, Davis and Coltrane liberally spread the free aesthetic among their constituents. In Coltrane's classic quartet and Davis's second quintet, these leaders offered a moderate free approach that became the basis for the neo-bop movement that has dominated mainstream jazz for the past thirty years.

The Radicals

Simply defined, free jazz was a music "freed" from the constraints of established practice. It may be helpful to consider musicians associated with it along a continuum of comparative "freedom." On one end would be a conventional hard bop style, with well-defined instrumental relationships, melodies, chord progressions, swing rhythms, meters, and forms. On the other would be a musical world of ostensible chaos lacking all of these traditional elements. Most free players fall somewhere between these two extremes. Despite a bewildering diversity of approaches, it is possible to divide most free musicians into two broad camps: the radicals who more or less dispensed with at least one cornerstone of mainstream jazz (such as meter), and the moderates who absorbed free elements into a fundamentally traditional framework (see Table 23.1).

Table 23.1 A Free Jazz Continuum

Hard Bop			Total Freedom
Tonal melodies			Atonal melodies
Triadic harmonies	*Moderates*	*Radicals*	No triadic harmonies
Meter/swing feel			No meter/swing feel
Chord progressions	←——————————→		No chord progressions
Standard forms			No standard forms
Standard intonation			Unorthodox intonation
Standard instrumentation			Unorthodox instrumentation

Ornette Coleman

Chief among the radicals was alto saxophonist **Ornette Coleman** (b. 1930). Coleman had one of the least auspicious musical backgrounds of any prominent jazz musician. Growing up in Fort Worth, Texas, he took up the alto saxophone and began playing in local R&B bands. But Coleman's already abstruse bebop style got him fired from one band after another. At one dance hall a man summoned him outside where thugs beat him up and destroyed his saxophone. After recovering he moved to Los Angeles, where he sat in with local jazz musicians with similarly disastrous results. Dexter Gordon once famously ordered him off the stage. When he came up to jam, rhythm section players would often leave the stage themselves. During this period Coleman supported himself as an elevator operator at Bullock's department store.

Despite these problems, Coleman manifested a raw musical power that eventually impressed musicians open to eccentric approaches. He found kindred spirits in trumpeter **Don Cherry** (1936–1995) and drummer **Billy Higgins** (1936–2001) and began jamming with them and a few others in a friend's garage. Around this time a young white bassist named **Charlie Haden** (b. 1937) heard Coleman sit in at a club: "He played three or four phrases, and it was so brilliant," Haden recalled. Crucially, Coleman was playing, not on the chord changes, but "on the inspiration and feeling of the song." What this meant in practice was that Coleman followed a roving muse, improvising variations on the melody or parts of the melody or related ideas that arose en route. Harmonically, he drifted wherever his melodic explorations took him, freely changing tonal centers at whim. Inspired by the possibilities inherent in this approach, Haden sought him out and soon became his regular bass player. Coleman organized a pianoless group featuring Cherry, Haden, and Higgins that critics now call his **classic quartet.**

In 1959 Coleman and Cherry attended the Lenox School of Jazz, where they created a sensation. "In some deep sense [Coleman] wasn't a student there," said one of the teachers. "He could have taught any of the faculty at Lenox. He burst on

Ornette Coleman, *The Shape of Jazz To Come* LP record jacket, 1959.

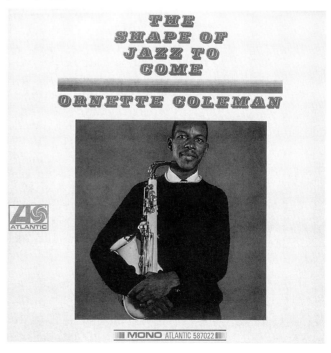

Venues

THE FIVE SPOT

The Five Spot Café, located at two different East Village sites in the 1950s and 1960s, hosted the most self-consciously progressive jazz of its time. The club was established in the mid-fifties by Joe and Iggy Termini, brothers who later opened another noted club, Jazz Gallery. At its original location at 5 Cooper Square, the Five Spot started as a seedy bar with sawdust on the floor. In 1956 Cecil Taylor made his debut there, immediately attracting the modern artists and writers who would thenceforth constitute the club's principal clientele. As the Termini brothers cleaned up the club's interior, other stellar engagements followed. The Thelonious Monk Quartet (featuring John Coltrane) made a celebrated six-month run in 1957, and—most famously—Ornette Coleman introduced his shocking new jazz idiom at the Five Spot in 1959–1961. In the 1960s the Five Spot continued to hire controversial artists, including Eric Dolphy (1961) and Charles Mingus (1964–1965). The second Five Spot opened in 1962 at 3rd Avenue and East 7th Street, and lasted for ten years. ■ ■ ■

the scene completely intact." Under the auspices of John Lewis, Coleman signed with Atlantic Records and made the first album with his new quartet, *The Shape of Jazz To Come.* On such pieces as "Lonely Woman" and "Congeniality," this album unveiled a music of strident horn cries and diffuse harmonies, though still within a relatively stable metric context. The following year Coleman recorded *Free Jazz,* which gave the new music its name. The title track features a double quartet, including two rhythm sections which heavily obscure—although again do not eradicate—the pulse. "Free Jazz" ventures into the realm of **atonality,** often eliminating any sense of home key or mode. The piece also presents thirty-seven minutes of **collective improvisation** by the eight musicians, thereby opening the door to communal stream-of-consciousness jazz playing. Perhaps most disturbing to mainstream players, on these records Coleman and Cherry play out of tune by conventional standards. Coleman defended their intonation with the pithy comment, "You can play flat in tune and sharp in tune."

In November Coleman's quartet opened at the **Five Spot,** a New York club devoted to progressive jazz (see Map 7 and "Venues: The Five Spot"). His debut sparked a furor in the jazz community. *Down Beat* gave a sampling of musicians' reactions: "He'll change the entire course of jazz," "He's a fake," "He's a genius," "He swings like HELL," . . . "He's out, real far out," "I like him, but I don't have any idea of what he is doing." Roy Eldridge said, "I've listened to him all kinds of ways. I listened to him high and . . . cold sober. . . . I think he's jiving, baby." Max Roach was so offended by Coleman's playing that he came up on the bandstand and punched him in the mouth. But with a few notable exceptions, critics lionized Coleman. One called his concert at Town Hall later that year "a miraculous and perhaps even historic event" and "a vest-pocket history of most of the radical changes in jazz improvisation during the past couple of decades."

Cecil Taylor

If Coleman stood for untutored musical potency out of an impoverished southern background, his like-minded contemporary, pianist **Cecil Taylor** (b. 1929),

atonality a harmonic approach that eliminates any sense of home key or mode.

represented just the opposite. Born into a black middle-class family in Long Island, New York, Taylor graduated from Boston's New England Conservatory, admired Schoenberg and Stravinsky, and constantly concerned himself with the integration of jazz and classical elements. As a child he studied piano and tympani with a husband-and-wife team of music teachers across the street from his home. Taylor also admired—and later even worked for—popular black dance teams. His background and interest in percussion and dance produced a mature piano style of unusual physicality.

Taylor mixed European interest in musical structure with the African American emphasis on emotion. After an initial fascination with white pianists Dave Brubeck and Lennie Tristano, he fell under the influence of Duke Ellington, Thelonious Monk, and especially Horace Silver, all of whom approached the piano with unusual percussiveness. Though he believes his most important musical education took place in the streets and clubs of

Cecil Taylor during the recording session for *Unit Structures,* 1966 (see Listening Chart 25).

ORNETTE COLEMAN QUARTET, *"Lonely Woman"* (1959)

One day in 1954, during his lunch break at Bullock's, Coleman recalled, "I was walking down the street and I came upon a gallery. On display in this gallery was a painting of a very bourgeois, wealthy-looking white lady sitting there with the most sad and lonely expression; tears on her face, and she had everything that anyone could ever want. I said, 'It's amazing, but I can relate to this painting.'" That day he composed "Lonely Woman" under its inspiration.

The piece represents a midpoint between traditional and free elements. Traditional features include a clear pulse articulated by the drums, a clear tonal (or modal) center, and the standard chorus form: AABA. But the shock of new features overwhelms any sense of traditionalism. First, Haden does not play a walking bass line but instead thrums a sinuous drone conjuring Far Eastern music. On top of this, Coleman and Cherry play the melody in a much slower implied tempo from that established by Higgins. The mournful melody takes on the character of a lament. The horns are out of tune with one another, powerfully evoking the alienation of the title. Although the melody outlines a clear AABA pattern, during Coleman's solo the A-sections become one long vamp over which Coleman plays essentially in a wandering modal style.

LISTENING CHART 24

Ornette Coleman Quartet, "Lonely Woman" (Coleman)

CD 2 / Tracks 33–36

RECORDED 22 MAY 1959, LOS ANGELES / *THE SHAPE OF JAZZ TO COME* ATLANTIC SD 1317

Ornette Coleman (alto saxophone), Don Cherry (pocket trumpet), Charlie Haden (bass), Billy Higgins (drums)

Style: Free jazz

Form: AABA song form

			Introduction: Vamp
33	0:00	12 bars	Drums set up fast bop tempo on cymbals; bass adds Far Eastern–sounding drone on top
		1st Chorus	**Head**
34	0:18	A (16)	Ornette Coleman (alto saxophone) and Don Cherry (pocket trumpet) play mournful head in much slower implied tempo than the drummer's tempo, in (out-of-tune) *unison*
	0:43	A (16)	*A-section repeated*
	1:08	B (8)	Horns and rhythm section coordinate important accents
	1:20	A (16)	Return to three-layered rhythmic activity: drums, bass, horns
		2nd Chorus	**Alto saxophone solo: Ornette Coleman**
35	1:46	Vamp on A	Coleman plays harmonically wandering solo, emphasizing soulful bluesy gestures and heartfelt exclamations
	2:21	B (8)	Add trumpet background line
	2:33	Vamp on A	
		3rd Chorus	**Head**
36	2:54	A (16)	Coleman and Cherry play head as before
	3:17	A (16)	*A-section repeated*
	3:40	B (8)	Bridge more explosive this time
	3:52	A (16)	*A-section repeated*
	4:18		**Coda: Vamp**
			Bass and drums close the piece much as they began it

Further Listening from the *Prentice Hall Jazz Collection*
Track 9: Ornette Coleman, "Civilization Day" (1971)

Harlem, Taylor has never renounced his classical training. "I am not afraid of European influences," he said. "The point is to use them—as Ellington did—as part of my life as an American Negro." Yet he claims jazz as his aesthetic base: "The object of any jazz musician who has had [my] background [in classical music] is to bring it to jazz—combine it with jazz and see what happens. My particular field is jazz and therefore it will eventually become a complete jazz expression."

Taylor actually played avant-garde music on record and in New York clubs before Coleman did, but for some reason his critical acceptance came slowly and gradually rather than overnight. Although in the early fifties he played briefly for Johnny Hodges and Hot Lips Page, Taylor never worked as a sideman with a prominent hard bop group. Instead, he started out as a leader, making his first album, *Jazz Advance*, in 1956. In the same year he played a six-week engagement at the Five Spot, helping to establish it as a leading forum for the avant-garde. Publicity from these events won him a spot at the 1957 Newport Jazz Festival and favorable notices in *Jazz Review*. Despite these successes, Taylor struggled to make a living. As late as 1962 *Down Beat* voted him best "new star" even as his nightly drawing power ebbed to the point that he had to disband and support himself as a restaurant cook and dishwasher.

Musically, however, Taylor had reached a turning point. That fall he organized the **Cecil Taylor Unit** (the first of many bands by that name), a trio with alto saxophonist Jimmy Lyons and drummer Sunny Murray. During a seven-week tour of

Cecil Taylor Unit, *"Tales (8 Whisps)"* (1966)

In "Tales (8 Whisps)," from the album *Unit Structures*, we hear all the prickly characteristics listeners commonly associate with Cecil Taylor: atonality, a lack of pulse or meter, abstract melodic patterns, and an uncompromising rhetorical intensity. But in addition to these recondite qualities, the piece also has more traditional features, a great variety of moods, and a coherent and elegant shape. Nor, as we shall see, is it an exercise in total improvisation. Taylor evidently worked out some material in advance, which he sometimes repeats at strategic moments to articulate form. Furthermore, he clearly rehearsed with his collaborators certain details of form and even specific motives.

The piece divides into eight sections (the eight "whisps" of the title?), which Taylor calls "units." Some units are separated by pauses; others flow directly, without a break, into ensuing units (an effect indicated with the word *attacca* in Listening Chart 25). The units differ from one another in duration, character, rhythmic speed, and instrumentation. Some feature Taylor playing solo piano, some are piano-bass or piano-drum duets, and some feature a trio of piano, bass, and drums. Most of the units unfold with a constant sense of change and evolution, but Units 1 and 4 recapitulate important material virtually note-for-note, creating the traditional effect of a *reprise*; thus, Unit 1 is in ternary form (a b a') and Unit 4 is in binary form (c c'). Taylor frequently plays abstract material, which he intensifies with seemingly superhuman flights of virtuosity (see, for example, the lightning-fast runs in Unit 6). But occasionally he plays more familiar-sounding material; in Unit 4 he presents a brilliant modernist parody of earlier jazz piano styles, faintly echoing the great two-handed traditions of boogie-woogie and stride. In this unit (as well as in Unit 7) he establishes a sense of pulse, tempo, and even meter.

LISTENING CHART 25

Cecil Taylor Unit, "Tales (8 Whisps)" (Taylor)

CD 2 / Tracks 37–44

RECORDED 19 MAY 1966, ENGLEWOOD CLIFFS, NEW JERSEY / *UNIT STRUCTURES* BLUE NOTE 84237

Cecil Taylor (piano), Henry Grimes or Alan Silva (bass), Andrew Cyrille (drums)

Style: Free jazz			**Form: Eight units of varying duration, character, rhythmic speed, and instrumentation**

Unit 1: Duet

Fast, frantic: Cecil Taylor (piano) + Andrew Cyrille (drums)

37	0:00	a	Introduces main idea of section: short, explosive figures
	0:12	b	Develops the idea in various ways . . .
	1:35	a′	Returns to opening material

Unit 2: Solo

| 38 | 1:46 | | Slow, more gentle: Taylor plays *chord clusters* unaccompanied
Attacca . . . |

Unit 3: Duet

Taylor + bass player (Henry Grimes or Alan Silva)

39	2:09		Bassist plays eerie high-register *harmonics* (with a bow)
	2:38		Burst of frantic mood, fast rhythms of Unit 1
	2:55		Return to calmer mood

Unit 4: Solo

Medium tempo; more regular rhythms: Taylor

| 40 | 3:11 | c | Taylor plays modernist parody of earlier jazz piano styles, gradually yielding to total abstraction |
| | 3:30 | c′ | Begins again with the same material, again dissolves in abstraction, but this time much more violent in speed/rhythm . . . |

Unit 5: Duet

| 41 | 4:01 | | Taylor + bass player (Grimes or Silva): isolated chords, jabbing figures
Attacca . . . |

Unit 6: Trio

| 42 | 4:27 | | Taylor, bass player (Grimes or Silva), + Cyrille Taylor alternates touchstone chord with lightning-fast runs
Attacca . . . |

		Unit 7: Trio
43	5:41	Medium pulse established in piano, then drums, then bass (reiterated pedal point); trio reaches point of maximum density of texture
		Unit 8: Solo
44	6:27	Taylor closes the performance by himself, recalling many ideas presented in earlier units

Denmark starting in November, the band forged a new type of group improvisation, one that abandoned the beat—and hence any possibility of swinging—in favor of a freely unfolding rhythmic environment, producing a "group chain reaction," in Taylor's words. "The first day I started rehearsing with him," recalled Murray, "I asked him, 'What should I play?' He said, 'Just play.' I said, 'What do you mean? Like a drum solo?' 'No, I mean just let yourself play your drums, but listen too.' And it happened." One characteristic feature of Taylor's music from this period forward is a preference for hurricane speeds that push the boundaries of human capacity to execute (by the performer) and comprehend (by the listener). Such violent playing, together with seemingly unfettered expressive passion, came to be known as **energy jazz.** Two of Taylor's former sidemen, tenor saxophonists Albert Ayler and Archie Shepp, became especially prominent exponents of energy jazz. We will assess their contributions, along with that of Pharoah Sanders, in Chapter 24, in the context of our discussion of John Coltrane.

The Avant Garde in Chicago

For the first time since the 1920s, Chicago emerged in the sixties as a major jazz center. In addition to assimilating the advances of celebrated New York players, Chicago musicians built upon the achievements of Chicago's father of the avant garde, at that time an underground figure named Sun Ra, to develop their own free traditions.

Sun Ra   A product of the Swing Era, pianist and composer **Sun Ra** (born Herman Blount, 1914–1993) was considerably older than most other free players. In the late forties, he played piano and arranged for Fletcher Henderson's aging big band. In 1953 he organized his own big band in Chicago. Over the next few years his music evolved from a sort of big band hard bop to a percussion-heavy group conception blending esoteric, exotic, and kitschy elements. From 1956 he began playing electric piano, becoming a pioneer of that instrument. By this time he had adopted the name Sun Ra, called his band the **Myth-Science Arkestra** (among other cosmic-sounding names), and begun formulating a startling identity for himself based on ancient Egyptian black history and science fiction. According to Ra (a native of Birmingham, Alabama), he was born on the planet Saturn and came to earth with a mission to help earthlings turn away from evil through music.

Whatever the meaning of his eccentricities, Ra established a basic aesthetic that strongly influenced free jazz in Chicago. Above all, his musical vision prized group empathy and cooperation. Unlike practitioners of energy jazz whose

energy jazz a subcategory of free jazz that emphasizes speed, rhythmic intensity, and expressive passion.

music often appeared to embody the anger and anxiety of black nationalism, Ra's band seemed more allied with the peace-loving side of social activism. In place of the howling frenzy of energy jazz, Ra promoted transcendence, theatricality, and even humor. Recalling his counsel to young sidemen, one musician said, "He just wants you to live clean and think brotherly." According to Ra himself, his music came from heaven: "I'm actually painting pictures of infinity with my music, and that's why a lot of people can't understand it. But if they'd listen to this and other types of music, they'd find that mine has something else in it, something from another world."

Association for the Advancement of Creative Musicians (AACM) In 1961 Sun Ra moved to New York. As if taking up the torch, Chicago pianist **Muhal Richard Abrams** (b. 1930) in that year organized the Experimental Band, a large ensemble of unspecified number devoted to exploring new musical ideas. Indifferent to commercial success, the Experimental Band rehearsed privately but made little attempt to perform in public. The band inspired young musicians to abandon some of the more destructive aspects of inner city life. One of its founding members, saxophonist Joseph Jarman, said that prior to joining the band, "I was like all the rest of the 'hip' ghetto niggers; I was cool, I took dope, I smoked pot, etc. I did not *care* for the life that I had been given. In having the chance to work in the Experimental Band with Richard and the other musicians there, I found the first something with meaning/reason for doing. That band and the people there was the *most* important thing that ever happened to me."

The communal, mutually supportive ethos of both Sun Ra's group and the Experimental Band led Abrams, in 1965, to found a cooperative, the **Association for the Advancement of Creative Musicians (AACM).** A nonprofit organization in the best tradition of sixties idealism, AACM sponsored concerts of various avant-garde bands, helped musicians find work, encouraged experienced players to teach the younger ones, and demanded high ethical standards of its members. As Jarman recalled, AACM was a peaceful response to the social turmoil of the time. With race riots proliferating in the northern cities and the various protest movements intensifying, "it was a very exciting, nervous period." But among South Side musicians, "we had experienced a view of union. And that's how the [AACM] came about, because we were experiencing unity in the various communities. The intent of the whole idea was to allow us to perform . . . with dignity, with pride, without humiliation, without limitation."

Under the aegis of AACM, free jazz took a different path from that espoused by the New Yorkers. Instead of *only* pushing the borders of abstraction through such techniques as atonality and ametrical playing, such groups as the **Art Ensemble of Chicago** and woodwind player **Anthony Braxton** (b. 1945) incorporated diverse elements—R&B, bebop, the blues, African rhythms, as well as European-based modernist sounds—within a grand holistic framework. In the spirit of Sun Ra, they also used poetry, dance, theater, and primitivistic costumes and makeup in their performances. In their rigorous interdisciplinary eclecticism, the AACM bands represented the first stirrings of *postmodernism* in jazz (see Chapters 28–30).

The Moderates

Many mainstream jazz musicians rejected free jazz in all its manifestations. But a sizable number of younger players experimented with free elements, eventually absorbing them on a limited basis. The music of these moderate free jazz musicians is frequently called **postbop.** They typically retained conventional standards of tuning, tone quality, and attack, and often asserted a clear meter and a repeating chord progression. However, they diluted standard harmonies and "played with the time," undermining metric accents through boisterous, irregular drumming and group interaction. One of the bands that did the most to reconcile free jazz with the mainstream was led by Miles Davis.

postbop a subcategory of free jazz that explores limited harmonic and rhythmic freedom while retaining such traditional jazz features as swing, meter, and chord progressions.

Miles Davis's Second Quintet

The early sixties represented a fallow period for Miles Davis. At first he emphatically rejected free jazz, for the first time in his career assuming a reactionary posture toward new developments. "If something sounds terrible," he explained, "a person should have enough respect for his own mind to say it doesn't sound good. It doesn't to me, and I'm not going to listen to it." Yet ultimately Davis could not resist the tantalizing avenues uncovered by the rising generation. Indeed, it was his youthful sidemen's fascination with free developments that finally compelled him in the mid-sixties to probe the avant garde himself.

Shortly after completing *Kind of Blue,* the Miles Davis Sextet began to dissolve. By 1962 all the original players had left, and Davis had to reassemble his band from the ground up. The first members, Detroit bassist **Ron Carter** (b. 1937) and a very young, seventeen-year-old drummer from Boston, **Tony Williams** (1945–1997), joined in early 1963. In May Davis summoned Chicago pianist **Herbie Hancock** (b. 1940) to his home. For the next three days Hancock,

Miles Davis's second quintet. *Left to right:* Herbie Hancock, Miles Davis, Ron Carter, Wayne Shorter, Tony Williams.

interaction the dialogue that occurs between soloists and rhythm sections in the idioms of free jazz and postbop.

outside playing in postbop, the practice of deliberately and temporarily transgressing the chord progression.

Carter, Williams, and tenor saxophonist George Coleman rehearsed in the basement while Davis listened on the intercom. Finally he came in and told them to appear for a Columbia recording session the following day. In February 1964 the quintet performed a civil rights benefit concert, which Columbia later released on two LPs: *Four 'n' More* and *My Funny Valentine.* Despite the concert's success, Coleman left Davis a few months later, explaining to a reporter that "the band was heading into areas he wasn't convinced about."

Those areas related to the avant garde. Tony Williams recalled that "before I joined Miles, Ornette Coleman's music had become very important. . . . So I was interested in expressing the drums and the drum set in a different way." According to Herbie Hancock, "What we were trying to do in Miles's band . . . was to . . . take these influences . . . and amalgamate them and personalize them in such a way that when people [heard] us they were hearing the avant-garde on the one hand and they were hearing the history of jazz that led up to it on the other." Davis's sidemen sought to balance past and present practices in a type of "controlled freedom." They wanted to drink deeply from the avant garde, but at the same time, "keep the groove [i.e., the beat] happening."

George Coleman may have resisted these experiments, but tenor saxophonist **Wayne Shorter** (b. 1933) embraced them. With Shorter's addition to the band in the summer of 1964, the personnel of Davis's so-called "second" great quintet was complete. For the next four years the band dominated the jazz world, recording six studio albums: *E.S.P.* (1965), *Miles Smiles* (1966), *Sorcerer, Nefertiti* (both 1967), *Miles in the Sky,* and *Filles de Kilimanjaro* (both 1968). Unlike earlier Davis groups that emphasized standards, the second quintet recorded evocative originals by Davis and his sidemen, especially Shorter. The relentless exploration of free elements produced exciting performances. Williams was the chief source of the tremendous energy in the rhythm section. Unlike traditional bop drummers, Williams played freely and propulsively on his drums and cymbals, producing a lively sense of **interaction** with the other players. In both solos and accompaniment, the musicians pushed the boundaries of harmony by deliberately transgressing the chord progression from time to time, a technique called **outside playing.**

Davis's youthful sidemen treated their boss with great respect, calling him "Mr. Davis" and committing their whole hearts to his music. But the respect ran both ways. "I was learning something new every night with that group," Davis said. Tony Williams, for example, "was the only guy in my band who ever told me, 'Man, why don't you practice!' I was missing notes . . . trying to keep up with his young ass. So he started me to practicing again because I had stopped and didn't even know it."

Bill Evans, 1964.

Bill Evans

Cecil Taylor and Sun Ra notwithstanding, most radical free jazz groups dispensed with piano. As the traditional bearer of the harmony, the piano was not considered essential in the absence of standard chord progressions. Even so, important changes took place in jazz piano style that relate directly to the free movement. In 1965 John Mehegan, an

MILES DAVIS QUINTET, *"Ginger Bread Boy"* (1966)

"Ginger Bread Boy," from *Miles Smiles*, captures well the raw excitement and turbulence of Davis's second quintet. The head consists of a twelve-bar blues plus a four-bar extension; the solo choruses omit the extension. The horns blurt out the unison head while drummer Tony Williams thunders away in the background, adding fills between the horn entries; in the last phrase of the head the horns play upward glissandos known—onomatopoeically—as *doits*.

The solos by Miles Davis, Wayne Shorter, and Herbie Hancock present highly chromatic inflections of the blues tonality, Hancock being the most aggressive in actually stepping away from the key to play *outside* from time to time. Hancock refrains from playing during the two horn solos and does not comp during his own solo, leaving the stark texture of bass and drums favored by many free jazz soloists. All the soloists develop their ideas motivically at certain places; Shorter, for example, builds much of his solo around the *doit* figure at the end of the head.

Williams's intermittent explosions on the drum kit and the soloists' irregular phrasing often disrupt the sense of pulse and meter articulated primarily by Ron Carter's walking bass lines.

---

influential theorist and jazz pianist, wrote: "In recent years there has appeared a trend in jazz pianism which, in terms of the rugged history of jazz piano, represents a rather startling, but musically effective [development]." Pianists who developed this trend, producing a truly postbop piano style, include Herbie Hancock, McCoy Tyner, Chick Corea, and Keith Jarrett. But the major jazz piano innovations of the sixties, according to Mehegan, are "generally attributed to pianist Bill Evans."

Bill Evans, whom we first encountered as a sideman for Miles Davis (see Chapter 21), was born and raised in Plainfield, New Jersey. He received thorough training in classical piano and graduated from Southeastern Louisiana University in 1950. After three years in the service, he moved to New York and began studying at the Mannes School of Music. His association with composer George Russell at Mannes brought him to the attention of leading jazz figures. His first recordings as a leader, *New Jazz Conceptions* (1956) and *Everybody Digs Bill Evans* (1958), generated some interest, but it was his brief stint with Miles Davis and especially his prominent role in Davis's *Kind of Blue* that brought Evans fame.

What was special about Evans's playing? An old girlfriend recalled his practice routine: "He would usually play classical music ... Rachmaninoff ... Beethoven and Bach. He would play that and then just drift into jazz in a very fluid sort of way." Evans's easy bilinguality produced an exceptionally refined and subtle jazz style. Prior to Evans, jazz pianists typically comped with third-based "shell" chords, often hollow sevenths or thirds, in the left hand. His love of French impressionist composers Debussy and Ravel prompted him to explore rich left hand harmonies. He often played clusters, chords built in *seconds* (as well as thirds). In Evans's hands, such **secundal harmony** sounded "pretty" or ethereal rather than strident. He also pioneered the use of stacked fourths in the left hand. McCoy Tyner, whom we will discuss in Chapter 24, became the foremost exponent of **quartal harmony.** Very soon other postbop pianists had incorporated secundal and quartal voicings into their comping style as well. These

secundal harmony the use of chords built on the interval of a second.

quartal harmony the use of harmony built on the interval of a fourth.

LISTENING CHART 26

Miles Davis Quintet, "Ginger Bread Boy" (Heath)

CD 2 / Tracks 45–49

RECORDED 25 OCTOBER 1966, NEW YORK CITY / MILES SMILES COLUMBIA CL 2601

Miles Davis (trumpet), Wayne Shorter (tenor saxophone), Herbie Hancock (piano), Ron Carter (bass), Tony Williams (drums)

Style: Postbop			**Form: 12-bar blues**

Head

		1st Chorus (12 + 4)	Miles Davis (trumpet) and Wayne Shorter (tenor saxophone) play head in unison:
45	0:00	a (4)	First phrase (horns, then drums)
	0:03	a' (4)	Second phrase (horns, then drums)
	0:07	b (4)	Third phrase: *doits* (horns, then drums)
	0:10	c (4)	Fourth phrase (drum solo: Tony Williams)
	0:14	*2nd Chorus* (12 + 4)	*Head repeated*

Trumpet solo: Miles Davis (twelve choruses)

46	0:28	*3rd Chorus* (12)	Miles Davis plays accompanied only by bass and drums; he
	0:38	*4th Chorus* (12)	inflects the blues tonality with many chromatic auxiliary notes
	0:49	*5th Chorus* (12)	(but little genuine *outside* playing); his irregular phrasing
	0:59	*6th Chorus* (12), etc.	undermines the meter and obscures the form

Tenor saxophone solo: Wayne Shorter (eleven choruses)

47	2.34	*15th Chorus* (12), etc.	Wayne Shorter, also accompanied only by bass and drums, organizes his solo around the *doit* motive of the head . . .

Piano solo: Herbie Hancock (eleven choruses)

48	4:28	*26th Chorus* (12), etc.	More than Davis or Shorter, Herbie Hancock reaches beyond the key to explore *outside* playing; alternates between long bebop-style lines and motivic development . . .

Head

49	6:25	*37th Chorus* (12 + 4)	Davis comes in with the head halfway into Hancock's twelfth chorus
	6:38	*38th Chorus* (12 + 4)	*Repeated*
	6:52	*39th Chorus* (12 + 4)	*Repeated* (Davis comes in a half-measure early)

Coda

	7:06		Ron Carter (bass) + Tony Williams (drums)

refractory harmonies diluted the tonality in a controlled and organized way, without destroying it altogether.

Many people do not think of Evans in connection with the avant garde. His style was far more lyrical and romantic than that of Coleman, Taylor, or even Davis's second quintet. And yet Evans was at the forefront of one of the most important free developments: group interaction. In late 1959 he organized a trio with bassist **Scott LaFaro** (1936–1961) and drummer **Paul Motian** (b. 1931). The three musicians developed a highly sensitive and dynamic group rapport, specializing in multitextured three-way conversations in which the drums and especially the bass "spoke" on almost an equal footing with the piano. The seemingly telepathic relationship between Evans and LaFaro was profound. Watching them, Motian recalled, "brought tears to my eyes." The trio became a mainstay at the **Village Vanguard,** a dark basement club and major jazz venue in Greenwich Village (see Map 7). On June 25, 1961, the trio played five sets at the Vanguard. (Riverside Records released some of the performances on two now classic albums, *Sunday at the Village Vanguard* and *Waltz for Debby.*) Ten days later, tragically, LaFaro died in a car accident. Devastated by the news, Evans stopped playing for almost a year. As he later put it, "When you have evolved a concept of playing which depends on the specific personalities of outstanding players, how do you start again when they are gone?"

BILL EVANS TRIO, *"Gloria's Step"* (1961)

CD 2 / Track 50

The Bill Evans Trio recorded this composition, by bassist Scott LaFaro, twice during the famous live sets that took place at the Village Vanguard less than two weeks before LaFaro's death. When Evans finally went into the studio to choose the material to be released on an LP, he insisted that LaFaro's work (both his compositions and his bass playing) receive prominent placement. Accordingly, "Gloria's Step" appeared as the first track on *Sunday at the Village Vanguard.*

The piece shows LaFaro's inventiveness, both as composer and as bass player. The form is unusual—twenty measures within an AAB chorus structure (5 + 5 + 10 measures). The phrase lengths thus defy expectations and seem to render the music perpetually off-balance by conventional standards. As bass player on "Gloria's Step," LaFaro takes an unusual approach, to say the least. Never quite settling into his traditional role as time-keeper and articulator of the harmonies, he teases the listener with furtive moves toward walking *in two* (half as fast as the actual tempo) while instead carrying on a running dialogue with Evans. The flexible and unpredictable interaction between LaFaro and Evans (and to a lesser extent Paul Motian) marks this recording as experimental within the moderate wing of the free movement.

Evans himself reveals his progressive tendencies through the elastic rhythmic sense and refined harmonic language that made him famous. Hearing Evans might be compared to watching a master watercolor painter capture a scene of deep mystery or nostalgia. For a good example of his sensitive use of harmony, listen to the sixth chorus of "Gloria's Step," in which he closes his solo with two-handed chords rather than the right-hand lines plus left-hand comping with which he began.

Create your own listening chart (CD 2 / Track 50)

Chapter 24 John Coltrane

Just as Sonny Rollins dominated the tenor saxophone during the 1950s, John Coltrane became the undisputed leader on that instrument in the 1960s. When Rollins temporarily retired in 1959 Coltrane lost no time filling the leadership void, recording brilliant, pathbreaking solos on his own *Giant Steps* album and on Miles Davis's *Kind of Blue*. As the sixties progressed, Coltrane's stature grew to colossal proportions. Through the work of his classic quartet and his later experiments with unfettered free playing, Coltrane riveted musicians and critics alike. By the time of his premature death in 1967, only Davis himself could boast similar authority or influence. Many writers now consider Coltrane the last great jazz innovator.

Coltrane cast a powerful spell over the black community in the 1960s. Particularly as he embraced the radical avant garde under the influence of strong spiritual convictions, Coltrane became a visionary figure to many young blacks. In this sense he offered a source of inspiration similar to that provided by Davis in the fifties. Davis himself acknowledged that "Trane's music . . . during the last two or three years of his life represented, for many blacks, the fire and . . . anger and rebellion and love that they felt, especially among the young black intellectuals and revolutionaries of that time. . . . Coltrane was their symbol, their pride. . . . I had been it a few years back, but now he was it, and that was cool with me."

Coltrane also shared with Davis a restless musical temperament, changing and evolving in his aesthetic outlook throughout his life. His career may be divided into three main sections corresponding to his shifting approaches to harmony—his chordal period (through 1960), his postbop/modal period (1960–1965), and his atonal period (1965–1967).

Musical Beginnings

John Coltrane was born in Hamlet, North Carolina, in 1926, the same year as Miles Davis. His mother was the daughter of the local preacher and his father was a keen amateur musician who played violin and ukelele. His parents thus represented an alliance of religion and music that would eventually characterize every aspect of Coltrane's life.

As a teenager Coltrane took up alto saxophone after hearing Johnny Hodges play with Duke Ellington on the radio. Upon graduating from high school he moved to Philadelphia, where he became an ardent Charlie Parker devotee and imitator. Yet like other young players of the time—such as Clifford Brown and Ornette Coleman—he began his professional career playing in R&B bands. Even in this early period he manifested his characteristic blend of ambition and humility, wanting to excel but eager to defer to and learn from more experienced musicians. R&B singer and saxophonist Eddie "Cleanhead" Vinson, with whom Coltrane toured in 1948, recalled, "Yeah, little ol' Coltrane used to be in my band. He never wanted to play. I used to have to play all night long. I'd ask him, 'Man, why don't you play?' He'd say, 'I just want to hear *you* play.'"

Coltrane's first big break in jazz came in 1949, when he joined Dizzy Gillespie's band playing second alto. Around this same time Coltrane had a revelatory dream in which Charlie Parker advised him to switch to tenor, a change Gillespie himself had been urging. Within a short period Coltrane devoted himself exclusively to the tenor, cultivating a solo style based on that of Dexter Gordon, Sonny Rollins, and Sonny Stitt. Unfortunately, his addiction to heroin and alcohol interfered with his musical progress. Habitually late and prone to sleep on the stand, Coltrane finally lost his job with Gillespie. In 1954 he got another promising opportunity when he was hired to play in the septet of his youthful idol, Johnny Hodges. But within a few months Hodges also fired him for drug-related irresponsibility. After these high-profile jazz engagements, Coltrane made his living playing in R&B bands around Philadelphia.

Apprenticeship with Davis and Monk

In 1955 Coltrane got the break that raised him to fame. Miles Davis, after his dazzling "comeback" performance at the Newport Jazz Festival in July, was assembling a permanent band—his so-called first quintet (see Chapter 21). Davis's pianist, Red Garland, and his drummer, Philly Joe Jones, both knew Coltrane from gigs around Philadelphia and urged Davis to hire him. Though unconvinced, Davis had bookings lined up for the fall and needed a tenor. Reluctantly, he called Coltrane and offered him the job.

Many critics did not approve of Davis's choice. Like Davis himself, Coltrane was a late bloomer who in 1955 still had not found his mature voice. His early recordings reveal a stammering, uncertain style. Writers faulted his intonation, his meandering conception, and, perhaps above all, his lack of originality. Reviewing a Davis record for *Metronome* in July 1956, one critic upbraided Coltrane for being on a "Rollins-Stitt kick" and for playing "out of tune." Even **Nat Hentoff,** who later became one of Coltrane's staunchest advocates, complained that "Coltrane . . . is a mixture of Dexter Gordon, Sonny Rollins, and Sonny Stitt. But so far there's very little Coltrane." Yet Davis, a true musical soothsayer, heard what Coltrane was doing and recognized the embryonic brilliance in his playing. And as far as his basic sound was concerned, some critics saw that Coltrane fit well in the Davis band. As one writer put it, Coltrane had "a dry, unplaned tone that sets Davis off like a rough mounting for a fine stone."

And yet, as we have already seen, Coltrane's problems with substance abuse marred his tenure with Davis just as they had done with Gillespie and Hodges. Davis recalled that Coltrane appeared on the bandstand in clothes "that looked like he had slept in them for days." One night, frustrated with Coltrane's erratic and unprofessional behavior, Davis slapped him across the face and punched him in the stomach in an attempt to reform him. Finally, in the spring of 1957

Davis had had enough: he fired both Coltrane and Philly Joe Jones, another incorrigible junkie creating problems in the band.

A Spiritual Awakening

Being fired by Davis, the most celebrated jazz musician then living, brought Coltrane to the lowest point of his life. He returned to Philadelphia where he and his wife, Juanita (aka Naima) Grubbs, moved in with his mother. In despair, he retired to a room determined to overcome his habits cold turkey, in the manner of his former boss, Miles Davis. He lay in bed, drinking only water, and waited for the agonizing withdrawal symptoms to pass.

Unlike Davis, however, he did not beat his addictions through sheer willpower. By his own account, Coltrane had a profound encounter with God during this period. This transforming experience enabled him not only to defeat heroin and alcohol but literally to begin life anew, invigorated with confidence and new purpose. As he recalled years later: "During the year 1957, I experienced, by the grace of God, a spiritual awakening which was to lead me to a richer, fuller, more productive life. At that time, in gratitude, I humbly asked to be given the means and privilege to make others happy through music."

Coltrane's newfound religion was not orthodox or conventional. He had been raised attending his grandfather's African Methodist Episcopal Zion Church; his wife Naima was a Muslim. Yet while Coltrane felt spiritually sympathetic to Christianity, Islam, and indeed many religions, he aspired more simply to unite with the "force that is truly good." His life after 1957 can properly be seen as an intense spiritual search. He explained that "my goal is to live the truly religious life, and express it through my music. If you live it, when you play there's no problem because the music is part of the whole thing. . . . My music is the spiritual expression of what I am, my faith, my knowledge, my being." As the years passed, music increasingly became his express vehicle to spiritual transcendence. His musical quest and his spiritual quest became one.

Transition with Monk

When Coltrane returned to New York in the summer of 1957, he took a job playing with Thelonious Monk. He used to go to Monk's apartment in the morning, drag him out of bed, and together they would practice Monk's compositions. "Working with Monk brought me close to a musical architect of the highest order," Coltrane recalled. "I felt I learned from him in every way— through the senses, theoretically, technically. I would talk to Monk about musical problems, and he would sit at the piano and show me the answers just by playing them." Monk's band with Coltrane was known as the **Thelonious Monk Quartet.** It only lasted six months or so, but during that period the band played a now legendary engagement at the Five Spot, the same venue that hosted Cecil Taylor, Ornette Coleman, and other experimentalists of the late fifties and early sixties.

During his time with Monk, finally freed from the paralyzing effects of drugs and alcohol, Coltrane began practicing with almost compulsive dedication, a commitment that he would keep until the end of his life. He became obsessed with mastering harmonic progressions. His wife recalls twenty-four-hour practice sessions during which he would neither eat nor sleep. During this period Coltrane made his first major album as a leader: *Blue Train.* This album, recorded for Blue Note, contains some of Coltrane's most memorable compositions, including "Moment's Notice" and "Lazy Bird." Most important, it shows Coltrane in full command of his instrument and aesthetic: here is a newly powerful and voracious voice in jazz.

Miles Davis, Second Term

One of the frequent visitors at the Five Spot was Miles Davis. He could see that Coltrane had conquered his addictions and was playing better than ever. When the gig at the Five Spot ended in December, Monk disbanded. Davis immediately asked Coltrane to rejoin his group, now a sextet, with alto saxophonist Cannonball Adderley also on the front line.

By this time Coltrane had developed a distinctive solo approach based on a blunt, exclamatory tone and streaming torrents of notes. In 1960 he recalled that in the last two years he had been "trying for a more sweeping sound." He had wanted "to play the entire scale of each chord. Therefore, they were usually played fast and sometimes sounded like glisses [i.e., glissandos]. . . . Sometimes what I played didn't work out in eighth notes, 16th notes, or triplets. I had to put the notes in uneven groups like fives and sevens in order to get them all in. I thought in groups of notes, not of one note at a time."

The ravenous, searching quality of his playing generated considerable controversy. Reviewing the Davis Sextet at the 1958 Newport Jazz Festival, one *Down Beat* critic misinterpreted Coltrane's emotional stance, famously denouncing his "angry tenor." Far from being "angry," Coltrane viewed his music as an attempt to make contact with, or at least to celebrate, the infinite. But others characterized his solos more positively. In a *Down Beat* article from October 1958, Ira Gitler offered a vivid rebuttal to the "angry tenor" charge: Coltrane played in **sheets of sound,** said Gitler, thereby deflecting attention away from the affect of his music and toward its purely sonorous qualities. Interpreting the emotion of Coltrane's solos in a positive vein, a French writer praised his playing as "exuberant, furious, impassioned, thundering."

In his search for musical truth Coltrane began playing longer and longer solos, a practice Monk had encouraged. Already in 1958, according to one observer, Coltrane was playing the longest solos in the Davis Sextet. "He was beginning to play rhythmic patterns over and over again. I remember him playing one phrase in particular twenty-nine times, and then seeing Miles pull the cuff on Trane's pants so he would move into something different—at which point Trane sprang into a completely new line, like being launched out of Cape Kennedy." Davis wavered between indulgence and impatience regarding Coltrane's prolixity. Adderley said that "once in a while, Miles might say, 'Why you play so long, man?' and John would say, 'It took that long to get it all in.' And Miles would accept that, really." But at bottom Davis seemed annoyed by such lengthy solos. When Coltrane once explained that he didn't know *how* to stop, Davis replied curtly, "Take the horn out of your mouth."

sheets of sound Ira Gitler's term for the streaming torrents of notes in John Coltrane's solos of the late 1950s.

John Coltrane, *Giant Steps* LP record jacket, 1959.

CD 2 / Track 51

JOHN COLTRANE, *"Giant Steps"* (1959)

In the spring of 1959, just one month after recording *Kind of Blue* with Davis, Coltrane entered the studio and made a landmark album of his own: *Giant Steps*. He had conceived the compositions for the album several months previously. Before the session Coltrane diligently practiced "Giant Steps" and "Countdown," both extremely fast pieces with busy chord progressions. "Giant Steps" is particularly unusual: because the bass line rises in alternating (minor) thirds and (perfect) fourths, the piece changes keys frequently and irregularly. By the day of the recording Coltrane had mastered these harmonic intricacies even at the fastest tempos. One can sense the degree of harmonic challenge from the struggle pianist Tommy Flanagan had with "Giant Steps." Unlike Coltrane's effortless performance, Flanagan's solo gradually disintegrates, from complete bop lines in the beginning to fragments in the middle to sustained chords in the end. Coltrane had brought the piece to Flanagan's apartment so he could prepare for the session, Flanagan recalled, "but I didn't realize he was going to play it at that *tempo!*"

"Giant Steps" offers a good example of Coltrane's *sheets of sound* approach—the streaming torrents of notes he often played in solos of the late 1950s. As others have pointed out, the piece also represents Coltrane's farewell to bebop. For here he takes chordal (i.e., vertical) improvisation to its ultimate limit in terms of accurately "running the changes" at a fast tempo. Like Charlie Parker, he relied on memorized formulas in order to match the harmonies at such speeds. "A lot of the scalar material Coltrane was playing [came from] Nicolas Slonimsky's *Thesaurus of Scales and Melodic Patterns*," one musician recalled. In this reliance on outside material, including cross-instrumental influences, Coltrane was part of a trend in the late fifties: "Most of the reed and trumpet players played out of different violin books, and also scale books [for piano] like [Carl] Czerny."

Create your own listening chart (CD 2 / Track 51)

The Classic Quartet

In May of 1960 Coltrane left Davis, formed his own group, and accepted a twenty-week engagement at a new club, **Jazz Gallery** (see Map 7). A writer for the *New York Daily News* exclaimed, "Run, do not walk or otherwise loiter on your way down to the Jazz Gallery. The reason is John Coltrane, a tenor saxophonist who has the future coming out of his horn." Listeners heard Coltrane's new group as bridging the old and new worlds of jazz. A *Variety* review stated that Coltrane's "range of tonal effects covers both the Colemans, Ornette and Hawkins." A couple of years later, LeRoi Jones wrote that "John's way is somewhere between the so-called mainstream . . . and those young musicians I have called the avant garde. John is actually in neither camp, though he is certainly a huge force in each."

Almost as important as his own playing was the music of his band. This group featured fellow Philadelphians **McCoy Tyner** (b. 1938) on piano, **Jimmy Garrison** (1934–1976) on bass, and **Elvin Jones** (1927–2004) on drums. Widely thought to be Coltrane's greatest ensemble, the band is aptly called his "classic quartet." Tyner and Jones played an especially vital role. Tyner developed an aggressive piano style dominated by quartal harmonies and jabbing rhythms. Jones is often described as a "volcanic" drummer who explodes unpredictably in a bubbling stream of polyrhythms. This rhythm section provided just the right intensity for Coltrane's anguished solos.

In the fall of 1960 Coltrane made his first album with his new quartet (but with Steve Davis on bass)—a record called *My Favorite Things.* Recorded for Atlantic, this album immediately captured attention for Coltrane's use of the soprano saxophone on the title track. The only jazz player widely known to have played this instrument, New Orleans pioneer Sidney Bechet, died in 1959; now Coltrane reclaimed it for use in a modern context. In Coltrane's version the harmonic progression of the solo section is reduced to two alternating chords over which Coltrane plays modally. The album became a jazz hit, selling over five hundred thousand copies. In late 1960 Coltrane won his first *Down Beat* poll for best tenor soloist, an honor he would receive five more times before he died.

Mounting Controversy

In mid 1961 Coltrane signed a five-year contract with **Impulse!,** a new jazz label that would especially foster the avant garde (see "Record Labels: Impulse!"). As one sign of Coltrane's new celebrity status, Impulse! gave him a hefty $50,000 advance (spread over five years). Despite his strong independence as a soloist, Coltrane yearned to play with other saxophonists. For his first few albums with Impulse he asked his good friend reedman **Eric Dolphy** (1928–1964) to join his band, initiating a collaboration that would last intermittently until Dolphy's untimely death of a heart attack in June 1964.

Dolphy, who played bass clarinet on Ornette Coleman's groundbreaking album, *Free Jazz,* inspired Coltrane to probe the avant garde more deeply—to the dismay of some critics. In November 1961, a *Down Beat* critic denounced a performance of Coltrane's group at the Renaissance Club in Hollywood: "I listened to a horrifying demonstration of what appears to be a growing anti-jazz

Record Labels

IMPULSE!

The most important jazz record label of the sixties, Impulse! Records, began as a subsidiary of ABC/Paramount in 1960. The following year the company hired Bob Thiele to replace the original producer, Creed Taylor, and assured its future by signing John Coltrane to its fledgling roster of artists. Together with Blue Note engineer Rudy Van Gelder, Thiele began recording some of the most exciting and progressive jazz of the day, living up to its house motto: "The New Wave in Jazz." Over the next five years the company released over 100 albums.

In addition to Coltrane, Impulse! recorded avant-garde players Cecil Taylor, Albert Ayler, Archie Shepp, and Pharoah Sanders, as well as mainstream boppers (or postboppers) like Charles Mingus, Freddie Hubbard, Curtis Fuller, Oliver Nelson, and McCoy Tyner. To make plain its commitment to quality, the label took care to produce albums with a handsome and distinctive appearance, featuring "gatefold" (double-spread) jackets and spare artwork in modernistic rectangular blocks. After Coltrane died and jazz itself began to dissipate in 1967, Impulse! declined as well. By the mid-seventies the company had ceased activity, but it was revived a decade later and continues to record in this second incarnation today. ■ ■ ■

trend exemplified by these foremost proponents of what is termed avant-garde music. I heard a good rhythm section . . . go to waste behind the nihilistic exercises of the two horns. . . . Coltrane and Dolphy seem bent on deliberately destroying [swing]. . . . They seem bent on pursuing an anarchistic course in music that can but be termed anti-jazz."

The cry of "anti-jazz" was taken up by other conservative critics who wanted to justify their antipathy to the latest Coltrane. But Coltrane had not abandoned tonality, meter, or swing. He was, however, playing ever longer and more furious solos—above an hour long in some cases—over static modal vamps, that is, without chord progressions. Critics chastened him for not "editing" his solos. Club listeners responded in divergent ways. One recalled hearing one of Coltrane's marathon solos live as a cathartic experience: "The feelings it engendered were closer to the awe one felt for a volcano or a mind-boggling religious revelation. My body felt exhilaration, transport, even as much as my mind and spirit." His female companion, however, reacted very differently: "It was like a total assault on all my senses, like being raped by music." Tenor player Archie Shepp considered Coltrane's expanded dimensions to be "his big breakthrough" and greatest contribution to jazz aesthetics. As Coltrane himself explained it, the length was a necessary part of his search. "You just keep going," he said. "You keep trying to get right down to the crux." More simply, "It seems like it does me a lot of good to play until I don't feel like playing anymore."

A Love Supreme

In the early sixties Coltrane fashioned his lifestyle in accordance with his musical/spiritual quest. He became a vegetarian, practiced yoga, and read constantly from the sacred books of the world, including the Bible, the Torah, the Koran, the Kabbalah, and the Bhagavad Gita. He avidly read the scientific writings of his idol, Albert Einstein, but he also put faith in astrology. Based on the ominous message of his astrological chart, he accurately foretold, "I won't live to be old."

In December 1964 Coltrane took his quartet into the studio and made what many critics consider his greatest album, *A Love Supreme.* The liner notes, written by Coltrane, explain that the entire album is a thankful tribute to God: "Dear Listener: ALL PRAISE BE TO GOD TO WHOM ALL PRAISE IS DUE. Let us pursue him in the righteous path. Yes, it is true; 'seek and ye shall find.' Only through Him can we know the most wondrous bequeathal. . . . This album is a humble offering to Him. An attempt to say 'THANK YOU GOD' through our work, even as we do in our hearts and with our tongues. May He help and strengthen all men in every worthy endeavor."

The album is divided into four parts presumably corresponding to Coltrane's own spiritual journey: "Acknowledgement," "Resolution," "Pursuance," and "Psalm." The playing of the quartet is ferocious in its intensity and stunning in its beauty. Primarily organized around vast modal plateaus, the music progresses from the bright illumination of the Latin-flavored "Acknowledgement" to the determined swing of "Resolution" to the exhilarating flight of "Pursuance" to the reverent gratitude of "Psalm."

Total Freedom

In March 1965, LeRoi Jones organized an avant-garde concert called **New Black Music.** To widespread surprise, the young Turks on the program were joined by the most progressive of the bop veterans, John Coltrane. Rather than view him as

JOHN COLTRANE QUARTET, *"Resolution"* (1964)

The second part of *A Love Supreme,* "Resolution" is a hard-swinging composition that the quartet had played several times in live performance before recording it in the studio. This particular recording represents the last of seven *takes* (including false starts). The form is that of an eight-bar blues in the minor mode (i.e., a twelve-bar blues without the middle phrase). The performance opens with Jimmy Garrison playing an unaccompanied bass solo almost entirely in *double-stops* (playing two notes at a time). Then Coltrane roars in with the head, which consists of three chorus-length statements of a descending exclamatory melody, each with a slightly different ending.

During the solos the band does not obscure the form the way the Miles Davis Quintet does in "Ginger Bread Boy." But Coltrane and his men use in abundance what jazz theorists call *tension-building devices.* In the first extended solo, pianist McCoy Tyner generates tremendous energy, pounding out driving lines in the right hand, *quartal* harmonies in the left, and a recurring open fifth in the low register—a trademark of his that appears with increasing frequency through the course of the solo. Near the end of his solo Tyner sets up a syncopated *two-against-three* rhythmic pattern (also known as *hemiola*) that lasts for three full choruses. The two-handed chords he plays to this pattern are *outside* chords.

In the second chorus of his first solo, Coltrane likewise plays *outside* figures; he also "breaks up the time," emphasizing random places in the measure that do not always correspond to the underlying meter. In his extended solo Coltrane repeatedly steps outside the tonality to explore other keys, however briefly. Like Tyner, he develops motives and patterns through repetition (e.g., see crying figures #1 and #2) both to impart coherence to his solo and to generate tension. One gets a sense in this solo of the kind of ecstatic expression that listeners must have heard in his live performances.

an outdated fuddy-duddy, the young tenor players considered Coltrane to be a shamanlike role model. The rhythmic and sonorous violence as well as the ecstatic length of his playing in the early sixties had inspired free-leaning tenor saxophonists to push the limits of their idioms. By 1965 many had surpassed Coltrane in the "freedom" of their conceptions but not in the mastery of their materials. They revered him for his total commitment to the principle of musical (and spiritual) evolution and for the overwhelming emotional impact his music had on audiences. For his part, Coltrane admired the young players for the audacity of their technical experimentation.

Two rising tenor players at the New Black Music concert would have a particularly strong influence on Coltrane: **Albert Ayler** (1936–1970) and **Archie Shepp** (b. 1937). Both musicians were practitioners of energy jazz who learned their craft playing with Cecil Taylor. Ayler developed an approach in which individual notes were sometimes indistinguishable, producing a holistic and continuous saxophone sound. In place of discrete motives and phrases, Ayler played sweeping cascades of shrieks, honks, and wails. "It's not about notes anymore," he said, suggesting that the proper domain of jazz was now pure sound. In one sense this style reflected Ayler's pop music beginnings as a "honking" tenor in R&B bands. But, in another, it represented the most uncompromising manifestation of free jazz. Ayler remained an enigmatic figure to the end of his short life: in 1970 his body was found in the East River; the cause of death has never been determined.

LISTENING CHART 27

John Coltrane Quartet, "Resolution" (Coltrane)

CD 3 / Tracks 1–6

RECORDED 9 DECEMBER 1964, ENGLEWOOD CLIFFS, NEW JERSEY / *A LOVE SUPREME* IMPULSE! GRD-155

John Coltrane (tenor saxophone), McCoy Tyner (piano), Jimmy Garrison (bass), Elvin Jones (drums)

Style: Postbop/modal jazz   Form: 8-bar (minor) blues

			Introduction: Bass solo (Jimmy Garrison)
1	0:00	16 bars	Jimmy Garrison plays halting solo in *double-stops*
			Head
2	0:21	*1st Chorus* (8)	John Coltrane (tenor saxophone) plays head; bass plays octave pedal points; drums play embellished accompaniment
	0:31	*2nd Chorus* (8)	*Repeated*
	0:42	*3rd Chorus* (8)	*Repeated*
			Tenor saxophone solo: John Coltrane
	0:53	*4th Chorus* (8)	As Coltrane begins to solo, the bass walks and the drums settle into a hard-swinging groove
3	1:04	*5th Chorus* (8)	. . . Coltrane plays *outside,* moving short angular motives around among various key centers; breaks up the time
			Head
	1:15	*6th Chorus* (8)	Return to the head and rhythm section accompaniment of the beginning
	1:26	*7th Chorus* (8)	*Repeated*
	1:37	*8th Chorus* (8)	*Repeated*
			Piano solo: McCoy Tyner (twelve choruses)
4	1:48	*9th Chorus* (8)	Tyner plays a fiery solo; notice the *quartal* harmonies in the left hand and sporadically repeated open fifth in the low register
	1:59	*10th Chorus* (8)	
	2:10	*11th Chorus* (8)	
	2:21	*12th Chorus* (8), etc.	
5	3:27		. . . sets up 2 against 3 syncopation (*hemiola*) with two-handed *outside* chords; the pattern lasts for three choruses

**Tenor saxophone solo: John Coltrane
(fourteen choruses)**

6	3:59	*21st Chorus* (8), etc.	Coltrane plays probing solo rich with sonorous intensity
	4:31		. . . develops crying figure #1 in upper register . . .
	5:03		. . . plays *outside*, repositioning short motive in various key centers . . .
	5:35		. . . develops crying figure #2 in upper register . . .

Head

	6:28	*35th Chorus* (8)	Coltrane plays head as in the beginning
	6:39	*36th Chorus* (8)	*Repeated*
	6:50	*37th Chorus* (8)	*Repeated*

Coda

| | 7:01 | | Coltrane repeats and extends last figure of the head |

Coltrane formed a close relationship with Archie Shepp. Shepp, a communist and avant-garde playwright as well as a musician, was perhaps the most outspoken free jazz player on political matters. For Shepp, the avant garde was the musical embodiment of the teachings of Malcolm X and the black power movement. The screaming paroxysms of Ayler, which Shepp also cultivated in his own playing, bespoke the rage of blacks over persistent, systematic racism in the country. Coltrane, of course, was the original "angry tenor" in the minds of some critics. As early as 1958 he had had to defend himself against this charge: "If [my music] is interpreted as angry, it is taken wrong. The only one I'm angry at is myself when I don't make what I'm trying to play." Nor had his mood changed with the upheavals of the sixties. Coltrane's attraction to the music of Ayler and Shepp was musical and spiritual and had nothing to do with anger. "I think what [Ayler's] doing," he said, "it seems to be moving music into even higher frequencies . . . he filled an area it seems I hadn't got to."

Coltrane eased into the pool of the radical avant garde gradually. At first he invited players like Ayler, Shepp, and another like-minded tenor, **Pharoah Sanders** (b. 1940), to sit in with his quartet during nightclub sets. Then in June of 1965, Coltrane recorded *Ascension*, a watershed album marking his unqualified embrace of radical free jazz. Based to some degree on Ornette Coleman's *Free Jazz*, this album alternates collective improvisation with solos in an atonal, ametrical context. In addition to his classic quartet, Coltrane added two trumpets, two altos, two more tenors (Shepp and Sanders), and an extra bass player. The resulting cacophony ignited the fiercest controversy of Coltrane's already controversial

John Coltrane.

Great Debates

THREE PERSPECTIVES ON COLTRANE'S LAST YEARS

The most controversial part of John Coltrane's career was his total embrace of radical free jazz in the last few years of his life. In the September 2002 issue of *JazzTimes*, three distinguished critics weigh in on the matter. Stanley Crouch, in keeping with his traditionalist perspective, argues that the stylistic shift launched by *Ascension* was a big mistake. Considering swing, the blues, ballads, and Afro-Latin rhythms to be "the essential elements of jazz," Crouch writes that Coltrane "turned his back" on jazz after 1965. Further, he played "emotionally narrow" and "largely one-dimensional" music even on its own terms. Crouch speculates that "few professionals want to say publicly what they really think" of Coltrane and his late music.

Gary Giddins is perhaps one of those few willing to speak his mind. In defending Coltrane's foray into the avant garde, Giddins marshals not rational arguments but personal testimony. He tells of hearing Coltrane's late albums, when they first came out, while living as a young freshman college student in southern France. Giddins and his friends responded to *Ascension* with humility borne of respect for Coltrane. "We might have loathed [the record] . . . , but we would never have simply dismissed it," he recalls. And yet he did not loathe *Ascension,* either then or now: "I love it, both takes, and, in those days, played it so often that now it has a ring of nostalgic familiarity." Giddins sees Coltrane's music as an ongoing "adventure," and his most difficult works as a stimulating "challenge" for the listener.

Nat Hentoff, a veteran jazz critic who knew Coltrane well, takes an entirely different approach. From many long discussions with Coltrane, Hentoff concludes that "his reason for being in music . . . was to become part of the source of consciousness from the beginning of time. . . . He wanted to connect, to enter into, that universal, transcendent peace. To keep trying to get there, he, through his music, had to continue to search deeper and deeper into himself and exorcise his own dissonances, his own demons—as you can hear in 'Ascension,' among others of his later recordings." Though he does not say it, Hentoff seems to imply that Coltrane's late music might sound different if one viewed it as Coltrane himself did—as part of his intense spiritual quest. ■ ■ ■

career. "This is possibly the most powerful human sound ever recorded," began one *Down Beat* review of the album. But many formerly loyal Coltrane fans found it necessary to forsake him after *Ascension.* His friend and admirer Ravi Shankar expressed puzzlement that Coltrane, a person so devoted to spiritual enlightenment, could produce a music in which Shankar "still heard much turmoil." Even his sidemen struggled with the change. By December McCoy Tyner could take it no longer and left the band; Elvin Jones followed in January.

When Coltrane died of liver cancer at the age of forty, his spiritual commitment and saintly character rapidly became the stuff of legend. One writer confessed in 1970, "I am not a religious person, but John Coltrane was the one man whom I worshipped as a saint or even a god." The following year Bishop F. W. King founded in San Francisco the St. John Coltrane African Orthodox Church, a body of Christian believers, still active today, whose liturgy is based on *A Love Supreme.* Jazz musicians, meanwhile, have spent the last forty years supping from the bounteous table laid out by Coltrane.

Modern Big Bands and Male Singers

Chapter **25**

A powerful dimension of the much-discussed generation gap of the 1960s was musical. With rock and (in far fewer numbers) free jazz capturing the politically conscious youth market, mainstream jazz appealed primarily to middle-aged and older listeners—the same ones, essentially, who had followed jazz in previous decades. Appalled by their teenagers' musical tastes—the Beatles and Rolling Stones on one hand, Ornette Coleman and Cecil Taylor on the other—parents longed for the sweet and swinging big band music of their youth. In view of their grievance, it seems poetically just that big bands made a comeback in the sixties. Yet these were not the big bands of old; most of them had assimilated all the developments of modern jazz, even including, in some cases, the avant garde.

As in the thirties, modern big bands often accompanied singers. Ella Fitzgerald, Sarah Vaughan, and other veteran female singers profited from the big band renaissance. But in a marked change from the Swing Era, now male jazz singers had come into their own. Starting in the 1950s Frank Sinatra, Joe Williams, Mel Tormé, Tony Bennett, and others began building reputations for singing with as much swing, sass, and pathos as any of the great female jazz vocalists who had preceded them. In the 1960s and 1970s these figures often struggled for success against the tide of rock. But they found acceptance in Las Vegas, a town that may have lacked the artistic sophistication of a place like New York but was surely unrivaled in its commitment to good old-fashioned entertainment.

Big Bands after World War II

As times and tastes changed after World War II, many of the great swing bands eventually folded. The bands of Jimmie Lunceford and Fletcher Henderson died with the passing of their leaders in 1947 and 1952, respectively. Benny Goodman stopped leading a big band in 1949 and spent the rest of his career performing as a single. Charlie Barnet disbanded permanently in the same year. Artie Shaw, after several previous retirements, left music for good in 1954 to write books.

Other swing bandleaders soldiered on through the fifties and beyond. Duke Ellington and Count Basie not only survived, they continued to evolve musically and (after some lean times in the early 1950s) to prosper financially. In 1955 sweet bandleader Lawrence Welk began hosting his own television show, a highly successful program that became a bastion of nostalgia for Depression-era audiences. Tommy and Jimmy Dorsey reunited around the same time to host their own TV show. After Tommy died in 1956, the show was canceled, but the Dorsey legacy lived on through a permanent Tommy Dorsey memorial band organized to tour the country playing Dorsey's most beloved hits in vintage style. Similar **ghost bands** devoted to the music of Glenn Miller and other deceased swing legends also came into existence in the fifties; some—including those of Dorsey and Miller—are still touring today.

With a few exceptions (notably Ellington and Basie), these relics of the Swing Era did little more than recycle their old music for nostalgic listeners. But a forward-looking and even experimental big band tradition did arise in the late forties. We have already mentioned Billy Eckstine's and Dizzy Gillespie's pioneering bop big bands. In addition to these, swing bandleader **Woody Herman** (1913–1987) organized his First Herd, an exciting, brass-heavy group, and in 1947, his saxophone-based Second Herd. Both bands incorporated the latest bebop innovations. One important center of modern big band developments was Los Angeles. The LA tradition began with the ambitious (and some would say, pretentious) music of pianist **Stan Kenton** (1912–1979). Kenton produced a big, loud, and complex big band sound that made full use of modern developments in both jazz and classical realms. A shrewd marketing strategist, Kenton termed his music "progressive jazz" to distinguish himself from his swing predecessors. Nearly every prominent West Coast (white) player and most of the jazz-oriented Hollywood composers of the fifties worked for Kenton at one time or another. Kenton's lead trumpet player, **Maynard Ferguson** (b. 1928), left the band in 1953 to play in the Los Angeles studios; in 1957 he formed his own big band. Ferguson, who specialized in bebop trumpet solos in the extreme upper register, continued the "high-octane" big band style favored by Herman and Kenton.

Further Listening from the *Prentice Hall Jazz Collection*
Track 5: Jimmy Giuffre, "Four Brothers" (1947), featuring Woody Herman's Thundering Herd

The Sixties Revival

In 1966, *Down Beat* noted that "Ellington, Basie, Herman (and on and off, [Lionel] Hampton and Kenton) notwithstanding, few jazz-oriented big bands have thrived during the last two decades, and none that has emerged has been able to survive." Though many regarded big band jazz as a dead genre, it was actually not so much dead as underground. Ever since the Swing Era, musicians had gotten together informally to play in **rehearsal bands,** groups organized not to perform publicly, nor to record, but to play for the sheer joy of it. For years devoted souls led New York rehearsal bands in the quixotic hope of someday finding an audience. In the mid-sixties, one especially distinguished rehearsal band realized that hope.

ghost band a touring band maintained to perpetuate the music and memory of a deceased bandleader of the Swing Era.

rehearsal band a band organized not to perform or record, but to play in private settings simply for the pleasure of playing.

Thad Jones-Mel Lewis Big Band

The origins of the **Thad Jones-Mel Lewis Big Band** can be traced back to July 1955. One night, at a gig in Detroit, Stan Kenton and Count Basie faced off in a "battle of the bands." Between sets, Kenton's drummer, **Mel Lewis** (1929–1990), and one of Basie's trumpet players, **Thad Jones** (1923–1986), got into a conversation about forming a band together. Lewis was a West Coast musician and Jones was an eastern player, the older brother of Elvin Jones. In the early sixties they revisited the idea while playing together in Gerry Mulligan's band.

Then in late 1965, perhaps in exasperated response to British invasion and free jazz, Jones and Lewis finally carried out their plans. "Mel and I made a few phone calls to some of our friends," Jones said. "They called some of their friends, a chain phone call thing, and we ended up with more than we had bargained for. And they *all* showed up, plus some who just heard about the gig." The "friends" were all top professionals who worked in the studios during the day, often in the NBC Tonight Show Orchestra, and played jazz at night for fun. Unlike studios in the thirties, the studios by this time were completely integrated. Jones and Lewis's rehearsal band thus demonstrated a model of racial harmony at the height of the civil rights movement. The band, an ensemble of eighteen, played primarily Jones's highly original compositions; Jones played flugelhorn solos on ballads and Lewis played drums.

Through the intermediary of a local disc jockey, the band—then known simply as "the Jazz Band"—was booked for four Monday evenings in December at the Village Vanguard. The packed audiences responded so enthusiastically that the club's owner made the band a permanent feature on Mondays. In March the band played an entire week at the Vanguard, performed its first concert (at Hunter College), and followed up with a benefit at Town Hall. The following month a *Down Beat* article called "The Big Bands: In New York . . . Signs of Life" focused particularly on the surprising emergence and success of the Jones-Lewis group. As quoted in the article, the co-leaders were ecstatic. "It's fantastic," said Jones. "I'm thinking about nothing else but this band." Lewis added, "This is a joyful band. We're having a good time on the stand—that's what has been missing on the [jazz] scene. . . . If we can keep rolling now, I think it will last for a long time."

In a 1971 review of *Consummation,* an outstanding album the band made for Blue Note, a *Down Beat* writer gave the maximum five stars, exclaiming, "I can't conceive of a big band playing much better than this." This assessment might stand as the received opinion even today. From its inception, the band continued as a part-time labor of love until 1979, when Jones moved to Denmark; Lewis then became sole leader until his death in 1990. (For an example of the Jones-Lewis band, see CD 3/Track 14: Joe Williams with the Thad Jones-Mel Lewis Big Band, "Woman's Got Soul.")

Other Big Bands of the New Generation

The enthusiasm that greeted the Thad Jones-Mel Lewis Big Band encouraged others to form bands as well. **Buddy Rich** (1917–1987), a swing veteran and powerhouse drummer, started his own big band in 1966. Through such records as *The Roar of '74* (1974) he came to epitomize an aggressive, hard-swinging idiom of fleet saxophones and scorching brass. In the early 1970s, Maynard Ferguson reconstituted his own big band with a similarly muscular emphasis. Some critics accused Ferguson of straying into the realm of hype, producing music that was "higher, faster, louder," but not necessarily better. But the sheer excitement of his screaming trumpets on albums like *Chameleon* (1973) drew large and enthusiastic audiences.

Toshiko Akiyoshi-Lew
Tabackin Big Band.

In 1973 a rehearsal band arose in Los Angeles that represented the West Coast response to Jones and Lewis. Pianist-composer **Toshiko Akiyoshi** (b. 1929) and her tenor-playing husband, **Lew Tabackin** (b. 1940) gathered together some of the best musicians in the LA studios and organized the **Toshiko Akiyoshi-Lew Tabackin Big Band.** Admiring critics immediately hailed the band as another high point in the continually unfolding big band renaissance. Akiyoshi, who grew up in China but relocated to Japan after World War II, brought a refreshingly "Eastern" quality to her compositions. She wedded jazz rhythm with melodies, harmonies, and voicings from traditional Japanese music. In the sixties Tabackin had played with both the Jones-Lewis band and Maynard Ferguson. With his own band he played husky tenor solos inspired by Ben Webster and Sonny Rollins, and flute solos that show the influence of his wife's Asian heritage. The band lasted until 1982, after which time Akiyoshi became the sole leader with Tabackin participating occasionally as guest soloist.

Male Singers

During the Swing Era, as we have seen, it was primarily women who established the conventions of jazz vocal style. After World War II, however, male vocalists began making their own contributions. Perhaps the testosterone-rich music of modern big bands prompted a sympathetic response from male singers. Their increasing importance in jazz corresponded with the rise of Las Vegas as the country's premier center for gambling and spectacular nightime entertainment.

TOSHIKO AKIYOSHI

Reflects on Her Unusual Place in the Jazz Tradition—c. 1975

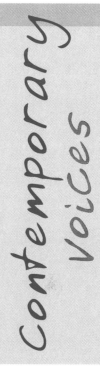

Contemporary Voices

The most important developmental years in anyone's life are, I think, between sixteen and twenty-five. That is the time that your character is built, when what you are as a human being is defined. My whole life was jazz during those years, so I really became an adult through jazz music. To me, jazz is mine. I can't pretend that it's someone else's music, or that I just play it because I love it—I can't separate myself from it at all.

And yet, I realize that jazz is purely American music, and since I am Japanese, what is my position in the jazz world? I've heard a lot of black musicians say that white musicians took their music and profited from it, leaving them with nothing. . . . I feel I'm involved in that, too. Am I an invader, too? Am I taking from jazz and giving nothing back? The only way I am able to resolve this dilemma is to give what I am back to jazz by composing. If I have developed my music to the point where a listener can sense my attitudes—this is, my history as it reflects Japan and as it reflects what I've learned of America in the past twenty years—if the listener can hear my history and my individuality, then I have accomplished the solution.

Composer's note, "Road Time Shuffle," conductor's score (Delevan, New York: Kendor Music, 1977).

THE TOSHIKO AKIYOSHI-LEW TABACKIN BIG BAND, *"Road Time Shuffle"* (1976)

As one writer put it, Toshiko Akiyoshi composed "Road Time Shuffle" "in celebration of the orchestra's precedent-setting trip to Japan in 1976." This live recording was made during that tour. (One can hear the enthusiastic audience clapping to the beat in the background.) A *shuffle* is a piece in which the drums (and possibly other instruments) overtly state the swing eighth notes in a continuous (eight-to-the-bar) *chunKA-chunKA-chunKA-chunKA* pattern. In "Road Time Shuffle" the shuffle rhythm is articulated by the trombones and piano in addition to the drums.

The piece is in ABAC song form. Two saxophonists—altoist Dick Spencer and tenorist and co-leader Lew Tabackin—play powerhouse solos, as if trying to match the entire ensemble in the forcefulness of their expression. Akiyoshi's ingenuity as a composer appears throughout, but especially in the *soli* for mixed woodwinds and trombone in the fourth chorus. She voices this group, which includes flute, piccolo, and three kinds of clarinets, in such a way as to reveal her Japanese heritage. This piece also reflects the expanded ranges and greater power of big band trumpet players of the postwar era. During the third chorus and again in the coda, Akiyoshi calls for wide upper-register *shakes* in the trumpet section. (Compare these high, sliding shakes with the more modest and choppy shakes of Benny Goodman's 1938 trumpet section on "Don't Be That Way" [CD 1/Track 71/3:06].) On the lead trumpet part she twice wrote the word, "scream," indicating a freely sliding effect up in the region of high F, G, and beyond.

LISTENING CHART 28

Toshiko Akiyoshi-Lew Tabackin Big Band, "Road Time Shuffle" (Akiyoshi)

CD 3 / Tracks 7–13

RECORDED 1976, LIVE IN JAPAN / COLLECTION: THE TOSHIKO AKIYOSHI-LEW TABACKIN BIG BAND: NOVUS SERIES '70 RCA 3106-2-N

Steve Huffstetter, Bobby Shew, Richard Cooper, Mike Price (trumpet), Bill Reichenbach, Jim Sawyer, Jimmy Knepper (trombone), Phil Teele (bass trombone), Dick Spencer (alto saxophone, flute), Gary Foster (alto saxophone, B-flat clarinet), Lew Tabackin (tenor saxophone, flute, piccolo), Tom Peterson (tenor saxophone, E-flat alto clarinet), Bill Byrne (baritone saxophone, B-flat bass clarinet), Toshiko Akiyoshi (piano, composer), Don Baldwin (bass), Peter Donald (drums)

Style: Modern big band; shuffle | **Form:** ABAC song form

			Introduction
7	0:00	1 bar	One-bar introductory break features a wailing Dick Spencer on alto saxophone
		1st Chorus	**Melody**
	0:02	A (8)	Saxophones play unison melody to shuffle rhythm in trombones, piano, drums
	0:17	B (8)	Alto saxophone solo: Dick Spencer
	0:33	A (8)	Saxophones play melody as before . . .
	0:49	C (8)	Spencer solos again . . .
			Interlude
	1:04	4 bars	Full ensemble shouts brief interlude
		2nd Chorus	**Alto saxophone solo: Dick Spencer**
8	1:12	A (8)	Spencer now offers a fuller solo statement, while band supplies shuffle-rhythm background figures
	1:27	B (8)	
	1:43	A (8)	
	1:58	C (8)	
		3rd Chorus	**Ensemble chorus**
9	2:14	A (8)	Full band plays *soli* homophonically . . .
	2:29	B (8)	

10	2:45	A (8)	Ensemble breaks up, trading brief motive among various instruments and registers; notice the wide *shakes* in the trumpets (and the lead trumpet's screaming high A at the end of the phrase)
	3:00	C (8)	Call-and-response: trumpets vs. saxophones/trombones
	4th Chorus		**Woodwind/trombone soli**
11	3:15	A (8)	Heterogeneous group: 2 flutes, B-flat clarinet, E-flat alto clarinet, B-flat bass clarinet, trombone
	3:31	B (8)	
	3:47	A (8)	(Second flute switches to piccolo)
	4:03	C (8)	
	5th Chorus		**Tenor saxophone solo: Lew Tabackin**
12	4:19	A (8)	Husky and full-throated, Tabackin closes out the performance with a masterful chorus . . .
	4:35	B (8)	
	4:50	A (8)	
	5:06	C (8)	. . . ensemble becomes increasingly prominent behind Tabackin
			Coda
13	5:21	C′ (16)	Full band recapitulates last C-section and adds a call-and-response between brass and woodwinds; this coda features plenty of trumpet *shakes* and other high-note pyrotechnics

The future of Las Vegas was determined in 1946, when mobster Bugsy Siegel opened the Flamingo Hotel, the first gambling casino on the Strip. Under the direction of the Mafia, similar establishments sprouted up throughout the fifties. Along the way, Las Vegas became a glamorous, fast-living town, attracting thousands of tourists from all over the country. All the big casinos sponsored live entertainment, complete with singers, dancers, and showbands. By the early sixties Vegas hotels and casinos were a booming industry.

Although Vegas hardly subscribed to the modern ideal of jazz for jazz's sake, the city's showbands required players fluent in mainstream idioms. In the sixties and seventies Vegas drew many jazz musicians to its secure job market, including Basie saxophonist Eddie "Lockjaw" Davis and Gillespie reedman James Moody. A few surviving swing bands played lengthy stints there;

Harry James, for instance, spent six months a year in Vegas in the early seventies. But singers, who suffered most directly from competition with rock, had the most to gain in Vegas. With its ethos of high-rolling, hard-drinking, and womanizing, Vegas was a man's town known for its beautiful showgirls and fabulous male singers: Johnny Mathis, Robert Goulet, Wayne Newton, Elvis Presley, Tom Jones, Engelbert Humperdinck, Harry Belafonte, the list goes on. Most of these were pop singers, but some performed jazz, including four of the greatest male jazz singers of the period—Frank Sinatra, Joe Williams, Mel Tormé, and Tony Bennett. As Bennett succinctly put it, "By the late sixties all the action [for vocalists] had moved to Vegas."

Frank Sinatra

Often viewed as an icon of popular culture, **Frank Sinatra** (1915–1998) is also regarded by many critics as one of the greatest jazz singers. Born and raised in an Italian immigrant family in Hoboken, New Jersey, Sinatra grew up listening to Italian opera in addition to the normal popular fare. Operatic tenors sang in *bel canto* style—a nineteenth-century romantic idiom from which Sinatra would derive, in the words of one authority, "his legato attack . . . his handling of portamento and rubato, and his sensitive modulation of vowel sounds."

Sinatra began his career singing for Harry James and Tommy Dorsey in the late thirties. He became a teen idol to the bobbysoxers for his tender, crooning performances on such ballads as "I'll Never Smile Again" (1940). But despite an already impressive command of phrasing—learned primarily from Dorsey and Billie Holiday—he did not swing on these early recordings. One would be hard-pressed to call Sinatra a jazz singer in the Swing Era.

After World War II Sinatra initially rode the crest of popularity enjoyed by other pop vocalists, but by the early fifties he had lost his audience. Fortunately, he landed a major acting role in *From Here to Eternity*, which won Best Picture in 1953. His acting success rejuvenated his musical career. He signed a contract with **Capitol Records** and produced a series of highly successful LPs in what was for him a totally new and jazzy style. Accompanied by a studio big band and orchestra playing Nelson Riddle's arrangements, Sinatra swung consummately (though he did not scat). He also perfected a sound and persona that epitomized coolness, confidence, and devil-may-care worldliness.

By the early sixties Sinatra was spending much of his time in Las Vegas. He became the ringleader of a group of entertainer-friends known informally as the Rat Pack. Consisting of Dean Martin, Sammy Davis Jr., Peter Lawford, and Joey Bishop, as well as Sinatra, the Rat Pack became something of an institution in Vegas, where they performed frequently at the Sands Hotel. They shared (or at least projected) a worldview centered on drinking, gambling, and sexual promiscuity. Some of those who knew Sinatra believe that the jolly camraderie of the Rat Pack masked a profound loneliness. Be that as it may, his music of this period undeniably transported his audiences to a realm of pure romantic fantasy—a fantasy of true twenty-four-karat love that momentarily transcended all the sordid realities of Las Vegas nightlife. Today's listeners can enjoy this experience through *Sinatra at the Sands: with Count Basie & the Orchestra* (1965), one of the great live albums of the sixties. On songs like "Come Fly with Me" and "I've Got You Under My Skin," Sinatra powerfully celebrates the exhilaration—and illusion—of romantic love in first blush.

Joe Williams

If Sinatra drew inspiration from Italian *bel canto,* **Joe Williams** (1918–1999) built his style on the blues. Born and raised in Cordele, Georgia, Williams was thirty-five years old before he got his big break: in 1954 he joined Count Basie, replacing long-time Basie singer, Jimmy Rushing. Williams immediately galvanized the Basie band, then on the verge of a comeback that would gather increasing strength in years to come. Williams, a rich, full-throated bass, sang the blues with great authority. In 1955 he made an album with Basie called *Count Basie Swings—Joe Williams Sings* that became widely popular, especially for Williams's "Everyday I Have the Blues." Williams welcomed the acclaim for his blues singing, but wanted greater expressive range. It took several years to convince critics that he could sing ballads.

In 1960 Williams left Basie to start his solo career. Reviewing a live recording of one of Williams's Birdland engagements, a *New York Times* critic praised his ballad singing and continued: "He swings overtly, too, and much more effectively than he did with Basie. He seems to have come through a period of adjustment that he was caught in when he left the surroundings of a big band and had to create his own momentum. And he has emerged on this disc, as he is in person, as one of the more forcefully communicative singers to be heard today." Accompanied by a small band led by Basie trumpeter Harry "Sweets" Edison, Williams continued to build his reputation. When Thad Jones and Mel Lewis looked around for a singer to record with their big band, Williams was the obvious choice. In 1966, with Jones and Lewis, Williams recorded *Presenting Joe Williams and Thad Jones Mel Lewis: The Jazz Orchestra.* On tunes like "Woman's Got Soul" and "Get Out of My Life," Williams projects his characteristic mix of funky, down-home vocals and warm, charismatic personality. The Jones-Lewis band, meanwhile, provide superb backgrounds in arrangements by Jones.

Joe Williams, 1961.

JOE WILLIAMS WITH THE THAD JONES-MEL LEWIS ORCHESTRA, *"Woman's Got Soul"* (1966)

CD 3 / Track 14

Like "Road Time Shuffle," this piece is also a shuffle. "Woman's Got Soul" was composed by the great R&B singer and guitarist Curtis Mayfield, and arranged for the Thad Jones-Mel Lewis Orchestra by Jones. The appropriating of this sort of R&B material by a jazz band allies the piece (conceptually, at least) with the soul jazz movement, a topic we take up in Chapter 26. At any rate, "Woman's Got Soul" is *soulful,* especially in the hands of consummate blues singer Joe Williams and the impeccable Jones-Lewis Orchestra. Mayfield's lyrics pay tribute to that rare individual—a woman with "soul," a value mixing hipness, authenticity, and decency, and one cherished above all within the black community in the late 1960s. Williams sings the words with down-home conviction, underscoring the song's timeless message that it's the inside and not the outside of a person that counts. Meanwhile, the Jones-Lewis men wail out sympathetic solo obbligatos and groovy background figures, as if shouting "Amen!" to Williams's impassioned secular sermon.

Create your own listening chart (CD 3 / Track 14)

In 1968 Williams moved to Las Vegas, where he would live and perform for the rest of his life. At the 1974 Newport Jazz Festival (held by this time in New York City) he reunited with the Basie band for an electrifying performance. According to one reporter, "The most powerful catalyst of the evening was Joe Williams. . . . Reunited with the Basie band, singing some of the blues he had once sung along with other things that have become part of his repertoire since he has been working as a single, Mr. Williams built up a long, utterly triumphant performance that was a masterpiece of pacing, projection, and a fascinatingly winning personality." By this time Williams had long since transcended his journeyman period to become, with Sinatra, one of the leading male jazz singers of the late twentieth century.

Bossa Nova and Soul Jazz

Chapter **26**

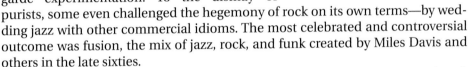

As we have seen, jazz musicians in the sixties responded to the juggernaut of rock in a variety of ways. Some fled to Europe or Las Vegas, some stoically persisted in playing mainstream jazz, some withdrew into an anticommercial sphere of avantgarde experimentation. To the dismay of purists, some even challenged the hegemony of rock on its own terms—by wedding jazz with other commercial idioms. The most celebrated and controversial outcome was fusion, the mix of jazz, rock, and funk created by Miles Davis and others in the late sixties.

Two previous attempts at musical alchemy, however, laid the groundwork for fusion. Both grew out of musical developments of the fifties. Cool jazz musicians borrowed popular dance rhythms from Brazil to produce a soft, sensuous music that especially appealed to white audiences. At the same time, hard bop players dug deeper into soul music and gospel, the favored genres in the black community, to expand their own listening base. The results, bossa nova and soul jazz, forever broadened the potential rhythmic character of jazz.

Latin Jazz before the Sixties

Latin-American influences on jazz are as old as jazz itself. Jelly Roll Morton insisted—and scholars have confirmed his claim—that New Orleans jazz depended heavily on a "Spanish tinge" brought from the Caribbean. Social dances from the Southern Hemisphere reached the United States early on. During World War I Vernon and Irene Castle helped popularize the Argentine **tango** and the Brazilian maxixe. In 1930 a Cuban dance band in New York introduced the **rhumba,** which became the most popular Latin dance of the decade. Duke Ellington, among others, brought Latin rhythms into jazz with "Caravan" (1936), written by his Puerto Rican trombonist Juan Tizol, and his own "Conga Brava" (1940) (the conga was a bowdlerized version of the rhumba).

Another Cuban dance, the **mambo,** became the key ingredient in modern Latin jazz. The mambo, a hot, energetic idiom, emerged in Havana in the late 1930s. In the early forties a Cuban bandleader named **Machito** (born Francisco Grillo Jr., 1912–1984) organized his seminal mambo band in New York. At the same time, Machito's brother-in-law, trumpeter Mario Bauzá, began playing in Cab Calloway's band. During his stint with Calloway he influenced the young

rhumba a Cuban dance that became popular in the U.S. in the 1930s.

mambo a hot, energetic Cuban dance that became popular in the U.S. during the 1940s.

player sitting next to him, Dizzy Gillespie, to experiment with Cuban rhythms. Gillespie's piece, "Night in Tunisia" (1942), represents one of the first successful hybrids of mambo and bebop. In the white community, meanwhile, Stan Kenton made his recording debut, revealing a strong taste for spicy Latin jazz, including one Afro-Cuban piece.

By the late forties the mambo had found a congenial home in the high-energy music of modern big bands. Gillespie organized his bop big band with a strong Afro-Cuban element: he hired conga player **Chano Pozo** (1915–1948) and, with Pozo, wrote several mambo-based compositions, including "Manteca" and "Tin Tin Deo." Kenton explored Afro-Cuban rhythms with equal enthusiasm. "Rhythmically, the Cubans play the most exciting stuff," he told *Metronome* in 1947. "We won't copy them exactly, but we will copy some of their devices and apply them to what we are trying to do. And while we keep moving toward the Cubans rhythmically, they're moving toward us melodically. We both have a lot to learn."

Despite the popularity in the fifties of yet another Cuban fad dance, the **cha cha cha,** the mambo continued to thrive. Xavier Cugat and Desi Arnaz represented mambo to the masses. Arnaz even played a hot-blooded Cuban band-leader (and loving husband) on the hit television show, *I Love Lucy.* In jazz the now commonplace mix of bebop and mambo was known, as mentioned previously, as "Cubop" (see Chapter 17). In 1956 Kenton recorded *Cuban Fire,* a classic twenty-six minute work in six movements. Percussionist **Tito Puente** (1923–2000) and singer Tito Rodriguez absorbed elements of big band jazz, attracting large numbers to their more "authentic" native Cuban style. They and their followers would epitomize Cuban-based Latin jazz for the next half century.

Bossa Nova

In 1959 the cultural influence of Cuba on the United States waned when Fidel Castro made Cuba a communist state, reigniting Cold War fears and precipitating a series of confrontations with the United States that culminated in the Cuban Missile Crisis in 1962. As Cuban music declined in the United States, Brazilian music arose to take its place. The most popular urban dance of Brazil was the **samba,** a fast dance in duple meter and straight eighth notes used especially during carnival season. Widely heard in Brazil since the 1920s, the samba entered American popular culture via movies and musical theater. Early samba hits in the United States included Vincent Youmans's "Carioca" (1933) and Ary Barroso's "Aquarela do Brasil" (known popularly as "Brazil") (1939).

Bossa nova, a Brazilian term meaning something like "new trend," was essentially a subdued, slowed-down samba with an emphasis on pretty melodies, rich harmonies, and romantic lyrics. The style emerged in the late fifties through the songs of **Antonio Carlos Jobim** (1927–1994), Luis Bonfá, and **João Gilberto** (b. 1931). Jobim, the most celebrated of the three, greatly admired American cool jazz, especially that of Gerry Mulligan. Jobim thought of his own music as uniting cool jazz harmonies with samba rhythms. According to Jobim, the mood of bossa nova was, above all, plaintive: "It is in our music, this sadness of the Africans, the Portuguese, and the Indians. . . . Our music is beautiful because sadness is more beautiful than happiness." In 1958 Jobim and Gilberto made the first bossa nova recordings in Brazil. Bossa nova was introduced to

samba a fast Brazilian dance in duple meter and straight eighth notes used especially during carnival season.

bossa nova a slowed-down samba with cool jazz harmonies and romantic lyrics.

the United States in the following year by the award-winning French and Brazilian film, *Orfeu Negro* (*Black Orpheus*), which featured songs by Jobim and Bonfá.

Stan Getz

The first American jazz musician to experiment with bossa nova was guitarist **Charlie Byrd** (1925–1999). In the spring of 1961 Byrd made a State Department tour of South America, performing in Venezeula, Brazil, Argentina, Paraguay, Chile, and Peru. Of all the indigenous musics he heard on the tour, none impressed him as much as Brazilian bossa nova. He returned to the United States determined to incorporate the new style into his jazz performances. But he could not convince any record companies to take a chance on bossa nova.

Byrd turned to tenor saxophonist **Stan Getz** (1927–1991). Born in Philadelphia and raised in the East Bronx, Getz began his career playing with Stan Kenton. He rose to fame as part of the "Four Brothers" saxophone section (together with Zoot Sims, Herbie Steward, and Serge Chaloff) in Woody Herman's Second Herd (see Chapter 25). In the fifties he emerged as the most distinguished tenor player in the cool orbit. Like many of his peers, he became addicted to heroin and almost ruined his career. Nevertheless, Getz scored high in the polls and earned the respect of a broad cohort of his fellow jazz musicians. By 1961 his opinion carried considerable weight with record executives, and Byrd hoped to benefit from Getz's influence.

Getz himself was scrambling to regain his footing on the shifting terrain of the early 1960s. Ornette Coleman and other free players dominated the press and John Coltrane led the polls for best tenor saxophonist. When Byrd took Getz to lunch and played him tapes of Jobim and Gilberto, Getz heard magic in the Brazilian sounds. Getz contacted Creed Taylor and arranged to make a

Stan Getz and João Gilberto.

bossa nova record with Verve. An initial session went awry when the contracted New York rhythm section failed to comprehend the subtle Brazilian rhythms. Then in early 1962 Getz and Byrd assembled with Byrd's rhythm section in Pierce Hall at the All Souls Unitarian Church in Washington and recorded seven tracks. The resulting album, *Jazz Samba,* sold briskly that summer. By the end of the year Getz had edged out Coltrane for first place in the *Down Beat* poll. In March 1963, *Jazz Samba* rose to first place on the pop charts—the only jazz album ever to do so.

As a follow-up to *Jazz Samba,* Creed Taylor arranged for Stan Getz to record in a more "authentic" rhythmic environment with Jobim, Gilberto, and other Brazilian musicians. The album, *Getz-Gilberto* (1963), featured Jobim's songs, Gilberto's guitar-playing and soft, almost whispered, vocals, and Getz's solos. While rehearsing one day, Getz suggested that Gilberto's wife, Astrud, sing on one of the songs. Astrud, a nonprofessional singer who was present mainly to interpret for the non-English speaking musicians, turned out to have a delicate voice with an entrancing mix of innocence and sensuousness. Over the vigorous objections of João Gilberto and Jobim, Getz saw to it that she sang on most of the cuts on the album. *Getz-Gilberto,* containing such bossa nova classics as "Girl from Ipanema," "Desafinado," and "Corcovado," won a Grammy in 1965 for Album of the Year, and "Girl from Ipanema" was voted Best Single. Astrud went on to become a pop music star.

The Bandwagon

Getz's tremendously successful recordings secured him financially. He used to introduce "Desafinado" as "the tune that's going to put my children through college—all five of them." Not surprisingly, given the unstable jazz economy of the sixties, many other jazz musicians tried to succeed with bossa nova as well. In October 1962, alone, bossa nova albums appeared by two dozen musicians, including Sonny Rollins, Coleman Hawkins, Cal Tjader, Shorty Rogers, and Herbie Mann. Miles Davis collaborated with Gil Evans on their last and weakest

CD 3 / Track 15

Stan Getz-João Gilberto, *"Girl from Ipanema"* (1963)

"Girl from Ipanema" is in AABA song form, with a B-section twice as long as usual: 8 + 8 + 16 + 8. Composed by Jobim, it has come to epitomize bossa nova for many listeners. The medium tempo, undulating rhythms, and soft dynamics of this recording are typical of the idiom. So is the melody, which in the beginning emphasizes *triadic extensions*, the "pretty" notes of the chord that lie a sixth, seventh, or ninth above the *root* (or fundamental pitch upon which the chord is based). The notes of the opening phrase, for example, align with the lyric as follows: "Tall [ninth] and tan [seventh] and [sixth] young [ninth] and lovely [seventh]. . . ." (You can only hear these harmonic relationships once the bass has come in, after the first A-section.) These rich harmonies, together with the multiple layers of gently lilting rhythmic activity, immerse the listener in an ambiance that is part smoldering heat and part exquisite coolness. Getz seems perfectly at home in this world, playing a solo that combines economic restraint with deeply felt lyricism.

Create your own listening chart (CD 3 / Track 15)

joint project, a bossa nova collection entitled *Quiet Nights;* Duke Ellington produced more substantial music in his *Afro-Bossa* (both 1962). Horace Silver wrote a classic bossa with his "Song for My Father" (1964), as did Lee Morgan with his "Ceora" (1965).

But within a short period the market was saturated. In 1963 Mel Tormé praised bossa nova as "the first exciting thing in popular music and jazz since the progressive era began. The only thing that scares me," he continued, "is that something new like this comes out, and, immediately, everybody jumps onto the bandwagon, and they drive it into the ground." Ephemeral pop treatments like Eydie Gorme's "Blame It On the Bossa Nova" and a bizarre album called *Boogie Woogie Bossa* seemed to confirm his fears. Stan Getz himself seemingly mocked the bossa nova craze by routinely announcing "Desafinado" as "Dis here finado"—an apparent word play on "Dis Here," Bobby Timmons's anthem of soul jazz, a genre that could hardly be further removed from the gently swaying music of Jobim, Gilberto, et al.

Soul Jazz

Like bossa nova, **soul jazz** came to prominence in the late 1950s. Coinciding as it did with the rising civil rights movement, soul jazz spoke for black values and culture with unabashed directness. In this sense it represented a populist counterpart to free jazz. As one writer noted in 1962, "Soul Jazz trades heavily on the social and ethical forces that are uniquely identified with the Negro in America today. As such it has become a rallying point for the rising young Negro jazz musician. It is music which he can accept as being uniquely his own, drawn from the personal heritage of the Negro and unavailable except in borrowed or artificial form to the white jazzman." Despite (or because of) these political factors, soul jazz became every bit as commercialized as bossa nova. As a result, critics have tended to dismiss it as an empty fad. Yet in the hands of the right players, soul jazz could rise to high artistic levels.

Soul jazz, a subcategory of hard bop, emerged when musicians fused modern jazz with the popular idioms of the blues, gospel, and soul. As we have seen, Horace Silver pioneered this development with gospel-based tunes like "The Preacher" and "Doodlin'" (both 1955). Philadelphia keyboardist **Jimmy Smith** (b. 1925) further emphasized the church connection by adopting the electronic Hammond B-3 organ as his main instrument. The Hammond organ, an inexpensive keyboard with fast vibrato and neon sonority, had been standard in black churches since the mid-thirties. It had become closely associated with the sound of gospel as performed by Mahalia Jackson and Roberta Martin. Smith's achievement, on albums like *The Sermon* (1958) and *Prayer Meetin'* (1960), was to transfer the Hammond to the realm of jazz virtuosity and improvisation without losing the gospel spirit of revivalist ecstasy.

Cannonball Adderley

Perhaps the most influential early purveyor of soul jazz was **Cannonball Adderley,** an alto saxophonist whom we first encountered in connection with Miles Davis (see Chapter 21). Adderley began his career as an ardent bebopper. His New York debut in 1955 has taken on the aura of legend. One night at the Café Bohemia, where Oscar Pettiford's band was playing, Pettiford's saxophonist failed to show up. When someone suggested that Adderley sit in with the band,

soul jazz a blend of hard bop with elements of the blues, gospel, and soul.

Pettiford scoffed. Adderley was a complete unknown, a high school band teacher from Fort Lauderdale, Florida, visiting the big city. How could he possibly keep pace with the best New York jazz musicians? As if to prove his point, Pettiford counted off "I'll Remember April" at a "murderous" tempo, according to Adderley's brother, Nat. But Cannonball, unfazed, "just flew across the top, and left everybody with their mouths hanging open." Taking place just a few months after the death of Charlie Parker, this incident quickly earned Adderley another nickname: "the new Bird."

Adderley's solos always manifested a strong bluesy element. But Adderley's blues were cheerful, even jubilant. Attracted by this quality, Miles Davis hired him in late 1957 to act as a foil, as he put it, "against [John Coltrane's] harmonic, chordal way of playing, his more free-form approach." Adderley's solo on "Freddie Freeloader," from Davis's album, *Kind of Blue,* beautifully demonstrates his stylistic blend of fluent bebop and extroverted blues lines.

In October 1959, Adderley left Davis to form his own quintet with **Nat Adderley** (1931–2000), his cornet-playing brother. The rhythm section included pianist Bobby Timmons, bassist Sam Jones, and drummer Louis Hayes. The rising popularity of soul jazz made it a logical and pragmatic avenue for Adderley, given his own funky tendencies. Moreover, his new gospel-leaning pianist Bobby Timmons shared Adderley's soulful strengths. Timmons composed "This Here" (aka "Dis Here"), a soul jazz piece which the band performed on its first record, a live set for Riverside entitled *The Cannonball Adderley Quintet in San Francisco.* Cannonball introduced "This Here" to his San Francisco audience with a little sermonlike speech, effortlessly imitating the rhythms and inflections of a black folk preacher to his delighted listeners. The combination of humor, religion, and earthy music proved immensely successful; the record became a hit, eventually selling a million copies, and established Adderley as the new leader in soul jazz.

Adderley built on this success with albums with such down-home titles as *What Is This Thing Called Soul? Them Dirty Blues,* and—his favorite off-hand expression—*Know What I Mean?* With Riverside and Capitol Records, Adderley made a series of live recordings with a "churchy" atmosphere, hoping to duplicate the success of his debut album. In 1966 he realized this goal with his runaway hit, *Mercy, Mercy, Mercy.* Before playing the title track, written by his pianist, Joe Zawinul, Cannonball sermonized in a manner reminiscent of his introduction to "This Here," while the audience murmured responses over the tinkling of glasses. Only long after the record was released was it made known that the "live" setting had been concocted in the studio, and that the "audience" had been paid with drinks to participate as if in a real club.

Lee Morgan

Some of the most inspired recordings in the soul jazz idiom were made by Philadelphia trumpeter **Lee Morgan** (1938–1972). Regarded by one authority as perhaps *the* "quintessential hardbopper," Morgan came of age under the spell of his idol, Clifford Brown. As a young teenager he used to go to Brown's house for lessons and encouragement. Just as Adderley made his national debut shortly after Charlie Parker's death, so Morgan seemingly took up the torch from Brown, auditioning successfully for Dizzy Gillespie's big band just months after Brown's premature death in 1956. Yet Morgan was no mere acolyte; in his earliest solos he already manifested a unique persona that critics would characterize with

Lee Morgan during a performance with Art Blakey's Jazz Messengers, 1959.

adjectives like urgent, fiery, impetuous, cocky, sarcastic, swaggering, and ebullient. In 1958 he began a three-year stint with Art Blakey's Jazz Messengers, where he first garnered critical acclaim.

By the late fifties Morgan was the standard-bearer of the virtuosic Gillespie-Brown trumpet tradition and the chief alternative to the introspective style of Miles Davis. Nevertheless, Davis suggested to Morgan that he "slow down and play less," advice he admitted taking to heart. Thus, in the sixties, he began yielding more and more to his natural inclination toward soul jazz. During his time with Blakey, Morgan had already revealed his ample gifts in this idiom, playing on pieces like "Moanin'" with expressive bends, smears, and wails, many of which he produced through half-valving. Now, whether the material was bop, blues, or ballads, Morgan often enriched his solos with such "soulful" devices.

In 1961 Morgan's career faltered due to heroin addiction, and, like Miles Davis, Sonny Rollins, and John Coltrane before him, he retreated to his home (in Philadelphia) to try to get control of his life. Two years later Morgan had beaten back the demons, apparently with the help and support of his longtime girlfriend, Helen More. He now entered a new period of creative activity, for the first time devoting himself to composition as well as improvisation. In 1963 he recorded "The Sidewinder," a twenty-four-bar blues. This piece features a so-called boogaloo beat, a loping dance rhythm based on straight eighth notes and their sixteenth-note subdivisions. The **boogaloo,** a black adaptation of the Latin bugalú, was one of many fad dances that emerged in the mid-sixties (along with the twist, the watusi, the monkey, and the shrug). In layman's terms, the beat

boogaloo a black adaptation of the Latin bugalú, a fad dance of the 1960s.

LEE MORGAN, _"Yes I Can, No You Can't"_ (1965)

CD 3 / Track 16

Lee Morgan recorded "Yes I Can, No You Can't" on _The Gigolo,_ an album that includes a restless title track in 6/8, three blues pieces, and a ballad. For the recording he borrowed Miles Davis's tenor saxophonist, Wayne Shorter, with whom Morgan had played with Art Blakey. Pianist Harold Mabern and bassist Bob Cranshaw both came out of soulful backgrounds, having accompanied blues master Joe Williams in the early sixties. And Billy Higgins, who played drums in Ornette Coleman's classic quartet, represented the group's closest tie with the avant garde.

"Yes I Can, No You Can't" appears to be one of Morgan's many attempts to duplicate the popular success of "The Sidewinder." Like the earlier piece, "Yes I Can, No You Can't" is a twenty-four-bar blues with a _boogaloo_ beat. Yet it seems far more expressive, and less glib, than "The Sidewinder." In the original liner notes, Nat Hentoff evocatively describes the piece as follows: "Lee [is] a writer who gets down to basic emotions, shapes, grooves. The opening _Yes I Can, No You Can't,_ for instance, which defies any listener to remain passive. How can you not move to it and with it? Wayne Shorter's walloping solo is followed by the kind of crackling power I've mentioned as Lee constructs what I'd call a talking solo—the sort of conversation held with vehement ease and wit by someone who really has something to say and the equipment with which to say it. Harold Mabern gets down and stays with what even _New York Times_ editorial writers call the nitty-gritty these days when they mean the core of it all."

Create your own listening chart (CD 3 / Track 16)

goes something like this: RATTA-tat-tat-RATTA-TATTA-tat-tat-tat. Outfitted with the popular boogaloo groove and a catchy melody, "The Sidewinder" became Morgan's first and biggest hit. Chrysler Motors even used it in a television commercial during the 1965 World Series.

After "The Sidewinder," Morgan recorded some of the finest music of his career. Initially, he had no qualms about blending jazz with popular music; indeed, as jazz players struggled in the late sixties, he said, "I don't want to hear that stuff about they can't sell jazz, because the music's gotten so now that rock guys are playing sitars and using hip forms, and Miles is using electric pianos. Music's gotten close. There are no natural barriers. It's all music. It's either hip or it ain't." And yet Morgan was not willing to participate fully in the burgeoning fusion movement. To the end of his life he continued to lead acoustic bands, and to defend jazz for its own sake. In 1972 his trumpet-playing colleague, Freddie Hubbard, by then deep into fusion himself, confessed in a *Down Beat* interview that "one reason I admire Lee today is that he's not jumping on bandwagons. He's sticking to Lee Morgan, and you either accept it or you don't."

Barely a month after this interview, on a cold February night, Helen More entered Slug's, a jazz club on New York's Lower East Side where Morgan was playing. Sick with jealousy over Morgan's affair with a younger woman, More confronted him between sets. The ensuing argument escalated until More pulled a gun and shot him dead. Ever since, the violent death of Lee Morgan has symbolized, as one writer has put it, both the "badness" of his life and music and the demise of hard bop itself.

Fusion

Chapter 27

Around 1967 the struggle of jazz to survive amid the overwhelming popularity of rock reached a point of crisis. In that year the hippie movement exploded with the Summer of Love and its associated psychedelic music, including the Beatles' landmark album, *Sgt. Pepper's Lonely Hearts' Club Band* and the Doors's number one hit, "Light My Fire." As protests against the Vietnam War and other social injustices grew ever louder, so did the music of electrified rock, eventually reaching ear-splitting levels. The powerful mix of rock and politics proved too much for mainstream jazz; as one observer recalled, "It was almost as though jazz had had a stroke in late 1967." Indeed, it was around this time that writers in *Down Beat* began speaking somberly about the "death of jazz," even as that magazine expanded its coverage to include rock.

Although many in the jazz community viewed rock as a curse, others saw it as a catalyst for injecting new life into jazz. As so often happened, Miles Davis spearheaded this effort, becoming the leader of a new hybrid style: jazz-rock, or **fusion.** Through his audacious music and the equally exploratory work of bands organized by his former sidemen—notably Lifetime, the Mahavishnu Orchestra, Headhunters, Return to Forever, and Weather Report—fusion gained widespread popularity. Inevitably, as with bossa nova and soul jazz, the number of ephemeral fusion recordings far outweighed the more ambitious treatments. As a result, many critics saw fusion players as cynically hastening the demise of jazz for commercial gain. Whatever the merits of this position, most agree today that fusion represents, thus far, the last genuinely progressive substyle in the life of jazz.

Forerunners

The drive toward fusion came from both the rock and the jazz camps. Sixties "rock" distinguished itself from fifties "rock 'n' roll" in part through its absorption of the jazz ideals of self-conscious artistry and improvisation. Psychedelic rockers, in particular, were fascinated by the long modal vamps and free-form improvisations of progressive jazz musicians like John Coltrane. By their own admissions, the Byrds based "Eight Miles High" (1966) on Coltrane's "India," while Grace Slick drew inspiration from Miles Davis's *Sketches of Spain* for Jefferson Airplane's "White Rabbit" (1967). Frank Zappa and Jimi Hendrix both flirted with jazz in club jam sessions and recordings. In the fall of 1967, a new band, Blood, Sweat & Tears, opened at the Café au Go Go in New York. In forming the band,

fusion a stylistic blend of jazz, rock, and funk that became popular in the 1970s.

singer Al Kooper had been inspired by Maynard Ferguson to combine rock guitars with a (reduced) big band horn section. The band's first album, *Child is Father to the Man* (1968), introduced a refreshing and powerful new sound drawing equally on rock and jazz.

Young jazz players likewise gravitated toward rock. As guitarist **Larry Coryell** (b. 1943) recalled, "We were in the middle of a world cultural revolution. Everybody was dropping acid and the prevailing attitude was, 'Let's do something different.' We loved Wes [Montgomery] but we also loved Bob Dylan. We loved Coltrane but we also dug the Beatles. We loved Miles but we also loved the Rolling Stones." Coryell himself is sometimes viewed as the father of fusion. In the mid-sixties he began performing in New York with two different bands—a jazz quartet led by Chico Hamilton and an experimental rock band called Free Spirits. In 1966 Free Spirits made one of the first fusion albums, *Out of Sight and Sound.* That same year saxophonist **Charles Lloyd** (b. 1938) led a proto-fusion band at the Monterey Jazz Festival. Including pianist Keith Jarrett, bassist Ron McClure, and drummer Jack DeJohnette, Lloyd's group dazzled the crowds at Monterey and recorded a seminal fusion album, *Love-In,* the following year. In 1968 *Rolling Stone* magazine hailed the music of these still isolated hybrid experiments: "Whether you can dig it or not, there is little doubt that this is going to be the young jazz of the future."

Miles Davis and Fusion

It took the prestige and leadership of Miles Davis to shape fusion into a coherent movement. After three years, the ever-restless Davis was beginning to tire of his second quintet. Since he had little appetite for continuing further into the avant garde, he began looking for fresh sounds. At the same time, like other jazz musicians, Davis was losing his audience. In the late sixties his record sales dipped below 50,000 from a high of 150,000 in the fifties. Bassist Dave Holland was shocked to see only thirty or forty people in the audience at one of Davis's concerts in San Francisco.

In 1968 Davis married a twenty-three-year-old pop singer and songwriter named Betty Mabry. Mabry introduced him to the counterculture of her own generation, particularly turning his attention to black popular music. Under Mabry's influence, Davis became deeply immersed in the music of Jimi Hendrix, James Brown, and Sly and the Family Stone. Davis especially admired Hendrix, who—by some accounts—used to come over to Davis's house where the two jammed together. Hendrix's distortion-laced guitar playing allied him with psychedelic rock, but James Brown and Sly Stone represented a new, intensely rhythmic brand of soul called **funk.** By the late sixties funk had become the dominant musical expression of the Black Power movement, even seducing free jazz exponents like Archie Shepp with its insistent rhetoric. By tapping into funk, Davis showed implicit solidarity with the most pressing concerns of black society.

Davis began experimenting with rock and funk in his second quintet. At first he simply added electric instruments. In late 1967 he recorded "Circle in the Round," an over thirty-minute-long track that included studio player Joe Beck on electric guitar. A few weeks later Herbie Hancock came into the studio and found a Fender Rhodes electric piano in the place of his regular acoustic grand. With Beck on electric guitar and Hancock on the Fender Rhodes, the quintet recorded "Water on the Pond." In May 1968, Davis followed these experiments with

funk in the 1960s and 1970s, an intensely rhythmic brand of soul characterized by interlocking polyrhythms.

"Stuff," a rock-based piece that featured Hancock on electric piano. Finally, in June and September he recorded *Filles de Kilimanjaro,* his last album with the second quintet and a transitional work in his move toward fusion. Although the solos, melodies, and harmonies reveal the group's jazz language, the rhythms played by Tony Williams consist of rock-oriented straight eighth notes. Moreover, every track features electric as well as acoustic piano.

In February 1969 Davis recorded his first full-fledged fusion album, a quiet atmospheric work entitled *In a Silent Way.* The band consisted of Davis, Wayne Shorter, and an expanded rhythm section: three electric pianists, bass, drums, and a brilliant electric guitarist from Great Britain, **John McLaughlin** (b. 1942). Hancock and Carter had left the band the previous year; when Williams left a couple of months later, the old rhythm section was gone and so was any sense of fundamental continuity with the past.

Bitches Brew

Although *In a Silent Way* represented mature fusion, it somehow escaped the critical commotion that greeted Davis's next album. Recorded in August of 1969, **Bitches Brew** officially launched the fusion movement. It also divided the jazz community between those who claimed that Davis had "sold out"

Miles Davis changed his wardrobe along with his music in the early 1970s.

and those who saw him powerfully reinventing jazz yet again. At the record's thirty-year anniversary *Down Beat* proclaimed *Bitches Brew* "the most revolutionary jazz album in history."

For *Bitches Brew* Davis expanded his ensemble to thirteen musicians, mostly rhythm section players: Davis, Shorter, bass clarinetist Bennie Maupin, John McLaughlin, three electric pianists (Corea, Zawinul, and Larry Young), two bassists (Harvey Brooks on electric and Dave Holland on acoustic), two drumset players (Lenny White and Jack DeJohnette), and two percussionists (Don Alias, and Jim "Jumma Santos" Riley). Over three days various combinations of this pool of musicians recorded under Davis's direction. "*Bitches Brew* was like a big pot and Miles was the sorcerer," recalled Lenny White. "He was hanging over it, saying, 'I'm going to add a dash of Jack DeJohnette, and a little bit of John McLaughlin.'" "There wasn't a lot said," added DeJohnette. "Most of it was just directed with a word here and there. . . . He was trying to capture moods and feelings and textures. He always went for the essence of things, and that was much more important to him than going back and redoing a note that wasn't perfect."

During the entire process Davis kept the tape rolling. The resulting master recording consisted not of separate takes, but of one long stop-and-start "performance," complete with spoken comments, "mistakes," and silent stretches, as Davis shepherded the musicians from one section to another. The final album depended heavily on **postproduction techniques** developed by rock bands over the previous three years. The Beatles pioneered these techniques—which

Great Debates

BITCHES BREW: ARTISTIC ADVANCE OR COMMERCIAL SELL-OUT?

Miles Davis's decision to move in the direction of fusion was the most controversial of his career. His landmark album, *Bitches Brew,* became a lightning rod for critical acclamation and dissent. Citing the clear intention of both Davis and Columbia Records to reach a larger, more youthful audience, some writers charged Davis with cravenly selling his jazz soul for financial gain. John Litweiler wrote that "Davis's bosses [at Columbia] ordered him to make a hit record, or else; *Bitches Brew* was the response." For Stanley Crouch, Davis's most vociferous critic, *Bitches Brew* shows Davis "firmly on the path of the sellout. It sold more than any other Davis album, and fully launched jazz-rock with its multiple keyboards, electronic guitars, static beats, and clutter."

Davis's defenders countered that, beyond superficial similarities, the music on *Bitches Brew* bore little resemblance to his rock or funk models. Davis's fusion was a fiercely experimental and densely polyphonic music with no catchy melodic "hooks," no lyrics, and no coherently repeating form. If he intended to pander to the masses, the apologists say, he chose a strange way to do it. Stuart Nicholson argues that the problem hinges on definitions. Fusion's detractors "wanted jazz to be what it used to be, not what it is." Paul Tingen takes the opposite view, freely admitting that Davis was playing rock, not jazz, in *Bitches Brew.* Indeed, that is why jazz critics couldn't appreciate the album: they didn't understand the musical language of rock. Even most sympathetic jazz writers "simply don't 'get it,'" he says, when it comes to Davis's electric music: "At best their portrayals and narratives lack depth and substance, and at worst they are rife with snobbery and narrow-mindedness, expressing the prejudice that rock music is inferior to jazz." ■ ■ ■

involved splicing, overdubbing, playing the tape backwards, slowing down the tape, creating tape loops, and so forth—on their groundbreaking concept album, *Sgt. Pepper's Lonely Hearts Club Band* (1967). This album demonstrated the potential for creating art from the master tapes *after* the musicians had left the studio. Surprisingly, Davis abdicated his own role in postproduction, turning the whole process over to Columbia producer **Teo Macero.** "I had carte blanche to work with the material," Macero said of *Bitches Brew.* "I could move anything around and what I would do is . . . say, 'This is a good little piece here, this matches with that, put this here,' etc., and then add in all the effects—the electronics, the delays and overlays. . . . [Then] I'd send it to Miles and ask, 'How do you like it?'"

When it was released in 1970, *Bitches Brew* sold over four hundred thousand copies and won a Grammy for Best Jazz Record of the year. In order to reach younger audiences, Columbia persuaded Davis to perform at the leading rock emporiums, Fillmore East in New York and Fillmore West in San Francisco. Over the next few years he opened concerts for such rock groups as the Grateful Dead, Blood, Sweat & Tears, Carlos Santana, the Band, and Crosby, Stills, Nash, and Young. His towering stature as a jazz artist persuaded younger jazz players to follow his lead, and the fusion movement was born.

Lifetime

One of the signs of Miles Davis's centrality to fusion is the fact that the outstanding early fusion bands were almost all led by his former sidemen. The first of these so-called **alumni bands** was organized by Davis's longtime drummer, Tony

Williams. In 1969, together with John McLaughlin and Hammond organist Larry Young, Williams formed **Lifetime,** a power trio inspired by the high-voltage music of Jimi Hendrix and British blues-rock trio, Cream. "I wanted to create a different atmosphere from the one I had been in," said Williams. "So I said, 'What better way to do it than to go electric? Organ, guitar and drums, but do it in a real aggressive manner with a lot of rock 'n' roll kind of feeling, energy, power . . . BAM!!'"

In May, three months before *Bitches Brew,* Lifetime made its first album, *Emergency!* Bursting with virtuosity and brute power, this album electrified many listeners. A reviewer for *Rolling Stone* exclaimed of the album: "Here is where we take a giant step into the future. Williams and his associates stand at the frontier." *Down Beat* concurred that Lifetime was producing "the freshest and most original sounds being made today." Indeed, Lifetime might have emerged as the dominant voice of fusion were it not for inept management by the band's promoters and its record label, Polydor. Lifetime's subsequent recordings proved disappointing, and the band finally dissolved in April 1971. But few bands have left behind such a sense of opportunities missed. "Everything but the music was incredibly bad," lamented McLaughlin. "Management, economics, administration, organization . . . incredibly bad." Cream bassist Jack Bruce, who performed with the band in its final days, gave the wistful summation: "Lifetime was, without a doubt, the best band in the world."

The Mahavishnu Orchestra

Three months after the demise of Lifetime, McLaughlin organized his own five-piece band. In addition to McLaughlin, the band included violinist Jerry Goodman, keyboard player Jan Hammer, bassist Rick Laird, and a young wizard of the drums, Billy Cobham. Shortly after arriving in the United States from his home in Great Britain in early 1969, McLaughlin had begun practicing yoga and studying meditation with an Eastern guru named Sri Chinmoy. Somewhat like John Coltrane, he came to see his life and music in highly spiritual terms; he professed the desire to become "the cosmic instrument of God." At the recommendation of Chinmoy, he named his new band the Mahavishnu Orchestra.

The Mahavishnu Orchestra showcased music of spectacular virtuosity, especially on the part of McLaughlin and Cobham. The band played in complex meters like 14/8, 17/8, and 20/4 at blisteringly fast tempos. And it featured unusual sonorities, including the use of **synthesizers**—electronic keyboards that produced "synthesized" sounds from a broad timbral spectrum. McLaughlin played a novel double-necked guitar—a twelve-string for arpeggios and a six-string for solos. The band's first album, *The Inner Mounting Flame* (1971), became a jazz hit, reaching eighty-nine on the *Billboard* chart. "Its coherence and control comes as a shaft of light on the muddied and confused," asserted the British jazz magazine, *Melody Maker.* The next album, *Birds of Fire* (1973), did even better, taking fifteenth place on the *Billboard* chart. The musicians' sudden success kept them on the road for over two hundred nights a year.

But by the end of 1973 the pressures of success and internal conflicts began taking their toll. McLaughlin's outspoken religious devotion and his open evangelizing for Sri Chinmoy at concerts and on album covers annoyed his sidemen; at the same time, some of his musicians wanted to use their own pieces, and the Mahavishnu Orchestra mostly played compositions by McLaughlin. The end came in December, with a final concert in Detroit. Although McLaughlin briefly formed a second edition of the Mahavishnu Orchestra in 1975, it never reached the creative heights of those first two albums.

synthesizer an electronic keyboard that produces synthesized sounds from a broad timbral palette.

Headhunters

If Lifetime and the Mahavishnu Orchestra took inspiration primarily from Jimi Hendrix and electric guitar–based rock, then Herbie Hancock built his fusion style on James Brown, Sly Stone, and funk. In 1973 Hancock formed what he thought was a funk band called **Headhunters.** In fact, it turned out to be one of the first ensembles to successfully wed jazz (improvisation) and funk, complete with the latter's interlocking polyrhythmic grooves. "I knew that I never heard any jazz players really play funk like the funk I had been listening to," Hancock said. "Instead of getting jazz cats who knew how to play funk, I got funk cats who knew how to play jazz." The band consisted of reed player Bennie Maupin, bassist Paul Jackson, drummer Harvey Mason, percussionist Bill Summers, and Hancock on assorted electronic keyboards: Fender-Rhodes piano, mellotron, Hohner D-6 Clavinet (with Fender fuzz, wah-wah, and echoplex), and ARP Odessey and ARP Pro-Soloist Synthesizers.

The band's first album, *Headhunters* (1973), defied all expectations, climbing to 13 on the *Billboard* pop chart, producing a hit single, "Chameleon," and eventually going platinum. More than any of the other alumni bandleaders, Hancock now geared his music primarily toward commercial success. After his next album, *Thrust* (1975), he said, "I felt I had to meet the challenge of going towards the simple." Critics castigated Hancock for betraying the sixties tradition of uncompromising experimentation on which he was weaned. Hancock defended himself by insisting that his Headhunter albums were *not* jazz per se, and therefore should not be evaluated as if they were: "The very fact I come from a jazz tradition means there are certain expectations built into anyone who knows my history. So when I do the more commercial side of me, they use those expectations, which don't apply, and I wind up getting unfairly treated." The problem with his argument is that many people still heard jazz in the Headhunters, a jazz defanged for public consumption but jazz nonetheless. As so often happened, the issue turned on a question of definitions, on the perceived difference between jazz and mere dance music.

Further Listening from the *Prentice Hall Jazz Collection*
Track 10: Herbie Hancock, "Chameleon" (1973)

Herbie Hancock's Headhunters, 1974. *Far left,* Herbie Hancock; *far right,* Bennie Maupin.

Return to Forever

After leaving Miles Davis in September 1970, Chick Corea initially moved away from fusion and toward free jazz. Then he reached a turning point in his life and career: he accepted the teachings of L. Ron Hubbard and became a devout Scientologist. His new worldview changed his musical convictions. Corea began to view his music less as a vessel for art and more as a means of communication. Recalling this change a few years later, he said that "musically my intentions were no longer to satisfy myself. I really wanted to connect with the world." Accordingly, he repudiated the avant garde and embraced fusion.

In the fall of 1971 he organized a band with a mystical name reflecting his spiritual awakening, **Return to Forever.** The band included the saxophonist and flutist Joe Farrell, the electric bassist Stanley Clarke, and two Brazilian musicians, the percussionist Airto Moreira and his wife, the vocalist Flora Purim. The following year Return to Forever made two acclaimed albums, *Return to Forever* and *Light as a Feather.* Under the influence of Moreira and Purim, Corea's music on these records represents a blend of jazz, funk, and the uptempo Brazilian samba. Corea's compositions, including "La Fiesta" and "Spain," strike a just balance between catchy accessibility and artistic sophistication.

In 1973 Farrell, Moreira, and Purim left the band, which thenceforth moved in a different direction. Corea had been very impressed with the almost

CHICK COREA AND RETURN TO FOREVER, *"500 Miles High"* (1972)

In "500 Miles High," Chick Corea and his band Return to Forever demonstrate their characteristically "Brazilian" approach to fusion. Like many fusion pieces, this one features an unconventional form by jazz standards; the form of the chorus is *binary,* divided into two distinct and balanced parts—A and B. The presence of electric piano and electric bass, together with the rock beat in the rhythm section during the melody, also mark this as a typical fusion performance. But Flora Purim's nonnative vocal accent, Airto Moreira's use of Brazilian percussion instruments in the rhythm section, and the shift to a *samba* double-time feel during the tenor saxophone and electric piano solos—these all reflect the fundamentally Brazilian orientation of the piece.

Much of the interest and excitement of "500 Miles High" come from *postbop* techniques employed by Corea and his sidemen. All the soloists are concerned with motivic development, group interaction, and with shaping the music through dynamics and rhythmic intensification. Notice, for example, how tenor saxophonist Joe Farrell and Corea interact on a rapid three-note motive in the sixth chorus and, similarly, how bassist Stanley Clarke and Corea cross paths on a walking triplet figure in the fourteenth chorus, creating an effect of true polyphony. Aided by the rhythm section, both Farrell and Corea build to intense climaxes during their solos—Farrell at the top of the sixth chorus and Corea at the top of the eleventh. An element crucial to the process of musical shaping is the shift in the rhythm section to a *samba,* double-time feel, in the second chorus of Farrell's and Corea's solos. Note, also, the corresponding "braking" effect in the last B-section in each case, which prepares for a return of the original time feel. (Listen to Stanley Clarke's bass lines to hear clearly the process of changing from one feel to another.)

LISTENING CHART 29

Chick Corea and Return to Forever, "500 Miles High" (Corea-Potter)

CD 3 / Tracks 17–23

RECORDED OCTOBER 1972, LONDON / *LIGHT AS A FEATHER* POLYDOR 827 148-2

Chick Corea (electric piano), Joe Farrell (tenor saxophone), Stanley Clarke (electric bass), Airto Moreira (drums, percussion), Flora Purim (voice, percussion)

Style: Fusion				**Form: Binary—AB**

				Introduction (tempo rubato)
17	0:00			Electric piano solo: Chick Corea
				Vocal melody: Flora Purim
18	0:31	*1st Chorus*	A (8)	Tempo rubato: *Someday you'll look into her eyes* *Then there'll be no goodbyes; and yesterday . . .*
			B (10)	*. . . will have gone!* *And you'll find yourself in another space—*
19	1:16			Electric piano completes the phrase; rhythm section begins playing in a fixed tempo
	1:22	*2nd Chorus*	A (8)	*You'll see, just one look and you'll know* *She's so tender and warm; you'll recognize . . .*
			B (10)	*. . . this is love!* *You'll find yourself on another plane—* *Five hundred miles high.*
	1:51	*3rd Chorus*	A (8)	*Be sure that your love stays so free* *Then it never can die. You realize . . .*
			B (10)	*. . . this is truth!* *And above the skies you will always stay—* *Five hundred miles high.*
				Tenor saxophone solo: Joe Farrell
20	2:22	*4th Chorus* (18)		Joe Farrell plays inventive and lively solo . . .
21	2:50	*5th Chorus* (18)		Rhythm section switches to *samba* (double-time feel)
	3:19	*6th Chorus* (18)		Climax . . .
	3:33			. . . Farrell and Corea interact on three-note motive
	3:48	*7th Chorus*	A (8)	
	4:02		B (10)	Rhythm section begins "braking" to prepare return of original time feel . . .

				Electric piano solo: Chick Corea
22	4:18	*8th Chorus* (18)		Original time feel; Corea begins soulfully . . .
	4:47	*9th Chorus* (18)		*Samba* (double-time feel); Corea turns up the heat . . .
	5:17	*10th Chorus* (18)		
	5:46	*11th Chorus*	A (8)	Climax . . .
	5:59		B (10)	Rhythm section begins "braking" as before . . .
				Electric bass solo: Stanley Clarke
23	6:16	*12th Chorus* (18)		Original time feel; Clarke plays virtuosic solo full of dancing double-time figures . . .
	6:44	*13th Chorus* (18)		
	7:12	*14th Chorus* (18)		
	7:16			. . . Clarke and Corea cross paths on walking triplet figure
				Vocal melody: Flora Purim
	7:41	*15th Chorus* (18)		*Someday, etc. . . .*
		16th Chorus (16)		*Be sure, etc. . . .*
	8:37			**Coda** (on "Five Hundred Miles High" motive)

otherworldly electronic virtuosity of the Mahavishnu Orchestra. "John's band . . . led me to want to turn the volume up and write music that was more dramatic and made your hair move," he said. On albums like *Hymn of the Seventh Galaxy* (1973) and *Romantic Warrior* (1976), Corea cultivated an ostentatiously virtuoso approach, often playing head-spinning unison lines with Clarke and, later, guitarist Al DiMeola. Critics responded negatively to the apparent reliance on virtuosity for its own sake, as well as to Corea's penchant for grand orchestral backdrops in the manner of "symphonic rock" groups like Yes and Emerson, Lake, and Palmer.

Weather Report

Most of the Davis alumni bands lasted for a short period of time, often flourishing brilliantly before capitulating to the forces that so often destroyed rock and pop groups: overexposure, formulaic musical practices, poor management, and internecine conflicts. The principal exception to this pattern was **Weather Report,** a group founded by **Joe Zawinul** (b. 1932) and Wayne Shorter that stayed together for fifteen years, from 1971 to 1986. Zawinul was born and raised in Vienna, Austria, where he studied at the Vienna Conservatory and learned jazz through American recordings. He immigrated to the United States in 1958 and soon landed a job playing for Maynard Ferguson. In 1961 he began a nine-year

Weather Report, 1979. *Left to right:* Joe Zawinul, Wayne Shorter, Peter Erskine, Jaco Pastorius.

stint as Cannonball Adderley's pianist. With Adderley he composed several soul jazz standards, including the hit, "Mercy, Mercy, Mercy." Shorter, as we have seen, emerged in the sixties as a John Coltrane–influenced tenor saxophonist who went on to develop an entirely individual sound and style. After a four-year tenure with Art Blakey's Jazz Messengers, Shorter joined Miles Davis, with whom he stayed until 1970 (see Chapter 23). By this time he was widely acknowledged as the leading tenor player of his generation.

In early 1971 Zawinul and Shorter got together with a young bassist from Czechoslovakia, Miroslav Vitous, and decided to organize a band. They chose the name Weather Report, according to Zawinul, "because that would allow us to change, just like the weather, so the [stylistic] scope is limitless." After adding a drummer and percussionist, the band made its first album, *Weather Report,* for Columbia. At this point it was hardly a fusion band, using no electric instruments. But striking features on the album, including sensitive three-way interaction among Zawinul, Shorter, and Vitous, drew critical praise. *Down Beat* awarded it the maximum five stars, and it won a Grammy for Jazz Album of the Year. Zawinul himself characterized the album as "a soundtrack for the imagination."

During the next few years the music increasingly came under the direction of Zawinul. The group dynamic was democratic to a point; "no one solos, everyone solos," was Zawinul's paradoxical decree. But Zawinul did not want to entrust the band's music to the whims of inspiration. He wanted the illusion of complete spontaneity but the control of composition, so he wrote out many of the interactive passages. Over time, the band embraced electrification as well. Like Hancock and Corea, Zawinul began using stacks of electric keyboards and synthesizers.

Zawinul and Shorter, who formed the creative hub of the group, went through many bassists, drummers, and percussionists. In 1975 an electric bass

WEATHER REPORT, *"Birdland"* (1977)

Joe Zawinul intended "Birdland," from the album *Heavy Weather*, as a tribute to the venerable but long-defunct New York nightclub dedicated to Charlie Parker (see Chapter 18). If the inspiration for "Birdland" came from jazz, the fusion that produced it involved the hottest pop trend of the day: disco. In 1977, the same year that *Heavy Weather* was released, John Travolta starred in *Saturday Night Fever*, the film that started the whole disco dance craze. The actual melodies of "Birdland" have little if anything to do with disco. But the disco beat, defined by an equal emphasis on all four beats in the measure, is the underlying beat in "Birdland," and appears especially prominently during the vamp sections of the piece.

The form of "Birdland" is even more idiosyncratic than that of "500 Miles High." As presented in Listening Chart 30, the piece divides into four sections: A, B, C, and D. The A- and B-sections basically constitute a lengthy introduction to the catchy main melody in section C; the D-section serves as an interlude. The main melody, however, is not necessarily the most interesting part of the piece. Some of the most creative moments occur during the ostensibly subordinate sections. Each section unfolds according to an essentially additive process, with new material being added successively to old layers. For instance, A begins with a synthesized bass line (A1), expands to include a bluesy riff played by Fender bassist Jaco Pastorius in the upper register (an effect achieved through the use of *harmonics*) (A2), and culminates in a syncopated passage for the whole band, with tenor saxophonist Wayne Shorter playing the lead (A3). A more dramatic intensification occurs in the final C-section, which gradually absorbs several embellishing layers over the course of fifteen statements of the basic tune.

sensation from Fort Lauderdale, Florida, made his first solo album. In a display of unconventional virtuosity worthy of Paganini, **Jaco Pastorius** (1951–1987) astounded the jazz world with this record. Particularly amazing was his tour-de-force solo performance of Miles Davis's torrid bebop anthem, "Donna Lee." Such facility, which included chordal playing, parallel octaves, and high lead guitar–style melodies (through the use of *harmonics*), had never been heard before on any bass, electric or acoustic. But Pastorius had to pester Zawinul with letters and demo tapes before a vacancy opened and the latter finally hired him in early 1976. Pastorius soon came to dominate live performances by the band, giving crowd-pleasing virtuoso solos with a tremendous knack for showmanship. "Every band needs what I call a warhead—the driving force, the motor," recalled Zawinul. "And in this band, Jaco was the warhead." Unfortunately, Pastorius's mental instability and fast lifestyle—including alcohol and cocaine addiction—created problems for the band. By 1982, said Zawinul, it was "time for him to go." After a brief solo career, Pastorius tragically succumbed to his demons, eventually becoming a homeless person. He died from injuries sustained during a brawl at the Midnight Club in Fort Lauderdale.

The recordings that included Zawinul, Shorter, and Pastorius, reveal Weather Report at its most exciting and inventive. Two of the best albums were *Black Market* (1976) and *Heavy Weather* (1977). The latter sold over five hundred thousand copies, lifting Weather Report into the ranks of its predecessors, The Mahavishnu Orchestra and Headhunters, in terms of popularity. The first track, "Birdland," became a hit single and, subsequently, a jazz standard.

LISTENING CHART 30

Weather Report, "Birdland" (Zawinul)

CD 3 / Tracks 24–29

RECORDED OCTOBER 1976, NORTH HOLLYWOOD / *HEAVY WEATHER* COLUMBIA CK 65108

Joe Zawinul (Oberheim Polyphonic, Arp 2600, Melodica, acoustic piano, voice), Wayne Shorter (soprano saxophone, tenor saxophone), Jaco Pastorius (bass, mandocello, voice), Alex Acuña (drums), Manolo Badrena (tambourine)

Style: Fusion   **Form: Four sections A B C D, the main melody being C**

				Introduction
24	0:00	A	1	Bass line: synthesizer
	0:18		2	Add bluesy riff: Fender bass *harmonics*
	0:43		3	Syncopated motives: tenor saxophone lead
25	0:55	B	1	Vamp
	1:02		2	Bluesy riff: synthesizer + piano
	1:31		3	Fanfare: tenor saxophone lead
	1:45		4	Vamp + soulful improvisations
				Main melody
26	1:59	C		Basic tune stated 6 times (with gradual thickening of texture)
				Interlude
27	2:36	D	1	Vamp
	2:48		2	Bluesy riff
	3:07		3	Harmonized descending chromatic line/tenor saxophone solo: Wayne Shorter
	3:28		4	Vamp
				Introduction
28	3:35	A	2	Bluesy riff: Fender bass *harmonics*
	3:46		1	Add bass line: synthesizer
	3:59		3	Syncopated motives: tenor saxophone lead
	4:12	B	2	Bluesy riff: synthesizer + piano
				Main melody
29	4:23	C		Basic tune stated 15 times, first with hand claps on back-beats . . .
	4:36			. . . then with crooning vocals added . . .
	5:00			. . . then with synthesizer countermelody . . .
	5:31			. . . then with synthesizer improvised solo: Joe Zawinul
	5:43			. . . then with hand claps quadrupled, coming on every eighth note
				Fade ending

Postmodern Jazz

(c. 1975–Present)

The Neo-Bop Movement

Chapter **28**

B Y AROUND 1975 AMERICAN SOCIETY HAD REACHED A STATE OF POLITICAL, ECONOMIC, and cultural exhaustion. The cultural revolution of the sixties had waned for several reasons. The youth who had led the revolution were taking jobs and raising families, thus becoming part of the establishment they had decried; at the same time, elements of the hippie movement had by now infiltrated mainstream society (in diluted form), thus taking the edge off the movement itself. Moreover, Americans were starting to worry about money, forcing the idealistic concerns of the sixties into the background. In 1973 members of OPEC (Organization of Petroleum Exporting Companies) sharply raised oil prices, precipitating an energy crisis in the United States that led to long gasoline lines, a glut of American luxury cars, and ultimately, a recession.

But two watershed events truly marked the end of an era. On August 9, 1974, President Richard Nixon resigned over the Watergate scandal. Over the previous eighteen months Americans had become increasingly indignant as revelations of White House corruption emerged on an almost daily basis. Nixon's resignation (and Gerald Ford's subsequent pardon of him) concluded a "long national nightmare," as Ford put it. The second event occurred the following year, when the United States finally capitulated in the Vietnam War and brought the last

U.S. troops home. Like the end of the war, Nixon's resignation brought widespread relief to American citizens, but also left them disillusioned, if not cynical, about their government and indeed their society.

Black Americans felt disillusioned for other reasons as well. Ever since Martin Luther King's assassination in 1968, they had felt increasingly convinced that white bigots would stop at nothing to keep blacks in a subordinate role. The convicted assassin, James Earl Ray, was only one man, but he represented entrenched racism on a wide scale. The urban riots following King's death expressed black anger and despair over their fallen leader and all he stood for. The black power movement sought to continue the cause of civil rights, but internal strife fractured the various black power organizations and membership declined. By the mid-1970s, several organizations had dissolved and their leaders had found more conventional outlets through which to express their views.

All these signs of cultural decline indicated a slowly growing backlash against the entire previous era in American history. The genuine advances of the sixties, including in the area of civil rights, had come at a cost. Many Americans were sickened by the deception of political leaders, tired of the cultural excesses of the sixties, and seemed to long for a return to stability. The swinging of the pendulum toward more traditional values is evident in the next two presidents. Jimmy Carter was a Democrat, but an austere one, urging people to turn down their thermostats and wear sweaters. And the ecstatic reception of Ronald Reagan, the reactionary Republican governor of California during its most strident counterculture years (1967–1975), showed that cultural conservatism now prevailed.

As in American society, jazz, too, had reached a turning point by the mid-1970s. Fusion was ebbing as a coherent movement. Miles Davis's abrupt retirement and apparent withdrawal from society in 1975 was symbolically traumatic in view of his relentless dominating leadership during the previous twenty-five years. The most audacious and creative fusion bands folded around the same time. The second edition of the Mahavishnu Orchestra disbanded in 1975; a second edition of Lifetime in 1976; Headhunters in 1977; and Return to Forever twice, in 1976, and again, in another edition, in 1977. Of the Davis alumni bands, only Weather Report continued to flourish into the eighties. The ossification of fusion seemed confirmed by the prominence of more commercial bands in the late 1970s and 1980s.

Certainly fusion continued to be a viable idiom—witness the remarkable artistic and commercial success of groups like Pat Metheny and Steps Ahead (see Chapter 29). But, at the same time, every other previous jazz style remained equally viable. The coexistence of old and new styles had begun in the 1940s, when Dixieland, swing, and bebop first vied for listeners, and continued with each new wave of stylistic change. The difference after 1975 was that now there was no longer a "new thing," a cutting edge, an avant garde leading all the outdated styles in its train. Instead, all styles were equally familiar and therefore, in theory, at least, equally significant. The ethos, even the possibility, of "modernism" had spent itself in jazz as it had in classical music, the visual arts, and literature. Jazz had entered its **postmodern** stage.

This is clear from the fact that the "new thing" after 1975 was really an old thing—the revitalization and reinterpretation of acoustic, mainstream jazz: in other words, bop. The renewed interest in bop, now called **neo-bop** by some commentators, can be seen as a jazz counterpart to the conservative political

neo-bop the revival of hard bop and postbop by players after c. 1975.

movement spreading through society. Neo-bop was no avant garde, but it did represent the single most coherent and influential movement in jazz of the late seventies and eighties.

Return to Tradition

In August 1977, *Newsweek* magazine featured a cover story bearing the sensationalistic title, "Jazz Comes Back!" "Pushed into a neutral corner by rock in the '60s, jazz has at last come out fighting," the article said. "The signs of rebirth are everywhere. . . . Ten years ago in New York there were fewer than ten jazz clubs. Today there are 80. Seven years ago in Boston there was just one. Now there are 21." Record sales were back up. "A mainstream artist like pianist McCoy Tyner, whose releases sold 20,000 copies five years ago, now sells 100,000 an album. Even avant-gardist Anthony Braxton has doubled his sales." A Detroit guitarist interviewed for the article said, "It's just barely possible to sustain life as a jazz musician—that's new."

The article continued, "If there is no one style around which musicians can rally today, as they did around bebop in the fifties, there are riches to choose from." With this statement, the writer aptly described the new postmodern environment, in which artists could self-consciously "choose" from a menu of old and new styles, mixing and matching at will, combining and recasting and reinterpreting, to serious or ironic or humorous effect. The writer could not have foreseen the rise of neo-bop to a position of dominance out of this egalitarian stylistic milieu. But the first signs of that rise were already evident.

In the mid-seventies several struggling bop players received unexpected boosts to their careers. In 1974 the outstanding but hitherto unsung postbop trumpeter **Woody Shaw** (1944–1989) made his first album as a leader, launching an illustrious career as "the last in the line of trumpet players that really added something new to trumpet jazz," according to his trumpet-playing contemporary, Randy Brecker. The following year *Village Voice* writer Gary Giddins heralded "The Return of Jackie McLean," an alto saxophonist who at one time apprenticed with Charlie Parker. Most dramatically, perhaps, veteran bebop tenor player **Dexter Gordon** (1923–1990) returned to New York in the summer of 1976 after a fifteen-year sojourn in Europe. His highly celebrated "homecoming" engagement at the Village Vanguard gave hope to diehard bop fans that perhaps the music they loved wasn't dead after all. In that same year **Albert Murray,** a protégé of Ralph Ellison, wrote *Stomping the Blues,* a paean to mainstream jazz that eventually became an artistic manifesto within the neo-bop movement.

Reunion Bands

One of the most impressive early manifestations of neo-bop was the all-too-brief career of the **V.S.O.P. Quintet,** which consisted of the sidemen from Miles Davis's second quintet—Wayne Shorter, Herbie Hancock, Ron Carter, and Tony Williams—plus the great 1960s trumpeter **Freddie Hubbard** (b. 1938) acting in the place of Davis. All of these musicians had spent the early seventies playing fusion; Hancock and Hubbard endured especially bitter criticism for turning their backs on jazz to "go commercial." The reunion of these five friends and colleagues to play acoustic, swinging music in the postbop tradition of the sixties heartened the capacity audiences that turned out to hear them at concerts and festivals.

The V.S.O.P Quintet began with Hancock. In 1976 George Wein, the organizer of the Newport Jazz Festival, called Hancock's manager and asked if Hancock would perform at the festival. His manager feared that a public association of Hancock with "jazz" might hurt his fusion record sales. But he agreed on condition that the performance be a retrospective of Hancock's work. So on July 29, Wein sponsored a concert at Town Hall called "A Retrospective of the Music of Herbie Hancock," featuring three groups: the Davis quintet of the sixties (plus Hubbard) referred to above, Hancock's sextet from 1969–1973, and his current fusion band, Headhunters. A recording of the concert was released under the title *V.S.O.P.*—meaning Very Special One-time-only Performance.

To universal surprise, the acoustic quintet generated the most enthusiasm. The following summer, the group—now called the V.S.O.P. Quintet—toured the United States and gave performances in Tokyo and London, playing some tunes from Davis's sixties repertory as well as some new ones. Wayne Shorter acknowledged the novelty of five fusion leaders returning to acoustic jazz: "When we go out on the V.S.O.P. tour, generations who never saw us perform in the sixties will get a chance to see what we look like playing together. It's like seeing if an actor can play more than one Shakespearian role." Sensitive to charges of reactionism, Ron Carter added: "Playing this music once again might require a few changes from a physical standpoint—Herbie's using only the acoustic piano, and Tony's playing the cymbals differently than with his own band—but it's not a change from an emotional point of view. Just because some of the forms we're playing date back ten years doesn't mean they're not contemporary."

V.S.O.P. Quintet, 1977. *Left to right:* Herbie Hancock, Ron Carter, Tony Williams, Wayne Shorter, Freddie Hubbard.

The members of the V.S.O.P Quintet saw the band as a momentary diversion from their own independent activities; in 1979 the band reunited one last time for a concert in Japan. But the V.S.O.P. Quintet spawned other, similar projects. In 1982 the veteran drummer **Lenny White** (b. 1949) approached record producer Bruce Lundvall about making a bop-oriented record with singer Chaka Khan and four distinguished musicians that White had played with in the past. Lundvall agreed, and suggested they also do a record with the same group but without a singer. For these record dates, White reunited with Freddie Hubbard and tenor saxophonist **Joe Henderson** (1937–2001), horn players for whom he had worked as a sideman many years previously. He also teamed up with his former rhythm section partners of Return to Forever—pianist Chick Corea and bassist Stanley Clarke. This all-star lineup entered the studio and in four days completed both projects, including a thrilling album by the acoustic quintet entitled *The Griffith Park Collection*. Like the V.S.O.P. Quintet, this group was a short-lived enterprise, recording one live sequel before dissolving. It was left to the rising generation to bring commitment and longevity to the neo-bop movement.

LENNY WHITE, ET AL., *"L's Bop"* (1982)

"L's Bop," by drummer Lenny White, is the first tune on *The Griffith Park Collection*. As the title suggests, White intended the piece to stir memories of past bop idioms: "The feeling I wanted to get was that of the early '60s, the Blue Note sound." The chorus has an unusual form: AAB (8 + 8 + 12) plus three measures in 5/4 time followed by two measures back in 4/4. The 5/4 section constitutes a *turnaround,* a brief transitional passage that completes one chorus and introduces the next. The 4/4 section is a break for the upcoming (or continuing) soloist. The head consists of two lines that combine contrapuntally. Trumpeter Freddie Hubbard states the rather ornate main melody (which descends three times in sequence), while tenor saxophonist Joe Henderson adds a somewhat less florid countermelody.

The soloists turn in brilliant performances on this recording. Henderson plays an exceedingly graceful and lyrical solo that nonetheless contains many unexpected twists and turns. Among other unusual effects he plays rapidly flowing *arpeggios* in his second break and a high-register *trill* in his last break. Hubbard lives up to his reputation as a "fiery" trumpet player, deploying his trademark *lip slurs* (a narrow, rapidly oscillating zigzag pattern) in the first B-section, and soaring into the upper register with his equally recognizable squeals at the top of the second chorus and the close of his solo. More than the other soloists, pianist Chick Corea seems concerned to develop a series of motives. He intersperses these developments with wide-ranging and continually surprising bop lines—all in a driving swing eighth-note style.

Bassist Stanley Clarke does far more than walk, picking up on motives introduced by the soloists and echoing their ideas without ever losing forward momentum. The composer of the tune (and instigator of the session), drummer Lenny White, accompanies with tremendous energy, pounding cross-rhythms behind the soloists and exploding sporadically with assaults on the tom-toms or cymbals. White himself assumes the role of soloist in a passage of *trading eights* with Corea.

LISTENING CHART 31

Lenny White, et al., "L's Bop"

RECORDED 1982 / *THE GRIFFITH PARK COLLECTION* ELEKTRA/MUSICIAN E1-60025

Freddie Hubbard (trumpet), Joe Henderson (tenor saxophone), Chick Corea (piano), Stanley Clarke (bass), Lenny White (drums)

Style: Neo-bop

Form: AAB + (5/4 turnaround + 4/4 break)
(8 + 8 + 12 + 5 = 33 measure chorus)

			Introduction = 5/4 turnaround + solo break
			Rhythm section: three measures of 5/4 + two of 4/4:
30	0:00		1 2 3 4 5 (short-LONG / short-LONG)
			1 2 3 4 5 (short-LONG / short-LONG)
			1 2 3 4 5 (short-LONG / short-LONG)
	0:03		1 2 3 4 (solo drum break: Lenny White)
			1 2 3 4
	1st Chorus		**Head**
31	0:05	A (8)	Freddie Hubbard (trumpet) plays ornate main melody three times in descending sequence; Joe Henderson (tenor saxophone) adds somewhat less florid countermelody
	0:12	A (8)	*A-section repeated*
	0:20	B (12)	B-section contrasts with A-section, containing mostly sustained notes
	0:31	5/4 (3)	Turnaround
32	0:34	4/4 (2)	Solo tenor break
	2nd Chorus		**Tenor saxophone solo: Joe Henderson**
	0:36	A (8)	Henderson plays highly melodic but quirky and unpredictable solo . . .
	0:44	A (8)	
	0:51	B (12)	

	1:02	5/4 (3)	Turnaround
	1:06	4/4 (2)	Solo tenor break: rapidly flowing *arpeggios* . . .
	3rd Chorus		
	1:07	A (8)	. . . begins chorus with descending sequence, develops motive which Stanley Clarke (bass) then picks up . . .
	1:15	A (8)	
	1:22	B (12)	
	1:34	5/4 (3)	Turnaround: ends solo on high *trill* . . .
33	1:37	4/4 (2)	Solo trumpet break
	4th Chorus		**Trumpet solo: Freddie Hubbard**
	1:39	A (8)	Hubbard begins his solo developing short, two-note motive . . .
	1:46	A (8)	. . . then shifts to long-flowing bop lines
	1:54	B (12)	*Lip slurs* into upper register . . .
	2:05	5/4 (3)	Turnaround
	2:08	4/4 (2)	Solo trumpet break: squeals into high range . . .
	5th Chorus		
	2:10	A (8)	. . . continues high squeals, adding *alternate fingering*
	2:18	A (8)	. . . Hubbard's brief "jackhammer" figure picked up by Chick Corea (piano) . . .
	2:25	B (12)	
	2:36	5/4 (3)	Turnaround: solo ends with more squeals
34	2:40	4/4 (2)	Solo piano break
	6th Chorus		**Piano solo: Chick Corea**
	2:41	A (8)	Corea plays imaginative solo stressing development of short motives . . .
	2:49	A (8)	

2:56	B (12)	
3:08	5/4 (3)	Turnaround
3:11	4/4 (2)	Solo piano break

7th Chorus

3:13	A (8)	
3:21	A (8)	. . . repeats syncopated riff, disrupting meter . . .
3:29	B (12)	
3:40	5/4 (3)	Turnaround
3:44	4/4 (2)	Solo piano break

8th Chorus — **Trading eights: Corea (piano) vs. White (drums)**

35	3:46	A (8)	Corea . . .
	3:53	A (8)	White . . .
	4:01	B (8)	Corea . . .
	4:08	(4)	White . . .
	4:12	5/4 (3)	Turnaround
	4:16	4/4 (2)	Solo drum break

9th Chorus — **Head**

4:17	A (8)	Horns play contrapuntal head as at the beginning
4:25	A (8)	
4:33	B (12)	
4:45	5/4 (3)	Turnaround
		Turnaround
		Turnaround . . . etc.
		Fade ending

Wynton Marsalis and the Young Lions

In the 1980s a crop of young, mostly black musicians sought to reclaim jazz from the forces of pop music, avant-garde experimentation, and excessive white influence. Their style of choice was the sixties postbop of Miles Davis and John Coltrane. By championing an idiom that was twenty years old, they emulated the Dixielanders of the 1940s; accordingly, some critics called them "new traditionalists." Most often, however, they are referred to as the "Young Lions." It seems fitting that the advance guard of these youthful guardians of tradition should hail from New Orleans, the birthplace of jazz.

The Rise of a Virtuoso

The undisputed leader of this group was a trumpet player named **Wynton Marsalis** (b. 1961). Raised in New Orleans in a musical, jazz-playing family, Marsalis began playing trumpet at age twelve. A musician of extraordinary talent and immense discipline, he quickly mastered his instrument, performing the Haydn Trumpet Concerto with the New Orleans Philharmonic at age fourteen. In 1979 Marsalis moved to New York where he dazzled classical adjudicators, winning a four-year scholarship to the Juilliard School of Music.

Although he loved classical music, Marsalis increasingly gravitated toward straight-ahead, acoustic jazz in New York. The way to make it as a jazz musician, a friend told him, was to play for Art Blakey's Jazz Messengers, then in its fourth decade of training young players. When Marsalis first sat in with Blakey's band, pianist James Williams recalled, "he didn't really know the music. He wasn't really a strong jazz player, but he was an excellent trumpet player." Yet Marsalis practiced very hard (long into the night, according to his roommates), and by 1980 was playing jazz well enough that Blakey hired him with the Messengers.

Wynton Marsalis, 1989.

The combination of transcendent classical virtuosity, rapidly growing jazz abilities, and obsessive practicing made Marsalis an *enfant terrible* of the music world. In 1982 Columbia offered him a record contract; accordingly, he left Blakey to form his own quintet with his equally gifted older brother, tenor saxophonist **Branford Marsalis** (b. 1960). The following year the Marsalis brothers played in a reconstituted V.S.O.P. Quintet (billed as V.S.O.P. II), with Hancock, Carter, and Williams. The collaboration seemed to symbolize a passing of the jazz torch from one generation to the next. In 1984 Wynton made history by becoming the first musician to win a Grammy in both jazz and classical categories. He soon became, as well, the most celebrated and controversial jazz musician in memory.

The New Traditionalist Agenda

The rise of neo-bop, a music cultivated mostly by young blacks, carried a strong element of race pride. Although the civil rights movement had flagged by the 1970s, its positive consequences were real and included affirmative action programs, the virtual elimination of statutory segregation, and a widespread interest in black American history. In 1977 ABC broadcast a twelve-hour, eight-night, miniseries called *Roots*. Telling the story of several generations of a black slave family, the program was spectacularly successful. More than 250 colleges and universities planned courses around the program and over thirty cities declared "Roots" weeks during the broadcast.

The growing interest in black history—indeed, in a black American cultural legacy—strongly influenced the artistic direction taken by Wynton Marsalis. While he was still playing with Blakey, Marsalis met a jazz writer for the *Village Voice* named **Stanley Crouch.** Marsalis soon became a protégé of Crouch, who himself had learned from Albert Murray, who in turn was a disciple of Ralph Ellison. Under the guidance of Crouch, Marsalis began expanding his awareness of jazz before the sixties. He developed a zeal for earlier jazz figures such as Louis Armstrong, Duke Ellington, and Thelonious Monk. He also came to view the blues and swing as cornerstones of any valid jazz aesthetic. At the same time, Crouch reinforced in Marsalis his natural aversion to fusion, pop music in general, and the avant garde.

A Divisive Figure

Because Marsalis saw acoustic, mainstream jazz as a pure and lofty expression of the African American worldview, he had little patience with those who broke with the true faith, regardless of their previous contributions to jazz. An outspoken, articulate, and opinionated individual, Marsalis publicly criticized both Miles Davis and Herbie Hancock for their fusion music. When Marsalis received his first Grammy in 1984, he made a speech condemning much music then marketed as jazz, and made a veiled attack on Hancock's recent fusion hit, "Rockit." In 1985 *Musician* magazine arranged for Marsalis and Hancock to debate their aesthetic views in a joint interview. In that same year Wynton and Branford had a falling out when Branford and pianist Kenny Kirkland left Wynton's quintet to play for the rock artist, Sting.

These confrontations, together with several uncompromising statements to the press, positioned Marsalis as the leading arbiter of taste and of proper definitions of what constitutes jazz. His authoritarian pronouncements, however, invited criticism of himself. Many pointed out that Marsalis's musical vision was an old one, and that Marsalis himself was, to all appearances, not an innovator. More damning perhaps, some critics charged that Marsalis lacked the creative genius of earlier jazz leaders, notwithstanding his undeniable technical skill. To his credit, Marsalis admitted this possibility in such self-effacing statements as this one from 1986: "I don't feel that I can make really great records because I'm not great." But such admissions, whether justified or not, only begged the question of what authority he had, then, to dictate the direction jazz should take or to deny the status of "jazz" to the imaginative work of avant-gardists like David Murray and Henry Threadgill or fusion players such as Pat Metheny. Thus, despite his impressive musicianship, Marsalis became a divisive figure in the eighties, singlehandedly generating much of the controversy in the jazz press of the time.

WYNTON MARSALIS, "Skain's Domain" (1985)

Wynton Marsalis recorded "Skain's Domain" on *J Mood*, the first album he recorded with his quartet, after the departure of his brother Branford and pianist Kenny Kirkland. (The title refers to Marsalis's nickname, "Skain.") "Skain's Domain" harks back to the freewheeling postbop of John Coltrane and Miles Davis in the sixties. With a chorus consisting of a series of harmonic plateaus, the piece invites a modal approach to improvisation. Marsalis goes beyond his 1960s models, however, in the adventurousness of phrasing and meter in the composition itself.

Listening to "Skain's Domain," you might find it difficult to figure out how the chorus works. The chord structure does not adhere to any of the standard patterns, such as AABA, ABAC, or the blues. Instead, the harmonies change somewhat capriciously, complicating the task even of counting out a complete chorus. Fortunately, in the liner notes to the album Stanley Crouch gives us a vital clue: "For those interested in the structure, the song is twenty-seven bars long, with a 2/4 measure at the nineteenth bar." This hidden 2/4 measure (a measure with only two beats rather than the usual four) adds a rhythmic hiccup in the middle of the form. Other odd rhythmic features include the 27-bar chorus length and the irregular rate of change from one chord to another. To illustrate the latter I have provided symbols for each of the chords in Marsalis's first solo chorus (e.g, C minor 7, D♭ minor 7, etc.). Don't worry about what the symbols mean in a technical sense; just observe the different lengths of each chord: 4 bars, 8 bars, 2 bars, 4 bars, 5 bars, 2 bars, and 2 bars. How unlike the balanced regularity of most chord progressions we have seen, with their hierarchical organization into 4-, 8-, 16-, and 32-bar sections!

The head follows the same basic pattern as the solo chorus, but includes small modifications in harmony and meter. The head begins with a *motto* (X), an opening figure that returns later at important structural moments (such as just before the piano solo). The head alternates between prominent trumpet figures (indicated in Listening Chart 32 as five phrases, including the *motto*) and straight time-keeping in the rhythm section, without Marsalis. The alternation becomes narrower until no more textural distinction can be made and the head merges seamlessly into Marsalis's solo.

Of course, one cannot discuss this recording properly without saying something about Marsalis's amazing technical facility and the unusual musical effects he achieves with it. Notice, for example, the myriad types of articulation and phrasing that he explores over the course of six choruses, or the virtuoso acrobatics that he occasionally undertakes—for example, when he rapidly states an oscillating motive in three different octaves near the end of his first solo chorus. Marsalis also has a keen sense for motivic development, which often appears as part of a rhythmic interaction between him and pianist Marcus Roberts. Both aspects—development and interaction—are used to build tension and increase excitement during the solo.

The Movement Expands

The first players who came to prominence on Marsalis's coattails were fellow New Orleanians, trumpeter **Terence Blanchard** (b. 1962) and alto saxophonist **Donald Harrison** (b. 1960). These players replaced the Marsalis brothers in Art Blakey's band in 1982 and later formed their own quintet. Other New Orleans

LISTENING CHART 32

Wynton Marsalis, "Skain's Domain" (Marsalis)

CD 3 / Tracks 36–42

RECORDED DECEMBER 17–20, 1985, NEW YORK CITY / *J MOOD* COLUMBIA CK 40308

Wynton Marsalis (trumpet), Marcus Roberts ("J Master") (piano), Robert Leslie Hurst III (bass), Jeff "Tain" Watts (drums)

Style: Neo-bop / modal jazz	Form: 27-measure chorus structure (19th measure is in 2/4)

				Introduction
36	0:00			Drum solo: Jeff Watts (free time feel)
	0:15			Add bass on pedal points: Robert Hurst
	0:19			Add piano: Marcus Roberts
				Gradually a medium tempo emerges . . .
				Head
37	0:33	1st phrase: X		Wynton Marsalis begins head with *motto* (X) in new, faster tempo
	0:35	*1st Chorus*		*Rhythm section keeps time . . .*
	0:39	2nd phrase		Rhythm section doubles trumpet rhythms . . .
	0:42			*Keeps time . . .*
	0:47	3rd phrase		Doubles trumpet rhythms, keeps time on sustained notes . . .
	0:51	4th phrase		
	0:56	5th phrase		
		2nd Chorus		**Trumpet solo: Wynton Marsalis**
38	1:00	C minor 7	(4)	Beginning his solo at a simmer, Marsalis gradually builds tension over several choruses, often through motivic development . . .
	1:05	D♭ minor 7	(8)	
	1:13	C minor 7	(2)	
39	1:15	B♭ major 7	(4)	
		F♯13–G13–A♭9	(5)	(Section begins with a 2/4 bar, then returns immediately to 4/4)

	1:20	12		
		1 2 3 4 (F♯13)		
		1 2 3 4 (G13)		
		1 2 3 4 (A♭9)		
		1 2 3 4		
	1:25	C 7 (♭5)	(2)	. . . states oscillating motive rapidly in three different octaves
	1:27	B major 7	(2)	
40	1:29	*3rd Chorus* (27)		. . . Marsalis and Marcus Roberts interact with isolated pops across pitch space
	1:57	*4th Chorus* (27)		
	2:25	*5th Chorus* (27 + 2)		. . . sputters and crackles in upper register, creates more rhythmic interaction with Roberts (Band extends last chord by two measures)
	2:55	*6th Chorus* (27)		
	3:23	*7th Chorus* (27)		
	3:32			. . . more rhythmic interaction between Marsalis and Roberts
	3:51		X (2)	Marsalis introduces Roberts with *motto*
41	3:53	*8th Chorus* (27)		**Piano solo: Marcus Roberts**
	4:21	*9th Chorus* (27)		Marcus plays solo emphasizing motivic development
	4:49	*10th Chorus* (27)		
	5:17	*11th Chorus* (27)		
				Head
42	5:45	First phrase: X		Roberts begins head with *motto;* band plays head largely as before, with minor but interesting changes; closes with *motto* again
	5:51	Second phrase, etc.		

players who benefited from Marsalis's example or patronage included Harry Connick Jr., a popular jazz singer and big band leader who studied piano with Wynton's father, Ellis Marsalis; flutist Kent Jordan and his younger brother, trumpeter Marlon Jordan; and trumpeter Nicholas Payton. When Blanchard left the Jazz Messengers in 1986, Philadelphia trumpet player **Wallace Roney** (b. 1960) took his place. The next year Marsalis discovered another gifted young trumpeter at a high school clinic in Waco, Texas: **Roy Hargrove** (b. 1969). Other Young Lions included trumpeter Philip Harper and his drum-playing brother Winard Harper, pianists Marcus Roberts, Geoff Keezer, and Benny Green, saxophonists Christopher Hollyday and Vincent Herring, guitarists Mark Whitfield and Howard Alden, and organist Joey DeFrancesco. Remarkably, almost every one of these players recorded as a leader at a very young age, a feat made possible by Marsalis's success.

Meanwhile, Marsalis toured constantly, playing, teaching, speaking, writing, adopting a role of advocacy unlike that of any of his jazz predecessors. Increasingly, he seemed less interested in making fresh music than in bringing the Jazz Tradition to those unfamiliar with it. Speaking of the power of jazz to lift society, he said, "I know this music can work. To play it, you have to have the belief in quality. And the belief in practice, the belief in study, belief in your history, belief in the people that you came out of. It is a statement of heroism against denigration."

Free Jazz and Fusion in the 1980s

Chapter **29**

Despite the triumph of **Wynton Marsalis** and the Young Lions, the 1980s brought continued soul-searching for musicians, critics, and fans worried about the future of jazz. It was reassuring that a new generation of predominantly black musicians had dedicated their lives to playing mainstream acoustic jazz. But on the other hand, postmodernism was an unsettling reality for listeners accustomed to a music that for sixty years had periodically rejuvenated itself through innovation. For all his brilliant musicianship, Marsalis had merely elaborated an old style, after all, rather than pioneering a new one. Where were the Armstrongs, the Parkers, the Coltranes of the 1980s?

Heedless of these philosophical concerns, a host of creative musicians perversely continued to make excellent music, proving in the process that retrenchment and consolidation have their advantages over innovation. Among modern big bands, Rob McConnell and the Boss Brass and Bob Florence performed ingenious, swinging charts in the grand tradition of their predecessors. Singers Abbey Lincoln and Bobby McFerrin devised imaginative pathways for the human voice. And live performances by legendary figures from Woody Herman to Dizzy Gillespie to Sonny Rollins continued to attract large audiences. But the freshest music of the period carried on the most suggestive trends of the 1960s: free jazz and fusion. In these domains, the World Saxophone Quartet and Pat Metheny, in particular, fashioned musical visions of startling originality.

Free Jazz in the Reagan Era

In the 1960s radical free jazz was sustained, in part, by militant black politics. Listeners who might ordinarily have recoiled from the raucous dissonance of the music took strength from its harrowing indictment of social injustice. But as the seventies dawned and the civil rights movement began to fade, free jazz faltered as well. Long banished from the nightclub scene, avant-garde players continued to hold forth in privately organized loft concerts for sympathetic friends and fans. In the absence of countercultural discontent, though, the old strategies of anarchy and disruption rang hollow. "It all started sounding the same," recalled soprano saxophonist Steve Lacy. "It wasn't free anymore."

To be sure, Cecil Taylor continued to perform his trademark uncompromising brand of energy jazz. And, although the avant garde languished in the

United States generally, it flourished in Europe, where unappreciated American musicians had fled during the 1960s. But the experience of Taylor's fellow revolutionary, Ornette Coleman, better represented the larger trend. In 1975 Coleman organized **Prime Time,** a band mingling elements of free jazz and fusion. While keeping his usual tendency to drift among tonal centers in his own solos, Coleman employed jazz-rock instrumentation, often using two electric guitarists, two bassists, and two drummers in his various editions of Prime Time. After the tribulations of the late sixties and seventies, other avant-garde players likewise decided to make peace (in varying degrees) with the mainstream. As a result, much free jazz in the 1980s assumed a friendlier character, incorporating elements of postbop, fusion, the blues, and other familiar idioms. Like neo-bop, free jazz thus mirrored the cultural conservatism of the Reagan era.

Henry Threadgill

Free jazz musicians from Chicago adapted more gracefully to these developments than did their New York-based counterparts. The Chicago players, after all, had always embraced outside influences. Thus, while the careers of energy jazz practitioners Archie Shepp and Pharaoh Sanders declined after the sixties, such AACM veterans as members of the Art Ensemble of Chicago and Anthony Braxton built international reputations. By the early 1980s another AACM alumnus was ready to make his mark on jazz: woodwind player and composer **Henry Threadgill** (b. 1944).

Born and raised in a Chicago ghetto, Threadgill encountered a wide range of music as a child. "There was never any talk of *this* kind of music or *that* kind of music," he recalled. "I grew up with hillbilly music on the radio, Polish music on the radio, Tchaikovsky, gospel. . . . We listened to it all." Like many young blacks of his generation, he especially treasured R&B: "Howlin' Wolf was my greatest hero, my favorite."

Perhaps because of his catholic tastes, Threadgill was rejected by mainstream jazz musicians. As a young player he toured with gospel companies and played in blues bands. But jazz players wouldn't let him sit in with them. "They didn't like the way I played," he said, "because I wasn't playing bebop the way they were. They said I didn't know what I was doing." This didn't make sense to Threadgill, who valued expressiveness over orthodoxy. "What would generally be the case is that they manipulated the licks [i.e., played standard bebop patterns], and I never wanted to do that. I wanted to *say* something."

In 1982 Threadgill proved that he had something to say when he organized his "Sextet," an odd name for a band consisting of seven players: Threadgill (woodwinds), Olu Dara (cornet), Craig Harris (trombone), Diedre Murray (cello), Fred Hopkins (bass), Pheeroan Aklaff (drums), and John Betsch (drums). On albums such as *Just the Facts and Pass the Bucket* (1983) and *Rag Bush and All* (1988), Threadgill conjured musical environments of tremendous emotional power, recalling the work of his spiritual forebears Duke Ellington and Charles Mingus. And like the Art Ensemble of Chicago and Braxton he drew from a varied stylistic palette, tapping gospel, R&B, and the blues, as well as the avant garde. But ultimately, Threadgill's music is *sui generis.* Permeated with irreverence, pathos, and sheer zaniness, it takes the listener into another world, where even familiar routines are never predictable.

HENRY THREADGILL

on Free Jazz after the Sixties—1979

I think by the time you get into the late sixties and early seventies people had matured, and the whole period of the charlatan had really come to an end. Either people had now learned their craft and really knew something about what they were doing, or they were fooling people. Anyway, the musicians that were working in the area that we were working in had been so badly labeled and abused, not only by the press, but by older musicians who were working in other styles. We had been slandered something awful, you know. "They don't know scales. They don't know how to play 'All the Things You Are.' They don't know all the previous things." That wasn't true, but of course nothing is born without a price. You have to pay the price for that music coming on the scene.

So by the time you got to the seventies, with all these things having gone against you, the people who lasted were people who really knew what they were doing. Sure, there were a lot of cats who got up and couldn't play. I mean, they used the times as an excuse not to learn the craft and to learn their instruments correctly. A lot of people got up there in the bandwagon screamin', hollerin', and got famous for different things, you know. But they didn't last, and like I said, only those people who knew what they were doing lasted.

The community of Chicago alone could not support what we were doing. Those initial years of putting an organization together [i.e., AACM] and setting up concerts—you couldn't do that for the rest of your life and support families, or even support yourself, working infrequently. The support of your comrades, that works for a while, but you can't go through ten years of that. You got to have money to live. You know, the same thing everybody else has. The cat that works at the post office, you got to have the same thing he has.

Quoted in Wayne Enstice and Paul Rubin, *Jazz Spoken Here: Conversations with Twenty-Two Musicians* (Baton Rouge and London: Louisiana State University Press, 1992), 290–91.

Contemporary Voices

The World Saxophone Quartet

The AACM was not the only free jazz collective of the sixties to produce influential artists in subsequent years. A St. Louis organization called the **Black Artists Group (BAG),** formed in 1968, nurtured the development of woodwind players Julius Hemphill (b. 1940), Oliver Lake (b. 1942), and Hamiett Bluiett (b. 1940). In 1976 these musicians joined California tenor saxophonist David Murray (b. 1955) to form the **World Saxophone Quartet,** with Hemphill and Lake on altos and Bluiett on baritone. Within a few years the band had inspired the organization of a number of similar bands, especially in Europe. By the 1980s the World Saxophone Quartet "had established themselves as the foremost chamber group in jazz by virtually unanimous critical acclaim."

As a cooperative the World Saxophone Quartet had no official leader, but **David Murray** was the band's most illustrious soloist. Like Threadgill, Murray grew up on R&B, not jazz. As a very young teenager he led a fifteen-piece R&B band, with a six-man horn section. He listened mostly to James Brown and Jimi Hendrix; "I had never even heard Duke Ellington's band," he said. But in the

World Saxophone Quartet.

seventies he rapidly absorbed the entire jazz tenor saxophone tradition, acquiring a dark, romantic sound reminiscent of Ben Webster and Sonny Rollins. Although he frequently performed in avant-garde contexts, he also saw the need to revitalize tradition. "The music has to start swinging again," he declared in the early 1980s.

The World Saxophone Quartet definitely swung, though with a wonderful freedom of movement in the individual voices. The band effectively balanced opposing elements: composition and improvisation, homophony and polyphony, avant-garde and traditional styles, soloistic and ensemble textures. Murray soloed frequently, but so did each of the other players. All the players doubled (or tripled) on other woodwind instruments, including variously pitched flutes and clarinets. Working without a rhythm section, the Quartet provided its own steady groove (or lack thereof) through the correspondences of individual lines. Some of its most exciting performances took place, as one critic put it, when the players were "collectively improvising in a kind of contemporary projection of New Orleans style."

Group improvisation is especially prominent on early recordings such as *Steppin'* (1978) and *Live in Zurich* (1981). As the band evolved and matured, the four players began to regulate improvisation within carefully wrought composed

CD 3 / Track 43

WORLD SAXOPHONE QUARTET, *"For Lester"* (1987)

In this poignant ballad showcase for tenor saxophone solo, David Murray—as composer and soloist—pays tribute to one of the great tenor saxophonists of the Swing Era, Lester Young (see Chapter 14). As soloist, Murray more readily channels the gruff, full-throated tenor voices of Coleman Hawkins and Ben Webster than the light-footed lyricism of Young. But the sheer melodic beauty of the piece together with an indefinite buoyancy of spirit make this performance an apt tribute to Prez, who was himself a master of these very qualities.

Equally subtle are the faint resonances that reveal the quartet's roots in free jazz. Strands of free jazz mingle in "For Lester" with numerous other threads from the music's past in an eclectic blend that shows the Quartet's debt to the free traditions of Chicago. This is only partly apparent in the head, which allies a mainstream melody with a nontraditional, heterogenous woodwind ensemble (flute, alto saxophone, tenor saxophone, alto clarinet) and mildly dissonant harmonies (in the A-section). But in his unaccompanied cadenza at the end, Murray evokes a wide range of sources, including R&B, mainstream jazz, and the shriek-and-squawk pyrotechnics of radical free tenor players such as Albert Ayler and Pharoah Sanders.

Create your own listening chart (CD 3 / Track 43)

frameworks. They also began using more familiar musical materials. In *Plays Duke Ellington* (1986) and *Rhythm and Blues* (1989) the Quartet paid tribute to two sources of musical inspiration: mainstream jazz and R&B. When Hemphill left in the fall of 1989 he was replaced, but the band's influence declined thereafter.

Fusion in the Prosperous Eighties

In 1975 an eminent rock critic noticed the artistic decline of fusion: "Electric jazz-rock fusion music is a mutation that's beginning to show signs of adaptive strain. . . . Fusion bands have found that it's a good idea to . . . stick with fairly simple chord voicings. Otherwise, the sound becomes muddy and overloaded. This means that the subtleties of jazz phrasing, the multilayered textures of jazz drumming and the music's rich harmonic language are being abandoned." As we have seen, it was in or around this year that Miles Davis retired and most of the bands run by his former sidemen dissolved. In their place arose a generation of fusion musicians concerned less with experimentation and more with commercial success. At some level, of course, fusion had always existed to make money; the movement had originated, in part, as a way of reversing jazz musicians' dismal financial prospects in the late sixties. But the best early fusion bands were animated by an intense idealism as well. For better or for worse, one cannot always say that about their successors.

The new generation of fusion players thrived in the prospering economy of the 1980s. Saxophonists such as **David Sanborn** (b. 1945) and **Kenny G** (b. Kenneth Gorelick, 1959), and bands like **Spyro Gyra,** The Yellow Jackets, and The Rippingtons, crafted an unobtrusive, pop-oriented kind of fusion emphasizing flawless execution and glossy production instead of risk-taking improvisation. In this respect the music represented a latter-day version of the tightly arranged and well-rehearsed commercial numbers of the Swing Era. Indeed, comparing the musical worth of the talented artist David Sanborn with that of someone like Artie Shaw would not be out of place. Yet, critics and purist jazz fans disdained this music, even as it became immensely popular on FM radio stations. The burgeoning radio audience led in the 1990s to the *smooth jazz* craze, a development we will take up in Chapter 30.

Miles Davis Comes Out of Retirement

Despite the highly commercialized environment, a few gifted musicians bucked the trend toward homogeneity and commodification. Fittingly, an important source of inspiration came from Miles Davis, who in 1980 astonished the jazz world by coming out of retirement to begin recording and touring again. One writer mused on the meaning of this momentous event: "Five years of silence from one of the four or five great creators of jazz, when all the others are dead and the music is stagnating, creates a mythology: the myth of the Messiah. Miles Davis, and this should be good enough to give us joy for the time being, is back."

Over the next several years, until his death in 1991, Davis fully embraced the new easy-listening brand of fusion. Though his music shows a characteristic vein of experimentation, Davis recorded pop songs by Michael Jackson and Cyndi Lauper, and publicly associated himself more with Prince than with his distinguished jazz colleagues from the past. Not surprisingly, critics generally viewed his music from this period as the least interesting of his career. But as the above quotation suggests, the mere symbolism of Davis's presence again on the

Pat Metheny, 1985.

jazz scene proved inspiring. Moreover, as before, Davis hired talented sidemen who went on to enjoy successful careers as leaders. Electric guitarists John Scofield and Mike Stern and tenor saxophonist Bob Berg are some of Davis's late-period alumni who rose to prominence in the 1990s.

Pat Metheny

Probably the most original fusion artist of the 1980s, however, had no direct connection with Davis. Guitarist **Pat Metheny** (b. 1954) grew up in Kansas City, Missouri, a city with a rich jazz history (see Chapter 11). As an adolescent in the mid-1960s, he fell in love with the Beatles, seeing *Hard Day's Night* twelve or thirteen times. But he also became a jazz addict and listened constantly to Miles Davis, Ornette Coleman, Gary Burton, and others. By age fourteen he was playing professionally in Kansas City. Before his twentieth birthday he had taught guitar on the faculties of the University of Miami and the Berklee College of Music in Boston.

In 1974, Metheny joined the band of his idol, vibraphonist Gary Burton. In that same year he met pianist **Lyle Mays** (b. 1953), then a music student at North Texas State University (now the University of North Texas). As both composer and pianist/synthesizer player, Mays would become his principal collaborator, sharing with Metheny an uncanny unity of conception not unlike that shared by Duke Ellington and Billy Strayhorn. In 1977 the two formed the **Pat Metheny Group,** a band of varying size and instrumentation, and began recording for **ECM Records** (see "Record Labels: ECM"). Together with bassist Steve Rodby, Metheny and Mays became the unchanging core of the group, as other band members came and went over the years.

Record Labels

ECM

ECM Records was founded in Cologne, Germany, in 1969, by Manfred Eicher. The letters ECM stood for "Editions of Contemporary Music," a name that said much about the wide-ranging, nondoctrinaire musical agenda adopted by Eicher. In the 1970s and 1980s, ECM made some of the most distinctive records on the market. ECM artists mingled elements of classical music and jazz, world music and American vernacular styles. Notably, ECM also blended free jazz and fusion traditions, long before it became fashionable to do so. A common thread running through many of ECM's albums was a seemingly "European" sense of refinement, a rarefied ambiance often stemming from an extremely subtle use of electronic sounds. Some criticized the label for fostering a New Age–like wispiness, but the best ECM records demonstrated true artistry on the part of both performers and producers. A glance at the ECM roster, containing names like Keith Jarrett, Chick Corea, the Art Ensemble of Chicago, Pat Metheny, and Norwegian tenor saxophonist Jan Garbarek, suggests both the stylistic range and—paradoxically—the aesthetic unity of the company. Perhaps more than any other label, ECM anticipated the freewheeling international eclecticism of the 1990s. ■ ■ ■

By the early 1980s Metheny had developed a unique sound, in both his guitar playing and his compositions. As a soloist he balanced breathtaking virtuosity with poignant lyricism. His electric guitar had a warm, personal tone, and his articulation and phrasing were equally distinctive. As a composer Metheny created emotionally broad settings, often suffused with romantic yearning or midwestern nostalgia. Drawing upon folk rock, the Brazilian samba, minimalism, and other diverse sources, Metheny's music did not fit easily into predetermined categories. (Metheny himself refers to "fusion" as "the F word.") Not surprisingly, critics seemed flummoxed by it. While conceding Metheny's obvious talent and musicianship, many condemned his "Brahmsian" soundscapes as precariously sentimental.

PAT METHENY GROUP, *"The First Circle"* (1984)

"The First Circle," one of Pat Metheny's best-known recordings, reveals the imaginative compositional skills of Metheny and his co-composer Lyle Mays. Structurally, the piece divides into five parts: a lengthy two-part introduction, the complete head, a piano solo by Mays, an interlude, and the second half of the head (with a brief coda). The form of the head is AABA, but the sections are about twice as long as the sections in traditional song form, and extra measures are occasionally added.

The piece represents an ingenious adaptation of the uptempo Brazilian samba. Instead of using the standard 2/4 or 4/4 meter, Metheny uses a *changing meter*, alternating between 12/8 and 10/8 from one bar to the next. (You may find it easier to count in 6/4 and 5/4, for example: 1 2 3 4 5 6 / 1 2 3 4 5 / 1 2 3 4 5 6 / 1 2 3 4 5 / etc. If it's difficult to locate the beat, get a metronome and set it to 160. This approximate tempo will help get you started.) The 10/8 bar throws the meter off-kilter, creating a slight instability that drives the music forward. Within this metric context, Metheny employs a two-bar rhythmic pattern (*pattern X* in Listening Chart 33) throughout the piece that goes as follows:

> <u>long</u> *short*-<u>long</u> *short-short* <u>long</u> <u>long</u> *short-short* /
> <u>long</u> *short*-<u>long</u> *short-short* <u>long</u> <u>long</u> *short-short* / etc.

This pattern appears first in the high guitar-bell pedal point of the introduction and in the rhythmic accompaniment to the head, but is perhaps easiest to hear in the synthesized French horn accents during the interlude.

"The First Circle" demonstrates a common theme in Metheny's music: a quest for the ecstatic. Using affective harmonies, gradually accumulating textures, and naturally increasing dynamics, Metheny builds several climaxes into the composition: first, at the end of the head, second, at the end of Mays's solo, and third, at the end of the entire piece. Pedro Aznar's *vocalise* (wordless vocal) doublings of the melody, especially in the upper register, dramatize this structure. And Mays beautifully shapes his solo to match the upward trajectory of the composition. Refraining from soloing himself, Metheny plays acoustic steel-string guitar as accompaniment, in the folkish plucking of the introduction and in the ferocious rapid-fire strumming later on, which—although he uses a pick—has sometimes left him with bloody fingers in live performances. "That kind of strumming takes a certain kind of physical energy that is more like drumming than conventional guitar playing," he once remarked.

LISTENING CHART 33

Pat Metheny Group, "The First Circle" (Metheny & Mays)

CD 3 / Tracks 44–49

RECORDED FEBRUARY 1984, NEW YORK / *FIRST CIRCLE* ECM 1278

Pat Metheny (steel-string acoustic guitar), Lyle Mays (piano, synthesizers), Steve Rodby (acoustic bass), Pedro Aznar (nylon-string acoustic guitar, voice, bells, percussion), Paul Wertico (drums)

Style: Fusion		Form: AABA song form with lengthy introduction, interlude, and coda

			Introduction
44	0:00	*Part 1*	Hand claps (in alternating 12/8 and 10/8 time; *count in 6 and 5*)
	0:12		Add high pedal point: guitar + bell play rhythmic *pattern X:*
			long *short-*<u>long</u> *short-short* <u>long</u> <u>long</u> *short-short*
	0:21		Add vocalise chant melody
	0:41		Sustained synthesizer chords
	0:50		Return to vocalise chant
	1:02		Sustained synthesizer chords
45	1:11	*Part 2*	Guitar-bass trio: steel-string acoustic guitar (Pat Metheny) + nylon-string acoustic guitar (Pedro Aznar) + acoustic bass (Steve Rodby); cymbal swells in background . . .
	1:53		Add high sustained counterpoint: piano + bells
		1st Chorus	**Head**
46	2:29	A	Synthesizers + steel-string guitar play unison melody to *pattern X* in background
	3:05	A	Add vocalise to unison line
	3:41	B	Back-beats, then down-beats
	4:08	A	Now vocalise an octave higher
		2nd Chorus	**Piano solo: Lyle Mays**
47	4:44	A	Mays plays lyrical solo, starting soft with sparse accompaniment and building to a climax, as percussion and guitar lines are added successively

	5:22	A	
	6:01	B	
	6:27	A	
			Interlude: Synthesizer (Lyle Mays) + Bass drum (Paul Wertico)
48	7:07		Mays plays *pattern X* on synthesizer (simulating French horn sound); Wertico inserts booming bass drum fills in the gaps
		3rd Half-Chorus	**Head (second half)**
49	7:44	B	Band plays head (from the bridge) as before
	8:11	A	
			Coda
	8:53		Final crescendo of guitar strumming and percussion

His fans and fellow musicians held no such reservations. Early on, Metheny built up a cult following that has only expanded with time. From the beginning he toured relentlessly, averaging between 120 and 240 concerts per year. The Pat Metheny Group scored high among his peers, receiving an unparalleled seven consecutive Grammy Awards for seven consecutive albums, starting with *Offramp* (1982). Not one to rest on his laurels, Metheny has constantly explored new sound worlds. "That's part of the reason why people like us," he said. "We think of music as research. When we get a record contract, it's like a grant. Funding for research. There aren't too many bands like that."

Michael Brecker, Steps, and Steps Ahead

One of Metheny's frequent outside collaborators on various recording projects was the tenor saxophonist **Michael Brecker** (b. 1949). The younger brother of the trumpeter Randy Brecker, Michael Brecker grew up in a musical family. Through marathon practice sessions, he developed into a brilliant all-around player with a gift for inventive improvisation. Throughout the seventies, Brecker played in hundreds of studio sessions, recording for jazz and pop stars alike. By the 1980s, he had become "the most influential saxophonist since John Coltrane," setting the standard for "tone, technique, energy, and . . . harmonic methodology."

In 1979 Brecker joined a band that came to be known as Steps. The band, which also featured Mike Manieri on vibraphone, Don Grolnick on piano, Eddie Gomez on bass, and Steve Gadd on drums, was an all-star ensemble similar to the V.S.O.P. Quintet, the Griffith Park group, and other star-studded cooperatives of the time. But Steps departed from those groups in its style, which lay somewhere between postbop and fusion. The musicians played on acoustic instruments but used fusion-oriented rhythms, textures, and forms. Manieri called the music "contemporary bebop"; sympathetic critics called it "the new acoustic fusion."

After successful tours and recordings in Japan, Steps signed a recording contract in the United States and began building its stateside reputation. But because another band had already registered the name Steps, they changed their name to **Steps Ahead.** Now with pianist Eliane Elias and former Weather Report drummer Peter Erskine, the band recorded an eponymous album in 1983. Presenting sophisticated, forward-looking compositions such as "Islands" and "Pools," and inspired virtuoso solos from Brecker in particular, the album drew enthusiastic praise from European critics but apathy from American ones, who couldn't figure out where to place the band stylistically. As Manieri lamented, "One critic said 'It would be great to hear them play the blues, that would help,' but I've played the blues for thirty years, who wants to keep playing the blues? We were trying to come up with new music." For their next album, *Modern Times* (1984), the band "went electric," using electric bass and synthesizers; Brecker even began playing an EWI (electronic wind instrument) in addition to acoustic tenor. Now a recognizably "fusion" band, Steps Ahead began to enjoy greater recognition. But ultimately the band was too creative for its own good. The music got little airplay because, as Manieri recalled, "more than half of the tracks have to have an acoustic bass before [they'll] play your record on jazz radio and the commercial stations won't play it because it's too edgy." By 1987, Steps Ahead had dissolved (although Manieri continued to lead a different band of the same name).

In the 1960s free jazz and fusion represented opposite extremes: the former alienated listeners through dissonance and abstraction, while the latter achieved commercial success by absorbing popular styles. By the 1980s, however, the two idioms had moved closer together. This is clear in the music of nearly all the major figures discussed in this chapter. As we have seen, Ornette Coleman mixed the two styles in his band Prime Time. In 1990 both Henry Threadgill and the World Saxophone Quartet followed suit, adding electric instruments to their bands. Pat Metheny collaborated with Ornette Coleman, bassist Charlie Haden, and drummers Jack DeJohnette and Denardo Coleman (Ornette's son) on a free-fusion blend for his acclaimed album *Song X* (1985). On his first album as a leader, from 1987, Michael Brecker explored both free and fusion traditions. Such experiments paved the way for an explosion of similar hybrids in the 1990s. As we shall see in Chapter 30, the free funk of visionaries like alto saxophonist Steve Coleman and trumpeter Dave Douglas supplied some of the most interesting jazz of the late century.

Jazz at the Millennium

Chapter **30**

The condition of jazz at the turn of the millennium is difficult to diagnose. Positive vital signs in the early nineties seemed to suggest that the proselytizing of Wynton Marsalis and the accessibility of contemporary fusion had broadened the jazz audience. A study from 1992 indicated that roughly a third of all Americans "liked" jazz (up from 26 percent in 1982), 25 percent wanted to hear more live performances of it, and 5 percent claimed jazz as their favorite kind of music. Not bad numbers for a centenarian product of poverty and discrimination.

But the problem of artistic leadership remains. Although more musicians perform at higher virtuoso levels than ever before, the sheer number of talented players paradoxically blends individuals into relative anonymity. Moreover, the fragmentation of styles and substyles begun during World War II started in the 1990s to accelerate at a geometric pace. The diversity made the very possibility of dominant leaders and movements, in the traditional sense, unlikely.

Some jazz lovers view this state of affairs with trepidation, but not everyone. As one critic usefully analogized, the posture of jazz "has become horizontal. . . . It was once vertical, with so many towering peaks—graceful soaring spires named Pops, Prez, Bird, Duke, Monk, Trane, Miles, and Ornette. There is a lack of height now; jazz is hugging the ground. Not because it is sick or tired or dying but because it is flourishing in a new way. It is covering more and more ground. Who knows where it will overflow next? Where will it plant roots next?" Today's jazz may lack the charismatic individuals of earlier periods, but it compensates with head-spinning kaleidoscopic plenitude. This rich stylistic environment was made possible by the most significant political event of the late twentieth century: the end of the Cold War.

The Postmodern Surge

To universal astonishment, the communist system of Eastern Europe collapsed in the late 1980s, ending almost fifty years of hostility between East and West. The end of the Cold War changed the world in profound and far-reaching ways. The Cold War world was a bipolar one, pitting America and Western Europe against the Soviet Union and its allies. After the war, global strategists began speaking of

"*Take my hams, I want to lose them. Take my slaws, I'll never use them.*"

Michael Crawford, *New Yorker,* February 29, 1988. This cartoon pokes fun at jazz's accelerating tendency in the late 1980s to unite with seemingly distant cultural phenomena. The deli owner is singing a variant of the popular standard "All of Me": "Take my lips, I want to lose them / Take my arms, I'll never use them."

of a multipolar world in which countries interacted within a complex matrix of myriad, often shifting relationships. The new fluidity of borders in previously insulated communist countries encouraged this interaction on every level, from transnational politics to trade to tourist travel. The creation of the Internet in the early 1990s dramatically intensified international contacts, shrinking the "global village" even further. These new realities opened American society to international and cross-cultural influences on a scale hitherto unknown.

These influences prompted a surge of postmodernist expression in the arts. Although we introduced the concept of postmodernism in Chapter 28, let's take time now to define it more fully. **Postmodernism** is a broad philosophical and artistic movement that emerged in the late sixties and early seventies. Its goal was to make sense out of a world in which the ethos of European-based *modernism*—that is, the prizing of innovation for its own sake—no longer dominated the artistic landscape. Postmodernism recognized that a vast knowledge of the world and its history, together with improved technology in transportation, photography, and sound recording, now made it convenient to experience art and culture from almost every time and place. The fall of communism enriched this global heritage, inspiring postmodern artists further to emphasize *pluralism* and *eclecticism* in their work.

As defined by theorists, postmodern music manifests at least some—although not necessarily all—of the following characteristics:

- A self-conscious appropriation and reinterpretation of past styles
- The free interplay of traditions from various world cultures
- Blurred boundaries between "high" and "low," or elitist and populist styles
- The juxtaposition of quotations and references from disparate sources, sometimes in a manner suggesting the technique of collage
- An emphasis on fragmentation and discontinuity at the expense of structural coherence
- An ironic, parodistic, or satirical attitude toward borrowed styles

Within a jazz context, overt postmodernism usually involves mixing styles from different periods (e.g., Dixieland and bebop) and/or with musical traditions generally considered alien to jazz. These traditions might include world music, avant-garde classical music, electronic art music, and even pop music if the blend somehow went beyond the standard approaches to jazz-rock fusion (see cartoon by Michael Crawford). But in this paradoxical era, even diehard modernists (e.g., radical free players) and reactionary traditionalists (e.g., neoboppers) were "postmodernists" in the larger sense by virtue of their conscious borrowing of artistic ideals from an earlier time.

postmodernism an artistic movement that arose in the late 1960s in which all styles, from every time and place, were equally available and viable.

The Institutionalization of Jazz

The multiculturalism inherent in the postmodern worldview transformed American universities and cultural institutions. In the 1990s, the Western European canon of cultural achievement came under attack and marginalized traditions were championed. Thus, really for the first time, jazz assumed an honored place in the academy alongside the classical works of Bach, Beethoven, and Stravinsky. Graduate programs welcomed aspiring jazz scholars, and academic presses published important historical, ethnomusicological, and theoretical studies of jazz. Queens College opened the Louis Armstrong Archives and the Smithsonian Institution the Duke Ellington Collection, each housing music and personal effects of those seminal figures. Such bastions of high art as Carnegie Hall and Lincoln Center began concert series devoted to jazz, featuring **repertory orchestras** that performed solos and arrangements painstakingly transcribed from historical recordings.

New respect for the music even found its way into politics, the last stop toward cultural legitimacy. In 1987 Congress passed a resolution declaring jazz to be "a rare national treasure," and in 1992 the country elected Bill Clinton, the first U.S. president to play jazz tenor saxophone in public appearances. The institutionalization of jazz reached a climax in 2000, when Ken Burns made his lavish, celebratory, ten-part documentary film. Funded by thirteen august benefactors, including General Motors, the PEW Charitable Trusts, the National Endowment for the Humanities, the National Endowment for the Arts, and the John D. and Catherine T. MacArthur Foundation, such an ambitious project would have been improbable even ten years earlier.

The Recording Industry

All this reverential activity tended to exalt the music's past, a preoccupation which also haunted the recording industry. Because classic recordings often turned far higher profits than new recordings did, mainstream record labels released a flood of compact disc **reissues** of records from the entire history of jazz. In a related trend, leading players made **tribute albums** to the jazz greats; Joe Henderson, for example, recorded *Lush Life: The Music of Billy Strayhorn* (1991), Joe Lovano recorded *Celebrating Sinatra* (1996), and Chick Corea recorded *Remembering Bud Powell* (1997).

The abundance of reissues and retrospective recordings saturated the market, making it difficult for musicians with original material to succeed. In a *JazzTimes* article on trends of the 1990s, one critic wrote that "even the larger jazz stars, who on a good album cracked 100,000 copies, were plummeting down into the 30,000 level, while the average jazz album, if it sold 5,000 copies was doing better than well. Putting out records by unknowns became harder to justify." As a result, many young players skipped the major record companies and recorded for **independent labels.** With the cost of making a CD recording dramatically reduced by new technology, the number of "indies" exploded in the 1990s, and included such labels as Thrill Jockey, Delmark, Criss Cross, Winter and Winter, Aum Fidelity, Palmetto, and Fresh Sounds.

To carve out their own niche in a tight market, some musicians took advantage of Internet technology. With personalized Web sites and online stores for their own music, enterprising players could eliminate the need for capitalist

repertory orchestra a band that performs the music of historical ensembles, often from parts painstakingly transcribed from recordings.

reissue a recording that makes newly available the music of an old, often classic recording.

intermediaries and interact directly with customers from all over the world. Offering free **MP3 files** (computer-generated copies of sound recordings) allowed unknown artists to advertise their music at very little expense.

Traditionalism on the March

The retrospective leanings of universities, concert halls, and major record companies tilted the advantage toward traditionalist performers. The leading traditionalist, Wynton Marsalis, expanded his stature and influence. In 1991 he became artistic director of New York's **Jazz at Lincoln Center**, from which prestigious post he continued to expound his controversial views. Working under the influence of Stanley Crouch and Albert Murray, Marsalis programmed concerts at Lincoln Center devoted to great black musicians of the past—Louis Armstrong and Duke Ellington, above all. His decision to avoid programs based on the music of white, free jazz, and fusion players raised heated protest from some quarters. Marsalis responded that the great black figures deserved to be treated first, since they created and developed the music, and that free jazz and fusion were corruptions of the jazz tradition. Nevertheless, in an age that valued "political correctness," critics accused Marsalis and Jazz at Lincoln Center of reverse racism and ideological intolerance.

In his own music Marsalis moved further away from his neo-bop beginnings toward the reinterpretation of earlier historical styles. This process began in earnest in 1988 when he recorded *The Majesty of the Blues,* an album featuring New Orleans polyphony, old-fashioned plunger style, and plenty of blues playing. He followed this with other retrospective projects like *In This House, On This Morning* (1992) and *Jump Start and Jazz* (1996). In 1997 Marsalis became the first jazz musician to win the Pulitzer Prize for his three-hour, twenty-seven-movement work, *Blood on the Fields,* an oratorio about slavery that echoes the spirit and intent of Duke Ellington's *Black, Brown, and Beige.* While some criticized Marsalis's backward orientation, his music of this period often went far beyond its historical models, refashioning them in new and unpredictable ways.

Further Listening from the *Prentice Hall Jazz Collection*
Track 11: Wynton Marsalis, "Express Crossing" (1993)

The Bop Legacy

Many of Marsalis's fellow Young Lions disappeared as quickly as they had appeared. But in the 1990s new young players emerged to carry the neo-bop banner. **Joshua Redman** (b. 1969) pursued a successful career as jazz tenor saxophonist, updating the full-throated tenor tradition with tremendous authority. Pianist **Brad Mehldau** (b. 1970), in a series of albums called *Art of the Trio,* performed thoughtful glosses of Bill Evans, whereas bassist **Christian McBride** (b. 1972) proved himself a worthy successor to the likes of Ray Brown and Paul Chambers, recording with such diverse artists as Roy Hargrove, David Sanborn, and Sting.

In addition to these youngsters, veteran bop-oriented performers burnished their reputations or rose to prominence for the first time. **Tom Harrell** (b. 1946), despite an ongoing battle against schizophrenia, boasted one of the most lyrical trumpet styles in jazz, echoing that of Clifford Brown and Art Farmer. Tenor saxophonist **Joe Lovano** (b. 1952) cultivated a fascinatingly refractory melodic

MP3 file a computer-generated copy of a sound recording.

CHRISTIAN McBRIDE

on the Influence of Marketing in the 1990s

T he whole "young lions" hype, which, unfortunately, I was a part of, peaked in the early 1990s. I say "unfortunately" because the hype was so strong, I don't think any musician from that movement will ever be looked upon by certain people as serious musicians. We'll be looked at as puppets for record companies and managers, or *People* magazine–type personalities as opposed to, well, *Down Beat* magazine–type personalities. Record companies, of course, jumped on the hype to sell some records, and they did . . . for a while. After the young lions hype died down, the focus was put on what's known as "concept" records (i.e., X plays the music of Y; X plays love songs; X plays music for driving to). Fortunately, there have been some concept records that have been wonderful, but I believe that when a record company tries to *force* a "vibe" on a record, rather than letting the music flow on its own power, we will hear some very untrue CDs. Which, in my opinion, flooded the market in the '90s.

"Artists' Perspectives of the '90s," *Down Beat* (January 2000): 33.

Contemporary Voices

sense, while managing to evoke the entire history of his instrument without suggesting any single dominant influence. Working in a conventional bop context, **Jeff Hamilton** (b. 1953) developed an approach to the drum set that was so melodic that in some solos listeners could recognize actual melodies. Meanwhile, postbop figures of the 1960s remained active, casting large shadows wherever they performed. The still towering stature of players like Herbie Hancock, Chick Corea, Wayne Shorter, and Tony Williams indicated just how much jazz in the 1990s relied on its history.

The Big Band Legacy

As in previous years the Swing Era continued, at various removes, to inspire young musicians. One of the most creative big bands to emerge in the 1990s was led by **Maria Schneider** (b. 1960), a protégé of Gil Evans. In her charts Schneider perpetuated the pastel impressionism of Evan's classic scores for Miles Davis, but with an unmistakably personal stamp. Another important group was the **Mingus Big Band,** an ensemble that has met weekly since 1991 to explore the music of Charles Mingus. Featuring an all-star roster, including Randy Brecker, Lew Soloff, Ronnie Cuber, Ryan Kisor, and Chris Potter, the Mingus Big Band stands as a proud descendant of the great rehearsal bands of the sixties and seventies.

In a more surprising development, small combos began playing a high-spirited party music based on big band swing and jump blues of the 1940s. **Retro swing** began as an underground movement among teenagers and twenty-somethings in Los Angeles. But after the success of the 1996 film *The Swingers,* featuring the band Big Bad Voodoo Daddy, retro swing became a nationwide phenomenon. Musicians and fans resurrected not only the music but the dances, clothing styles, and slang of previous generations, forming a cultural blend of equal parts Cab Calloway and Rat Pack–era Frank Sinatra. In typical postmodern fashion, retro swing bands often played through a filter of slapstick distortion, producing a cartoon version, so to speak, of the original swing music.

Groove Merchants

Although traditionalist musicians enjoyed high profiles in the press, players working in the fusion idiom generally fared better financially. The dominant fusion movement of the period was driven almost entirely by marketing strategies of radio programmers. Mainstream acoustic jazz, it must be remembered, had not appeared on commercial radio for decades (being confined primarily to public radio and college stations). In the early 1990s the one type of jazz with a limited presence on commercial radio—the easy-listening fusion of Kenny G, David Sanborn, and Spyro Gyra—began showing the potential for huge revenues. Using "research groups" of prospective listeners, programmers narrowed down the style of this music and coined the advertising term to best describe it: **smooth jazz.**

The name "smooth jazz" served the same purpose as "soft rock"—to announce that the rough edges had been sanded off of a once daunting idiom. One critic described smooth jazz as an amalgam of "syrupy alto and soprano saxes, reverb-heavy guitars, pristine digital keyboards and funky but light synthesized drum patterns." Pioneered at FM stations such as Chicago's WNUA and Los Angeles's KTWV ("The Wave"), smooth jazz appealed to fairly well-to-do adults between thirty-five and fifty who, as one writer put it, "like the idea of jazz but don't really like jazz." Critics had little patience with smooth jazz, dismissing it as "jazz lite" or "elevator music." Whatever its artistic merits, no one could dispute the financial rewards of this music. In 1997 the top fifty smooth jazz stations forecast combined advertising revenues of $190 million.

Acid Jazz

The "edgy" counterpart to smooth jazz was a British-born idiom known as **acid jazz,** probably the most resistant to definition of any substyle in the music's history. Coined in 1987 by a London disc jockey, the term originally referred to a mix of 1960s soul jazz, Brazilian rhythms, and "acid house" dance beats. In 1993 acid jazz group Us3 recorded "Cantaloop (Flip Fantasia)," an acid jazz record that became a pop hit. In this piece the band used **samples** (originally recorded excerpts) of Herbie Hancock's soul jazz classic "Cantaloupe Island" as the backdrop to a vocal rap about a new genre fusing jazz and hip-hop.

Yet acid jazz was much more than a jazz/hip-hop hybrid. In 1995, one writer called it "a fertile fusion of traditional jazz, '70s soul and funk, Latin percussion and hip-hop rhythms." Even this definition was incomplete. Some acid jazz recordings emphasize the funk side of the equation, others the Latin, still others the hip-hop—and some absorb electronica or world music. Some use vocals and some are entirely instrumental. What seems clear is that acid jazz represented the multicultural egalitarianism of the 1990s. As a percussionist for Groove Collective explained, "We're a microcosm of what we'd like the world to be—less separation and segregation, more interactivity and intermingling of cultures and styles."

smooth jazz in the 1990s, an unobtrusive, pop-oriented kind of fusion emphasizing flawless execution and glossy production values.

acid jazz a 1990s stylistic blend drawing upon soul jazz, Brazilian rhythms, hip-hop, world music, and "acid house" dance beats.

Medeski, Martin & Wood.

Many acid jazz musicians possess semi-amateur-level abilities and do not improvise extensively. But the movement inspired seasoned jazz musicians to explore new possibilities in groove-based music. Some first-rate bands to do so were: the groups led by Miles Davis's most distinguished guitarist of the 1980s, **John Scofield** (b. 1951); **Bela Fleck and the Flecktones,** whose leader plays—of all things—jazz banjo; and **Medeski, Martin & Wood (MMW),** an acid jazz trio featuring John Medeski on Jimmy Smith–style Hammond organ, Billy Martin on drums, and Chris Wood on bass.

Postmodern Eclectics

As major record companies fetishized the past, the independent record scene reflected the multiplicity and ethnic diversity of post–Cold War society. It also produced some of the most adventurous jazz of the period. With low overhead costs, the independents could afford to target eccentric, specialized tastes and musicians could afford to experiment. Thus, whereas jazz in the eighties manifested a central movement (the Young Lions), jazz in the nineties splintered into countless paths, yielding new hybrids—and hybrids of hybrids—at a tremendous rate. The 1990s saw the emergence (or ascendancy) of M-Base jazz, klezmer jazz, ecstatic jazz, flamenco jazz, Hasidic jazz, township jazz, Eastern European jazz, and any number of other fusions with world music.

The most eclectic and experimental players often participated in the so-called **downtown scene** in New York—the area in East Greenwich Village that supported alternative jazz, rock, and other fringe genres. The leading venue for new jazz was the **Knitting Factory,** which Michael Dorf opened in 1987 (see Map 7). "The New York music scene . . . was desperate at this time for a new

MEDESKI, MARTIN & WOOD, *"Take Me Nowhere"* (2002)

Medeski, Martin & Wood is sometimes cited, accurately, as an acid jazz group. The band members themselves, however, describe their style as "avant-garde instrumental hip-hop trance-funk," an unwieldly formulation that nevertheless says more than "acid jazz" does about the band's remarkably inventive and unpredictable music. On "Take Me Nowhere," MMW overlays hypnotic dance club beats with a fascinating collage of electronic keyboard sounds, interactive textures, and soulful rhythmic figures. There are echoes of the electronic music of avant-garde classical composers such as Karlheinz Stockhausen and Edgard Varèse in some of the effects produced by Medeski on this recording. Indeed, the more you listen to this piece, the more there is to hear.

Calling into question the meaning of such structural conventions as "head," "break," "solo," and "coda," "Take Me Nowhere" manifests the band's postmodern interest in disunity and discontinuity. Shortly after Groove #1 is established, bassist Chris Wood plays what sounds like an important melody. But is it the head, or just a bass line? The ambivalently incomplete restatement of this melody only compounds the confusion. Similarly, at the end of the first statement of the "head" (if that is what it is), Medeski and Martin drop out to allow Wood to play what seems like a solo break in the traditional sense. In later contexts, however, such openings appear less like spotlights for the soloist and more like literal fractures in the texture, signaling a larger disintegration that intensifies as the piece proceeds.

This disintegration becomes palpable during the section after Wood's "solo" (a solo, it should be said, that is more atmospheric than declarative). For here, surprisingly, the band starts playing an entirely new rhythmic groove (Groove #2). Is this a departure from the material we just heard—a new, contrasting section? But no, the music winds down shortly thereafter; it must be a coda. But it doesn't sound like one. . . . Such are the mental arguments one often has with oneself while listening to Medeski, Martin & Wood.

venue," Dorf recalled. "The 'jazz clubs'—the Blue Note, Sweet Basil, The Village Vanguard, Carlos I, the Angry Squire, and so on—were all in line with the George Wein (Newport, Cool, and JVC Jazz Festivals) definition of jazz. . . . The only alternative spaces were what has been historically referred to as the loft scene—individuals setting up concerts in their own spaces. But the loft scene was very cliquey and underground; word of these shows basically never made it beyond downtown." In his new club Dorf actively encouraged experimentation, as his first press release made clear: "The Knitting Factory considers many things art and is open to suggestions."

Steve Coleman and M-Base

Out of the heady exploratory milieu fostered by Dorf and others, several composer-performers rose to prominence in the 1990s. In 1985 alto saxophonist **Steve Coleman** (b. 1956) formed his band Five Elements and invented a name for the kind of music they played: **M-Base,** meaning "macro-basic array of structured extemporization." This highfalutin acronym said little about Coleman's actual style, but that was beside the point. By naming his own music, Coleman sought to prevent critics from pigeonholing him into the usual categories.

LISTENING CHART 34

Medeski, Martin & Wood, "Take Me Nowhere"

CD 3 / Tracks 50–56

RECORDED 2002, ENGLEWOOD, NEW JERSEY / BLUE NOTE RECORDS 7243 5 35870 2 4

John Medeski (electronic keyboards), Billy Martin (drums and percussion), Chris Wood (acoustic bass)

Style: Acid jazz	Form: No conventional form

Introduction

50	0:00	Synthesizer (with heavy vibrato) + bongos, then cymbals
	0:22	*Groove #1 established;* synthesizer bends pitch slowly and fluidly . . .

Head?

51	0:44	Bass melody stated by Chris Wood (acoustic bass) to synthesizer and drum accompaniment
	1:02	"Solo break": Wood (bass) . . .

Interlude 1

52	1:08	Band presents constantly shifting mélange of electronic sounds and percussion effects

Repeat of head?

53	1:26	Wood plays varied version of "head," which soon changes beyond recognition; electric piano adds tremolos in upper register
	1:50	. . . synthesizer drops out, giving effect of partial break

Interlude 2

54	1:53	Synthesizer produces electronic wah-wahs, etched with distortion
	2:03	. . . *drums stop,* but it no longer feels like a break
	2:07	. . . various layers of floating synthesizer sounds, the kind from the beginning, slowly interact

Acoustic bass "solo": Chris Wood

55	2:20	Wood plays bluesy bass solo based on soulful riffs and sustained notes
	2:35	. . . *drums stop,* as before; Wood resumes soloing amid two interweaving synthesizer sounds (one like the rustle of tiny sea shells, the other like the wind) and a low-register hum produced by string bass played with a bow

		Coda? (or new section?)
56	2:58	*Groove #2 established* by Wood; + pulsating, nasal-sounding synthesizer
	3:03	. . . drums gradually enter, accompanied by slowly and ominously rising wind effect
	3:26	John Medeski resumes synthesized pitch-bending of beginning but more actively, as if playing a solo
	3:44	. . . groove and texture begin to disintegrate; band closes on abrupt, luminous sustained chord

In fact, his music, which combined boppish improvisation with complicated funk polyrhythms, free jazz, and world music, itself defied categorization. Although he used electronic instruments, the music was too experimental to fit most people's definition of fusion. Coleman's vision inspired other musicians to probe M-Base principles in the late 1980s and early 1990s, including alto saxophonist Greg Osby, pianist Geri Allen, and singer Cassandra Wilson.

John Zorn

The fortunes of alto saxophonist **John Zorn** (b. 1953) rose concurrently with those of the Knitting Factory and, indeed, the two provided each other mutual support. Inspired by everything from avant-garde classical music to heavy metal rock to Ornette Coleman to cartoon music, Zorn fashioned a jazz approach of unprecedented eclecticism. In the late 1980s he recorded albums full of cross-cutting lurches from one idiom to another in the manner of his idol Carl Stalling, the venerable soundtrack composer for Warner Brothers cartoons. The violence of his juxtapositions gave the music shock value, enhancing Zorn's iconoclastic image. While continuing in this hectic vein in the 1990s he also formed the quartet Masada, with which he has explored a somewhat calmer blend of jazz and the Yiddish music of his Jewish heritage.

Dave Douglas

Zorn's trumpet player in Masada was **Dave Douglas** (b. 1963), another musician who became a mainstay at the Knitting Factory. An eclectic from a young age, Douglas cites classical composer Igor Stravinsky, pop music icon Stevie Wonder, and John Coltrane as his main influences. He first attracted wide attention in 1994 with recordings and performances by his Tiny Bell Trio, a group composed of trumpet, electric guitar, and drums. With this band Douglas played personalized renditions of traditional Balkan music. Heading various other small groups over the next few years he continued to explore Eastern European hybrids, together with other world music blends, electronic experiments, and more conventional postbop settings. Not surprisingly, given his interest in Stravinsky, Douglas has spent a lot of time composing and on finding the right balance between composition and improvisation.

Great Debates

THE FUTURE OF JAZZ: A CRITICS' ROUNDTABLE

In 2002, ten jazz critics agreed to collaborate on a book entitled *The Future of Jazz.* In it they debated (entirely by email) such topics as repertory ensembles, vocal jazz, the music business, jazz in the world, and jazz and race. One theme which arose repeatedly, regardless of topic, was the current tension between traditionalists, those who relied principally on the past for inspiration, and the fusionists, those who sought new sounds by mixing jazz with other idioms, whether they be pop, classical, or world musics. Here are some of their opinions on three aspects of this debate:

1. *The New Traditionalists*

   "Today the main thrust of jazz . . . is a kind of retro jazz that orbits the hard-bop style of the 1950s and early '60s. . . . It is as if the jazz clock has stopped. Jazz has become a museum of older styles and tried-and-tested methods of articulation. Walking into a New York jazz club in 2001 has become no different from what it was forty years before."

   —Stuart Nicholson

   "The problem with the 'you're not playing anything *new*!' argument is that it's only half right. Yes, jazz has depended on lots of very individual voices to evolve it. But—in case we haven't noticed—it also has a delicious side to it that is about refinement of tradition."

   —Ben Ratliff

2. *Jazz-Rock Fusion*

   "I'm doubtful that I'll ever bet the farm on a future of jazz-rock, and here's why: there's something inherently graceless about it. . . . From Lifetime to Last Exit, all but the best moments of jazz-rock have been somewhat ham-fisted. . . . To over-generalize, rock beats just don't get the job done, 'cept in rock."

   —Jim Macnie

   "There are lots of people reconsidering the good 1970s fusion stuff; the bad taste [of lesser efforts] is dissipating and now we can hear how good those Miles records are, how they teem with possibilities that were never fully explored. Davis . . . reached way out and swept everything into one glorious sound. I'd like to think that's about to happen again."

   —Peter Margasak

3. *World Fusion*

   "The globalization of jazz is not just another engaging story, another sign of the music's growing acceptance. To my mind, it is the main story, the overwhelming trend, the key evolutionary thread taking us to the world's future."

   —Ted Gioia

   "As for the idea that European jazz is the future, I'd just say it's early to tell. . . . One can argue all one wants about the Nordic approach to jazz, but numbers argue in favor of American jazz retaining popularity: more people in the world have been exposed to it."

   —Peter Watrous   ■ ■ ■

Yuval Taylor, ed., *The Future of Jazz* (Chicago: A Cappella Books, 2002), 46–60, 154–55.

Reflecting on the music of his time, Douglas said, "With love and dedication, musicians [today] build a new music on the remains of the old—sometimes in fits and starts, sometimes through gradual expansion and evolution. The only way to go is forward; yet there are as many forward directions as there are musicians. . . . The beauty of this time is that musicians are free to choose which elements they use from moment to moment, creating an infinite range of possibilities and variations."

Further Listening from the *Prentice Hall Jazz Collection*
Track 12: Dave Douglas, "Kidnapping Kissinger" (2001)

Jazz Outside the United States

The long-simmering internationalization of jazz finally reached a boil with the fall of communism. For years musicians outside the United States made contributions to jazz in small, infrequent doses, starting with Belgian guitarist Django Reinhardt and French violinist Stephane Grappelli in the 1930s. The totalitarian regimes of Hitler, Stalin, and their successors in Eastern Europe tried to eradicate jazz in their own countries. But as a potent symbol of freedom and democracy—and, thus, of subversion—black-market jazz flourished at the

Orchestre National de Jazz, 2002.

subterranean level for decades. When the iron curtain finally lifted in Poland, a Hungarian stepped to the microphone during a public meeting at a Warsaw jazz club and declared his ideology: "I am not a communist. I am not a socialist. I am a saxophonist."

In Western-style democracies the role of non-Americans grew in the 1960s and 1970s, first through the extensive European free jazz movement and then through prominent positions given them in the top fusion bands of the United States. As we have seen, the Austrian pianist Joe Zawinul, British players John McLaughlin and Dave Holland, Czech musicians Miroslav Vitous and Jan Hammer, and Brazilians Airto Moreira and Flora Purim made crucial contributions to fusion (see Chapter 27). At the same time, Japanese pianist and bandleader Toshiko Akiyoshi (see Chapter 25), Cuban trumpeter Arturo Sandoval, and Danish bassist Niels-Henning Ørsted Pedersen brought new life to bop-oriented acoustic jazz.

The international openness of the nineties greatly increased the influence of non-Americans. Indeed, one critic asserted in 2000 that jazz "is no longer United States–exclusive. You can put together a serious jazz band to make a world-class recording in any major city in the developed world." A prominent British writer went even further, arguing that, as America recently became preoccupied with jazz's past, it lost control of its future: "The vanguard of jazz has moved to Europe." Norwegian pianist Bugge Wesseltoft confirmed this perspective by expressing his disappointment in recent American jazz: "I think American jazz

ORCHESTRE NATIONAL DE JAZZ, *"Estramadure,"* PART 1 (2001)

Characterizing the spirit of *Charmediterranéen,* a recent album by the Orchestre National de Jazz, musical director Paolo Damiani mused: "What do I hear, what do I see? A journey undertaken without preconceptions during which I find images of spell, of incantation, something that leads us to another place, we don't know where. . . . I don't know what I'm looking for, but I know how to recognize the marvellously unexpected when I come across it."

"Marvellously unexpected" is a good way to describe "Estramadure," one of several multimovement pieces on *Charmediterranéen.* The piece was composed by François Jeanneau, a saxophonist and codirector of the orchestra. The name *Estramadure* refers to a historic region of Spain in the southwestern provinces of Cáceres and Badajoz, bordering on Portugal. And indeed, the music evokes in many elusive ways the exotic spirit of the Iberian Peninsula. In particular, furious violin and cello solos (by Régis Huby and Paolo Damiani, respectively) conjure images of folk and gypsy music characteristic of this mountainous and agricultural region.

The piece has five main sections: an introduction, a chaconne, the head, a violin solo (which closes with the second half of the head), and a final unaccompanied cello cadenza. A *chaconne* is a baroque variation technique based on a brief, recurring harmonic progression; in this case the progression appears five times. This appropriation from the classical tradition is one of several hints at the European origins of the musicians themselves. The introduction and chaconne, for example, manifest a restraint and a refinement of harmony and sonority that seems indebted to the centuries-old French musical tradition. The ONJ Web site may deny that the band plays exclusively "French jazz," but French elements appear, nonetheless.

LISTENING CHART 35

Orchestre National de Jazz, "Estramadure," Part 1 (Jeanneau)

CD 3 / Tracks 57–61

RECORDED 15–16 OCTOBER 2001 / *CHARMEDITERRANÉEN* ECM 1828

Paolo Damiani (cello, artistic and musical director), François Jeanneau (soprano saxophone, flute, musical co-director), Thomas de Pourquery (soprano, alto, and tenor saxophones), Jean-Marc Larché (soprano, alto, and baritone saxophones), Médéric Collignon (pocket cornet, bugle, voice), Alain Vankenhove (trumpet, bugle), Gianluca Petrella (trombone), Didier Havet (soubassophone), Régis Huby (violin), Olivier Benoit (guitar), Paul Rogers (bass), Christophe Marguet (drums); guests: Anouar Brahem (oud), Gianluigi Trovesi (piccolo clarinet, alto saxophone)

Style: European jazz		Form: Baroque chaconne / AABA head

Introduction (no rhythm section)

57	0:00		Soprano saxophone plays lyrical solo melody to accompaniment of violin, cello, and (later) trumpet and soubassophone

Chaconne (no rhythm section)

58	0:45	1st statement	Brass play meditative theme in harmony . . .
	0:58	2nd statement	. . . add soubassophone
	1:12	3rd statement	. . . add alto saxophone, then tenor saxophone
	1:25	4th statement	. . . add unison obbligato line: violin + oud (a Middle Eastern lute)
	1:38	5th statement	. . . add still more winds to theme

Head (first 3/4 of form)

59	1:59	Vamp	Drums set up a loping groove; bass joins in with an ostinato figure . . .
	2:11	A (8)	Woodwinds (with soprano saxophone lead) play earnest melody of odd phrase lengths . . .
	2:28	A (8)	*A-section repeated (with the addition of strings)*
	2:44	B (8)	More instruments added to B-section, which dies down to low dynamic level; AABA form interrupted by . . .

Violin solo: Régis Huby

60	3:01	Vamp	Huby improvises highly virtuosic and impassioned solo that owes much to the classical tradition . . .

			Head (second half)
	4:18	B (8)	Huby continues to solo over the ensemble . . .
	4:35	A (8)	(Soloist out . . .)
			Cello cadenza: Paolo Damiani
61	5:00		Unaccompanied, Damiani plays a virtuoso cello cadenza, reflecting avant-garde classical influences as well as more traditional ones
			(This passage segues, without a break, into Part 2 of "Estramadure")

somehow has really stopped, maybe in the late '70s, early '80s. I haven't heard one interesting American record in the last twenty years. It's like a museum, presenting stuff that's already been done. . . . I was taught it is no good copying Bud Powell or Bill Evans, there are already hundreds of musicians in America who do that. We [Norwegians] want to find our own voice, that speaks of where we come from. I haven't grown up in New York, so I see things differently."

As non-Americans have begun to find their own voices the cross-pollination of jazz and various world musics has accelerated, producing a genre known as **world fusion.** Chano Dominguez, a Spanish pianist, has ingeniously merged jazz with flamenco music, complete with characteristically flamboyant guitar playing and accompanimental clapping and foot-stamping. South African musicians have developed a mix called township jazz, a beguiling combination of jazz and traditional marabi music. And in France a government-funded big band has been exploring jazz from a cosmopolitan European perspective. Organized in 1986 at the instigation of the French minister of culture, the **Orchestre National de Jazz (ONJ)** began as an entirely French production. In recent years, however, musicians from other European countries have started participating. The latest edition of the band is led by Italian acoustic bassist and cellist Paolo Damiani. According to the ONJ Web site, "Damiani's nomination to head the most important big band in France (which in no way means 'French jazz'), is another way of affirming an inspiration and an identity that are *European.*"

Whither Jazz?

Not everyone regards Europe as the source of jazz's most hopeful prospects in the new century. But recordings like *Charmediterranéen* suggest the enormous potential of international cross-breeding. Irish jazz, Bulgarian jazz, Indonesian jazz—such hybrids suggest a future for the music unlike anything we have yet seen. Either that, or a future that jazz lovers don't *want* to see, namely atomization into a thousand idioms so different as to make any further reference to "jazz" meaningless. Awed by that dark possibility, some critics consider the 1990s as a fragmented, leaderless era ushering in the demise of jazz. Others,

world fusion a stylistic blend of jazz and musical traditions from countries outside the United States.

aware that such dire pronouncements have been made before, take a more optimistic view. "What's good about the fragmentation?" asks Peter Watrous. "By accentuating the local [developments], . . . a focus will be found in the form of a figure rising out of the mess. But those leaders won't exist if there is already a dominant figure or a dominant movement. They can only arise out of flux and darkness—what the '90s were about, in a good way—an era where jazz was pretty much without an aesthetic leader. So brace yourselves, because something important is going to show up, probably sooner than later. There's simply too much pressure, too much intelligent action for all the fragments to remain on the margin."

As the millennium begins we find ourselves, as usual, in the midst of uncertainty about the meaning and future of jazz. The big questions of the twenty-first century will be: (1) Has jazz become a museum music to be performed, studied, and appreciated primarily in historical perspective? (2) Will the present fragmentation eventually disintegrate jazz into nothingness? or (3) As Watrous predicts, will jazz yet rejuvenate itself to open major new frontiers of sound and style? For an answer to these questions, we will just have to wait and see.

Credits

Jazz record sleeve featuring John Coltrane, Unidentified photographer, Dorling Kindersley Media Library. © Dorling Kindersley

Jazz record sleeve featuring Ornette Coleman, Unidentified photographer, Dorling Kindersley Media Library. © Dorling Kindersley

John Coltrane, Institute of Jazz Studies, Courtesy of the Rutgers Institute of Jazz Studies

GIs carry a wounded soldier from jungle thicket. Photographer: Kyo Icki Sawada/UPI. Corbis/Bettmann

M. L. King delivering "I have a Dream" speech in Washington, D.C., 1963. Magnum Photos, Inc.

Charleston dance contest in front of St. Louis City Hall, November 13, 1925 (detail). Photograph, 1925. Missouri Historical Society, St. Louis

Jimi Hendrix Playing at Woodstock, Photographer: Henry Diltz. Corbis/Bettmann

Jazz Trumpeter Lee Morgan, Photographer: Francis Wolff. Corbis/Bettmann

Jazzs Guitarist, Pat Metheny at Hammersmith Odeon, Hammersmith, London, on May 2, 1985, Photographer: Derick A. Thomas. Corbis/Bettmann

Savoy Ballroom, New York City, Harlem, 1939. Photographer: Cornell Capa. Magnum Photos, Inc. © Cornell Capa/Magnum Photos

Bill Evans playing piano, 1964. Lebrecht Music Collection, Lebrecht Collection/NL

Medeski, Martin & Wood, Blue Note Records

"Take my hams, I want to lose them. Take my slaws, I'll never use them." The Cartoon Bank ©The New Yorker Collection 1988 Michael Crawford from cartoonbank.com. All Rights Reserved.

"Pop, tell me again how jazz came up the river from New Orleans." The Cartoon Bank ©The New Yorker Collection 1957 Eldon Dedini from cartoonbank.com. All Rights Reserved.

Sidny Bechet, Photographer: William P. Gottlieb

World Saxophone Quartet, February 13, 1987, at a performance at the Duke Ellington School for the Arts in Washington, D.C. Photographer: Michael Wilderman, Jazz Visions Photo/Graphics. Michael Wilderman/Jazz Visions

"What is Swing Music, Anyway?" April 24, 1936. King Features Syndicate. © Reprinted with permission of King Features Syndicate.

Scott Joplin, 1910, Frank Driggs Collection

Buddy Bolden and Band, 1900, Frank Driggs Collection

Freddie Keppard, Chicago, 1919, Frank Driggs Collection

Bessie Smith, 1923. Frank Driggs Collection

Carroll Dickerson Band at Sunset Cafe, Chicago, 1922, Frank Driggs Collection

King Oliver's Band in Chicago, 1923, Frank Driggs Collection

Jelly Roll Morton and his Red Hot Peppers, 1926, Collection of Duncan Schiedt

Louis Armstrong, 1927, Frank Driggs Collection

Louis Armstrong and his Hot Five, 1925, Frank Driggs Collection

Fletcher Henderson, New York, 1924, Collection of Duncan Schiedt

Duke Ellington and his Orchestra at the Cotton Club in New York, 1931, Frank Driggs Collection

Fats Waller, New York, 1936, Frank Driggs Collection

Albert Ammons and Meade Lux Lewis at Cafe Society, 1939, Frank Driggs Collection

Fletcher Henderson and his Orchestra, Chicago, 1936, Frank Driggs Collection

Count Basie Band at Columbia/Vocalion Studio in New York, March 1940, Frank Driggs Collection

Duke Ellington and his Orchestra, 1943, Frank Driggs Collection

Artie Shaw and his Orchestra, 1938, Frank Driggs Collection

Lester Young, 1941, Frank Driggs Collection

Ella Fitzgerald and Chick Webb at the Apollo Theatre, 1937, Frank Driggs Collection

Art Tatum, Collection of Duncan Schiedt

Charlie Parker, Dizzy Gillespie, John Coltrane, and Tommy Potter at Birdland, January 1951, Frank Driggs Collection

Sarah Vaughn, circa 1947, Frank Driggs Collection

The Modern Jazz Quartet, 1950s, Frank Driggs Collection

Charlie Parker, Los Angeles. 1947, Frank Driggs Collection

Duke Ellington, 1930s, Frank Driggs Collection

Billie Holiday, 1941, Frank Driggs Collection

Charlie Parker with strings, 1949, Frank Driggs Collection

Roy Eldridge, Charles Peterson, Don Peterson. Photo By Charles Peterson, Courtesy Of Don Peterson

Fisk Jubilee Singers, Fisk University Library, Fisk University Franklin Library's Special Collections

Miles Davis and his wardrobe along with his music in the early 1970s, Anthony Barboza Photography, Anthony Barboza Collection

52nd Street between 5th and 6th Avenues, New York, 1948, Photographer: William P. Gottlieb. © 1979, William P. Gottlieb from the Music Division of the Library of Congress.

Thelonius Munk, Howard McGee, Roy Eldridge, and Teddy Hill standing in front of Minton's Playhouse, New York, 1948, Photographer: William P. Gottlieb. © 1979 William P. Gottlieb from the Music Division of the Library of Congress.

Photo of Bunk Johnson, late 1940s, Collection of Duncan Schiedt

Art Blakey, Paris, 1948, Herman Leonard Photography, LLC. © Herman Leonard

Joe Williams, 1961, Collection of Duncan Schiedt. © Duncan Scheidt

Benny Goodman, "Don't Be That Way" cover, Collection of Duncan Schiedt

Bert Williams, Frank Driggs Collection

Charley Patton, Frank Driggs Collection

Dick Haymes and the Andrew Sisters, 1940s, Frank Driggs Collection

The Wolverine Orchestra with Bix Belderbeckle at the Gennet Studios, Richmond, Indiana, February 18, 1924, Frank Driggs Collection

John Coltrane, Cannonball Adderley, Miles Davis, and Bill Evans in the Columbia Records studio, New York, 1958, Frank Driggs Collection

Stan Getz and Joao Gilberto, Frank Driggs Collection

Miles Davis, 1958, Frank Driggs Collection

Bert Williams, London, 1896, Frank Driggs Collection

Paul Whiteman Band, New Amsterdam Roof, New York City, February 1929, Frank Driggs Collection

Toshiko Akiyoshi—Lew Tabackin Orchestra, Frank Driggs Collection

Louis Armstrong, California, 1956. Corbis/Bettmann

Cecil Taylor as he plays the piano during the recording session for his "Unit Structures" album in Englewood Cliffs, New Jersey, May 19, 1966. Photographer: Francis Wolff. Corbis/Bettmann

Wynton Marsalis, Saratoga Springs, N.Y., Photographer: Ken Frankling. Corbis/Bettmann

Charlie Mingus, April 3, 1960. Corbis/Bettmann

Miles Davis's Second Quintet, Photographer: David Redfern. Redfern's Music Picture Library

V.S.O.P. Quintet, 1977, Photographer: Kathy Sloane

$64,000 Jazz LP cover, Institute of Jazz Studies

Miles Davis 'Round About Midnight album cover. Institute of Jazz Studies

Clifford Brown, Jazzinstitut Darmstadt

Coleman Hawkins in the 1940s. Corbis/Bettmann

Gerry Mulligan and Chet Baker at the Haig, 1952, Photographer: William Claxton. Demont Photo Management. Photograph by William Claxton/Courtesy Demont Photo

Weather Report, 1979, Institute of Jazz Studies

Herbie Hancock's Headhunters, Institute of Jazz Studies

Orchestre National de Jazz, Mephisto, ECM Records. © Mephisto/Courtesy ECM Records

Jazz Band Performing, Photographer: Wally McNamee. Corbis/Bettmann

Index

Entries in bold indicate recordings from the accompanying 3-CD anthology or the Prentice Hall Jazz Collection. Page numbers in bold indicate major treatment; page numbers in italics indicate a photograph.